MAFIA COP

The Two Families of Michael Palermo

Saints Only Live in Heaven

By

RICHARD STANLEY CAGAN

As told by **MICHAEL GEORGE SABELLA**

Skyhorse Publishing

Skyhorse Publishing books may be purchased in bulk at special discounts for sales promotion, corporate gifts, fund-raising, or educational purposes. Special editions can also be created to specifications. For details, contact the Special Sales Department, Skyhorse Publishing, 307 West 36th Street, 11th Floor, New York, NY 10018 or info@skyhorsepublishing.com.

Skyhorse® and Skyhorse Publishing® are registered trademarks of Skyhorse Publishing, Inc.®, a Delaware corporation.

Visit our website at www.skyhorsepublishing.com.

10 9 8 7 6 5 4 3 2 1

Library of Congress Cataloging-in-Publication Data is available on file.
ISBN: 978-1-61608-857-6

Printed in the United States of America

I dedicate this book to my wife, Elizabeth Ann McDermott Cagan, whose loyalty, perseverance, and forty-nine years of married love have enabled me to persevere through the thousands of hours that were required to complete this very special story of the life of New York City Special Investigations Unit (SIU) Detective First Class Michael George Sabella.

I also dedicate this work to my loyal and generous literary agent, Sheri Williams of www.redwritinghoodink.net, who was an invaluable asset and friend in helping me to perfect this manuscript.

And finally, most importantly, I also dedicate this book to my good and valued friend, Michael George Sabella, who was, is, and will always be a stand-up guy and who was as "Tough as a Bullet" in fighting crime. He gave his life to the police force.

—R.S.C.

CONTENTS

PREFACE

Mafia Cop is the dramatic memoir of New York City Narcotics Detective Michael Palermo. Some of those who knew him called him the Mafia Cop because of his intimate relationship with leaders in law enforcement and his personal and business relationships with the dons of two of the major Families of organized crime in New York City.

Palermo worked in his official and unofficial capacities as a negotiator and conciliator in coordinating solutions to conflicts between the New York Families and the New York City Police Department.

Mafia Cop takes you inside the inner world of the New York City Police Department, which was riddled with corruption as a normal daily routine, and into the inner sanctum of the Crime Family organizations where you will meet dons, consiglieres, underbosses, button men, soldiers, and cowboys. Detective Michael Palermo was one of a privileged few members of the law enforcement community who were informed of the impending arrest of crime lord Vito Genovese by the federal government in what many believe was the government's contrived case against him.

Palermo maintained his underworld contacts while visiting with underworld informant Joe Valachi in his Castle Hill Avenue bar in the Bronx and spent many hours with his childhood friend and future Las Vegas underboss, Carmine Canicatti, in Canicatti's after-hours bar and gambling casino in New York City. He was one of only two cops ever allowed entrance there—despite his close relationships with leaders in organized crime, he never compromised his position as a police officer. He was a "stand-up guy" for both sides and never "double-banged" anyone.

Palermo carried out sensitive negotiations with major underworld figures while working clandestinely with retired Chief Inspector Collin Devlin. Chief Devlin spent many of his early years in the Catholic Protectory with his friends, many of whom would become leaders in the Cosa Nostra. It was Chief Collin Devlin who made Mike Palermo a "made man" of the shield.

Palermo was a member of the elite SIU (Special Investigations Unit) and in his career participated in more than 2,000 arrests. He served as an expert witness testifying in international drug smuggling cases, as well as fighting in the trenches of New York City against the illegal drug trade. One of his final major arrests was that of drug trafficker Albie Simmons, who was an underboss to Harlem drug kingpin Nicky Barnes. It was this arrest that triggered his final battle with the District Attorney, who wanted to be governor, over the body and career of Michael Palermo, the Mafia Cop.

INTRODUCTION

Remember that no matter what you are or what you may become, you will never be anything more than the seeds of two families. One is made of clay, the other of honor. —Alfonso Palermo

The story of *Mafia Cop* begins in 1953, before which many events had already taken place that would mold the life and character of Michael Palermo. It is a value and an entertainment that you read some of the writings and some of the inner mechanizations of this man you are about to meet, Michael Palermo.

I have collected these, his personal manuscripts, these bits of remembrances of his life on the police force in New York City. I found them buried beneath reams of papers encased and shrouded in dust in the bottom of his file cabinet. You will laugh or smile or even wince as you read them. You will learn things you never knew about a secret society of men, a society that lived and functioned behind the scenes, in basements and in stores, on rooftops and in bars, a society that lived another life in the public eye.

These files of Michael Palermo will give you some small insight into the pressures and highlights and street education of a New York City policeman in the middle of the twentieth century.

You will read his story in his own words. You will also read my reconstruction of the events that happened in his life, based upon his private notes; our treasured conversations in the private sanctuary of his home and in his favorite restaurants in which he recounted his triumphs, battles, tears, and laughter; and the testimony of persons who were eyewitnesses to the events that happened. These are all true accounts. Some of the names and places have been changed to protect the innocent. Others have been changed to protect the guilty, the storyteller, and the author.

—R.S.C.

FLASH-FORWARD

NOVEMBER 1969 ALTAMONT, CALIFORNIA

In a green fedora and a moss velvet suit, the black man danced in his own private world of smoke and pills—into a frenzy, spinning up and down, side to side, his elastic frame wedded perfectly to the rock, rhythm, and beat of the psychedelic lights and sounds. His inky pupils dilated and mirrored the straggle-haired lead singer, Mick Jagger, on the stage before him. Foggy images danced in his head. The thumping electronic bass beat tympanis deeper than a bullfrog's bloated throat. Through his eyes and ears, the black man wafted in a sea of opiate fantasy, in a world of melody and primeval beat.

His left eye squeezed closed, leaving aim to his right—aim down the chrome barrel of the .38 caliber revolver buried in his sweaty right palm. The lead singer screamed into the night, a scream of origin and roots buried in Africa. The audience cheered and the singer sang on, his voice piercing the music, triumphant like primal man in his early world.

The man in green squeezed the trigger and the stage began to tilt. Players stood sideways but didn't fall. Shooting stars spun and left a vapor trail in the black man's mind. Smoke and pills raced into his brain, filling it with numbness. The crowd swirled around his green fedora, a spinning wheel of lights and people, a merry-go-round of carousel sounds, a centrifuge sucking his breath into a central whirlpool.

Branch-like rakes clawed his cheeks. His eyes imaged the crowd. Tufts of hair with pulpy roots brushed his face, and his cheekbone cracked and caved like the snapped frame of a dry wishbone.

A hiss squeezed out. A gurgling, sucking noise. And his ribs parted. A probe, a twist, and a severed heart spilled life deep into the dead man's chest. The black man in green lay still and the lead singer ran away.

On the grass lies Meredith Hunter. He is a rock-and-roll fan. Broken pool cues are imbedded in the dewy pasture, their splintered ends muddied like a painter's brush in umber. Hunter is dead. A switchblade sticks in his belly. Its pearl handle glints in the starlight. Polished wood of natural oak has clubbed him into another world.

Woods and fields for miles around still echo the panic and fright of 300,000 rock fans gone wild. One hour ago, Altamont, California, was a world in rage.

CONCERT DAY MINUS TWO, ALTAMONT, CALIFORNIA

MICHAEL PALERMO

I watch the treetops swirl and fly away from the column of air that blows screaming from above. The chopper blades whirr, slicing through the damp, early-morning air. Waves of inversion bring sweet, earthy fragrances up from the forest floor and they settle in my nose and mouth. I am now Mike Scotti, and I am the chief of security for Britain's hottest rock-and-roll group, The Rolling Stones, that has stormed the world.

I can smell and taste the bits of soil and moist humus that had nested beneath redwoods and evergreens. It is dirt disturbed and volatilized by a wind stream of chopping steel. The aircraft blots its shadow softly over the countryside, leaving no print, no footstep, no mark at all. A perfect visitor to a virgin forest. Just darkness blackening treetops and valleys, second after second, leaving no sign that it had ever existed. It is a footstep without a print, like an empty life in a hostile world.

At an altitude of 800 feet, my eyes soak in every detail of the farmlands below, which ease into sight. Woodlands, pastures, brooks, ponds, and livestock. It's quiet and peaceful down there, I think to myself, like in a tale of Homer or Hercules. I float over a 100 acre meadow.

At 7:00 AM, people are converging on the concert field—the old raceway at Altamont. In cars, trucks, and motorcycles they swell the roads and crawl like ants to a piece of sugarloaf. Weaving serpentine trails snake over hillsides thick with people carrying bags, knapsacks, and overnight cases. At the last minute, the concert had been moved to Altamont because too many people had shown up and would have destroyed San Francisco.

Women walk and sing while breast-feeding infants hang suspended from belly slings. Small children bob up and down in papoose halters on their father's backs. Country lanes begin to choke and snarl from an eventual 300,000 rock fans that are going to laze in the sun and finally go wild over a full day of free concerts by the top rock-and-roll stars in the world: Santana; The Grateful Dead; Jefferson Airplane; Crosby, Stills, Nash and Young; The Flying Burrito Brothers; and The Rolling Stones. This concert is Mick Jagger's dream. Jagger and the Stones had held a free concert in Hyde Park, London, earlier that summer.

They march in faded, patched jeans and baggy shirts. I can see them step in time and tune with the birds and flowers. I know that pockets and bags hold their stash of drugs, needles, spoons, and pipes. I can make the biggest drug arrest of my career right here and now—and then go down in history as public enemy number one. It is all at once beautiful, awesome, and frightening.

I pan the crowd with binoculars from my 800 feet-up chopper box seat. Like a computer read out, details cram my brain on how to avoid the potential violence and destruction of a crowd in chaos. Sure, I eased the Stones through the insanity of exploding concerts before, but never like this. There's an atomic bomb down there just waiting to blow. I always had cordoned the group with six steel-shouldered bodyguards that I routinely snatched from the Bronx County District Attorney's office, right from D. A. Ross Simon's private police detail. I rotate them and arrange their tour with the Stones so that it coincides with their off-duty time. Simon doesn't even know they are moonlighting. He never would have dreamed that they were in California today sleeping in the bed of luxury at one of San Francisco's finest hotels.

* * *

"Hey, Scotti," yells the helicopter pilot. "That's an army down there. I never seen anything like it. The ground's black with them. How many do you think there are?"

"I don't know, Tommy. At least 100,000."

"A hundred thousand? It looks like an invasion down there. And the show don't start for two more days. It's so packed now that all the roads only go one way, right to the speedway, or what's left of it. Did you hear what they did to the stands at the track yesterday? They ripped the bleachers apart and used the wood to make campfires to cook on and to keep the bugs away at night. The guy who runs the place is going out of his mind. They ruined him. He says he's gonna sue. Sue who? Who the hell is he gonna sue? He's lucky he got away with his life."

Tommy banks the chopper in a turn to the left and we fly in circles around the perimeter. Special emergency tents are set up for those who overdose. Cocaine, heroin, Benzedrine (bennies), amphetamines, barbiturates, LSD, mescaline, hashish, and marijuana burn in the blood of the flowing masses. "Trip Tents," they call them. They are staffed by hippie, hyped-up doctors who share drugs with the kids. After emergency care the patients are whisked to area hospitals. The scene is that of a disoriented mob completely in Nirvana and at peace on farmland in Altamont, California. Backs and heads sway in arrhythmic serpentine tendrils. Dante's *Inferno* portrait of the youth of a nation bent on destroying itself. *How can they do this to themselves?* I wonder.

The pungent smoke steams up and makes my nostrils tingle. I know the flavor. At every rock concert with the Stones, the secondhand smoke gets into the clothes, bloodstream, and the minds of myself and my phalanx of the Bronx District Attorney's battalion of bodyguards, and we get high. To his fans here, Mick Jagger is a god. He is idolized by love-crazed, glassy-eyed, impressionable groupies of every sort. From communers, runaways, and adventurers, Jagger has slept with every sector. From thirteen to thirty in every tour city he is said to have a playmate. From the finely chiseled features of the Hispanic go-go dancer in New York to the thirteen-year-old in Los Angeles. Together, they all share "love." When I book the rooms, I always arrange for Mick to have a connecting room with his favorite guitar player down the hall from the rest of the Stones.

I won't ever forget the night in Chicago when I casually walked in on one of Mick's parties. The room bounced wildly with the rock of a Rolling Stones' album. A fourteen-year-old, freckle-faced, red-haired girl sat huddled in a corner, naked, inhaling hashish. A coal-black nude girl with glistening flower-oil-scented skin hung her long sweeping inky hair over Jagger and his glistening, ripped body. Strobe lights flashed through colored glass and twisted rainbows splashed on the walls. It was a scene from Dante's *Inferno*. It was hard rock and hard drugs.

* * *

"The cows are dying down there, Scotti. There's going to be hell to pay. The farmers say that their stock is dying of hardware from the 'freaks,'" yells Tommy over the roar of the droning chopper blades.

"Hardware?" I ask. I'm half-listening, still trying to figure out how I'm going to protect the Stones.

"Yeah. Cows will do that. They'll eat just about anything. Barbed wire, nails. You know. Stuff like that. But now when they cut them open, they find beer cans, bottles, needles, spoons, and knives. You name it and they eat it. The radio says there's going to be 300,000 of those kids down there by the time the show starts."

"Hardware? That's a damn shame," I say. "Let's go back, Tommy. Get me back to Frisco. Who the hell ever expected a scene like this? I haven't even started to secure the hotel yet. How the hell am I going to protect that psycho Jagger with a mob like this? He thinks he's Jesus Christ and these are his disciples."

MIKE SCOTTI

At every concert date, I would personally install traps in the rooms that the Stones occupied. I was like an artist. I used drills, saws, nails, and paint to create undetectable hiding places for their "valuables." I never asked. I never mentioned it and I was never told what the "valuables" were. But I knew what went into those traps. I left a trail of traps for stashing drugs in some of the most prestigious hotels in the United States. It was a work of art. It's my secret. While the Stones were under my protection, they were never busted as they had been before. Hell, I eat, breathe, and live deception all my life. "You gotta know it if you're gonna stop it." That's why the Howard Morris Agency gave me the job. That, and a word from some Friends of Friends.

I have standing orders to my men: "Protect the Stones, but never hurt the kids in the crowd." It isn't easy, but my guys do it. And they do it the best.

But Mick, whom I love like my own kid almost, is a problem at times. He's a prima donna, if you know what I mean. For this concert, he insisted on coming here three days early so that he could touch his fans. It was his idea to do something nice for the kids. He is a generous guy. It's his mystique that allures the other entertainers to perform at a day of free rock and roll. But not all of the fans are predictable. Yesterday, as he was mingling with the crowd with me at his side, a fist flew out from between two girls and smashed into Mick's face. His nose shot blood out all over his face. Man, we grabbed him and I almost threw him into the chopper that I always have waiting, and we got the hell out of there fast.

And still after that, he wanted to throw rose petals down on the crowd while he flew overhead. He settled for 1,000 roses instead. Like Caesar, he helped throw out the flowers from the chopper one at a time to a screaming crowd.

* * *

CONCERT DAY

MIKE SCOTTI

I look at 300,000 people. They are a sea of mad humanity. I see bodies writhing and bouncing, flesh to flesh, sweat to sweat. Legs and torsos roll in the trampled hay making love. The air is smoke, bottom sounds, and orgasm. The crusty farm topsoil shakes beneath the sneakers, boots, and sandals of an army of rock fans.

The sun rises and I see some of the sleeping worshippers wake up. From 7:00 AM there is continuous music. The Stones take the stage at 1:00 AM the next morning. I see candy-colored lights and an audience stoned out of its mind. I watch the show with my security officers from the side, front, and backstage areas. During the daylight shows I have received reports that members of the Hells Angels motorcycle club who were stoned on drugs were attacking kids in the audience. Mick Jagger and the Stones refuse to perform unless the beatings are stopped.

One of my men arranges a meeting for me and the leader of the Angels. We walk to a clearing behind the stage. My eighteen-passenger helicopter stands ready behind us.

"I'm Scotti. My people tell me you're out here to break heads. I don't want to believe that."

The leader spins a toothpick over and over between his teeth.

"That's those hippie disc jockeys. They're full of shit!"

"That may be, but my people are here to protect the group. The Stones won't go on unless the guys in black jackets stop breaking heads."

The leader swaggers back and forth looking down at the grass, from side to side. I know he has heard the rumors that I am connected with the New York mob syndicate.

"Yeah, well, it looks like you got your hands full, man. Those trip tents look like emergency wards full of freaks."

"They were set up for O.D.s, not broken heads. Sit on your people or the Stones don't go on," I answer.

"Look, Scotti. There are 800 Angels here to listen to some good music and have a big high. Three hundred thousand freaks are causing the trouble. They're looking to tear down the stage. We're here to make sure that they don't. So some get hurt."

"I'll worry about the stage and the groups. You keep your guys under control. Do we understand each other?"

"I'll go along with that. I understand what you're saying. We don't want nobody hurt either. We ain't animals. That's the trouble with these goddamn people. They got us all wrong, man. We're people, just like everyone else. We got hearts and brains.

We bleed if we get cut. We ain't looking for no trouble and we ain't goin' to start none. Just looking for highs, man. You know, highs." He stretches his hands up toward the diamonds in the black sky. On his back is a satanic red face.

"Listen, don't give me any of that bullshit. Save it for the press and for the heat. I don't give a fuck what you and your 800 goons screw around with here. Just don't hurt anybody. Leave the kids alone and we'll all walk away from this thing in the morning in one piece. You got that?" I had two big bodyguards on both sides of me. My face was on fire. My heart was a jackhammer in my chest.

With a toothpick clamped between his front teeth, he agrees. "You got it, man. We ain't here after no kids." He spits the tooth-pick out onto the grass and walks off into the crowd, flanked by two of his war counselors.

"'This is the craziest damn scene I ever saw," one of my guys says. "Mike, how the hell do we get out of here? You know these freaks ain't going to sit still when the Stones finish. We're going to have to move like a damn freight train to get out of here."

"It's OK," I say. "Tommy's got the bird spinning now. We'll get all our people on before they finish and then move the group. We'll treat it like every other concert, the same way we've been doing it. Instead of a limo, we have a chopper. When the Stones start the last set, I want those spotlights out. We move the group first. We'll be in the air before they know we're gone."

I leave and scan the crowd. People are screaming in front of the stage. Some are deeply inhaling from pipes, eyes rolling back into their hollow heads, leaving only almond-shaped sockets. I give the nod to my three other men. Mick Jagger and the Stones take the stage. In forty-five minutes, the show will be over. In thirty minutes, the group's girlfriends and support staff will be on board the big, brown army-type helicopter. It was built to carry eighteen people. At the end of the concert, the Stones will be cordoned off by security and retreat at once to the chopper. They will have to outrun the crowd. The sound systems will be left behind. A token, a tribute to the fans. Sound systems are expendable. Human lives aren't.

"I don't like it, Mike," one of my guys says. "I got a bad feeling. I think we ought to move now."

"No way," I say. "They've got to finish. We have to wait. We've got no choice. Keep your eyes open and keep on the horn if you see anything. As long as things stay like this, we let them finish. Hell, they came over 3,000 miles just to finish it. It's like the end of a pilgrimage for Mick and these people. Look at them. They think they're in Mecca or something. Would you take away their prophet? Not me, man. Keep your finger on the button and call me if you have to."

I see him nervously squeeze his walkie-talkie. It's his only link to sanity and civilization.

Deep in the crowd is Meredith Hunter. He is an eighteen-year-old black fan. He sings and waves his hands wildly. He had traveled to Altamont just to hear and see the people who made all the records that he had bought.

And it was free. All it will cost him is his life.

The crowd cheers as the Stones grow more primeval with their music. In the heat of the roar, Hunter reaches into the pocket of his jacket and takes out a .38 caliber handgun. Slashing into the air with his right hand and gun high, he races through the crowd straight at the Stones. When he gets to the stage, he points the gun at Mick Jagger and jabs it in time to the music.

My walkie-talkie screams: "Holy shit! There's a crazy sonofabitch with a gun out right in front of the stage. He's gonna shoot Mick."

I scream back, "Get those guys out of there! Tommy, pick that bird up just as we get there. We'll jump in. Get those guys out! I don't care if you have to carry them!"

Guitars drop, twanging an eerie resonance through the amp-
lifiers. People draw back from Meredith Hunter. He starts spinning around, singing and screaming, flailing his revolver at the
crowd. Girls shriek. People stumble and Hunter's eyes are shining
yellow lights. He dances in a consuming fever, oblivious to the
crowd. He is swallowed by paradise.

The open space around him grows larger, expanding as people
push out and run away from the maniac with the gun. Young girls
fall. Their faces are stepped on by boots digging for a foothold. A
group of Hells Angels and their girlfriends race into the center of
the circle. Four black motorcycle jackets grab Hunter and rip the
gun from his hands. Girls tear at his hair. Fingernails rip into his
cheeks and twenty-five members of the Hells Angels beat and club
Meredith Hunter to death with pool cues. A switchblade pierces
his lung and heart. Three hundred thousand people go insane and
Meredith Hunter dies as he wanted to live—singing. His gun
wasn't loaded. He had just lost control of his enthusiasm.

Altamont is a riot. A war scene of pasture and barbed wire, of
trampling and of death.

We all race to Tommy and the chopper, the Stones stumb-
ling in front of us. Cheering groupie faces urge them on through
windows from inside the bird. Faster and faster. Girlfriends for a
day. Run, more speed, before somebody gets a hand on us. Run
before our clothes become shredded souvenirs. Run before they
kill us all.

Tommy has the chopper a foot off the grass trying to set off
a wind stream to disperse the crowd. But the nose won't lift up.
It kisses the ground. It's too heavy. Much too much weight. The
tail blades waver, slowly floating from side to side, one foot off the
ground. The chopper has filled with kids who are after the Stones.
They are even hanging on the fuselage. Jagger reaches the door
and turns toward the onrushing throng. He reaches into the crowd
and pulls his drummer from the arms and hands of screaming

fans. Two panicked musicians jump into the aircraft. The rest of the Stones are stuffed through the doorway, layer by layer, by me and my guys. Fans force their way through the door and grab on to everyone and everything. Girls sit on the landing struts.

Tommy revs up the engines, trying to take off. The wind crashes down in a jet stream, scattering most of the crowd. There's still too much weight. We can't lift off. A voice booms: "Those crazy bastards, they're going to kill us all!"

I yell, "Throw those mothers off the struts! Let's do it now or they're going to tear us into little pieces!"

Tommy keeps the props at lift-off velocity and six pairs of steel arms peel and rip people off the outside of the chopper. The bird lifts up four feet and Tommy motions thumbs-up. My six guys jump back in and the brown bird very slowly gains altitude. Two diehards still hang on and cling to the lower grid work. I reach down to grab the hand of a young blonde girl in a red T-shirt. Across her chest is printed in big white letters: I'M STONED ON THE STONES. Twenty feet off the ground in the early-morning black sky she reaches for my hand, which will pull her to safety. An air pocket jolts the chopper and she loses her hold. She falls, back down into the smoky lights below, like a star burned out. The other hanger-on holds fast and makes the trip on a strut. He survives his open-air flight and near-crash landing at San Francisco airport.

We deplane. Bewildered strangers, rock stars, groupies, and bodyguards leave a concert and fields of ruin behind.

HOTEL ROOM, SAN FRANCISCO, CALIFORNIA

MICHAEL PALERMO

"It was crazy, Augie, I never saw anything like it. Three hundred thousand kids goin' crazy, out of their minds. All because some crazy black guy from Watts pulled a gun on Mick in the middle of the concert. The damn piece wasn't even loaded. The guy was just having a good time. He was stoned out of his mind. He couldn't have hurt a fly. Then the Hells Angels grabbed him and beat the shit out of him with pool cues. Let me tell you, it was a hairy situation."

Augie Coletti couldn't believe what I was telling him. Mick Jagger, Keith Richards, and the rest of The Rolling Stones and me and my men had just been through one of the scariest times of our lives.

Mick kidded about it, saying, in his British accent, that the kids were just having a good time.

"The Hells Angels were running security for the crowd. And, as you know, I've been doing my job to provide security for the Stones. And we haven't had any problems until now. We never had a problem until Altamont. And even that wasn't our problem. Our security was good. I had a chopper in back of the stage waiting to lift us out fast after Mick and the boys finished.

"I tell you, Augie, Mick Jagger is something else. He insisted on coming to the concert three days early so that he could walk around and shake hands with his fans. He wanted to do something nice for the kids. I couldn't stop him. I know you understand. Well, one day as he's walking through the kids, some bastard punches him in the face and bloodies his nose. I whisk him out by chopper and get him fixed up. He laughs and says that it comes with the territory.

"Then he wants to fly over the crowd and throw rose petals down on them from the air. He settles for 1,000 white roses and we do it. I tell you, he had me running around like crazy covering his ass.

"The place was packed with kids with knapsacks, women breast-feeding and carrying babies like papooses, overnight cases, tents, 300,000, they say, all on a 100-acre meadow. They had 'trip' tents set up for those who overdosed. The kids were having the times of their lives. The tents were staffed by hyped-up hippie physicians. There were ambulances running back and forth. And it was all free.

"I got with me six cops from Ross Simon's Bronx D.A.'s detachment. They've got steel shoulders. Big, strong guys. Only the best. My old partner, Richie, is with the D.A. now and he made the arrangements. Neat, eh? This bastard Simon is after my ass and I got his cops working for me in off-the-job security 3,000 miles away in San Francisco. If he ever finds out, he's going to crawl up the wall.

"The air is thick with marijuana and the Hells Angels are running crowd control and some biker gang is beating up kids with pool cues and chains. They're filling up the ambulances too. Mick and the boys say they're not going on until the beatings stop so I have a talk with the leader of the Angels and we come to an agreement. He thinks I'm mob-connected from back East, so I get some respect. Everywhere I look, there's cocaine, bennies, amphetamines, barbiturates, LSD, mescaline, hashish, and grass. You name it. It's like a scene from hell. You really put me in the hot seat with this one, Augie. But I got everybody out OK.

"I took care of the Stones all through the tour. I made these 'traps,' you know the kind, in all the hotel rooms we stayed at so that the boys could keep their 'valuables' in there so we could keep the cops off our backs. I used drills, saws, nails, and paint to make them. I didn't want any trouble with the cops like they got into before. And these guys would party every day and night with all the groupies that followed us around the country. It was one wild time. I thought I had seen everything on the NYPD but this tour really opened my eyes. It's a completely different world that these people live in. I don't see how they do it."

Augie just listens. What can he say? He raises the occasional eyebrow.

"So just before the Stones go on, there's a mad sea of people bouncing around and making love right out in the open all over the place. Really rolling in the hay. The whole farm shook like an earthquake was starting.

"You know these guys think my name is Mike Scotti. I want to keep my personal life quiet. I got my men all around back and front of the stage. The Stones go on and the crowd goes crazy. Everything's good until this one black guy from Watts stumbles down to the front of the stage and starts waving a gun, aiming it at Mick while he's singing and pulling the trigger. It's not loaded. Mick doesn't see the guy until the crowd grabs him and beats the hell out of him. I hear the guy got killed. Poor bastard. He was just having a good time. He didn't know what he was doing.

"The place breaks out into a riot. People are running everywhere. They storm the stage. I had the chopper warming up so we pack the Stones and their girlfriends in and take off and get the hell out of there. Kids are hanging on the struts. We can hardly lift off until they start to lose their grip and fall off. It was like war. The kids left all their instruments on the stage. We were lucky to get out in one piece. But I did it, Augie."

Augie Coletti looks at me like I'm telling him some kind of a fairy tale. He's in from New York to take care of business and visit with me and The Rolling Stones. He even brought a doll along with him and she thinks she's in heaven when she meets Mick and Keith. They are perfect gentlemen. She flips over their accents. They flip over her figure. She's one sharp dame.

Augie sucks on his Cuban madura Macanudo cigar, blows dirty brown circles in the air, sighs, and nods his head up and down as if he's going to say something really important, and he does with a soft whisper.

"Mike, I gotta tell you, you did one helluva job. Nobody could have done it better. I'm very happy. I'm glad everything worked out OK. I know you have to get back for that business you have back home. I got somebody else to fill in for you. I got good things happening, and when you're all finished with your business and you beat this thing, I got a lotta doors I'm gonna open for you."

"Hey, Augie, you did enough already and I appreciate it. But one step at a time. I'll be seeing you when I get back home and we'll talk."

"Mike, one last thing. Carmine wants to see you first thing when you get back tomorrow. I know it's important. He won't talk about it. That's how I know."

"OK. I'll get the first plane out in the morning."

"Good. And tonight we party. See you at eight."

* * *

INTROSPECTUS

MALOCCHIO

The evil eye. The curse of the *cornuto*, cast to inflict pain, terror, and death upon an enemy.

Malocchio lurks in the hills of Sicily. It slithers and crawls throughout the world, through the forests and swamps, into castles and hovels, into the hearts and minds of any man or woman, no matter how rich or poor. Wealth cannot buy deliverance from the Black Curse of the Evil Eye. There is only one release.

For over two centuries, a small fieldstone building has stood upon a windswept bluff in Camastra, overlooking the blue Mediterranean, a panorama before it. A view sensed unseen of ancient Greece, Crete, Sparta, and Mount Olympus; a silent penetration into the heart of Buddha and Mohammed; a glance across to the deep and mysterious dark secrets of voodoo. This church has stood for over two centuries as the Savior of last resort against evil, a place for a holy communion with God.

One man knelt among the hand-hewn pews. At forty-seven years old, he was a youngster to this ancient citadel of lost hope. The hands that had mortared its stone and planed its wood had long ago returned to the dust of the earth. Those hands had left a legacy beyond price, a transcendence to the Divine.

Bright sunlight filtered through stained-glass windows, painting a muted panoply of jeweled colors upon the marble floors and holy altar. A stillness and reverence spread out from the tabernacle and embraced the man. There was another presence within the holy walls, a sacred presence just beyond touch but not beyond feeling. Michael Palermo, for the first time in his life, felt the warm hand of his God upon his shoulder. He had never needed God before, at least not the way he needed Him now. He had come to the end of the road, and the road had led him back to Sicily and to the Camastra of his parents, to the rich soil where seeds grow and flourish; back to the generations of his ancestors, generations that held the answer to the arcane curse of *malocchio*. He had come to this church to fight the Prince of Darkness.

For one hour he prayed in a way he had forgotten—in a way he had not really ever learned. For he prayed this day with his heart, with his soul, and with his life. This was the last day, the last chance to break the chain of misfortunes that plagued him; to cure the pain of knives slicing into his brain; to remove the hot needles sizzling and pricking his mind; to release the tightness around his throat, the grip that was choking him, the Black Hand that would destroy him.

He had heard of *malocchio* many times before. He had seen the ceremony of exorcism when he was a young boy. In the back of his Uncle Aldo's grocery store in East Harlem, he had seen the lady dressed in black draw the curse from his uncle. He had hidden behind sacks of coffee beans and watched as the ugly black demon was dragged out of Zio Aldo. There was a great screaming and crying and the lady almost died. But she survived and Uncle Aldo lived.

Michael Palermo sat with his God, afraid to sit with a lady in black who could drive out demons. He was afraid of the monster that would erupt and leave his mind and his body; afraid that it would roam the world to torment someone else; afraid that the lady would die.

He could pray no more. There was a limit to everything, even for time praying with God. He felt some relief as he genuflected before the altar. With reverence, his shoes gently patted the marble floor as he left his sanctuary. He walked, and breathed, and lived as his parents and grandparents had done, as his ancestors had done. Now they were only ghosts. Perhaps they would walk beside him. Yes, he could feel them. He felt strength returning. He walked where they had walked, breathed the same air, seen the same mountains, the same sky, the same sea, the same earth and the church—the same church where they had been baptized and been purified before burial.

It was tradition that walked with Michael Palermo. It was the will and wisdom of the past that led him to the house of his cousin, Anna Palermo, the lady in black, the lady with the power to fight *malocchio*.

Somewhere in his past, there must have been a word, a gesture, or, as some say, perhaps even the sprinkling of some dried blood by an enemy who spelled the crushing pain of *malocchio* on Michael Palermo. Or did he perhaps bring the curse upon himself?

The door of Anna's house was open. As he entered, she was waiting for him.

"Michael, I knew you would be coming to see me now. I had a feeling."

"Anna, I don't know how or why, but I'm here. I was walking, feeling good. And I just followed my feet and, well, I'm here. I would like to talk."

Anna wore a belted black dress. It could have been a dress from the fourteenth century, for here in this little village things changed very slowly. People were reluctant to give up the ways of the past, the ways that worked.

"Come with me, Cousin." Anna led him into a small room. It was a tiny chapel with pictures of saints on the walls. At a little altar, a statue of the Blessed Mother held her infant son. On the stone wall above, a crucifix held him in death. Anna Palermo, at this moment in time, held life and death in her hands. It was a moment that never was and never would be again.

They sat at a table in the center of the room. Anna lit a small candle. The flame flickered and lapped at its red glass. Their faces turned scarlet in candlelight. She poured a drink into two glasses.

"Today you are with family, Cousin, and I will help you. I know you are troubled and through the power of God, I will help you, for it is through Him that we have the life and the power. Let us drink some Strega.

"Strega. The name means 'Witch.' It stings the mouth and throat. Feel how hot it is and how it burns as we swallow. It is also very sweet. It smells like flowers.

"Now that you are warm inside, relax. Breathe in deeply and let me look into your eyes."

Anna's eyes burned red as she looked into Michael's mind. He sat with his arms on the table, his hands clasped before him. He could not move. The air floated in trance.

"We shall see if there is a *malocchio* on your head," she whispered as she placed a drop of oil in a saucer of water before her. The two cousins watched as the oil beaded into a ball. It writhed in the water, changing shape. The drop moved as a snake, a gold strand, wiggling and coiling into a snail, then a man, and finally into a face, a face with horns—Satan.

Tears fell from Michael's eyes and he began to cry. Anna dropped her head into her hands, drained of strength.

Slowly she regained her composure, emptied the water and oil into a bowl, and said hoarsely, "Michael, I have done this many times and never have I seen a *malocchio* so strong. Never before have I seen the face of Satan. Tell me, my cousin, what has brought such a force upon you? Are you a killer of children? A stealer of wives? A Soldier of Satan? What have you done to make you like this?"

Michael closed his eyes, spilling the tears of the past over his cheeks. His teeth bit his lower lip, and he answered very slowly, as if he were very far away, at a distance of many years ago.

"I did what many people did, and they were honored as I was. I also did other things and still I am not sure why. I've often asked myself if, in my life, I've acted because I wanted to help others or because I wanted to help myself. It's like the doctor who heals people and then is paid with money and with respect. Now this is respect with honor. I was paid with money and with respect. This was not only the respect of honor but also of fear. If I have a *malocchio* on my head, I can only believe it is because at times I sought the respect that comes from fear and from power. Perhaps this is the way of a Soldier of Satan. I don't know. But if this is so, then the *malocchio* comes from within me. Even of this I am not sure. In a life such as mine, one can never be sure."

Anna just listened, nodding as he spoke, feeling the words, experiencing what he felt, bringing his torment inside her slowly, ever so slowly. From a saucer of warm oil, she chanted a prayer in Sicilian, half to herself and half in a whisper. Her thumb touched the oil and she reached out over the candle to mark a cross in oil on Michael's forehead. With more oil she crossed his temples and then each eyelid. Face to face, she concentrated and they locked minds.

A tension seized the air, a heaviness. Anna's eyelids became lead leaves and they began to close. Her face twitched around the eyes and mouth. Her cheeks sucked inward, drawing upon the spirit in her cousin's head. She yawned deeply, becoming very tired. Tears began to fall from her eyes. Michael's eyes opened wide with relief. He watched Anna, scarcely believing what he saw and how much better he felt. The candle dimmed and almost snuffed out as she lifted both her arms. With fingers outstretched, she grabbed at him slowly and pulled her arms toward her. With empty fists, she felt the *malocchio* draw out of him and sink into her chest. And then suddenly she collapsed onto the table.

"My God!" screamed Michael. "Not her, God! Don't take her! Let her live! Please let her live. Take me! I'm the one." He pressed his hand to her neck, feeling for a pulse. She was alive. Weak but alive.

"Anna," he whispered into her ear. "It's all right. It's Michael. It's over, Anna. It's all over."

Her pulse beat stronger and she opened her eyes. Michael helped her up. Together they walked.

"There is one thing I must do," she said softly. "Wait for me back at the table. I'll be all right." She entered the bathroom and forcibly retched the Black Curse out of her. Her cousin twinged as he heard the agony of her ordeal. He knew she was in deep pain. She returned, exhausted.

"I'm sorry, Anna. I didn't want this for you. I never should have come here and brought this into your life."

"Michael, that's what family is for. To help each other. It's good you have come to me. You never could have lived with that. I've never felt such a force before. Are you feeling better?"

"My pain is gone. I feel like I did when I was a boy."

"There's just one more thing to do," she said as she took a new saucer of water and placed a drop of oil into it. The drop did not move. It remained a round gold ball. The *malocchio* was gone. It was cast back into the days of many years ago, into the years of the stories of the life of Michael Palermo.

CHAPTER 1

The city gave me a living. A city of parasites and fat cows all living on each other. It took cops to make it work. Without cops, it would all be chaos and everything would grind to a halt. Without cops, the biggest guns would take over and be on the top. And the biggest guns would be bought by the people with the most money. Come to think of it, that's the way it is today. The cops protect the big money for the people in power. They keep the little guy from grabbing it all. They keep the little guy down and the big guy up.

Those cops on the job. They're little guys. They're keeping themselves down and they don't know it.

* * *

RYAN

I started on the job in 1953, and right from the get-go I ran into corruption. It was right after I shipped out of Korea and the Marines that I met Lieutenant Ryan. I had just filed my application for the police department and I was having a beer in the Bottiglia Tavern on Quimby and Castle Hill Avenue. My buddy

Angelo Poppi was a detective, and he was the one who introduced me to Lieutenant Ryan. As Ryan and I talked, I remember seeing Angie standing in the pantry nook with his arms around one of the waitresses. He pulled the curtain shut. Poppi really had big balls in those days. He could score anywhere, even in a restaurant at peak business hours. I always figured that that had something to do with him getting his gold shield. He was a popular guy.

Anyway, when he found out I was trying to make the department, this Lieutenant Ryan and I became good buddies for the evening. Then he made me a deal I couldn't believe. For 500 bucks he was going to guarantee that I pass the police test. He had friends in high places. He said that after he greased a few doors, I could walk right on in. He guaranteed that I'd pass or he'd give me my money back. I couldn't lose, he said.

Ryan was a heavyset, muscular, tough Irish cop. His eyes danced as he spoke and he spoke like he had kissed the Blarney. He was a perfect salesman and, like he said, 500 bucks was like buying an insurance policy. I told him I'd think about it. I didn't tell him that I needed time to figure out his angle. Everybody had an angle. The Marines had taught me that.

It was while walking home that night that I kept seeing Ryan's face in the street lamps. He was saying, "For 500 bucks, I guarantee you'll pass. I'm not trying to rip you, kid. You've got nothing to lose."

All the street lamps were talking and laughing just like Ryan. I figured he must have big connections downtown. He could get rich helping guys like me. If he helped enough guys, he could retire with big bucks. If he helped everybody, he couldn't lose, and that's when I realized that Ryan couldn't lose no matter what happened. He takes the money, does nothing, and if the guy passes the test, Ryan's made 500 bucks. If the guy fails, then Ryan gives him his money back. What a deal!

A few days later, I thanked Angelo Poppi for the introduction and told him that from then on, he could keep friends like Ryan to himself.

THE TEST

I passed the written test on my own and without any help from Ryan. Then I just had to take the physical. I was still in good shape from Korea, so the only problem I could see was the height and weight requirement. You see, I had to be at least five-feet-eight inches tall and weigh at least 135 pounds. I needed a quarter-inch in height that I didn't have. I also didn't weigh 135 pounds. I had two strikes against me.

Some of the guys who worked with Poppi told me that if I stuffed myself with bananas and water just before being weighed, that would put on the three pounds that I needed. Other guys said that if I slept on the floor at night, the discs in my spine wouldn't compress and I could pick up the quarter-inch I needed. They said that people get a little shorter as they walk around all day long and gravity squeezes the cartilage discs in the spine. Well, I'll tell you, I was willing to try anything. I really wanted to be a cop. Not only did I sleep on the floor on the night before the physical, but I even got dressed while laying on the floor. Poppi took the backseat out of the station wagon, and he and another buddy carried me down and laid me on the floor in the back of the car.

Now you've got to picture this. I'm lying there on my back and the only thing I can see is the ceiling of the car, and I'm stuffed to the throat with bananas and water. All through the heavy traffic I can hear myself sloshing from side to side and from front to rear. I start to get seasick. Like I'm on a banana boat or something.

When we get downtown I can't walk too much because I don't want to lose the bananas and the quarter-inch. I get inside quick, sign in, and hit the hard bench outside the examining room. I'm going to lay there on my back until they call me. A lot of little guys had done the same thing before. Some of them passed the physical, and some didn't. Now, while I'm waiting there for my name to be called, I start to get these real bad cramps in my insides. I try to hold them back, but they won't stop. They keep pushing hard. And nobody calls my name. I only need a few more minutes. But then my guts begin to heave and I can't wait. I can't hold it. I run down the hall like a crazy man and I lose three pounds in the men's room. Then, wouldn't you know it, as soon as I get back they call my name.

Inside I strip and get on the machine. First, they measure my height. And I tell you I never stretched so hard in my life. I never wanted anything so bad as to be five-eight. I needed what other people took for granted. There are two switch buttons that my heels have to keep pressed down. I feel like I'm made of elastic, straining, stretching, just to reach that rod with my head. My muscles start to hurt. I can feel the tendons and ligaments give a little. Let me touch, God, and I'll do anything you want. A novena. Anything. I touch and the attendant says, "You're five-eight." Whew!

Now for the scale. If only I hadn't lost those goddamn bananas. I should have eaten cotton and glue.

I get on the scale and the weight slides along the bar in front of me. One hundred and thirty-three pounds. The damn bananas! I don't make the weight. I figure it's all over. But after everything I had gone through to get on that damn scale in the first place, I'm not going to walk away like a damn fool. I turn to the attendant and ask him very quietly, "Would you mind adding two pounds to that?"

The guy looks at me, kind of surprised. I think I've blown it for sure. Then he shrugs and says, "Sure, what the hell is two pounds anyway?"

I'm 135 and five-eight. And I always thought that it was kind of funny, that in spite of everything else that had happened to me before—the Harlem streets as a kid, the two wars I was in, the shrapnel in my leg, the written police test—that it was only that one judgment call, that one executive decision, that one white lie that made Mike Palermo a cop.

THE FIRST ACT OF CORRUPTION

I remember my first week on the job, in the "bag." It was a hot day in May. As I walked, I had to be careful not to step in the tar that was melting in the frying sun; not to stick in the pink and white, flat button-blobs of chewing gum that the neighborhood kids had spit out; not to skid on the dog droppings that littered the steaming sidewalk and gutters. Beads of perspiration melted from my open pores and I tried to walk in the shadows of the buildings. I twirled my nightstick and jabbed at the low black-iron railings that surrounded the tenements.

Clang! Clang! Bing, bang, clang! Boy, I thought, I've got rhythm just like those black mothers on the front stoops. I whistled a catchy trolley tune as I chimed the musical rails, and I smiled to the natives as I passed them. At 138th Street I watched this big, black car with a white guy driving run a red light, real blatant-like, like he owned the road. He came down the street right at me. Great, I thought, here was my first moving violation. Just what I needed.

As I jumped into the tarry street and waved him down, I could feel the eyes of the stoop bunnies sticking in my back. Hell, I felt like I was on a stage, an actor, like Pat O'Brien, except O'Brien was Irish. The glossy new black Buick pulled over right in front of the tenement stoop. It was stuck with people in sleeveless pullover blouses, patchy skirts and trousers, curlered hair sticking through babushkas, and always the kinky, greased, slapped-back black hair and always the native scent of sweating indolence. In front of them all, I stepped up to the car. I was sweating bullets because of our audience and because of the driver with his annoyed surprised white face.

"May I see your driver's license and registration, please, sir?" My audience snickered behind me. The guy handed me his wallet. I should have known something was wrong right then and there. "No, sir! Please take them out of the wallet." The guy looked at me, surprised.

"Listen, Officer, trouble like this I don't need. I know there's a light there, but why shouldn't you take the wallet and take what you want?"

"Sir, please take your license and registration out."

"OK, Officer. All right. Here you are."

I grasped the documents, but he didn't let go.

"Look, Officer, what good is it going to do you or me if you give me a ticket? You give me a ticket, I'll have to pay $5 to City Hall. That does no good for you or for me. Why should City Hall get rich? Listen, why don't you take a chicken?"

He wouldn't let go of his license. "A chicken? Where's a chicken?" I asked in surprise as my eyes searched the car.

"I've got a nice chicken for you. Look, everybody takes one. Why should you be different? A ticket I'll pay and you'll get nothing. But a chicken, you'll have, you'll enjoy. You have a family? I'll give you a BIG chicken. I own the chicken market around the corner. Please, take a chicken."

"What's the name of your chicken market, Mr. Fleisher?"

"Fleisher's Chicken Market. What else? And it's kosher. But it doesn't matter. You'll enjoy. Everybody takes one. Come see me later."

I felt a tickle, a light tremble, and before I knew it I was howling in a big belly laugh. The stoops behind me were giggling.

"Mr. Fleisher, get the hell out of here, but watch yourself. If I stop you again, you won't just get a warning from me." I found myself cordially patting him on the shoulder as he stuffed his bulky wallet inside his jacket. A streetwise merchant with chickens for bribes. It was so funny to me at the time that he deserved to be let go.

"Thank you, Officer, and I'll be waiting for you later. Don't forget. A nice BIG chicken."

I really had no intention of going to get that damn bird, but fate must have been at work because, near the end of my shift, I found myself in front of Fleisher's Chicken Market. What the hell, I thought. I'm here. I might as well go in and say hello. As I entered and closed the glass door behind me, Fleisher's eye caught mine. The sawdust chips on the floor flew in all directions as he half-bounced and half-slid across the room toward me.

"Just a minute, Officer, and I'll have a nice chicken for you."

With that, he reached into a smelly wooden crate and hoisted a large black and speckled white, gurgling sputtering bird out by the neck. The chicken flashed its claws in a wild running motion and screeched. With feathers flying, Fleisher brushed past me into the back room where a yarmulked rabbi stood with a long, narrow, razor-sharp knife. I wanted to stop them, but the words never came out. They stuck like a lump in my throat. I felt a goose-pimply twinge as the rabbi held the feathers by the feet, slashed the chicken's throat, and thrust him headfirst into a large wooden funnel. His legs kicked, and feathers flew up from the flapping, poor, doomed bird. After the blood drained and the flapping stopped, my supper was handed to a young boy who worked in front of a steamy, stinking hot water kettle. After a short dunk in the cauldron, he quickly plucked the bird and Mr. Fleisher neatly covered it in light brown wrapping paper and stuffed it into a brown paper bag.

"It's a beauty, Officer. You'll love it. You'll enjoy. You did the right thing, Officer. Now, I know you can't go into the station house with a chicken in a bag, so when you're finished work you come back here and pick it up."

I nodded, thanked him, and went to the station house to sign out. I felt a little funny. I had just witnessed a murder. Sure, it was only a chicken. And I was going to eat it. I wondered if Fleisher thought he owned me and had me in his pocket for a chicken. Oh, what the hell.

I got out of uniform and returned to the market. As Fleisher handed me the chicken, I quipped, "Are you sure this is kosher?"

He winked and answered, "Sure it's kosher; everybody takes a chicken."

That damn chicken was the toughest damn big old soup rooster I ever had. How the hell did I know that I shouldn't have broiled it on the grill? We could hardly eat it. I'm convinced that five hours of boiling wouldn't have made any difference.

That was my first act of corruption on the job. A tough old chicken and a savvy old merchant. Corrupt or not, everybody on the force knew it was "kosher."

THE AMBER LIGHT

I was eight weeks on the force and Sergeant Halloran's driver, Tommy Lynch, was out sick. I got his seat that night. It was a drizzly, wet night in August. I remember how the traffic lights had a misty halo about them as they burned. Red, amber, green, like a Christmas ornament. I checked out the car and waited for Sergeant Halloran. I had never had much to do with him before this day, but I had heard from some of the guys that he was into whiskey and bucks. I was supposed to drive and not remember too much of anything that I saw that evening. "Just play it cool with 'Hollerin' Halloran'," they said.

"OK, Palermo, let's get the hell out of here," piped Halloran. "Do you know where Sullivan's be, lad?"

"Sure, Sarge."

"Well, let's go see O'Leary and be sure he's havin' no trouble. It's a wet night and there's some that's a bit dry in the throat on a warm, piddlin' night like this. O'Leary will be glad to see us."

I drove, mouth closed, eyes and ears open. Halloran settled into the bench seat and slipped his legs and body forward so that his head and neck could rest on the seat back. He made himself at home. After all, I guess this was his second home. Why shouldn't he relax and enjoy it? Eight hours of work, eight hours of sleep, two hours of traveling time to the job. That left only six hours with his family. He spent more waking time doing police work than with his wife and kids. Sure, relax, Halloran, make yourself at home. You've got a chauffeur, an easy chair, a rocking car to lull away your problems. What the hell else could you want?

"Very nice, me boy, now hop in there to Sulli's and pick up my flute from O'Leary. Tell 'em I send my best and may the green always be with him—and with me, too, of course. But don't tell him that last part. Let him say it so that we can be sure things are well with him."

"I'll give him your best, Sarge," I said.

"No, son!" Halloran laughed. "Let him give you HIS best."

I didn't know for sure exactly what he meant. What the hell did he want with a flute anyway? I hope he's not going to blow an Irish jig all night long in the car. Poor old Lynch. Maybe that's why he's out sick. I should have brought along earmuffs. That would be some helluva sight. An Irish sergeant tooting a flute, and a Sicilian driver wearing earmuffs. It wouldn't work. I'd just have to pretend I liked his playing and get him to play *Santa Lucia*.

"Hi, I'm looking for O'Leary," I announced to the man behind the bar.

"I'm he," said the red-haired, scarlet-cheeked bartender. His eyes beamed and his lips smiled, lightly curled at the corners.

He slapped two heavy-boned hands, palms down on the bar top. "What can I do for you, Officer?"

"I've come for Sergeant Halloran's flute," I answered, not knowing what the hell I was really saying.

"Ah, Sergeant Hal's got a new driver, does he? Where's Tommy Lynch tonight, home, nice and dry?" O'Leary glanced over my shoulder at the window and when I saw his eye wink I realized that Halloran had waved an OK from the squad car at the curb.

As I was told, I recited, "The sergeant says to tell you, 'May the green always be with you.'"

"May the green always be with him," O'Leary responded as he pulled a six-ounce fluted, amber-colored Coca-Cola bottle out from under the bar. He put it in a little brown paper bag along with an envelope. Would you care for a little something, Officer?"

"No thanks, O'Leary. Not when I'm on the job. But I appreciate the offer."

O'Leary burst out into a laugh, crashed his palms down on the bar, and chuckled. "Of course not, not on the job. Some other time, then."

I left, sat behind the wheel, and Halloran put the bag between his thighs. At his direction we drove to a street darkened by vandals' rocks. Rocks that had smashed the streetlights.

"Park here, Palermo. Keep your eyes and ears open and your mouth shut. I'm going to rest a bit while I plan our tour tonight."

He took the envelope out of the bag and smoothly slipped it inside his blue brass-buttoned jacket as if he had done it a hundred times before. With the brown bag crinkled and crushed around the fluted bottle, he pressed his lips on the exposed open throat and glugged down his amber delight. I could smell the whiskey. The aroma floated up from the bag, from his lips, even, it seemed, from out of his ears. As I sat watch for the people of the City of New York and for him, he slipped into a snoring sleep and I was in the middle.

While he slept and I watched, the car got hot and filled with the reek of whiskey. I opened the rear window for ventilation and the mist of rain washed the air clean. The rain sprinkled in lightly and the rear vinyl-covered seats started to smell like an old raincoat. I sat and Halloran slept. After about fifteen minutes the rain finally let up. Carefully, I opened the door to get out and stretch and breathe deeply. But not quietly enough. The snoring stopped and the wily Irish cop opened his left eye like a cat that heard a dry branch crack in a quiet forest.

"What's up, lad?"

"Nothin', Sarge. I just wanted to stretch my legs."

With that, a green Chevy passed through the intersection just as the light was changing from green to amber but not yet to red. Its tires splashed in a large puddle under the light and a spray of multicolored rainbow droplets veiled the air.

"Get your ass back in here and nail that bastard. He just went through that light," growled Halloran.

We raced after the Chevy and stopped it two blocks away.

"Let me see your license and registration."

"Hey, Officer, have a heart, will ya? If it's about that light back there, it was amber. I made it through while it was amber," pleaded the driver. He was a little guy, dark complexion, black hair, wiry. He could have been my brother. He could have been me.

"You know you're not supposed to go through an amber light. The light's a warning that the red light's coming on. You're supposed to stop on amber."

"But I made it through before it turned red. Look, I just got off work at Lincoln Hospital. I work in the emergency ward. It's one in the morning. I was just trying to get home. My wife's waiting up for me. We're having a baby. She works days. We don't get to see each other much. A ticket like this is really going to hurt. It's going to cost me half a day's pay just going to court to answer it. I'll stop at the amber from now on. I promise!" He was begging.

I felt like God. But then I remembered that God was in the squad car behind me.

"Just a minute." I went around to the rear of the car to check the license plate with the registration. They matched. I walked up to Sergeant Halloran who was licking the whiskey off his lips.

"Sarge, this guy's a working man at Lincoln Hospital, and you know the light was amber."

"Fuck 'em. Write him up. It'll make up for all the red lights he's gone through before. He needs to be taught some manners, lad. This'll be a sort of penance for all his past sins, all his past red lights, or whatever the hell else he's done that was wrong. Write him up! Now! And be quick about it. We've got a lot of ground to cover in the next few hours!" hollered Halloran. His nickname fit him perfectly. As I turned, I knew he was going to finish off his "Coke" flute behind my back. So I gave the little hospital guy a ticket. I didn't tell him that it was presumptuous Father Halloran's penance. I felt like I was giving a summons to myself. The poor guy sure could have been me.

That night, I was wedged in between an amber flute of whiskey and an amber traffic light. I didn't like it. It wasn't the last time that I'd find myself in the middle.

THE WIRE

I remember April 1955. It was a sunny Monday and I was working on 138th Street and Cypress Avenue. A glossy black Chevrolet pulled up across the street from me and parked. I knew it was one of our stripped-down, unmarked jobs. I saw a high-ranking officer in the rear seat. I could see the "eggs" on his cap. What the hell did I do now? I thought, as the uniformed driver walked up to me.

He said the Chief wanted to know my name. The Chief was a big boss. He was Bronx Borough Commander Ernest Hecter.

I gave him my name and he got my precinct number off my lapel—40. He thanked me and returned to the car. I watched the glossy black surprise package get lost in traffic.

The next morning, Commander Hecter called me down to his office. When I got there, there were a bunch of sharply dressed officers working like hell behind their desks. Hecter's second-in-command, Lieutenant Sanford Garelick, asked me if I knew why I was down there. I told him I didn't. And I tell you I was scared stiff. I took a seat and waited for three hours. Finally, Garelick called me into Hecter's office and the three of us sat down at the Commander's desk. The conversation went like this. Commander Hecter began.

"How'd you ever make this fuckin' job?"

"I took the test, Sir."

"I'm not talkin' about that. Are you five-eight?"

"Yes, sir, I am."

"And how much do you weigh?"

"One forty." I wondered if this guy was for real and if he was going to weigh me.

"Tell me about your background." Hecter seemed a little more cordial.

"Well, sir, I've got seven years in the Marine Corps."

"What did you do?"

"I was in the invasion of Okinawa, got my three stripes, and then went to Korea and got my first Louie bars."

Hecter threw his arms up in the air and yelled, "The goddamn job's loaded with Marines." Then he smiled like a Cheshire Cat. "What did you do after that?"

"I worked in Western Electric for a while after I left the service. I helped install telephones."

"You installed telephones?" Hecter's eyes widened. Garelick looked on with interest.

"I didn't install them. I used to draw the cables in and hook them into the new crossbar digital system. I was a good wireman. I did a lot of soldering."

"So you know about telephones. Do you know the color coding?"

"Yes, sir, I do. Blue, orange, green, brown, slate. That's the color code we used."

"Good, Palermo. Good. I've got a nice job for you. Do you have any friends on the job?"

"No, sir. I don't know a soul."

"Perfect!" Hecter smiled. Garelick beamed.

The next day, Hecter put me in a basement. It was under a haberdashery store. I was alone with him and a wiretap machine that was tapped into the six pay telephones of the United Cigar Store on 161st Street and River Avenue. It was opposite Yankee Stadium.

My job was to give Hecter the phone numbers that were dialed from the cigar store. At that point, I didn't realize that I was in the middle of a highly organized gambling operation and that the nine plainclothes men assigned to cover gambling in that district were all on the payroll. As I listened to the phones, I realized that every bookmaker or gambler who went to Yankee Stadium used those phones to call in bets. The calls to the betting parlors came in so fast that I couldn't leave the machine. Finally, I called Hecter. The guy was in heaven. He sounded like Teddy Roosevelt yelling into the telephone: "CHARGE!" And Hecter charged and raided. All the bookies were being cleaned out of the Bronx. Imagine that, all because of one new guy in a store basement who didn't know anybody and really didn't know what the hell he was doing. Well, as you see, this couldn't go on for long.

I received a visit from one of the borough white-shield plainclothes men. He was an Italian named Bratti.

"Hey, kid. Do you know what you're doing?"

"Sure. I'm in a goddamn basement tapping phones."

"Where's the wire?'

"The United Cigar Store."

"You see, you don't know what the hell you're doing. Let me set you straight. You're knocking every bookmaker in the Bronx out of business."

"What the hell do you mean?"

"You're ruining a lot of good guys. Good guys like Matti Green who just bought a tuxedo store and sunk a lot of money into the business. He's got a bank of phones that are gettin' wiped out. He's losin' big money. Everybody's mad. And I mean everybody! I was told to put you on the pad. We don't want you sending any more phone numbers to Hecter because he himself is being taken care of. But he doesn't want the whole world to know about it, so he's got this crap goin' out. He's double-bangin' everybody. He's takin' it with one hand, and with the other he's knockin' everybody over to show that he's gut-honest. Besides being mad, we're all very embarrassed. The whole squad is pissed off. Hecter's using you to make himself look good downtown."

Man, was I in a jam. Bratti told me about how cops had to stick together, never rat on each other, and had to live up to a contract. I had heard all that stuff before from the hoods when I was a kid. I tried to get out of that whole deal right then and there, but Bratti said that I couldn't get out and still look good with the Dutchman, as they called Hecter. So we agreed that I would first call Bratti with the numbers, and then call Hecter. Bratti told me which numbers I should give to the Dutchman. For the sake of the borough, I stayed on.

Now you can imagine how things went for Commander Hecter after that. Gambling operations under the padded umbrella didn't get raided anymore and those that were raided turned out to be lonely telephones ringing in a vacant loft.

Hecter and his men wound up answering them and booking the action.

After that I went back on patrol. I never forgot Commander Hecter and THE WIRE. And I never thought it would feel so great being back in "the bag."

THE COOP

Mike worked the early morning tour from twelve midnight to eight in the morning. It was a chilly December evening two weeks before the holiday season. He walked his beat, checked the dark storefronts, some of which burned a yellow glow from within. There was a shoe repair shop, a cleaners, Pringle's Bar, a barbershop, and rows of neighborhood stores that helped the district survive. Business was good at Pringle's. People were already celebrating the holiday, and those at the bar who weren't there for the partying were there lamenting privately and silently about their sorry lot in life. Careers that were stalled with despaired hopes of promotions, lost chances to make money that would guarantee financial security and freedom. These were people left with the hollow, broken visions of expensive, glittering cars and oceanfront suites that they now coldly realized were never to be. Some of the drinkers had had their essences scooped out by family tragedies, illnesses, or deaths. In drink, they saw an escape that they could never otherwise achieve in this life. The whiskey and beer flowed freely at Pringle's and the customers reveled or wept silently or to each other. Mike smelled the sawdust sprinkled with bourbon or beer foaming from draught. Pringle's Bar had a delicious, singular aroma of spirits, malt and hops, cigars, and cigarettes blended by the master brewer of tavern fragrances, the neighborhood bartender.

I was thirsty, and seeing those people inside Pringle's got me to thinking that maybe I should go in for a flute of my own. I could put to use some of the things that Sergeant Halloran had taught me during our tour together. Well, I thought, maybe later I would drop in, but not until the Sarge came around for his "see." I knew he would be making his rounds, collecting envelopes and amber coke bottles. I would just wait until after he came around with Lynch.

Every night Halloran would come by for my little salute, to make sure that I was on the job and that everything was under control. After a smile, a nod, a gag, and a wave, I could then hit Pringle's at closing time at 3 AM, get a flute, and sack out in "the coop" until I checked out at the precinct house at eight. The "super" at the Morrison housing project liked to have cops around. He let the cops use the basement in the main building. There were always twenty to twenty-five cops sleeping out their tour. They slept on benches, on the floors, sitting up in folding chairs, leaning on walls, and even on tables. And then there was one guy who was different. He slept on an inflatable mattress that he blew up every night. It cushioned his sleep, and in the morning he deflated it and stuffed it inside his jacket. His name was Leavitt.

Leavitt thought he was sharp, a smart guy. He never missed an angle. He always wanted the edge. He knew all the answers. A lot of guys thought he was a big bag of hot air, but they tolerated him because his uncle was a lieutenant in the Police Commissioner's office. He sure was a lot of hot air. The bastard, always blowing up his mattress and settling into it like he was sleeping on a cloud. If his uncle knew what he was doing in the coop, he would have skinned him alive. The rest of us slept on wood.

A few weeks earlier, Leavitt had started having some problems with his air mattress. Every night somebody kept sticking a pin into it, and with a slow leak he settled down into the wood like the rest of us. When he woke up he'd get real mad and curse the "pin bastard" who stuck his air bag. For two weeks it was a pin, a patch by Leavitt, a pin by "the bastard," and another patch by Leavitt, a pin, a leak and a patch and more hot air by Leavitt. He said some day he would catch the rat.

I walked into the Morrison coop with my Pringle's flute wrapped in a brown paper bag. It was half past three and Leavitt was just blowing up his balloon. I gave a few of the guys a slug from my bottle, and we threw the bull while Leavitt pulled a surprise on everyone. He dragged his bed into a maintenance closet and wedged the door shut from the inside. That night he had it all figured out. He'd be safe from that pinpricking bastard. We joked that he might suffocate in there and nobody would be able to get in to bury him. While Leavitt slept in "maintenance" and I was warming my insides with Seagram's 7; while guys rolled craps and played poker in the corner; and while others snored on wood cushions, a bold trio just seven floors above set into motion a plan that defied belief.

Little Herman, Tony T., and Sugarman Cobb activated a week of planning. With the aid of a stolen master key and a chain cutter, the three, systematically and with the quiet softness of cotton falling on velvet, opened apartment doors one by one, bound and gagged any residents they came upon, ripped out the phone lines as a precaution, and selectively looted the unguarded spoils. Their plan was to rip off the entire apartment building, to do something that would be a big score and would be talked about for years. By the time they reached the fourth floor, after hitting every apartment on their tour up to that point, they had collected money, jewelry, wedding rings, gold chains, marijuana, pills, heroin, and cocaine. Sugarman Cobb, a heavy-set, jolly-faced black guy with glistening, slicked-back straight black hair, looked and felt like Santa Claus as he hung on to a bulging canvas sack of loot that swung over his shoulder.

The trio had no way of knowing that apartment 4G was occupied by a lone man who slept fully clothed in a dark corner with his right index finger resting on the trigger of a double-barreled sawed-off shotgun. Fernando Mendato slept like a panther in a tree, holed up in his girlfriend's pad. He was wanted by the police for murder and by the black narcotics racket for hijacking and killing one of its dealers. Mendato's left eye and right index finger were poised to react instantaneously to the slightest vibration, even to the buzzing of a fly.

The lucky trio finished apartment 4F, and Little Herman softly slipped the master key into Mendato's willing tumbler. In the dark hole in the corner of the room, a left eye watched as three quiet figures slipped into apartment 4G. The beam of Tony T.'s flashlight cut through the black and scanned the room. It was one eye watching another, just Fernando Mendato and Tony T.'s light beam.

As the light swept across the tables and lamps, a right index finger tensed on the shotgun trigger. The beam swung over to the pitch-black corner, and the eye and flashlight met head-on with a brutal finality. A steel finger tensed, taut like a bowstring stretched to the limit. A hair trigger moved but a millimeter, and a deafening explosion roared like the tail end of a jet engine and tore into Tony T. blasting him two feet up in the air and hurtling him across the room, shattering lamps and chairs, mirrors and plates. On the white wall, in the spotlight of a brilliant full moon, he crashed with a deadening thud and stuck pasted like a mural, spread-eagled with a ragged, oozy, pulpy red wound emblazoned on the chest of his pink shirt. Glistening tabs of fresh flesh and crimson drops of dying blood were framed on the white wall by the jaundiced yellow full moon. The dead man slowly slipped into a hunched heap on the floor just as a duo with a bulging sack dove out the door and down the staircase. Mendato and his shotgun followed. As Herman and Cobb reached the lobby, they saw two police officers approach the building. They didn't know that Patrolmen Avery and Williams were on their way to the basement for a snooze.

They didn't know that the building was a "coop." They had planned the job well, they thought, but they also didn't know that a sleeping Mendato had a shotgun with a hair trigger. They were scared of the cops in the front of the building and of the shotgun that they knew would be coming down the stairwell after them, so they ducked down the stairs to the basement to hide or to exit through a rear door.

Mendato bolted down the staircase with his eyes stretched wide and glassy. He had reloaded and held his stubby, sawed-off shotgun at his right hip. When he saw Avery and Williams at the front door, he froze and jerked the trigger. The glass doors shattered into a fusillade of tinkling, splintering needles and buckshot. The two bewildered cops dove into the hedges lining the walk. After a side rollover, they recovered into a prone firing position. As Mendato ran past them, seven bullets ripped into the rear of his head and back. As the head shots exited, his forehead blew apart and dust puffs feathered off his back and shoulders, the dirt of days of being hunted in the street. As Mendato fell, Cobb and Herman were downstairs, opening the door of the basement room, which was full of sleeping cops.

Guys in uniform were snoring, stretched out on the floor, on the tables, propped up in chairs, playing cards, and shooting craps and Leavitt was in his private suite on an air cushion, oblivious to life itself, just waiting for his alarm clock to wake him up for his hourly check-in call.

I took one look at these two numbnuts that came busting into our place and I dropped my damn flute. They were more surprised than we were. Cobb let loose his sack, and piles of cash, jewelry, pills, and packages, which popped out and spilled over the floor. Haven't ID'd Hanley yet and I jumped up and drew our pieces and those two guys turned and ran into Avery, who was running down the hall to tell us what had happened out front. They stopped cold and just sat down in the hall with their backs to the wall.

By this time, the front of the building was jammed with ambulances, police cars, sirens, and spinning red lights. It was like something out of an old Cagney movie. By the time we searched and questioned our two prisoners, newspaper reporters and photographers were asking questions and popping flashbulbs.

Now, just imagine, twenty-two cops, all dressed neat and spick-and-span, looking like ideal policemen. Hell, Reed even spit on his brass and his shoes to shine them up. Twenty-two cops leading out two scared and confused prisoners into a sea of noise and flashing lights. We all got commendations, all except Leavitt, that is, because he was sleeping, and the Department's efficiency rating got a real boost. He had been sleeping on his air mattress locked in the maintenance room. When he came out to make his hourly check-in call, he didn't believe anything that we told him had happened. And wouldn't you know it, while he listened to us, somebody stuck his air mattress with a pin.

THE JUMPER

I can remember one afternoon's work as clearly today as on the day it happened. It was a quarter to five. I'll never forget the time because I was supposed to meet my wife for dinner at five-thirty at a restaurant in Downtown Manhattan. Lou Jenkel was my partner. We were two detectives counting the minutes, waiting to check out for the day, when the phone rang. The 42nd Precinct needed two detectives to talk a jumper out of leaving the fifteenth floor of a project apartment. This wacko wanted to take a long first step out the window. They called for detectives because the guy was armed with a knife. Lou took the call and said we would respond immediately.

"Hey, Lou, for Chrissake, I gotta meet my wife for dinner at five-thirty. She'll kill me if I screw up again like the last time. I was three hours late then."

"Come on, Mike, we got plenty of time. It'll be a breeze," laughed Jenkel, like he wanted to toy with me, tease me like a kid who didn't want to take a bath. "We'll have this bird down in no time, one way or the other. Who knows, maybe the kook can fly."

"Lou, I don't ask for much, do I? I mean, I laugh at your jokes, put up with your goddamn garlic salami and listen to you hiccup half the day. And what do I get? You owe me a little consideration. Take the call yourself. You go and get all the credit. Come on, it's ten to five. I really gotta meet her on time tonight. You don't need me." I was pleading with the guy and he was getting his kicks by being a ball-breaker but laughing the whole time. I guess we were both acting a little. We were really good friends and got along well, but every once in a while we'd crack each other's nuts.

"So you don't like my jokes, eh? Well, just look at this one." He picked up an umbrella and did a Chaplin waddle down the hall to the elevator. "Get your ass down here and walk this way."

I gotta hand it to him, he made me laugh again like he usually did and I followed. There was no use arguing with a guy who thinks he's Chaplin. Down the stairs, in the car, to the fifteenth floor and right to the windowsill where this black guy was ready to jump. I kept beefing and trying to get away to meet my wife. It was now 5:30—dinnertime. I took one look at the guy and knew what I had to do. There was a priest there, telling this black guy Charlie that he knew he was a good Catholic and that it was a mortal sin for him to take his own life. Life is in the hands of God, he said. God gives life and takes it away. Charlie's friends needed him, loved him. There was not a problem in the world that couldn't be solved. The priest would help Charlie. He would sit down with him, and together they would work out his difficulties.

An elderly woman was there and she pleaded with her son Charlie not to jump. She berated Charlie's wife. No woman was worth taking your own life, she said. God will punish her. Charlie would find another girl who would make him happy.

I stood through five minutes of the pleadings and kept hearing my watch ticking.

"Pardon me, ma'am. Excuse me, Father, but if I can have a word with him alone I know I can bring him in. It would be better if you both went outside into the next room so that Charlie and I can talk in private." I motioned them across the room to the door so that I could be alone with this idiot who was ruining my dinner and my life. As I approached the window, he started to grab the sill spasmodically, in a grasping, almost lurching movement.

He straddled the window ledge threateningly, like he was riding a horse. His left leg inside and his right leg outside. His hair was kinky-ribbed and pressed close to his long skull. There were drops of panicky perspiration on his jet-black slippery skin. His lips looked swollen and were three times the size of mine. His teeth were bleached-bone, ivory white. As he spoke, his yellow eyes dilated and with every forced breath his nostrils flexed and pulsed.

"Keep away from me, man, you hear, or I'm gonna fly. I'm gonna fly real good. You hear! You ain't gonna stop me, man. No way." He was screaming wildly.

I stepped aside and peered out the adjoining window. Fifteen floors below, there were hundreds of little ant-like creatures darting in and out, waving, screaming, and some were holding a circular net directly below. It was a jump net with vertical pole supports on the rim. From where I stood, it looked as big as a round oatmeal box top. How the hell could they catch anyone in that? Tiny specks of people were herded behind barricades. Some were quiet and still, looking up with their eyes glued on Charlie and me. He was the star and I was the supporting cast, along with the priest, his mother, and the extras. After all this, damn Lou Jenkel was only an extra! I'll show those bastards Charlie and

Jenkel. I figured I'd use a technique I'd used before. I even saw it used successfully in some police movies. I inched closer to Charlie.

"Look, you black bastard! Nobody loves you. Nobody cares what the hell you do. I'm not coming any closer because I don't want you grabbing me and taking me with you. Now you already made me one hour late for my dinner date with my wife. So why don't you either jump out the goddamn window and kill yourself, splatter all over the damn pavement, splash your stupid-ass head and brains all over the street, or get the hell back in here so I can go out for dinner." I gave him the option to come back in last so that it would be fresh in his mind and he would be more likely to accept it. I was using psychology.

Well, this guy Charlie did a double take. I mean I had shocked him and said just the opposite of what everybody else had said. He just sat there like he was thinking. Just looking down at the people on the ground and back at me like he couldn't make up his mind about what to do. That was all I needed. I took the opportunity to prey upon his uncertainty. Again, I used the psychology I had been taught.

"Listen, dummy. Make up your mind! I've got to get to dinner. If you don't get the hell in here, I'm going to push you out the goddamn window myself."

I got through to him. He turned, sat on the ledge, put both legs inside the room, threw his knife to the floor and stretched out his open hands toward me. As Lou and I reached out to grab him, he gave us a big, glaring, white, toothy smile, made two fists with the back of his hands toward us, raised his two middle fingers in an obscene gesture, and did a back flip out the window into the open air, into the specks of cheering observers, into his audience. He was the star. He was flying. Jenkel and I dove at the window to grab his feet but he was too fast. He was gone. I watched him float down fifteen floors and sail like a skydiver in free

fall, on his back, his outstretched fists with extended middle fingers, his black-framed white toothy smile. It seemed like minutes
as he fell, like he had wings that made him fly. Charlie was flying
and, miraculously, without even steering, he was heading straight
for the box-top-size jump net. His loose shirt and pants legs rippled and whipped in the breeze of flight, and crazy, dumb Charlie
smacked down right in the center of the jump net. I watched
the center cave in, the support poles buckle and bend. My God!
What did I do? And Charlie, poor Charlie, poor dumb, crazy
Charlie. Well, as I watched, I saw Charlie bolt out of the center
of the net and head back upward, back at me. It was like a dream
sequence, but this time he only traveled two stories up and fell
back down into the net.

Jenkel screamed, "Bull's-eye! How the hell did you do it,
Mike?"

Charlie bounced a few more times and then jumped out of
the net like a hero. Little speck Charlie started running around
the lawn and the sidewalks, in and out, and cops and firemen
were trying to catch him. And as he ran he was shaking the outstretched hands of his fans behind the barricades.

When they finally got him tied down and asked him why he
jumped, everyone expected a tale of family struggle, personal mis-
fortune, addiction, gambling debts, or just incoherence. Instead,
Charlie said, "Why'd I jump, man? I jumped because that little
white bastard cop up there told me that I was ruining his supper
and his date with his wife. Man, that mother said that if I didn't
jump, he was going to push me out the window. And nobody,
man, nobody pushes Charlie around."

They wrapped Charlie in a straitjacket and off he went to Bel-
levue. Now, I figure that you can't be right all the time, but I only
wish that Charlie hadn't had such a big mouth.

THE COLOMBIAN CONNECTION

Manuel Ortiz swaggered down Broome Street in front of the New York Narcotic Squad Headquarters in downtown Manhattan. Ortiz was from Colombia, South America, and he dealt in junk. He wore a luxurious mohair suit, shiny, pointed alligator shoes, a silk shirt and tie, gold jeweled rings that slipped over manicured nails, and a diamond-studded wrist watch. His clothes were elegant but on this day the man himself looked like a bum, like he had slept the night in an alley. He was unshaven with messy jet-black slippery hair. His unknotted tie was rumpled from a night of drinking. It draped around his neck. The full-cut powder-blue zoot jacket was unbuttoned and flopped as he walked. Ortiz snapped a hoary ash from the tip of his little cigar as he entered the Narcotics Squad building. He left the elevator at the sixth floor, shoulders hunched and nervously puffing his cigarillo. He shuffled down the hall and stopped before Gertrude Davis. Davis was a black undercover policewoman who, in the fledging Narcotics Squad, was taking her duty tour at the reception desk.

Ortiz' arms and legs flowed rhythmically as he and Davis talked. He demanded to see Inspector Phillips, but Davis kept shaking her head. Phillips was in a meeting. So Ortiz settled for the second-in-command, Captain Harry Anderson.

Manuel Ortiz dropped a bombshell in Anderson's office. This worn-out, tired junk dealer would give up his boss, Argento "The Gent" Diaz, the Colombian Connection. Ortiz wanted to even a score with Diaz. He would deliver him dirty to Anderson and Phillips. It would cost them nothing except that maybe they could do something for him in the future. The two cops were stunned. They had been after Diaz for years, and now one of his own people would finish him off. They accepted.

Now this story is interesting enough as it is, but as Ortiz and Anderson left Phillips in his office, the Colombian asked to speak to Anderson alone. The two men stood behind a closed door. Ortiz thought that things had gone far enough. He startled Anderson as he spoke without an accent.

"I'm not Ortiz. I'm a cop and my name is Mike Palermo. I'm assigned to the four-oh. Lieutenant Ryan guaranteed this would be the fastest way to get into Narco. I have to get off the street, and I feel I could do a good job here."

Well, I'll tell you, at that point Anderson just stood there with his mouth wide open. He didn't move. I didn't know if I had blown my job or if he was going to pop me one.

All of a sudden, like a block of ice cracking, his mouth split open and he began laughing. He said he was going to kill that bastard Ryan. And I knew how he felt. I felt like killing the bastard myself. He told me to get the hell out of the building and to go back to where I belonged.

A week went by and I heard nothing. After two weeks I received transfer papers, which put me into the Narcotics Squad. I worked there for fifteen years. Ryan and his guarantee really came through.

CHAPTER 2

"Carmine, the Senator is here."

The Havana cigar twitches as Carmine's teeth clench. A burnt haze of smoke swirls and wafts around his face like a veil before a man who doesn't want to be seen. The ash is round and perfectly formed like a large bullet. Brown streamers blow out through the ashen cork as Carmine groans.

"Tell the man I'll be right with him. Give him a cigar, a drink, and anything else he wants. Make him feel at home."

Carmine sits in his business office with Angelo Orabona, consigliere of the Marcante family, and Giorgio Amadeo, Don Alberto Marcante's lieutenant responsible for enforcement. Carmine Canicatti is an under boss and it is with him that the Senator has requested a meeting.

"Angelo, you know it's the same old story. Everything's different, but everything's the same. The same scenes with the same feds pulling the same damn strings." Carmine taps his cigar over a crystal ashtray and the ash falls off intact, like the head off a guillotine blade. A sign of a good cigar. The cigar is almost dead, almost all used up, ready to be thrown away. Like today's gourmet dinner is tomorrow's sewage.

"Yes, I know," says Orabona. "And the don is very concerned. This affair reaches deep into Washington, into the highest levels of the Administration. When our Friend was in the private sector, he and the Senator had a business arrangement. It was all perfectly legal. They took advantage of government programs designed to help minorities, and our Friend and the Senator set up a company to get government contracts that would only be given to the minorities. It was a good thing. The country wanted to help the underprivileged, and our Friend and the Senator also wanted to help. And what did they get in return? Did they get thanks? No! Instead, political enemies now want to embarrass the Administration and destroy our Friend with false accusations.

"The feds are looking to nail the Senator on a phony murder rap for killing a black stoolie over twenty years ago. But they say they'll drop the case if the Senator gives up our Friend. This he will never do. So he comes to us tonight to see if we can be of help. There are big investigations going on. Everybody's being called to the witness stand. It's the usual thing when a political vendetta gets out of hand.

"Our people and the Senator tell us there is one link, one man who, if he testifies, even though his testimony would be false, could cause trouble up and down. He's an ex-cop, retired over ten years. He doesn't know it yet, but tomorrow he's going to get a visit from the feds. If they can convince him to cooperate, he can bury a lot of good people. The feds can put his head in a vise from his past. They can make anybody say what they want them to say. It is the don's feeling that this man should be visited tonight to make sure that no one has any problems.

"I have brought Giorgio with me and he will help you do what needs to be done."

Orabona's hand gestures at Giorgio Amadeo. On the streets he is called "The Rock." He is a button who gets results—every time. He nods impassively.

Carmine raises his snifter of brandy, swirls the oaken cognac before his face, tastes the breath of fragrance welled in the bell of the glass, and toasts, "*Salute.*"

"*Salute,*" return his two business associates.

Carmine sets down his glass, crushes his cigar in crystal, licks his lips, and whispers, "Now, for the Senator. I won't be long. There's some good brandy in that bottle. Make yourselves at home."

* * *

The night air is crisp. Dead leaves carpet the grass. Crystal stars glitter in the black velvet sky just beyond reach of Mike Palermo's fingertips. The ground crackles beneath his feet as he walks with Bonnie and Clyde, his wife's two miniature poodles, the world's furry gift from France.

Briarcliff Manor, in Westchester County, New York, is October-cold on this Halloween night. Trick-or-treaters have ravaged the neighborhood hours before. Shaving cream and toilet paper stream from mailboxes and tree limbs. One good rain and a little clean-up and it will all be gone. Everything is biodegradable. Everything but plastic. Like the kind they use for body bags.

Palermo runs his own private investigating business in Manhattan. He keeps security tight at some of the biggest hotels in Midtown Manhattan. He knows all the tricks. He has staff to do all the work. He is the brains. He has been trained by the best, by the New York City Police Department as a cop and by the streets of East Harlem as a kid in the 1940s. He investigates everything. From security cameras in hallways and elevators and monitor banks in screening rooms, he is there with his crew. It is almost like being back on the job.

Now, on All Hallow's Eve, he walks with dogs on a constitutional. He walks on a sleepy Briarcliff Manor country road into a night air of cold ink. The dogs will find their way home by themselves. They will bark and cry and scratch on their back door in a panic. And Mike Palermo will disappear off the face of the earth.

* * *

"It's pleasure to see you again, Senator," Carmine extends his hand to his guest. "You're in good health?"

"Thank you, Carmine. That's why I wanted to speak with you. I need a doctor of sorts. Someone to prevent an illness. I wish to stay in good health."

Marcus Brown is a powerful New York State Senator representing one of the strongest and most crime-ridden minority districts in New York City. His manners and dress are impeccable. His hair is beauty parlor-new, streaked with black and silver elegance. The chestnut-paneled walls of Canicatti's private office reflect in the mirror shine of his shoes. An ivory cigar holder caresses a Canicatti Havana cigar. A large diamond ring hugs his right pinky finger. He has used that ringed finger to make many oratorical and evangelical points. His political strength is derived both from his alliance with God and from his affiliation with organized crime. He walks a thin tightrope in the middle. If he should fall, he would take many people with him. Many people watch to see on what side of the line he will land.

Marcus Brown is the only black man to ever enter Carmine Canicatti's private office, his inner sanctum. This is his first and last time. Carmine is doing a favor for some valued friends.

"How can I help you, Senator?"

"Carmine, before I ran for public office, I practiced law, representing clients from Harlem, people who had nothing; people just trying to keep life together; people with families; people who had to take the things they needed or their children would go hungry; things that they could never in this world ever get any other way than to take them from those who had them. Some of the people I represented were guilty and some were innocent, and, as for others, only God knows. Only God can be the judge.

"I handled all kinds of cases. Robbery. Murder. Drugs. Vice. You name it. I had a very large general practice. In 1960 a stoolie was murdered. They called him 'The Gimp.' I knew him. His real name was

Jerry Mackey. He was small-time. Two bits here and there. He actually helped the street get rid of the trash. And then the trash got rid of him. Life was hard in Harlem in those days—like now. And any little bit of trash removal helped. Up to a time, Mackey was tolerated.

"He apparently got in over his head and was fingered. They found his body in an alley. The Narcotics Squad worked with Homicide, but Mackey's killer was never found.

"The feds are now trying to build a case against me, alleging that I was behind the killing. Mackey's contact in Narco is going to be questioned and it will be suggested that he testify as to the accuracy of some new evidence against me that has just been unearthed.

"Of course, all of this is preposterous. All contrived. What they want is for me to testify against my friend in Washington about some business dealings of ours years ago. Everything was perfectly legal then and aboveboard, but you know how they can twist everything around, fabricate any fantasy, and produce phantom witness who never actually existed. They want to embarrass my friend, have him tried in the press, and assassinate his character by false charges and intimations.

"The key to their case against me is Mackey's police contact, an ex-narcotics cop. It has been suggested that you might have someone speak with him and refresh his memory about what actually happened. Then they have no case. Without his testimony, no one has any problems."

Carmine settles back into his huge leather chair uneasily.

CARMINE CANICATTI

I don't want to have nothing to do with this eggplant with the ivory cigar holder. I don't want to have nothing to do with him or with cops, retired or on the job, dead or alive. I don't need the heat. This stupid bastard is in here now because the don asked me to see him and see what I can do. I guess the don feels that he has to return a favor. And Marcus Brown's ass is part of that favor.

I look into his eyes and I see Cab Calloway singing and dancing. He don't belong in here.

Don Alberto controls all of Harlem. Nothing lives and nothing dies in Harlem without getting his OK. Nothin' gets in and nothin' gets out of his territory without him knowing about it and giving his nod. He brought my Uncle Mike up through the ranks, and now Uncle Mike's an underboss for the don. So this eggplant is something I got to do.

Like it or not. I gotta do it.

* * *

Carmine wears a brown silk shirt open at the neck, and a heavy gold chain hangs on a furry chest, bondage to an expensive lifestyle.

"Senator, you overestimate what is possible. Cops are very funny people," says Carmine softly. "I've known a few in my day, as I'm sure you have. There are some you can talk to and some you can't. I will promise you this. I'll do everything possible."

"It's been a pleasure seeing you again. I know you must be very busy with your district and all these other things going on all around you now. Before you leave, tell me one more thing. Who's the cop?"

"Maybe you know him," suggests Brown hopefully. "His name is Mike Palermo."

* * *

CARMINE CANICATTI

My fuckin' heart stops. My blood begins to boil. I feel like I was hit by a cannonball right in the chest. My head floats off into the cigar smoke. I catch it just in time.

"Mike Palermo? No! I never heard of him, Senator. Well, thank you, Senator. We'll keep in touch."

"Thank you, Carmine. I'm in your debt."

"My pleasure, Senator."

The Senator goes to a political rally. I go back into my office to Giorgio Amadeo with a contract.

* * *

Hobgoblins and witches haunt Briarcliff Manor. Invisible white sheets fly around on brooms, cackling and crackling in the dark forest. The specters of Halloween have a night of freedom to mix and dance with the Headless Horseman and Ichabod Crane in Sleepy Hollow at Washington Irving's village of Tarrytown just to the south. They will revel until sunrise and then rest for another year until Pandora's box of demons opens just a crack and then they will escape again for another night of ghostly charade.

* * *

MICHAEL PALERMO

Gotta stop smoking. But it tastes so good. Who am I kidding? I can't even taste it anymore. I just keep smoking like a goddamn robot. And I can't get away from it. I spent half my life busting junkies, and now I'm hooked on this weed. Like a fucking junkie.

Those dogs are great. Look at them wrestle with each other in the leaves. The match flame feels soft and warm in my hands in this cold air. That's it, cup the hands like in Korea, in the goddamn snow-covered mountains. And the cold wind. Block the wind. Don't let the flame go out.

His face glows in an eerie orange fire, like a head without a torso, a disembodied face floating in blackness, a death mask severed by a guillotine. He exhales and watches his smoky breath extinguish the flame. The moon is a curved, thin splinter in the sky. A falling star arches overhead, meteoric debris burning up in the atmosphere.

A red-hot cigarette tip burns through the night, a firefly of ash. He calls the dogs by name and catches them with his flashlight. Unleashed, the light is a signal for them to stay close by. The night is dead quiet except for the man and his dogs. The black car with the bright headlights seems out of tune with nature as it rumbles down the road toward them.

A cigarette burns in the backseat. Palermo stops and watches, waiting for the car to pass. It doesn't pass. It rolls to a stop alongside him. The rear window slips down, and Palermo's flashlight reaches back into time, deep into the blackness of old memories. Illuminated before him is the face of Giorgio Amadeo, as bright as the sun side of the moon.

"Get in, Mike," whispers Amadeo.

"Giorgio? What the hell are you doing here? What's up?"

"We have to talk."

"Talk about what?"

"It's important."

"We'll talk here," insists Palermo.

The black muzzle of Amadeo's .38 settles the question. Palermo takes the backseat between Giorgio and Frankie Faiella. A seat between two buttons.

"OK, let's talk," agrees Mike.

"Not here. There are some people who want to see you in person."

The black limousine glides quietly out of Briarcliff Manor, an invisible phantom that can never be traced. It leaves nothing but the footprints of a retired cop set in muddy clay that abruptly stop at the side of the road, a step into oblivion.

MICHAEL PALERMO

I'm inside this car and nobody's says anything. I got two huge sides of beef on either side of me. We're in the backseat. I'm in the middle again. Two bovines are in the front seat. It took an army of bulls to get me here. I can see straight ahead through the windshield. I watch the world roll by. It's like being in a motion picture show with people all around. I'm lucky. No one's sitting in the front seat to block the view. I can see perfectly. It begins to rain. Headlights flash in the glass and paint a kaleidoscope of glare. Images blur in the colored streaks and I begin to see shapes, fuzzy forms blinking with the road lights. My mind can see people—all the people in the world that I can think of who would do something like this to me.

Silent circular files whirr in my brain, flipping, trapping, clicking, and stopping. I remember everything in my life that has ever happened to me, everything that could have even remotely gotten me here. I can see everything like a photograph. A mind like a photograph can be dangerous to some people.

And then I stop wondering and thinking. I relax. First my toes. Then my legs. I feel a calm numbness sweep over my body. My head floats in a light trance, an escape into memories to find answers. Then, as suddenly as it all began, the lightness turns heavy and I see the face of Bob Long peering at me through the windshield screen of my mind. I see it all clearly. The phone rings by my head. It is 7:00 AM, Friday.

"Hello?"

"Mike, is that you?'

"Yeah. Who's this?'

"Bob Long."

"Bob. Hey! It's been a long time. How've you been?'

"Great, Mike. A lot of good things are happening. That's what I wanted to see you about."

"Sure, Bob, when?'

"How about dinner tonight at the Flamingo?"

"That sounds OK. How about eight o'clock?"

"Perfect, Mike. See you at eight."

"OK, pal."

I hang up the phone, sink into the warm, soft pillow, and remember Bob Long. He is a cop who was put through law school by the Department. He had retired and won an Assembly seat as the party's fair-haired boy. It had been an easy win with no real competition. It had also been preordained through deals and trade-offs. Bob Long played ball and he got to first base the easy way. He is now on his way to second base and some people say he is trying to steal it. Behind the scenes, behind backs, whispers hiss that he is going after a seat in the State Senate, and that he wants to steal it like he stole everything else. But the whispers are wrong. They don't know that the seat is his just for the asking. It is only another deal in Bob Long's race to home base. He doesn't have to do a thing. He can walk right in with his eyes closed. That is, if he didn't have one big problem named Linus Hawkins.

Hawkins had been on Long's assembly staff and he had accessed delicate personal dealings involving the Assemblyman and quiet commission payments he had received from the construction industry—commissions that a court of law would call bribery. These were payments received and never reported on his income tax filings. And now Hawkins wants a consultant's commission, a fee for silence.

Long knows many people. He knows the cops, the courts, and the hoods. But there is only one person he knows who can deal with them all equally. Only one person who can talk to Hawkins in one way or another, so that Hawkins will talk to no one. Only his old police partner, Mike Palermo, can do the job. Me.

The Flamingo Club is a posh nightspot with quiet corners for intimate couples. Me and Long share an intimate table.

"Mike, I want the guy whacked," whispers Long through pursed lips.

"Bob, I didn't hear that and don't say it again, because I don't want to hear it. That's not done anymore. It's not the old days."

I get very nervous. My head screws around automatically, looking for the wire or the plant; left and right, up and down. I am feeling the old nerves get upset again. Those nerves had helped me survive as a combat Marine in World War II and in Korea. And to survive again as a narcotics detective in the NYPD. I would do anything to survive. Well, almost anything—anything that was right. I would do the right thing. But it had to be right in my own mind and in the minds of those people I respected. Sure, I had killed before, but only when it was right to kill. When it was necessary, like in the war. There is an invisible line in my mind that I can't cross. No matter how hard I am pushed, I can't cross it. What the hell good is survival if I can't live with myself afterward?

"There are ways to handle these things, Bob. A lot of ways. And I know that what I didn't hear from you just now isn't the answer. There are approaches that can be made, like restrained violence. Even no violence. I'm sure this guy's a reasonable man. We can have someone reason with him."

"There's no time, Mike. And even if I give him what he wants, he's too dangerous to have around. He's going to sing any day now. And he says he's got a book deal. Magazines. A movie. He's unbelievable. And time's running out. There are some very heavy people who want this dealt with right now.

"We go back a long way, Mike. We did a lot of time together. Just one month of that time could be a book and a movie itself. I don't want to handle Hawkins myself, but I know it has to be done. Don't make me do it myself."

I can see tears in Long's eyes. They do not fall. They just sit there like a well of sadness.

"I'll tell you what, Bob, let's eat, have a few drinks, and then we'll solve this thing together. Whaddaya say? For old times' sake. Salute!"

The glasses clink and we drink. But I know I haven't helped him. Not even God can help him. But maybe Satan can.

I'll never forget the face and the last words I heard Bob Long say when we parted that night. He looked steady, right into my eyes when we shook hands, and said softly, "Thanks, Mike. But there are a lot of important people who can't take any chances with this thing. I'm sorry."

I watched a tear drop from Bob Long's eye as he turned and walked away alone.

And now, one day later in the backseat of Giorgio Amadeo's meat wagon, I see Bob Long's face in the windshield of my mind and I hear his words, "A lot of important people can't take any chances with this thing. I'm sorry."

What the hell was he sorry about? Sorry for me? I didn't do anything. Maybe that's it. He's sorry for me because I won't do anything. How can anyone connect me to Bob Long's problem? I'm not involved. It's not my business. It's not my way. It's not my honor.

But if it's not Bob Long, what is it? Who is it? I have no more time to wonder. The meat wagon slides into a black truck garage on Arthur Avenue in the Bronx. I'm back on my old turf. I know Little Italy like I know the wrinkles on my face in the mirror in the morning.

I sit in a small room with a little yellow light hanging from the ceiling by a dusty old cord. It's like one of the old precinct interrogation rooms that I used to question prisoners in. Suspects who were a threat to society. I can hear a faint conversation through the locked door, but the key words soak into the walls before my ears can grab them. Giorgio won't explain. He won't talk to me. I must really be on somebody's shit list. I sip black coffee and smoke a cigarette while I wait for the people who I know will come. They have to come if I'm ever going to get out of here. If they ever let me get out of here. Why the snatch? It all happened so fast. My wife? Dina will go out of her mind when I don't get back home. I better call her. And the dogs? We call them Bonnie and Clyde. Ah, they'll find their way back home. I better call her.

I bang on the door. "Hey, Giorgio, I want to make a call."

"Not now, Mike. It's not necessary. It's too late. You've got company."

The door latch snaps open and the door swings into the room, into my world of a dusty room and a little yellow light. I look at Carmine Canicatti. He is wearing a tan camel's-hair long coat, tan leather gloves, tan leather shoes, tan silk shirt, and tan-and-brown-striped silk tie. I get up.

"Carmine, what the hell is going on?"

"It's OK, Mike. Everything's gonna be OK. We got some trouble and you're in the middle." Carmine sits down at a chair at the tiny, dusty, round table, being careful not to dirty his camel's-hair coat.

"Sit down, Mike. We have to talk."

"Carmine, how can I be in the middle of anything? In the middle of what?"

"In the middle of twenty-four years ago. In the middle of a stoolie called The Gimp and a black lawyer named Marcus Brown."

"What? Are you crazy, Carmine? You pull me out of Westchester for ancient history? What's going on?"

"The feds, the fucking almighty feds have pulled a resurrection. They resurrected the Mackey killing and want to hang it on Marcus Brown. They want him to give up a good man. It's a bum rap all the way."

I fall back into time. Into fuzzy, hazy time. I can hardly see daylight.

"What's this got to do with me?"

"Tomorrow you're going to get a visit from our government, and they're gonna make you a proposition to help them build a case against Brown."

My mind clicks and snaps shots of Mackey, the alley, the knife wound in his chest, the blood.

"That's an unsolved case. We never came up with anything. There are thousands of Mackey cases out there. There was nothing to finger Brown. He's a Senator now. Are they crazy?"

"They've got new evidence. Brand-new. They just developed it. In fact, they just fuckin' made it up. And they want you to confirm it."

"Bullshit! That's past history. There's nothing there. They're out of their minds. Out of their goddamn minds."

Carmine's face gets cold like ice with all the blood drained out and it looks me straight in the eyes. It's like looking at the bottom end of a steel piling before it's driven into the ground.

"Mike, would you like to call Dina?"

"Yeah. Yeah, sure. But I'd much rather go home and see her."

"That can't be, Mike."

"Why not?"

"Because this morning you're going to take a little vacation."

"Yeah? Where am I going?"

"You're going to Freeport in the Bahamas—with me. Tell your wife you're on a new case. But don't tell her it's a case of Dom Perignon." Carmine squeezes a smile and it almost cracks his face.

Early that morning, federal agents arrive at my house, unexpected and unannounced.

They leave empty-handed.

I return home two weeks later with a tan.

The government never had a case. Not then, and not even back in 1957.

NARCOTICS SQUAD ROOM, 1957

"Captain, U.S. Attorney Brooks is on two."

"Thanks, Marcy."

Captain Harry Anderson ran the embryonic Narcotics Squad at its Broome Street Headquarters.

"Hi, Ben. You guys need some help again?"

"We've got something big going down, Harry. Too big to believe. If you want in on the action, send me someone down here at 1300 today."

Benjamin Brooks, the United States Attorney for the Southern District of New York, stayed on military time even after his separation from the Army Adjutant General staff.

"You're not going to believe this one. We've got one of the big boys by the balls."

"Love to see that and be there myself, but I've got a meet with the PC for lunch. I'll send you some of my heavyweights. Thanks for the call and my best to Lois."

"Will do. Be good."

Anderson bellowed out his open office door. "Johnny, you and Mike get your asses in here, now!"

In the far corner, next to the ribbed four-foot-high hot-water radiator, by the window overlooking a brick wall, John Patella was busy clandestinely taping a KICK ME sign on the back of Detective Vinnie Motta's sweaty white shirt. He accomplished this while getting up to see the Captain. He slapped Motta on the back while saying, "You're the only sonofabitch in here who does any work. You deserve some recognition. Someday soon I hope you get it."

"Hey, fuck you, Patella. Keep your hands off me. I don't know where those mitts have been." Motta flicked his lit cigarette butt through the air, hitting Patella's arm. A shower of sparks sprinkled over the police reports on Guy Hanson's desk. Hanson was in the john so he didn't care.

"Come on, Mike, Cap wants us."

Mike Palermo, smoking a Lucky Strike, crushed it in the full ashtray on his desk and followed Patella into Captain Anderson's office.

DETECTIVE FIRST GRADE JOHN PATELLA

Heavyweights. That's what Cap used to call us. We weighed about 150 pounds each. We were probably the only team under 300 pounds. The FBI and Treasury used to call down to Narco when they had a big operation going down so we could coordinate. We didn't want one hotshot puttin' holes in another on a stakeout or a takedown.

Mike and me had been partners for about a year and we had made some good arrests. I had another year to go for my twenty and then it was goin' to be Honolulu, Hawaii, and a helluva lotta good living. All that stuff I missed out on and had to give up while on the job. My pension and the bucks I had saved would put me on easy street. I didn't want to come back and be a bank guard like some guys do. Or run security in some hotel. Or open my own P.I. office. I just wanted to take it easy under the sun and surf. I was lucky. I still had the same wife I started out with. A lotta guys had broken up with their wives. The job was a big part of it. On call all the time. Crazy hours. The filth of the street. Not knowing if some gun-crazed junkie was going to take a shot at you or try to stick a shiv between your ribs. Too much pressure for anyone. Cops, wives, and kids. And then there was the money. There never seemed to be enough for everything. Food, rent, clothes, shoes for the kids, haircuts, tuition, cars, insurance. I think cops, on an hourly pay scale, were the most underpaid people on earth. That is, if they weren't on the pad. Some were, and you could tell by just looking at them and how they lived and how they dressed. Manicured nails (unless their doll was a manicurist); alligator shoes, custom-made shirts, silk ties, diamond rings. Hell, they looked like the bums we were trying to put away. Why is it the bad guys always have more money than the good guys?

Anyway, Mike and me, we were good guys. That meant we were poor, did our jobs, made good arrests, kept our noses clean and out of the trough, and dressed in Robert Hall suits like all good underpaid cops did. It was the pension that would make the difference and put us on easy street after twenty years. Then things would even out. If we lived that long.

Mike wasn't as lucky in love as I was. He had married his childhood sweetheart. The girl next door. An East Harlem kid named Rosalie. Everybody called her Rosey. They had two boys who were eight and ten. The job got to Rosey, and things started to go downhill. That's when Mike started looking around for some understanding. But it didn't afffect the job. He was always there when I needed him. He never talked much about Rosey after a while. Just about the two boys. He sure loved them a lot.

We got off at the fifth floor of the Government Building where the U.S. Attorney had his office. The place was covered with more marble than the Vatican. Did I tell you I had an audience with the Pope once? That he was a real gentleman? But he lives in another world. Not the real world of Narco. We sat for a while and then Brooks buzzed us in. Mike and I sat in this long, wide, elegant room like in a mansion. The walls were paneled with oak and briar. There were two seats left at a long table. I tell you, this was a far cry from the Squad Headquarters where guys sat around with their shirts open, feet on the desks, paper coffee cups in their hands, smoky and cramped, cigars burning, full of "Yeah" and "Fuck You." This place was class. Those lawyers really know how to live. They're not down in the trenches everyday like we are. We were the only two Robert Hall suits there.

There were guys from Treasury, the FBI, the U.S. Attorney's staff, and us. Brooks had hands almost as big as garbage pail covers. I heard he was from old money and he looked it. Manicured hair and nails, custom silk shirt and tie, pointed Italian shoes. He looked like either a cop on the take or a hood. At least he could have passed for one. He was six-foot-five, curly blonde hair, sharp nose, and clefted chin. A Harvard graduate.

He looked nervous. Like he had his hands in the cookie jar. He fumbled through some papers in his portfolio, looked up at all of us, and said coldly, "Gentlemen, we've got Vito Genovese on a heroin sale." Mike and I looked at each other and he raised his forehead into rippled wrinkles.

"We've got a top witness who personally bought heroin from Genovese."

Mike and I couldn't believe it. Vito Genovese was on the top of his game. He headed the largest and most powerful of the five New York Families. He had the most soldiers, the most political and judicial contacts. He owned some big cops, judges, senators. He even had juice with the clergy.

"We have a corroboration witness who was present at the sale."

Vito Genovese was the most powerful Mafia Don in the country.

"Marshalls, bring in the witness."

Two big Federal Marshalls wearing Western hats and cowboy boots brought in a little, chunky Puerto Rican named Cantelopez. He wore a blue mohair suit with the creases of the pants and sleeves as sharp as razor blades. He was plump for an addict. His eyes searched the red carpet like he was looking for a place to bury his head. His black hair was long and greasy and hung draped in a saw-toothed black-flame pattern as it straddled the collar of his suit. We found out later that he used to work as a heroin cutter for one of the other syndicate families.

"Mr. Cantelopez has done a great public service for his country by coming forward and reporting the criminal activities of Mr. Vito Genovese. Mr. Cantelopez, with the knowledge of the United States Attorney's Office, made a direct purchase of a quantity of heroin from Vito Genovese on April 13th, 1953, at La Segura Restaurant at Amsterdam Avenue and 79th Street in Harlem. The transaction was corroborated by a Mr. Pedro Sanchez who is being held in protective custody on the West Coast.

"If you have any questions for Mr. Cantelopez, please direct them through me."

Cantelopez twitched his left arm nervously to seat his new jacket more comfortably. His coal eyes needled the carpet. I know what was going through his mind. *You're all a bunch of fuckin' jerks. Just take care of me and I'll say and do anything you want.*

There were no questions.

"Thank you, Mr. Cantelopez."

The Marshalls took him out through two heavy oak doors and into a top-secret life in and out of hotel rooms with armed guards until he testified. Twelve years later, he was found stabbed to death with a syringe hanging from his arm, dying alone in a basement. The rats ate his face.

Brooks didn't bat an eye. He thanked us all with a straight face. We left and he must have gone to his office and laughed his ass off.

Mike and I didn't believe what had happened. Neither did Cap Anderson. We didn't know how they were going to make it stick.

Mike said that if they could do that to Vito Genovese, the most powerful leader of organized crime in the country, they could do that to anybody. Even to me and him. He was right.

On that day in 1957, one of the biggest cases of contrived selective prosecution in the history of the United States was spawned by a handful of men.

* * *

CARMINE CANICATTI, CAPOREGIME

Mike Palermo and me grew up in East Harlem. We were both born in 1927 and became best friends. We used to go down the avenue and shine the shoes of the guys in the mob. That's how I got my start in the outfit. He used to talk about Capone, Luciano, and Three-Finger Brown, who, by the way, didn't only have three fingers. He loved those guys. To him, they were like guys in the Cagney movies. And they had money. Plenty of it. That's why I went into the business. My uncle took me in with him. Under his roof, so to say. And now I got my own place in Vegas. Not bad for a guy who didn't get past the third grade.

We used to walk by those Italian restaurants with the smells of garlic and cheese coming right up the basement stairs into the street. We'd wait outside for the wise guys to come out. They felt good after the vino, antipasto, and lasagna. We'd charge them a quarter a shine, big money in those days, and they'd give us a coupla bucks' tip. They were good people and they took care of a lotta poor people during the Depression. Better than the government did. All the feds and the cops ever did was put our friends in jail. And then their families would have been thrown out into the street if it hadn't been for the wise guys. Now I know why they called them "wise." They knew how to take care of people. How to talk to people with respect. They respected their parents and their families.

That's how Mike and me got our education, on the street. We were streetwise. Then Mike went bad. He became a cop. Did you know that he volunteered for the Marines in World War II? I told him he was crazy. That they were going to work his ass off and maybe get him killed. The Marines are always the first guys to go ashore to take a beachhead. He went in as a private. And he was in combat. He saw action in the landing in Okinawa. Did you know they gave him a Purple Heart and a Bronze Star, and a Silver Star, and three Campaign Stars for Asiatic Pacific Action, and a China-Burma-India Patch? He was one of 200 Marines in Peking, China, who had to get Chiang Kai-shek's ass out of the mainland into Taiwan. He said that sonofabitch robbed China blind. Hey, Mike was there. He should know.

Then he was in Korea and they made him a Second Louie. He was in Marine Intelligence. Then the Marines made him a First Louie and got rid of him with an Honorable Discharge. We were all proud of Mike. All his old friends. The guy was a war hero. Too bad he had to go bad and become a cop. He had a good head on his shoulders. He could have gone a long way in the business. I don't know where the hell he went wrong. You think he would have learned something on the streets. Cops are no good. None of them. Except Mike.

So, like I was saying, back in 1957 I almost got my ass kicked in by my uncle, Mike Digs. They say that truth is stranger than fiction. And I believe it. I really do. How else after over twenty years could it turn out that Mike and me are living side-by-side as neighbors in the Bronx, in Throggs Neck? Him a narc and me a button with my own after-hours joint downtown called "The Rafters"?

One day Mike and me meet in the backyard and he lets slip after a little vino that the feds are goin' to take down Vito Genovese on a dope rap. Just like that. Like it was nothin'. Like he was saying, "Looks like rain." Then he clams up like he wanted to bite his tongue for lettin' it slip. One thing I have to say about Mike and me, we never talked business. It was like an invisible wall between us. We both knew what was goin' on but we acted like we didn't. I don't know what would have happened if it ever got to having to clip each other. I'm glad we never had to find out. You hate to whack your best friend, if you know what I mean. Mike Palermo and me were like family. And so was Vito Genovese. I was in his family. Sure at the time I was only a little shit, but my uncle Mike Digs was a caporegime. So the first thing I do is call my uncle and go over to his house because he don't want nothing said on the phone. You can't trust cops. Not with nothin'. And the firemen ain't no better. After a fire they'll come into your house and rob you blind.

So I tell my uncle about Vito and he doesn't believe me. He calls me names and then thinks it over and feels he should bring this right to the don at his house. That's when the shit hit the fan.

* * *

MIKE DIGS, CAPOREGIME

You gotta understand, Vito is not a guy you fuck with. He'll have you in the ground before you blink. So when my stupid nephew comes to me and tells me that the feds are goin' to bust Vito Genovese on a dope rap, I don't believe him. I tell him he's crazy. Vito never sold dope in his life. He wouldn't be that stupid. But I can't take a chance with not tellin' him what came down to me. So like a *chuuch* I go to his house. I call first to get permission. Vito lived in a castle—at least, it looked that way. It was a fortress. Sally Sciacca let me in. He's one big man. Got hands like meat hooks. I sit with the don and he asks about my family and offers me some espresso. We're the best of friends. How could I tell this man, this friend, what I gotta tell him? I know he once had a guy clipped for ratting on a guy who was skimming from the organization. Then he whacked the guy who was skimming.

Vito came up the hard way. He lived with the Camorra on the streets and in the sewers of Naples. He had a hole in the skin of his lower jaw. He told me that he got it from a storekeeper who had stabbed him in the face when he was a kid when he caught Vito stealing an apple. The hole never went away. Two years later, just before Vito came to this country, the storekeeper went away to sleep with the fishes. They found him with a fuckin' apple stuffed in his mouth. And there I am drinking espresso with this man, and I have to tell him the feds got him for selling dope.

He was fifty-eight at the time. Gray hair in a marine cut. He had sided with Maranzano in the Castellammarese War in 1920. Maranzano won, and so did Vito. Now he was Maranzano.

So we sat down and talked. The man was a perfect gentleman. He didn't allow no cursin' in his house. He respected women, except for those in his cathouses. But, like he said, they were just tryin' to make a buck. Like everybody else. Even like Vito and me, but we do it in different ways. Everybody's got his own business.

"Why did you visit with me tonight, my friend? You said it was something important."

"Vito, I don't know how to tell you this, and I know it makes no sense at all, but I feel I have to bring to you what my nephew told me. He lives next door to a cop who works in narcotics. My nephew, Carmine, and him were kids together in Harlem. I don't know how they started making conversation and I know he shouldn't be talking to these people, but he got something out of this cop about him being in Foley Square and them saying that they had Vito Genovese for selling junk to a Puerto Rican."

I felt like I had just vomited in the don's face. Vito said nothing. He didn't move a muscle. I looked for a sign that would tell me to stop. To shut up, so I could save my life. Then his face drained and hardened to white marble. The little muscles in his skin flexed in bands of ribbons like steel. The left corner of his mouth began to twitch. I saw fire in his eyes and felt the pain inside him. His left eye snapped closed, then wide open. And then I shut my mouth and sat back in the chair.

The don's hands grabbed the arms of the chair and his fingers choked the leather like he was strangling me. Squeezing my neck until there was no air left in my lungs. Then his right hand stroked the bullet-shaped hole in his face and I knew that he remembered the shopkeeper who slept with the fishes. I had just stabbed him again in the face.

He got out of the chair like he was a ghost looking at something far away. He clenched his teeth hard and whispered, "Mike, get up and come over here."

I didn't want to get up but I had to. I knew his brain was on fire. He put his arm around me, touched my ear with his breath, and hissed hoarsely, "Mike, don't you ever come to me with *escremento* like this again." I could hear his teeth grind together as he spoke. "Don't even think it. Do you understand?"

I nodded. It took all my strength. His hand dug into my shoulder. I could feel my skin swell.

Then his hand relaxed. The steel in his face softened to ropes. The fire in his eyes was now a warm glow.

"You know, Mike, we've known each other for a long time. We came up together, you and me. You've always had my trust for one reason. And that's because I know I will always have your loyalty. You're one of my right hands. I know you're not crazy, right?"

I nodded again.

"I know you're not out of your mind. But when you come to me with a story like this . . . well, I just don't understand you. I don't ever want to hear anything like this again. Don't even think it. Do you understand me?" His face got deep purple.

I had to say something so I wouldn't look like such a damn fool. "I know it's crazy, Vito. It makes no sense. I know it can't be true. I know there's no way you would ever talk to a spic, but I was just telling you what this guy said, and this is what my nephew told me. I don't know for sure if it's true. I'm sure the guy's gotta be crazy, but I couldn't sit on it. I had to bring it to you." I was sorry I had ever opened my big mouth.

From deep in his chest, Vito raised his voice. "Enough! Get the hell out of here right now! Your nephew ought to have both his legs broken to even tell you something like this. You tell your nephew:

number one, I don't want him near cops—with cops there's no friend-ship, no trust; number two, never to tell you this kind of bullshit again. This is a complete insult. I don't want to ever talk about it anymore."

I got up fast. I felt like a hollow piece of waste. "I meant no insult. I felt I had to tell you. I had to bring to you what comes to me. Whether it's true or not. I feel that my loyalty is to you and that you should know everything."

Then he paced the window and slowly calmed down. "Mike, look, I'm sure you can understand how this thing has upset me. I know that you're loyal and that you couldn't sit on this without coming to me. But understand you have nothing to worry about. You talk to your nephew and tell him it would be very healthy for him not to be friends with cops."

Then I left to meet with my nephew.

* * *

CARMINE CANICATTI

I was in Alfie's Restaurant when my uncle came back from mee-ting with Vito. He was very quiet and sat across the table from me.

"I feel like tearing you apart. You see these tables here? I feel like breaking them over your head. Chewing you up, spitting you out, and grinding you into the floor with my heel. When you were a baby, I used to rock you in the cradle and feed you cereal, hold you in my arms and kiss you on the cheek. Now I want to kill you. But I can't. You're my sister's blood. That means you're my blood too. How could you do this to me, you dopey bastard? I'm on the shit list so bad that it's going to take me years to get back to where I was. I don't want you around at all. You listen to me and you listen good. Number one, that little after-hours joint you have, that's closed. Number two, you're going on vacation and you're lucky it's not a permanent one. You got no business living next door to cops. I don't want you anywhere near cops.

"I want to make it very clear that if you weren't my blood, you wouldn't be walking out of this place tonight. Take a vacation. Now!"

For the first time in my life, I was scared. In just a few hours I had lost everything I worked for. My whole life was ruined. I would be lucky not to get whacked.

"Uncle Mike, I'm sorry. I didn't mean . . ."

"Get out of here now! Out of town. Far away. Go to Florida. Go see Torchia. He'll put you up till this blows over."

Sheepishly I left, went to my club, got drunk, got crazy, and finally erupted like Vesuvius and broke down Mike Palermo's door at three in the morning. He was standing there in his skivvies, a little 145-pound, five-foot-eight midget. I felt like a fuckin' grizzly bear.

"You dirty bastard. You ruined me. I have to leave town. I gotta close my joint. I gotta stay out of sight. I can't even come near the city for four months. You got me in big trouble. It's unbelievable what you did to me."

Mike was dumbfounded. He stood and listened and finally said, "What the hell did I do to you?"

"You and all that crap this afternoon. You and all that bullshit about a don." I wanted to kill him, but I couldn't touch him. Something from the old days held me back. I guess I remembered the Harlem kid I used to shine shoes with outside the mob restaurants. I left. It's a good thing I didn't touch Mike and it's a good thing that my uncle kept his head and didn't smash up Alfie's or me because eight weeks later I was back in town and things were right back to where they were before, except for one thing. Vito Genovese appeared on network radio and television. Newspapers carried his picture on the front pages. Vito Genovese, handcuffed and boxed between two big federal agents, was booked, fingerprinted, and photographed with those damn stenciled I.D. numbers like a license plate. He surrendered to the feds for the sale of heroin to a Puerto Rican junkie in 1953.

My uncle told me that Vito remembered meeting Cantelopez one time in La Segura restaurant on 79th Street and Amsterdam Avenue in 1953.

He liked the Spanish food there. One night when he had finished eating a garlicky paella, a Spanish don named Ernesto Fernandez, the owner, introduced Vito to a well-dressed Puerto Rican. Genovese invited him for dessert and coffee. He and Cantelopez talked. Cantelopez told him that he had his deep respect and that he was a loyal friend; in fact, he said, he worked for another family as a heroin cutter. Cantelopez then boasted to his friends about how he and Vito Genovese were amigos. This opened up a lot of doors for the spic who eventually became addicted to the heroin he cut and wound up a needleman junkie on the streets. Four years later, the feds made a case against Vito because he liked Spanish food.

* * *

FRANKIE FAIELLA, BUTTON

Sure I know Mike Palermo. He came out of the streets with Carmine Canicatti. He's a stand-up guy. He won't double-bang you. Still, I don't want nothing to do with him. I seen him over the years at the Copacabana and some other joints. He was involved in that bum rap that the feds laid on Genovese. I work for Marcante now. Alberto Marcante. He runs Harlem, you know. Nothin' goes down here that we don't get a piece of. He took over when Genovese went down. Some people say that Don Alberto pulled the plug on Vito, and that it started on the day we hit Johnny Ventura on Fordham Road. It was a beautiful contract. Giorgio "The Bull" Amadeo and me and two other kids filled it.

Ventura was close to Vito and thought that as long as the big man was on top he could do anything. It got so bad that he was keeping more and more of the take of the policy banks for himself and that he pissed off a lot of people who had big guns. He got too hungry. So when we took him out we gave Vito the finger. It was back in 1957 that Ventura went down.

I used to like to walk the streets of Arthur Avenue. It was like Mulberry and Mott Streets in the old days. I get a bounce and rhythm to my walk, a little sway, a little swagger, when I hear that Italian opera and those Neapolitan ballads that float out of the apartments. Caruso and Carlo Buti and Jimmy Sorelli. They tell me it's something like Naples and Palermo, Sicily on the Avenue, but I've never been there. Someday I'm going to go, though. There were glass storefronts with the gutted baby goats and sheep hanging from their hind legs; baccalà, dried and salted cod; salamis and cheeses; and caposella, sheep's heads. Fruit stands right out in the street. I used to like to think then of Garibaldi, Mazzini, and Count di Cavour, those guys who fought in the Risorgimento of Italy. I don't look like I read much, do I? I read, but only what I want. Italy and Italians, that's what I read. Roots, that's what it's about. We all got to stick together. Don't look like I read? Remember, you can't tell a book . . . nothing . . . except what horse you want in the third at Aqueduct. Hey, gotcha. You thought I was going to say "cover," right? I surprised you, right? Well, that's how we hit Ventura. We surprised him.

(As we talked, I could see the bulge of a handgun beneath Frankie Faiella's blue silk jacket. I knew it was a weapon with six chambers of death because he had a reputation for brutality. —R.S.C.)

As I walked down the street, people waved to me, young girls giggled, and small children came up to shake my hand. Sure, we kept the peace in that neighborhood, even today. We respect the people and they respect us. We do our business and they do theirs. Even the beat cop, Vito Cioppa, waved to me. He shook down so many crap games of kids in the alleys, he could retire early.

I waited in Romano's Pastry and Coffee Shop for the phone call. I was a kid again. I sat at a round bistro table, ate a cannoli, and drank espresso. My heart was filled with love. Three chambers of love and one of violence. Without the violence you get no respect, and without respect you get no love. So you gotta have the violence to have love.

The phone rang and I had it in my hand before the first ring ended.

GIORGIO AMADEO, THE BULL, BUTTON

I was singin' in Rosalie's shower in her apartment on Arthur Avenue. Her husband worked in construction. He was away on a job in Hoboken. I had my cousin, Tony, who's a union trustee, make arrangements for him to work on a bridge there every Wednesday so that Rosalie could get some peace and quiet and so could I.

I come out of the shower wearing Canoe and a white terrycloth towel. She's laying in the bed playing some kind of a game pulling the sheet tight over her nipples, popping them out in the open, and saying, "peek-a-boo." Well, I go over there and warm her up and I'm just about to ride the pony when I hear Frankie at the door saying, "It's time." Well, it was time, but not for Rosalie, so I tell her I'll be back but business comes first. Nothin' personal, but business before pleasure, because without business you can't have no pleasure.

I throw on my clothes, get my piece, and jump down two flights of stairs and into the hot '50 Ford that Johnny Boy heisted. Me and Frankie sit in the rear. Johnny Boy is the wheelman and Carlo the lookout. I was supposed to be the triggerman, and I was all set. I like being on the job. It's good to do something you like.

Nah, I didn't feel bad about clippin' Johnny Ventura. He was a killer, a bomber. Besides, he had his hand in the Family's pocket. He was all dressed in black. A badass. He looked like an undertaker or priest. A lot of people were afraid of him. He was

Genovese's top enforcer. I felt good about takin' him down. Real good. In fact, afterward we all went out for a pizza.

We watched him come out of the Fordham Social Club and walk down Fordham Road like he owned the street. People ran up to him and said hello. A fruit store owner handed him an apple with a big smile. They laughed at something Ventura said. He BS'd with some other merchants. And then, like he always did, he walked into the Sunset Pharmacy to buy his cigarettes. We were parked in front of the store but he didn't notice us. We didn't exist. He came out and lit one of his cigarettes. I could see the Lucky Strike package. He stood in front of us at the side of the car. I could touch him. He breathed in real deep like he was enjoying the best day of his life. Then he exhaled and looked down at me as I lowered the window. He couldn't move. His eyes froze. He stared into the end of my .38 with the silencer. His jaw dropped as he went for his gun inside his jacket.

I fired, and a silent hole opened in the center of his forehead. I watched the ragged edges suck inward, spilling a curtain of blood over his face. The storefront window behind him exploded as the bullet and bone pieces crashed into it.

Before Johnny Ventura hit the ground, he was dead and we were gone. Now that's what I call one great hit. One fine piece of work.

* * *

(According to one of the four dons at the meeting in the back room of a Harlem restaurant, a sit-down took place right after the Ventura execution. —R.S.C.)

Four men sat at a table set for five. They drank red wine and broke bread together. They were more than just friends, they were business associates. And their business was that of a don. They sat, these four: Francesco Colucino of the Brooklyn waterfront; Carlo

Gianini of Queens; Valerio Fredoni of Fordham; and Alberto
Marcante of Harlem. One man did not sit. He was Vito Genovese
and he had not been invited.

"My friends," began Marcante. "It's sad to meet like this.
We all thought we were finished with the old days. We thought
there was no place and no need for violence anymore. You know
as well as I that if we have problems we can sit down and work
them out. Up to now, that's been possible. There, in that empty
chair, sits a man with whom no one can talk, because he hears
nothing but his own words. He sees and eats nothing but his
own words.

"And it's those words which will choke him. And now he's
begun to choke himself. His head has gotten too big for his body.
He wants to consume everything. Every day he grabs into other
people's territory. Every day he buys soldiers from other families
to build an army that will take everything from everyone. Vito
Genovese has nibbled and bitten the hands of his friends, and
now, he has no friends except those that he can buy.

"As we agreed at our last meeting, something must be done
now, before it becomes more difficult. We've begun to remove
the teeth of the jackal. Johnny Ventura is no longer with us. An
example has been set for everyone to see. An example must be
greater than the lesson, so that the lesson will never be forgotten."

The three dons nodded in agreement.

"What is left now is the lesson from Segura called Cantelopez.
That is one lesson that Vito Genovese will never forget."

And so the great federal puppeteer pulled the strings that
put Vito Genovese away to die in prison. Up to this day, it was
only the four dons who knew that they had pulled the strings of
the government so that the puppeteer would do their work for
them.

* * *

MICHAEL PALERMO, DETECTIVE

I'm thirty-two years old, have two great kids and a wife who wants a divorce. What the hell did I ever do to deserve this? Can't sleep anymore. The job, the hours, the idiots and scum every day. She's next to me. I can hear her breathe and feel her heartbeat. Boy, she was beautiful when we got married. She still is. White gown that made her look like an angel. Her mother made it for her. Young, beautiful, and foolish. That's what we were. The South Pacific took too much out of me. A guy's only got so much to give. And then he's tapped out. Right now I'm scrapin' bottom. I can't let her go, but I love her too much to make her stay. I can't let her go. What about the kids? She said I could have visiting rights. To my kids I'm goin' to become a visitor. None of the "boys" would ever go for that. If they didn't whack her, they'd beat the shit out of her for even sayin' such a thing. That's the difference between a hood and a cop. A hood is either not bothered by his wife or he's a widower. A cop becomes a visitor to his kids.

I guess I can't blame her with everything that's gone down. I could never hurt her or the kids. *One more chance. Let's just have one last chance.*

"Is that you, Mike?" Rosey rolls over in bed, turns her head. "Were you talking to me?"

"Nah, I was talkin' to myself. Sorry I woke you up."

She looks at the alarm clock. "It's almost time to get up anyway. I'm going to take the boys to an early Mass. You going to come to church with us today?"

"Yeah. Yeah, I'm going to church with you today. I want to spend the whole day with you and the kids. The kids need a father around."

"You're not going to start that again, are you, Mike? I told you, we tried. We really did. We tried our best. Pauley, Mikey, me, and even you. But it just doesn't work anymore."

"Rosey, we can't just throw it all away. We've got too many years. We were kids together. We come up off the streets together. What the hell happened to us? I loved you so much. I still do."

"I loved you too, Mike. God knows, I loved you the first time I saw you when we were eight. You wore those ripped, raggy, black corduroy pants when you ran around the street picking up coal for the fire."

I sigh wistfully. "That was the Depression, '36. Thirty-six was a bad year all around. That's when my father died. Burst appendix. Didn't have money to go to the doctor. Hated hospitals. Said hospitals were a place where people went to die."

Rosey smoothes back her hair and stares up at the ceiling. "It's funny what kids can remember so far back. Some things they never forget. I remember Carmine, and Augie, and his sister Maria. The Canicattis and the Colettis. They were neighbors." Her lips purse. "They were good people. Where did Carmine go after he left the Neck? Some kind of trouble he was in?"

"I don't know. He's on the other side of the fence. I don't see him much anymore."

"People lose touch. It's a shame, Mike. Like us. We live together and sleep together and still we lose touch. Maybe that's the trouble. We don't touch anymore. Remember when you used to kiss me?"

"I'd still like to kiss you."

"It wouldn't be the same anymore."

"I'm the same. You're the same. What's different?"

"We are, Mike. We're different. We're not the same people we used to be. People change. Their bodies change. Their minds change. They see things differently. Things that once were the most important things in the world suddenly aren't important anymore. Take you, for instance. For you, the job is the most important thing in the world."

"That's not true. You and the boys are the most important things to me. You always will be. You gotta know that. If there's anything in this world that's the most important thing in the world to me, it's you and the kids."

"Do you mean that, Mike? I mean, do you really mean that? There's nothing more important to you than me and Mikey and Pauley?"

"I mean it, Rosey. With all my heart I mean it. There's nothing I wouldn't do for you and the kids. If a guy came in here right now with a gun, I'd give my life for you and the kids."

"I don't want you to do that, Mike. I just want you to be around more. The kids and me, we need you. It's no good, kids without a father. A wife without a husband. You're not married to the job, you know. You're married to me. You're a father with two sons who don't even know who you are. How many times can I tell them, when they ask me where you are, how many times can I tell them you're workin'? You're always workin'. The job is more important to you than we are."

"You know I do it for you, Rosey. So we can have something. So we can put something away. Make sure the kids grow up with everything they need. So we can both hold our grandchildren in our arms. I don't want all this only for me. I want it for us. The job is a way to get it for us."

"The job is taking it all away from you, Mike. Don't you see that? Don't you understand? I spend all day worrying about you when you're not home. That some jerk is going to shoot you, stab you, who knows what? I can't take it anymore. It was bad enough when you were in the Pacific. I cried every day you were gone. If it hadn't been for your letters, I couldn't have lived. That's how much I loved you.

"That's how much I still love you. But you're not giving me love back. The cops are taking it all. All your time and all your love goes to the Department. Give it up, Mike, and come back home to your family. Be a father and a husband again. Please."

I roll over, place my arms around Rosey and kiss her on the forehead. "My little Rosey. You weren't more than ninety pounds when we got married. Carmine had a dog bigger than you. A Shepherd, remember? But you still got the figure. You gonna give me one more chance?"

"I gave you one more chance last week, Mike. Remember?"

"Yeah, but this is different. We've got something good here. Too good to throw away. One more chance. Please."

She twists her face and raises her eyebrows.

"For the kids' sake, Rosey? One last chance?"

Ever so slightly, she nods. "OK. One last chance. For the kids' sake. One last chance. But you have to live a normal life. Be a normal father. Be my husband. I need you. I need you bad."

We embrace and hold each other tight. And Rosey cries.

The alarm clock goes off—8:00 AM on a Sunday morning. Then the phone rings. I answer it.

"Mike."

"Yeah, Cap."

"There's been trouble. I want you to get the Bandits and meet me at the Fontina at eleven. OK?"

My world crashes. Spinning faces of Rosey and Pauley and Mikey racing after Captain Anderson with kitchen knives. Blood. Tears. Crying. All sucked down the drain.

"Cap. This is a bad time for me now."

"Somebody put Jim Groty through a meat grinder. He's in intensive care at Pelham General. It doesn't look like he's going to make it."

Rosey shakes my arm. "What is it?"

"Just a minute, Cap." I turn over and look into Rosey's eyes. "Somebody put Jim Groty into intensive care. They don't think he's gonna pull through."

"Oh, my God," cries Rosey.

"Cap wants me to help. Can I go?"

Rosey turns away and buries her head into her pillow. She cries heavily and screams, "Go to your job. Go to your whore. Go and don't come back. Don't ever come back and do this to me again."

"Cap, I'll call you back."

When Rosey stops crying and we talk, we both agree that I had to go. A cop is down. Cops have to help cops. Wives have to help cop husbands. And cop kids just have to learn to understand.

And so I just had to learn to understand that cop wives and cop kids just can't live with cop husbands and cop fathers who are cops above anything else.

I, Mike Palermo, became a visitor to my sons.

And I became a cop with a vengeance.

* * *

ROSALIE TERRIO PALERMO

I just couldn't take it anymore. You understand, don't you? It breaks your heart to send somebody away that you love. But slowly that love started to die because Mike killed it a little more every day. Every time we had a dinner date, he came hours late or didn't come at all. A jumper, a drug bust, a raid, a stakeout, a drink with the guys after work. You name it. I know all the excuses. I'm a pro. All cops' wives are pros. It starts out that at first the excuses are true. Then the truth gets stretched a little and becomes a little white lie. Then the lies are as black as coal. Then there's no attempt to even cover up the lie. Like a little kid who wanted to get caught and be punished.

The money wasn't good, either. Some guys lived good, though. Their wives were at the hairdressers every three days. They had

furs and diamonds and fancy cars. You could tell who had their
hands out in the street. I don't know what Mike did, but we sure
didn't have lots of money. If he was on the take, he didn't hide it
at home because I looked everywhere.

One day I met Tina Canicatti, Carmine's wife, in Macy's.
She and Carmine and the kids moved to Country Club Road in
Pelham Bay. They were doing good. Had a waterfront place with
a dock and a fancy boat. She was driving a Cadillac. I was driving
a Henry J.

How could it be, I asked myself? Carmine went bad and he
was doing good, and Mike went good and he was doing bad? I
should have married a hood and did good.

Tina dropped little hints that Mike was fooling around,
playing the field. Some of those stakeouts were sleep-ins. He wasn't
on the job. He was doing a job on me. That's when we stopped
being husband and wife, and I told him I wanted a divorce. He
must have sweet-talked me 100 times and I fell for it. Until Jim
Groty got beat up by some cowboy. When he left that day, that
was the end. So we got a divorce. I got the kids and the house and
the alimony and the child support and a piece of his hide. He got
visiting rights to the kids, the Department, his little sluts, and his
freedom. I figured I was going to go to hell anyway for what I was
thinking that I was going to do to him, so a divorce wouldn't make
me burn any hotter.

Eventually I found another guy. An accountant who stays
home, even to work. I love him and the kids have a stepfather
who's great with them. No more lies or not coming home. No
more drug dealers, junkies, killers, or prostitutes. Who needs it?
Not me.

As for Mike, I wish him well. May he have a long life. And
then rot in hell for what he did to me, the bastard.

* * *

MICHAEL PALERMO, DETECTIVE, NARCOTICS

I got to the Fontina just as Dempsey and Goddard arrived in Dempsey's Chevy. Ferrara zipped in, in his little white Alpha Romeo. I tooled in, in my Henry J. We were the Bandits. Four guys that Anderson pulled from different precincts. We were unofficial. They could give us the chair for some of the things we did. We were a big secret, but somebody big upstairs must have been watching over us because no matter what we did, even if we screwed up, we never got into any hot water. Maybe the PC was our rabbi. I don't know. We took on every assignment Anderson gave us. Our job was to make sure that the "street" respected cops. Without respect, the hoods would run us out of town. Then the whole system would collapse.

Anderson's upper lip twitched as he spoke. "We've got big trouble. Groty was stomped at Ricco's last night. His gun and shield were grabbed, and he's busted up bad in Pelham General. There's no way this can happen to one of ours. What they did to him, they did to all of us. I don't know just what went down. I don't know if he was right or wrong. If he grabbed somebody's girl or if it was a righteous arrest that he took on himself. It doesn't matter. Nobody does this to a cop.

"I want this handled right. I want the gun and shield and I want the respect that's due. I want the bastard who did this handled in our own way. You know you guys function as outlaws. I got your asses covered upstairs like I always do. Whatever you do, you got nothin' to worry about." Anderson's hand trembled as he passed a sap over the table. Ferrara grabbed it.

"Do whatever you have to. Don't leave any garbage lyin' around. Understand?"

Ferrara asked, "How bad is Jimmy?"

"He looks like he went through a meat grinder," said Anderson.

"Do you have any idea at all what happened or why?" asked Dempsey.

Anderson's forehead was dripping with sweat from his curly red hair. His face furrowed with the hint of jowls attacking in middle age. He took out his handkerchief and wiped his face, like he was drying up after a bath. "No. All I know is that he took a bad beating. Ricco's has a rep as a no-problem place. I go there with my wife. Bodie doesn't take any crap like this from anyone."

"We'll start with Bodie then, all right, Cap?" asked Ferrara.

"I would. And Frank," Anderson stared Ferrara straight in the eye. "I want a good piece of the bastard with my Bessie you got in your pocket. She and me've been through a lot together. She won't let you down."

"We won't let you down, Cap," piped Palermo.

"I know you won't. Now get goin'." Anderson waved us away.

FRANK FERRARA, DETECTIVE, VICE SQUAD

That morning, we visited Ricco's place.

Ricco "Bodie" Bodugno was waiting for us in the kitchen. Before we could say anything, he handed over Groty's shield and gun. There was dried blood streaked on the shield case. He told us he was sorry this had happened. He wasn't there so he didn't know exactly what happened. I thought he was full of shit. He just didn't want to be a stoolie. We worked as two teams. Me and Mike were the Italian battalion, and Dempsey and Goddard were the Black Irish. Dempsey was Irish and Goddard was anything but. Black as raw oil. He coulda made a great vice cop. Instead they put him in Homicide.

* * *

CHEECH BASILICO, BARTENDER

Thirty-eight years old, 283 pounds, five-foot-eight, beer belly jiggling as he wipes his sweaty hands on his apron as he testifies. Brother-in-law of Ricco's owner, Ricco "Bodie" Bodugno.

Yeah, I called Captain Anderson. I was sick about this whole mess. I did all I could, but it happened so fast. After everybody ran out of the place, it looked like a morgue. Just me and this cop who didn't have a face no more. Nothing you could recognize, anyway. His eyes were maroon, closed and swollen. His nose was broke, and most of his front teeth were missing. There was blood everywhere. It made me sick. His jaw was broke too. He was layin' on the floor. I thought he was croaked. Ricco came right over with "The Scarf." The three of us carried the cop out to his car and left him there for his friends to get him. Ricco reached out and got the guy's gun and badge back. At least it was somethin' we could do. We don't want no trouble with cops. We run a good place here. This has never happened before, and it'll never happen again.

I threw the guy that did it out into the street. I tried to get him hit in traffic. But he was so drunk he just bounced off the cars and ran away. No, I didn't recognize him. Nah, I don't remember what he looked like. Nah, I don't know his name or where he lives. Hey, whatta you think I am? Some kinda rat? Get outta here before I throw you out.

* * *

DOMINIC BANDUCCI, MORTICIAN

Late sixties. Platinum hair with a bushy silver handlebar mustache. Elegantly dressed in garments of repose. An image rather than just a mere man. Smooth and consoling. Born in Palermo, Sicily.

Yes, I heard about what happened to that cop in the restaurant. People tell me a lot of things. They trust me with their secrets and with their loved ones. I would never tell a secret to a soul. Never, except in this one case. This Vinnie who did this, he's got something wrong in his head. He does this all the time. Everybody is afraid of him. It has to stop. It's not right.

The cop got to Ricco's at around midnight. He drank a lot. He laughed loud and danced by himself to the jukebox. He was really out of place in Ricco's. Nobody knew he was a cop. He was asking girls to dance with him. But they said no. I don't blame them. He went into the men's room, and on the way out he passed by a table of six—three men and three girlfriends. The cop stopped at the table, leaned over, and asked one of the girls to dance with him. He was drunk and she pulled away. This Vinnie stood up. He's tall and thin. Lanky. Six feet. Freckles, loose curly hair. I observe these things because we prepare the loved ones the way they used to look. I have an eye and an ear for these little details.

Vinnie told the cop that the girl didn't want to dance with him. The cop asked her again and grabbed her shoulder. Vinnie pushed him. The cop put his arm around Vinnie's shoulder like they were friends. He mumbled something in Vinnie's ear, and Vinnie hit him in the face with his fist. Broke his nose. He hit him more and more. Then when the cop fell, Vinnie kicked him in the face many times, kicking in his eyes and breaking his jaw. Then he took his wallet, his gun, and his badge.

Everybody ran out of the bar. Vinnie took the cop's gun and put it in his mouth. He pulled the trigger. Before it went off, Checch, the big bartender, grabbed Vinnie and threw him out into the street and closed the bar.

I'm glad I told you. I told Michael Palermo the same thing right after it happened. This Vinnie, he was not good. Not good for anyone.

His last name? Cannelli. Vincent Cannelli. He is not good.

* * *

DOTTIE MARKS, WAITRESS, THE STAR DINER

This young couple came in. Looked like they just came from a dance. Looked like they were in love. Ordered Adam and Eve on a raft. That's two eggs sunny-side-up with bacon. They sat down and talked while Ernie made up the order. Then I served it with toast and coffee.

Then these three creeps came in. Drunk. I've seen it before. The tall one with the red hair went over to the kid's table and started to yell at the boy. His name was Marty. The girl he called Sharon. Suddenly the creep started to vomit over the food. And picked up a ketchup bottle and smashed it on the kid's head. It made a sick sound. Like a thud and a squish, like busting open a melon. Blood spattered all over the place. The creep was still yelling and throwing up. The girl cringed in the corner. I went over to try to stop it, but the drunk's friends ran him out of the place. Then I got sick. I never saw the inside of a skull and a live brain before. It was terrible. A real nightmare. I had to take the rest of the night off after the cops and the ambulance came.

No, I never saw the creep or his friends before. No, I wouldn't recognize him if I saw him again. Sorry.

* * *

MRS. VINCENT CANNELLI

The sonofabitch is drunk again. Dried ketchup all over his clothes. Hasn't been home for a week. Stinks from liquor and is sleeping next to me in my bed. Snores so loud the neighbors complain. Tenement walls are made of paper.

Wonder where he was tonight? Probably whoring around with his friends. Doesn't give me and the baby enough money to live.

Thank God for my mother, or me and the baby would have died long ago. He said if I leave him, he's gonna kill me and the baby.

Why did I ever marry him? He's gotten worse. My mother warned me. I thought I could change him. He said he loved me. I used to be pretty. Some guy knocked on the door ten minutes ago. I let him in. He said he was one of Vinnie's friends. He went over to his jacket and took out what looked like a gun and a wallet. Oh, shit! I hope I didn't just let the guy rob Vinnie. He'll kill me for sure when he wakes up. I hope he doesn't wake up. I hope he never wakes up again. It's just going to start all over again. Maybe I can kill him while he sleeps. No jury would convict me if they see how he beat me and the baby. Babies cry. So what can you do? Feed it. Change it. Love it. But you don't beat it. Unless you're Vinnie Cannelli, the cowboy of Fordham. Maybe if I hit him with the frying pan, or the iron, or a hammer, or . . .

There's the baby. He's crying again. Gotta get up and get him quiet before he wakes up Vinnie. Or else I'll have to kill him while he's awake.

* * *

VINCENT CANNELLI, DOSSIER EXCERPTS, ORGANIZED CRIME TASK FORCE

Vincent Cannelli is known on the streets as a "cowboy." He belongs to no organized crime family structure. He is a headbreaker engaged in strong-arm tactics to invoke fear into victims. From time to time he has done jobs for different families with the hopes that this would some day earn him an invitation to join and be under its umbrella of protection. The more he tries to prove his usefulness to button men in the families, the more trouble he makes for himself. He is frequently ordered to sit at a table for reprisals and reprimands.

He is a player in one of the favorite inroads of the mob in which organized crime gains a foothold in legitimate businesses, forcing them into a partnership with organized crime figures. A favorite business is the neighborhood restaurant and bar because of the cash business involved.

The strategy follows a pattern in which a hood like Cannelli will stand at a bar and drink for a while and then provoke an argument with a patron. Cannelli and his friends then proceed to wreck the house. When the police come, the story is that there was a fight over a girl. The investigation of such a low-priority incident is very shallow.

The next day, a "wise guy," a man within the family, visits the owner, expresses his surprise and regrets and offers his influence to see that this type of destruction never takes place again. The "protector" then receives courtesies and payments every month.

Cannelli is often called to a table to set him straight because he invariably breaks up a bar that is under family protection. He is a hothead. He has a cruel temper and a vicious mouth. He leaves his wife and baby for weeks at a time, drinks a lot, and is in constant trouble with the streets.

* * *

MICHAEL PALERMO

After I got the name and the story from Banducci, the undertaker, me, Dempsey, and Ferrara set out to find Vinnie Cannelli. But he disappeared. Vanished. We thought that maybe the "boys" had got to him first. That would have been OK but not as sweet as us gettin' our hands on him. We became obsessed with finding him. We operated as "Bandits" just on our time off. We staked out his '55 Pontiac Bonneville, which had been parked outside of Ricco's since the beating. I recognized it because I had run into this guy once before. He beat some guy up in a traffic fight over a parking space. I just happened to be on my way home and I stopped and broke it up. I let them both off with a warning. What the hell did I know that he was going to waste Jim Groty?

Some people have special things that they do well. I remember license plates, where the hoods stashed their girlfriends, their favorite meeting places, their tailors, dentists, and physicians. There was one proctologist they called "The Rear Admiral." That one was easy to remember. I remembered Cannelli's license plate. It's like a picture permanent in my mind. In shifts of free off-duty time, we sat on that Bonneville around the clock. We knew that Cannelli lived in an apartment three blocks away from the Bronx Zoo. Monday, two days after Groty landed in the hospital, I visited Laura Cannelli and the baby.

Going up the staircase, I could smell the mixed tenement aromas that I remembered as a kid. It was like I had lived in this place all my life. This was the bowels of the streets. I felt for my .38. I didn't know if the maniac was home or not. I knocked on the door. From inside I heard the sound of a chair scraping on the floor, footsteps, and then a woman's thin voice at the door.

"Who's there?"

"Police. Open the door. I'd like to talk with you."

"He's not here. I haven't seen him in two weeks. And I don't know where he is." The voice wavered and got lower.

"It'll just take a minute. I won't be long. I might be able to help Vinnie."

The lock clicked open and the door opened a crack. Two sad, weary black eyes looked at my shield. The door closed again and the door chain clinked against the metal jam and the door opened wide. Vinnie's wife stood there with a baby in her arms.

* * *

LAURA CANNELLI

I was embarrassed when the cop came into the apartment. I wore a light summer dress that was frayed and had holes in it. I tried to sew them but there wasn't much left of the material. Like my life. Not much left. The dress floated on me. I was beautiful once. Everybody told me so. Not only the bums who were only looking for a good time.

This cop was a little guy. Half the size of Vinnie. As tall as me, and I'm only five-seven. He had skin the color of olives. Black hair and bright, black eyes. Another Sicilian. The neighborhood is full of them. I told him I ain't seen Vinnie in two weeks. I lied. It was one week. I told him he used to send me money for the rent and for food but now my parents help out. As I talked, I looked out the window, which had vertical bars on it like I was in jail. The cop searched the apartment. No Vinnie. I could have told him so. If he saw Vinnie I asked him to ask him to please send us a few bucks. I got more embarrassed. I felt like a beggar on the street.

This cop, Palermo, gave me his number and asked me to call him if I saw Vinnie. I told him I would. But I won't. After all, no matter how bad the guy is, he's still my husband and we had something good once. He let himself out when I went to feed the baby. He wasn't bad. The nicest cop I ever met. When I went to lock-up, I found a $20 bill on the hall table. He must have put it there. Yeah, he was a good cop. I never saw him again. I hope he's all right.

* * *

MICHAEL PALERMO

For five days, we watched the Bonneville, drilled the streets, searched the bars and pool halls, but Vinnie Cannelli disappeared into thin air. Either he was dead, on the mattresses or a magician. Anderson got mad. The pressure mounted. We gave up the car, but first I broke the left rear taillight to mark it if I saw it in traffic. Then I remembered that Cannelli had a girlfriend who was a hatcheck girl at Delmonti's Restaurant on the Grand Concourse. I didn't know where she lived, but Ferrara knew. He had dated the girl one month before. She lived somewhere on Kingsbridge Road and Jerome Avenue but he couldn't remember where. So we cruised to try to pick out the apartment house. We found nothin'. Then we went back to Ricco's to question the bartender, Cheech Basilico, again. The Bonneville was gone. Cannelli was back on the streets. In our turf. Now we just had to track him down and put out his lights. We cruised Kingsbridge Road.

On a steamy, hot August night we found him. He was puffing along like he owned the road with smoke and music pouring out of all four windows. We had the Bonneville but the license plate didn't match. But the car had my signature on the left taillight. The bastard knew he was hot so he switched plates. He was hot enough to burn. He parked the car on Kingsbridge Road and walked into a drugstore. While he was in there, Dempsey busted into his car and stashed an old empty .32 throwaway he had been saving in case he ever needed it. He hid it under the driver's seat. PC—probable cause when we grabbed him.

Cannelli came out of the drugstore, lit a cigarette, inhaled deeply, and walked down the street with a springy, cocky gait, opened the car door and pulled out into traffic. We followed the left rear white taillight. More probable cause. Although in those days, we didn't need any reason to stop somebody. It's not like it is today. But even today, we don't need cause. Just suspicion.

We followed him all around town, and then he made us and took off like a madman. Goddard was driving. Another madman. Finally Cannelli gave up, slowed down, and headed for the Bronx Zoo and his apartment building across the street. He pulled into the parking lot, parked, got out of his car, put his hands up in the air over his head, and leaned his ass on the front fender.

We walked like a wall and surrounded him on three sides. Cannelli played the tough guy and said he was waitin' for us. That it was only a matter of time. *Come on, do what you gotta do. I know I was out of order. I know what I've got comin'.* Like that was all there was to it. But there was a lot more. A whole lot more than he ever expected.

Goddard was a big, black burly pro-football type. He grabbed Cannelli by the neck. I saw his biceps flex under his silk shirt. He called Cannelli a dirty bastard and told him he'd never know how much we wanted him. His teeth were clenched as he spoke and I never saw hate in his eyes like I did that night. Dempsey opened the door of the Pontiac and searched it and found the .32 that he had stashed there a few minutes before.

"What did you think you were going to do with this?" yelled Dempsey as he waved the gun in front of Cannelli's face. "Blow somebody away? Waste some cop? Stomp him like you did to our friend?"

Cannelli's face turned purple. Goddard was strangling him. I felt good.

"That ain't mine," screamed Cannelli. "Somebody put it there."

Goddard picked him up six inches off the ground. Cannelli's face turned red. His freckles disappeared in a sea of scarlet. Ferrara threw a right to his gut. Dempsey hit him in the forehead with the butt of the .32. I popped him with a shot to the rib cage just under the heart. Goddard drove his knee into Cannelli's groin. We lost control and went crazy like we were being released from something. We broke his toes. His face became redder and swollen. Goddard squeezed his neck and Cannelli's eyeballs bulged, like they were going to pop out of their sockets. The whites of his eyes hemorrhaged. We were murdering him. Goddard let him drop. He slumped into a heap. He was still breathing and conscious.

"And now he's mine." Dempsey loaded the .32 and raised Vinnie by the neck and propped him up against his car. It was black like a hearse. He took the gun and rested the muzzle against Cannelli's forehead, between his eyes. "I want the sonofabitch to see it coming," he growled. "Now, you dirty bastard, you ain't never gonna beat up on nobody ever again, are you?" Cannelli started to cry. Dempsey's finger tightened on the trigger and the hammer drew back slowly. Tears and blood streamed out of Cannelli's eyes. Goddard had his left arm, Ferrara the right. "Good-bye, you sonofabitch," grinned Dempsey. He was going to kill him. Another second and Vinnie Cannelli would be a corpse.

Something snapped inside of me. A line broke. A line I couldn't cross. I saw Vinnie's wife and kid. I grabbed Dempsey's wrist and knocked the gun barrel up just as it went off. The bullet channeled through the skull bone above Cannelli's forehead, ripping a swath through his scalp. It ricocheted off the tenement walls. His head spurted like an open faucet, pouring blood over his face. I wrestled with Dempsey for the gun, and Cannelli slumped to the ground again.

I called Dempsey a crazy bastard and said that the radio cars would be on us in minutes. Dempsey put away the gun and kicked Cannelli in the face, breaking his nose and jaw. Just like Cannelli did to Groty. Then we all kicked him in the gut one last time and got the hell out of there.

It was 6:00 AM and we drove to the 46th Precinct. Ferrara walked into the station. He said the place was buzzing like a hornet's nest. Phones were ringing and radios crackling. He came back and told us that it seemed that some hood named Vinnie Cannelli had been the target of a mob hit. He was in intensive care at Fordham Hospital and under police protection.

I got home and called Anderson and told him that there was a bad accident and that the guy fell down the stairs and would be in the hospital for at least a month and that he damn near died.

Anderson told me that the guy should be more careful.

Eight weeks later, I'm eating at Amen's Restaurant in Pelham Bay. It's on Westchester Avenue under the El. Across from Tony Amendola's place, the Chateau Pelham. Tony owns both places, but he gave Amen's to his nephew to run. The Chateau does catering, and Amen's does dinners. I'm with Mario "Buck" Truccolini, a fed named Johnny Napolitano, and singer Jimmy Sorelli. Buck's into numbers and jukeboxes and horses and you-name-it. He's a heavyweight. Not only because he weighs 300 pounds, but because he's got some heavy connections. He's a good friend. We never talk business, only pleasure. Johnny Nap is a Treasury agent. He's busted some of my friends from the old days. But mainly guys I haven't seen in a lot of years. Jimmy Sorelli is an international vocalist and singing star that sings Neapolitan ballads and is in all the jukeboxes. Buck put him in those boxes and keeps him there and on the radio. Jimmy is in great demand to sing at a lot of wise guys' weddings. He's a popular guy with the "boys."

I love Amen's. It's warm and the food's delicious. Everybody comes here, good guys and bad guys. And those guys in between.

Buck is eating his favorite dish of escarole and beans and soaking bread into the olive oil and garlic sauce. I just finished my veal rollatini, and I hear a guy at the bar asking for me. I get up and talk to the guy. I recognized him from Fordham Road. I can't believe it when he tells me that Vinnie Cannelli is outside and he wants to talk to me. I don't know what his game is, but I have my .38 on me, and I unbutton my jacket before I go outside to meet him. What is it they say? "A brave man dies but once, a coward a thousand times." Anyway, I was never scared of no punk hood.

Cannelli's standing against a building. He blends into the shadows. He walks toward me. I can see he's in pain. He's walking with a limp.

"Thanks for meetin' with me," he starts out. "I wanted to thank you for saving my life. I know that guy was going to kill me. I owe you my life."

"You're damn right he was going to kill you," I say. "You're in a nutcracker, pal. Keep this up and you'll be pullin' the lid over your own box. You better get your act together and get into another business before it's too late. You got a lot of enemies on the street. And you're no friend of cops."

"You're right. I appreciate what you say. I'm going into something else. But I want you to know if there's ever anything I can do for you, anything at all, just let me know. I owe you."

"You don't owe me anything. Who you owe is your wife and kid."

Cannelli steps back, gives a wave, and climbs into his Bonneville with the smashed left rear tail light. He'll be easy to find again if anybody wants him.

I saw him only one more time after that.

When I get back to the table, Buck's patting his mouth with a red linen napkin. A candle flickers in a woven-straw wine bottle. The wax has melted in red, white, and green streaks. Nap is sipping some caffè espresso with a twist of lemon peel and some anisette. A light brown, foamy head floats on the coffee and coats his lips as he drinks. Jimmy Sorelli slices into the thick soft skin of a California navel orange. He peels it and separates the sweet meat. He offers sections of the orange around the table. He's riding on a wave of popularity. I loved his voice. It was silky smooth. He was a star in Italy as well as here. Buck is Jimmy's mentor, his rabbi. He got him into jukeboxes and on radio all over the country. He got him record deals and bookings in nightclubs. Jimmy showed Buck respect and made command performances for him. He does special shows for dons and underbosses and capos. They were good together.

"Hey, Mike," chuckles Buck. "Whatta got, a tomata out there? Come on, forget the tomatas. Have a orange. Jimmy, give him a piece a orange. I got a friend who's got a piece of a orange farm on the West Coast." Buck crunches down on an orange slice and drops of juice squirt from the corners of his mouth and drip down his chin.

"Come on, Buck," I laugh. "Your friend's got an orange farm. I got a whole tomata farm out there."

"Yeah, I know that's the trouble with you two guys," he punches his finger in the air at Nap and me. "Too many tomatas, not enough time for your friends, for listening to some good music. You tell 'em, Jimmy. Sing to 'em. Ask Tornese to put on that bellissimo 'Ritorno a Sorrento' that we got in the box."

Jimmy smiles, slips over to the bar, and talks to the bartender. In a few minutes, Sorelli's recorded voice fills the restaurant. Boy, it was a sweet moment. Good food, candlelight, friends, an international singing star, and the guy who had made him. The bartender keeps playing the song over and over again for twenty minutes and then steps over to the table with a smile. He bends over and whispers to Buck loud enough for everyone to hear, "Buck, that big guy at the bar is getting tired of hearing 'Ritorno a Sorrento.'"

Buck looks up at him, still chewing his orange, and snorts juicily, "Tell him I say he can go fuck himself!"

The bartender's lips crack into a little smile. "But Buck, that guy knows karate."

Buck stops chewing, swallows with a gulp, and smashes both fists down on the table. Everything on the table jumps into the air, including Jimmy, Nap, and me. Buck roars, "I don't care who the fuck he knows. Tell him if he don't keep his mouth shut I'm gonna break both his legs."

We all start to laugh. When Buck sees us go crazy, he breaks out into a belly laugh of his own. He was in his mid-forties, a robust, swarthy man of medium height with a lightly jowled, round face. He loves to eat, especially escarole and beans, especially at Amen's, especially with Sorelli, Napolitano, and Palermo.

When he speaks, his big, heavy belly jellies in little waves. He's formidable as an ally but demands the respect of common decency and loyal friendship.

"What should I tell this guy, Buck?" asks the bartender again respectfully.

The laughing dies down and Buck puts his hand on his cheek like he's thinking. "Tell him, who the fuck does he think he is? Tell him it's my box. If he wants a box of his own, tell him I'll plant him inside one and ship him off to Banducci, the undertaker."

Sorelli's "Ritorno a Sorrento" plays for another ten minutes, until Buck tells the bartender to play another one of his favorites, "Ritorna a Me."

We talk into the early morning hours. Black coffee, music, stories about the old days, food, family. But we never talk about business. For us, at Amen's it was just pure pleasure.

* * *

MICHAEL PALERMO

Captain Harry Anderson had just received word of his promotion to Deputy Inspector and would be leaving the Narcotics Bureau to assume a command of his own. He had asked me to meet him at noon at Patrick O'Leary's Restaurant on Fordham Road near St. Nicholas of Tolentine Church. I was told that I would be meeting a very good friend of Anderson's. After parking my car on a side street to minimize exposure as I usually did, I walked the half-block down Fordham Road to the meeting place. It was a beautiful, sunny Sunday and the church bells were chiming, heralding the Almighty. Patrick's was a fine Irish restaurant that drew a respectable clientele from the neighborhood and nearby suburbs. It specialized in Irish stew, Yorkshire pudding, Irish soda bread, and Irish coffee. The tablecloths were Dover white, with Kelly-green napkins and sparkling Waterford crystal perched proudly on top.

As I entered, I immediately spotted the captain at a far table in a corner of the dining room. Anderson was sitting with a distinguished-looking gentleman who was in his early sixties. The man's elegant platinum hair blended softly with his silver silk suit. Anderson waved me over. As I stepped along the parquet floor, I felt I was going to meet either a Tammany Hall politician or a judge. As I approached, Anderson rose, shook my hand and introduced me.

"Chief Collin Devlin, I would like you to meet Michael Palermo."

"It's a pleasure meeting you, Chief," I said as I shook his hand. His grip was firm but relaxed.

"It's my pleasure, son. Please have a seat and join us for lunch. We're going to have a nice, warm, relaxing afternoon." Devlin's eyes twinkled as he winked at Anderson. His ruddy cheeks dimpled as he spoke. "The Captain has given me your background, and I've looked forward to meeting you."

I found out later that Devlin had been briefed by both sides of the shield. He knew more about me than anyone else in the business. I found out that Chief Devlin had just recently retired. He was known to be a man of great charm and character. He had earned the respect of leaders in law enforcement and in the underworld. He was a man of great power and influence. To Collin Devlin, "respect" was an all-important two-way word. He believed that to deserve respect, a person had to dispense the same in all of his dealings. I learned later that it was through Chief Devlin that order and unity in the city were preserved.

I didn't know until later that Devlin was Harry Anderson's "rabbi"—his "hook," the guy who had brought him up and gotten him his last promotion, and his successor's promotion, and this very meeting in Patrick O'Leary's restaurant. A Chief Inspector has a lot of power. Even retired, he can make you or break you. He's like a

Police Department don. Devlin's speech was as pure as angel hair. When I was with him, it was like we were in the White House and he was the Irish ambassador. He was above vulgarity. Above the street.

I didn't know it then, but I was soon going to become a "made man" of the shield, sponsored by a police boss. I would be in the corridors of power. I would be connected within the circle of control. As long as Collin Devlin was alive, I would be an untouchable.

As we broke bread and spoke, I began to feel the power and smooth forcefulness in the Chief's speech and demeanor. I felt I was breaking bread with a Police Department don—a Vito Genovese in gold shield, with an eagle and two stars. I sat and listened and silently slipped into awe. I was the low man at this table hierarchy. The Chief respected everyone as he spoke. He never used the typical phrases or slurs that had become a part of police jargon, part of the rain of ethnic epithets that showered the streets and filled the squad cars. This was no locker room lunch. It was the White House and Devlin was the Irish ambassador. The "Ambassador" required that those in his presence follow his own personal code of deportment. He was above vulgarity, above the street. He was on the 101st floor penthouse. He spoke with deep respect for the street, with high regard for names that I immediately recognized and knew personally. I never imagined that a man like Chief Collin Devlin ever existed. He spoke like I felt. I was Devlin, only a younger version. We both had walked in the same footprints that in turn had been walked by thousands before us. Our destinies had always been set to cross at a table of Dover white and Kelly green in Patrick O'Leary's Restaurant on this day. Our life's trip plans had been chartered on the road map of East Harlem and the Upper West Side where we had both shared similar childhoods in consecutive generations thirty years apart.

I realized at that moment that I had just stepped over the threshold of the sand lot and into the major leagues; out of the world of the unsponsored and the ordinary and into the select realm of the *padrones* and the specially connected.

I was inside of the circle of control, the corridors of power. I was about to become a "made man" of the shield sponsored by a police boss.

I felt good. I felt as if someone was watching over me. Maybe even God. I hadn't talked with God for a long time. I felt something or somebody draw me toward the St. Nicholas of Tolentine church across the street from Patrick's restaurant.

I was drawn to the church and I found myself kneeling at the altar before the holy red flickering sanctuary candlelight that proclaimed that God was in the tabernacle.

My mind cleared and emptied and I felt lightheaded, as if a heavy weight had been removed from my mind. I felt like I had not felt since I was a little kid when my father bounced me on his knee and my mother gave me a bowl of cherries to eat with sweet cream. Life was now truly a bowl of cherries. And I had become the cream of the crop.

* * *

COLLIN DEVLIN, CHIEF INSPECTOR, RETIRED

The minute I saw Mike Palermo, I knew that we would hit it off just fine. He reminded me of my son, Donny. They would have both been the same age if Donny didn't catch a Jap sniper's bullet in Guadalcanal. Marines. He wanted to be a cop like his father. Never got the chance. He would have gone far in the Department. I could have seen to that. Lord knows, I've got friends everywhere.

Well, normally I wouldn't talk about myself too much, but since you asked me, I'll tell you.

I grew up in Washington Heights on the Upper West Side of New York City. I was always in trouble with the law. I spent years in and out of the Catholic Protectory in the east Bronx. Now the grounds are Parkchester. It's lovely there. MetLife put up the apartments. Parks, fountains, playgrounds. You can't walk on the grass there. They've got their own constabulary that'll write you up if you do. A lot of my friends from the Heights went to the Protectory too. I met a lot of other young men there. You may have heard of Alberto Marcante, reputed boss of Harlem, successor to Vito Genovese. He and I were roommates many a time.

Some of the boys went into the priesthood. Others became cops or firemen or sanitation workers. And still others, like Albert Marcante, made a living on the street. He did quite well for himself, as did I.

The Protectory was run by the Irish Christian Brothers. They ruled with an iron hand. Many was the lad that I saw get the tar beat out of him. If the Brothers had beaten up a guy on the street like they did in the Protectory, where the boys were under their protection, the Brothers would have been arrested for assault and battery and thrown in jail. When the property was sold to MetLife, the Brothers still had control of other boys who went to the nearby St. Raymond's School. They beat the boys up there too. But somehow, with perseverance and the grace of God, the kids graduate every year.

Besides losing Donny, my wife passed on just after I retired. A shame it is. Waiting all our lives to enjoy retirement, and then the good Lord takes her from me. I don't have anything left except my friends on the force, some cousins and my one-bedroom apartment overlooking the central fountains of Parkchester.

Many of my childhood friends are now bosses in the Irish and Italian mobs. None of us wants to see anybody get hurt. We want everything to run along smoothly. Like a well-oiled clock. And that's where Mike will come in. Sometimes you can avoid a fight by sitting down and talking things over. And that's just what we're going to do whenever there's a problem between the street and the police. We've done it before, and we can do it again. God willing.

* * *

CAPTAIN WILLIAM COSTELLO

I replaced Harry Anderson when he moved up to Deputy Inspector. Chief Devlin brought me up through the ranks. He told me to watch over Mike Palermo. Cover him like I would my own son. Now I answer to Inspector John Phillips, Chief of the Narcotics Bureau. Devlin speaks very highly of Phillips and put in a good word for me. The least I can do is watch out for Mike.

Devlin says that Phillips is a great credit to the police force because of his education and public speaking ability. And he's right. Every time the Commissioner needs a rep at a speaking engagement, Phillips fills the role. A lot of times I'm in charge here. Good thing, too, because Phillips doesn't know that much about police procedures. He's more of a showpiece. He promotes police imagery, packages the department in a Wall Street public relations wrapper. Captain Anderson, on the other hand, fought in the trenches like me. I know what it's like out there. You have to give a cop some slack and the benefit of the doubt. You can't go by the book all the time.

For instance, I know what's going down tonight with Chief Devlin and Palermo. Mike's going to "borrow" a license plate from the lost plate file at one of the precinct houses and spring-clip it on his car so that the street can't make him. Those guys have ways of tracing license plates of strange cars that hang around in a controlled neighborhood. In minutes, they can give you the detective's name, rank, and command. Just a call by a hood to

BCI, that's the Bureau of Criminal Investigation, while they use a legit cop's name and shield number. Yeah, something's going down tonight with Mike and the Chief. That's why he had me call him.

* * *

MICHAEL PALERMO, CHIEF'S AIDE

When I got the call from Cap Costello, I was makin' it with Connie at her place. She was the girl of a button in the Bronx named Angie Salamini. He was away at college in Sing Sing at the time so I didn't think I would have any trouble. And I was lucky. So was she. Not only because she had me, but because if Angie found out, she'd wind up in the river. Me? Well, I got a gold shield and it's like a bulletproof vest. But I would stand up for her. I guess. But she's a big girl now. Responsible for herself. Anyway, I didn't have to worry about Angie, and neither did she.

Rosey and the kids have been gone for a few years now, but I still get to see the boys whenever I can. Not as much as I'd like, because the job takes most of my time. I'm probably gonna have to cut back on Connie now too, what with the Chief and this meet tonight. This is the first time I ride with him. When I called him to confirm, he said we're goin' down to "The Hole." That's an East Harlem mob joint. An Italian restaurant, five steps down from the street, with no sign on the outside that you can read from the street. Just a little plaque near the door that says: RISTORANTE. It's family-run. Marcante umbrella. Old mustache Petes make the Chianti at home in their apartments or basements and send it down in unlabeled gallon bottles. The Hole's got great Italian food. I've been down there a few times since Rosey and me broke up. I've been there with Carmine Canicatti. Yeah, I run across him at Yonkers Raceway sometimes. In the Empire Terrace. The

Tannenbaums run the place. H.M. Stevens does the catering. One of the waiters, a guy I know, a little guy, Louie, and his partner, Paulie, book the bets for the help, the waiters, busboys, and kitchen staff. The maître d' books the bets on his own for some valued big-money customers. They make more money keeping bets out of the parimutuel system than they make as working men. I know, but it's none of my business. I'm in Narco, not vice. That's Frankie Ferrara's job, when he's not busy being a "Bandit" with me. What does he care? Louie and Paulie and the maître d' are small potatoes.

So I go to see the Chief that night and pick him up in an unmarked car with a license plate I picked up from one of the precinct house's lost-and-found storerooms.

"Good to see you, Mike," says the Chief. "You're right on time. That's important. Just keep smiling and let's take a spin around the oval and see those Christmas trees and flowers and lights. See how soft and warm they look from here? It's the spirit of Christmas, my boy. I remember how little Donny used to play under a tree like those with his wind-up tank."

"That was a long time ago, Chief. My kids did that too."

"Do you spend much time with your boys?"

"Not as much as I'd like. But I'm gonna take care of that. I've got some leave coming up."

"Good, because when you look back at it all, someday you'll realize that family is all you've got."

We circled the trees and decorations three times. Carols floated from hidden speakers. Reindeer, elves, and Santa Claus shared the scene with sheep and goats and the Holy Family and a manger.

"And now, Mike, let's go downtown to 'The Hole.' You know where it is, don't you?"

"Yeah, sure, that's Nickie Falco's place in upper East Harlem. Yeah, I was there a coupla weeks ago. I love Bud's cooking."

"Good, and on the way down I want to talk to you. First, I have no concern over anything that you do on the job. Captain

Anderson has told me that you keep out of trouble, and that's good. Whatever you do, you've covered your trail. My only concern is to keep a smooth working relationship between the Department and the street. I know about you and the 'Bandits.' They were my idea. Harry was my right hand. And you and Dempsey, Goddard, and Ferrara were my right and left hands. You did what had to be done if we were going to have law and order.

"From now on, you'll answer to me in regard to your assignments with me. When you're on the job, you're responsible to Captain Costello. If you ever need me for anything at all, call me, any time, any day. Understood?"

"Understood." I understood it, but I didn't believe it. It was just me and him, and nobody else knew what we were doing. What *were* we doing? He's a police don and I'm an underboss.

Devlin looked at his watch. "Good. Ten o'clock. Right on time. Park wherever you can and meet me inside."

"Right, Chief."

I was lucky. I found a place right in front of the restaurant. I got inside twenty seconds after he did. And, wouldn't you know it, standing at the bar was Carmine Canicatti.

"Carmine, what the hell are you doin' here? Followin' me everywhere I go?"

"Good to see you, Mike. How's everything? Whatta you doin' here?"

CARMINE CANICATTI, BUTTON

The last person I expected to see at The Hole that night was Mike Palermo. I knew that Nardino had a heavy meet with some police brass, and I'm here for him if he needs me. What the hell is Mike doing here? I see this Irish guy sit with Casper at a table in the rear. I seen the guy before but I never met him. Looks like an Irish politician. In here he sticks out like a cauliflower in an eggplant patch. Heavy meet. Casper and he always embrace like they're the best of friends. I know we got big troubles going down on the street. Maybe this guy is in Casper's pocket.

MICHAEL PALERMO

The last person I expected to see at The Hole that night was Carmine Canicatti. I see the Chief sitting in the back with a capo from the Marcante family. Casper Nardino. I never met him but I know he's strong with Marcante. Devlin and him embraced as I came in. I betcha the Chief went to school with him back in the old days. Nardino's got his back to the wall in the gunfighter's seat. Through Nardino, Devlin is connected to Marcante. Nardino has muscle in gambling, loan sharking, and hundreds of legitimate businesses. What the hell are they talkin' about? I better talk to Carmine.

* * *

"So, Carmine, how's the club doin'?"

"Good. When you comin' over? It's been a long time. That reminds me, we're gonna have to sit at a table about one of your boys."

"What are you talkin' about?"

"Johnny D. He's a pain in the ass. He's been pumpin' his brother Peter and then takin' down a lot of good people. You know, there's a right way and a wrong way to do things."

"I'll talk to him."

"Good. I'd hate to see anything bad happen to his brother."

So "Makeup" Johnny DeStefano, a hotshot narc, is getting names and places and things from his brother Peter again. Peter's one of Carmine's soldiers. The guy is using his own brother as a stool. Him and all the fancy makeup he wears. He thinks he's cool. Everybody else thinks he looks like a faggot jerk-off. Now

I gotta go talk with him again. It ain't easy. He made some good busts lately, but when you know what went down to get them, it kinda leaves a bad taste in your mouth. Yeah, I'll talk to Johnny D. again and then have a meet with Carmine at his club. How does Johnny get those broads that hang on to him all the time? What do they see in a guy who wears mascara, eye shadow, and pancake makeup? The world's gettin' worse every day. I don't know who's who anymore. The good guys from the bad. The guys from the broads.

GASPARE "CASPER" NARDINO—CAPOREGIME

"Dev, we've got a bad problem here. Angelo's office was hit today. Last week it was Tony Bats and Johnny Red. They come on strong. They say they're from downtown. We don't know them. We had them checked out. They don't fit but we're not sure. Our contracts are already filled. Even though they look like cops, talk like them, and act like them, they just don't smell right. They pull their guns and flash their shields, and right away they talk dollars.

"Collin, who needs a gun with a bookmaker? If anything, we look to square the beef and put them on if we have to. No, Collin, these guys are phonies, and they're givin' your guys a bad name. But we want to be sure. We don't want to ice nobody who belongs to you.

"Look, you reach out and let me know. We can't waste time. Your people are looking bad. Like they're out of control. If these guys are phonies, then our problems are over. If they're the real thing, then your problems are just beginning."

"If they're cops, then we have no problem," said Devlin. "It will be taken care of by our people. And if they're phonies, your people get some exercise. Either way, case closed."

"OK. As long as it's finished," agreed the capo.

"Now, about our problems," said Devlin. "Every day they get worse. We have wise guys breaking up bars with cops around. Fights with cops and disrespect for my people."

"Yeah, I know," said Nardino. "I heard what happened to that cop at Ricco's. But you got to understand that the guy wasn't one of my people. He was a cowboy lookin' to make a place for himself. I think that maybe pretty soon he ain't gonna be a problem no more.

"If the guys out of line are my people, they'll be dealt with in our own way. Meanwhile, we got some two-bit hoods who don't know how to keep their mouths shut. With all the money it takes to keep peace, it don't make no sense to have people around with big mouths who make trouble."

"This could be the same crew," said Devlin. "And the word's out that for forty big ones anybody can buy a button today."

Nardino stopped eating. He stared.

"Scarmello," whispered Devlin.

"Scarmello? Are you crazy?" asked Nardino. "He's not one of my favorite people, but those kind of balls he don't have. Forget about him. That's not why we're here. We'll take care of business like we always do, and then we'll have peace again. Right?"

"Right," agreed Devlin.

"Now bring your boy over here and let's have something to eat. It'll be good to meet him. I think I seen him around."

I was watching the back of the room while I talked with Carmine, and I saw Devlin and Nardino wave me over to the table. I was glad. I was hungry. Carmine comes along with me, so I stop and tell him I have to go. He says, "OK, go," and he keeps following me. Now this could be embarrassing if I bring a guy over who hasn't been invited. By the time I get there, Carmine was right in back of me when Nardino says, "Collin, I want you to meet Carmine Canicatti."

Carmine brushes past me with a smile and shakes hands with Devlin.

"Casper, I want you to meet Mike Palermo."

I shake hands with Nardino and we all sit down. Then we eat, and the big guys talk and we listen. It was like listening to my uncles. They talked about the old days, music, and good food. And Nardino told stories like fairy tales, but they all had a message like a stiletto in the night and deep in the heart.

"You see, Dev," said Nardino, "you got where you did because you got the education. You got a shot. I never had that. So while you were readin' books and goin' to school and Holy Name meetin's, I was on the street makin' a livin'. And like you made it work, so did I, but in a different way. It ain't easy bein' in business these days. A lot of overhead. But all you had to do was sit around and pick up a paycheck and wait for your pension. Is that why you became a cop?"

Devlin smiled, "There's a lot of truth in what you say. My grandfather was a cop. So was my father. It was that police money that gave me the chance. I could be sitting on your side of the table, or have become a wire lather or a steamfitter, but being on the force was in my blood. I guess even from the day I was born. I wonder how it would have been if I were in business like you and if you were the cop."

That's when Nardino broke out in a belly laugh and almost choked on his linguini.

"Me a cop?" said Nardino. "That would be like a miracle. A fairy tale."

Then the stories started, and Nardino told us an old Italian story about a frog and a scorpion and some guy he and the Chief knew.

"You know, Mike, you and Carmine are here because you two can be trusted. You're both good people. The Chief and I were just talkin' about a guy that you should hear about. You gotta keep your eyes open for guys like this. Here's the story.

"There was this frog in Italy. He was a happy frog. Very happy. Not a care in the world. His name was Cheech the Frog. One day, Cheech was going to swim across the Tiber to Rome to see his girlfriend. He was doin' real good in the world. Plenty of bugs to eat, water to drink, and lots of girl frogs to love. But on this day, Cheech the Frog stopped for a minute to get the sun before jumpin' into the river. A scorpion walked up to him real slow. Now Cheech knew he could jump away from the scorpion and be safe in the river.

"Suddenly the scorpion began to speak. 'Hello, Cheech,' he says. 'I wonder if you could do me a big favor.'

"The frog is curious and says, 'What kinda favor?'

"The scorpion says, 'I want to cross the river to see my mother in Rome, but I can't swim. Would you carry me across on your back?'

"The frog says, 'You think I'm crazy? If I let you sit on my back, you'll bite me and I'll die.'

"'Don't be stupid,' says the scorpion. 'If I bite you, you'll die and sink and I'll drown and we'll both die. I won't bite you. I want to live. I promise on my children I won't bite you.' Cheech the Frog thought about it and said, 'OK, that makes sense. I'll swim out into the river and you jump on my back while I'm in the water. That way I can be sure you won't bite me.'

"Cheech swam out a little from the shore and the scorpion jumped on his back from the tree limb. The two of them began to swim across the river. When they were in the middle, in the deepest part, the scorpion bit the frog on the neck. Cheech started to weaken and began to sink. He looked at the scorpion as he was dyin' and said, 'Why'd you bite me? You said you wouldn't. Now we're both goin' to die. Why'd you bite me? Are you crazy?'

"The scorpion looked at him as the water came up to his neck and he said, 'I don't know. It was a stupid thing to do. I just couldn't help myself. I guess it's just in my nature. In my character. I couldn't control myself.'

"You see," says Nardino, "you just can't change a man's character. A guy will say, 'I'm sorry, I won't do it again. I'm goin' to turn over a new leaf.' Don't believe him. You can't change a guy's nature. If you think you can, you're goin' to take a hit by the sin of stupid generosity. It's nice to be generous, but not to be stupid.

"That's what happened to Vito Genovese. He made friends with a spic. He was generous and he was stupid. Being stupid put him in the joint. He'll probably die there."

The Chief and I rode back to Parkchester and he told me that the frog in the story is Frank "Cheech" Scarmello, a capo in the Valerio Fredoni family that runs Fordham. Scarmello was selling "buttons" for forty G's to get "made" into the Family. These were people he hardly knew, unreliable and unproven. They really didn't belong in the organization. They hadn't paid their dues with years of loyal service proving their reliability. They had only paid Scarmello, who was cleaning up. He must have big bucks stashed away. The Chief said he'd never live to spend it. He was in trouble with the bosses and a table would be called where they would decide what to do with him.

Devlin smiled. "Casper should only know that we have the same type of trouble in the Department. Mike, did you know that some of our people are selling gold shields for 500 bucks? Their blood isn't as rich as Scarmello's."

"I heard stories, Chief."

Devlin chuckled. "Is that how you got yours, Mike?"

"Come on, Chief. Inspector Anderson told you how I got mine."

"Oh, that's right. The Colombian Connection. Quite a scam. You pulled the cap right over their eyes."

Then he laid out arrangements.

"In the future, you'll be dealing directly with Carmine on any matters between Nardino and me. Carmine will speak for him, and you'll speak for me. You'll be my right arm. You'll meet other men like Nardino, and you'll represent me and the Department when you meet with their people.

"By the way, I want you to know that the Scorpion in Casper's story was Frank Scarmello of Fordham, and the frog could easily have been his Family or our own Department."

The Chief was right. I met a lot of big people. In two weeks, I met Tommy Lucchese.

We drove back to Parkchester. The lights were out.

Everything was quiet.

* * *

MICHAEL PALERMO, FACILITATOR

Carmine and me got right on the job. He brought along some guys and we staked out Big Julie's tuxedo store on the lower East Side. The day before, some guys had come into his place looking for bucks. Julie never saw them before. They wore suits, had guns and shields. Julie told them to come back tomorrow when the collections came in.

Today is tomorrow, and Carmine, me, and two of his guys are in the back of Julie's, in the fitting rooms. Carmine is trying on a tux and his guys are laughing at him. There is a phone bank in the back room behind us. The door's got cartons in front of it on a platform that slides clear so that guys can get in and out, but not so that anybody not in the know could see there was a back room. Julie is helping a legit customer with a tux. He's ringing the sale up when these three guys walk in and they look like they're from the precinct house. They got the look. They wait while Julie finishes with the customer and then they talk with Julie. Carmine is standing there in his white jockey shorts, black shoes, formal white shirt, black bowtie, and black tux jacket, while the fitter is working on the pants. I see that Julie is bringing two of these guys into the back of the store. The third guy stays outside and keeps an eye open. I tell Carmine and he just makes smoke with the Cuban cigar stuck in the corner side of his mouth. His guys stand on either side of the door.

Julie brings the guys back and when they see Carmine standing there with no pants on, they stop in their tracks. They didn't know what was goin' on. Then Carmine takes a .45 out of his jacket and aims it at them and his guys grab them from behind. I'm standing behind a carton because if these guys are phonies Carmine doesn't need me. He can handle things himself and I'll just walk out the back door and go see Salamini's girlfriend, Connie. Why ruin a good day off?

Carmine has one of the guys call the third guy into the back, and he gets grabbed by Julie who is a very large man, six-two, 300 pounds. Julie is sweating. I guess he's mad about paying for protection and then not getting it. It makes the guys on the pad look bad. Carmine winds up with three .38 police specials and three gold shields. He brings them back to me behind the carton to check them out to see if they're real. I look at them up close. Then I take out my shield to compare. Carmine looks at the four gold shields. There's no doubt about it, I say. These guys are cops.

They're from the four-three, out of their precinct, shaking down honest bookmakers proprietors of a victimless crime. Nobody forces people to bet. Bookmakers are nonviolent. Nobody needs a gun with a bookmaker. But with these cops, we need a few cannons in their faces to get their attention so I could explain the facts of life on the job to them.

Carmine goes back out from behind the carton and puts these three rogue cops into chairs. They got four guns on them. Three of the guns are their own. Then I come out and walk in front of them. I pull out my gold shield and tell them I'm from I.A., that's Internal Affairs. These guys shit. I tell them this is a protected undercover operation of the Department. They got no right being here. They're going to blow the whole front. They could lose their jobs over what they did and be brought before a Grand Jury for felony prosecution. I tell them to get their asses back to the four-three and to stay there. If me, or any of my men (I wave at Carmine his guys and Big Julie) ever see them back here or working anywhere out of the four-three, I personally am going to throw them all in jail.

I explain that the Department has a lot of other undercover operations like this all around the city, and if they try this again anywhere else, they're either going to jail or going to turn up floating in the river. By this time, these guys are sheet-white. They look like they're going to throw up. They got four guns on them. Not much leverage to bargain with. They thank me for letting them go. Swear they'll never do it again. I thought they were going to kiss my ring. If I ever really was in Internal Affairs, I bet I would be a real bastard.

They didn't know it, but I had saved their lives. Carmine and his boys play for keeps. I give them back their guns and they leave like they had just pulled a robbery. I also told them to keep their mouths shut about everything that just happened. If I found out that they opened their mouths for anything but to eat, I would hear about it and all hell would break loose.

After they left, Julie sent out for pizza and beer and Carmine and his guys laughed their balls off. I went out for some excitement with Salamini's girl.

Carmine found out who the phonies were, and they were never heard from again. I only had to play Internal Affairs one more time to set two more guys straight.

And to take care of our problems, I put together reports of guys who didn't show the proper respect to the proper faces in public places, and Carmine reached out and set things right. Then it was back on the job.

* * *

FEBRUARY 1960, 23RD PRECINCT, BROOME STREET NARCOTICS HEADQUARTERS:

GERTRUDE DAVIS, DETECTIVE, NARCOTICS

A look-alike street hustler extraordinaire, ebony-skinned, pimp's delight, tight shiny skirt bulging at the buttocks, hemmed thigh-high with nigrous stockings in white-roped high-heeled shoes, white sweater-wrapped Gertrude Davis, Broome Street undercover cop.

I made the buy from Dominic Gatti in Patsy's restaurant a week ago. Mike Palermo was the corroborating witness. You should have seen me then. I looked like a hooker junkie. You got to do a lot of acting on this job. Today I've got my everyday going-to-market clothes on. Hell, I don't want to get arrested right here in headquarters. Yeah, I'm that convincing. You better believe it. I got a lot of good, solid arrests under my belt and under my garters.

Tommy Croft and Lenny Lombardi are the arresting officers. They just brought Gatti upstairs. Mike's here too, probably upstairs already so that we can make the I.D. The kids and George will be eating T.V. dinners again tonight. I don't even get time to clean the house anymore. This job is really getting to be a pain in the ass. I'm going to make the I.D., sign the deposition, and get back home before George thinks I'm fooling around.

DOMINIC GATTI, HOOD

It hurts, man. The cuffs they got on me are too tight. They're cutting my wrists. I told them they were too tight, and the big bastard just made them tighter. I'm goin' to keep my mouth shut from now on. They're not getting nothin' from me.

Goddamn old brick building. Steel staircase feels like it's falling down. When I tripped before, they dragged me on my knees.

Gatti's wrists were raw from the chafing of the steel bracelets. The handcuffs glinted in the thin light of the overhanging dusty lamp of the stairwell. His hands were lashed from behind. With each tug and drag, the strain on his elbows sent stabbing pains shooting up and down his arms. He felt like the bull who had been tamed with the cruel ring through his nose. He walked and followed into a noisy hallway busy with the fast-moving, blurred talking shapes of the 23rd Precinct.

Gatti stumbled along with his captors to a gray steel door. His head was cloudy and he felt nauseous. A deep, empty, spinning pit settled in his gut and his black eyes darted rhythmically from side to side. His legs woodened to clubs and he tottered as he stood before Interrogation Room 2. The door wobbled before him and squealed open as if a mouse was jammed in the hinges and crushed. On each arm, a hardened hand from behind clamped upon Dominic's triceps and hurled him into the room. He crashed into a chair hidden in a dark corner.

Downstairs, Jerry "The Gimp" Mackey stood before the desk Lieutenant. He was a stool for Palermo and his team. He was in for a bogus arrest for passing marijuana in a local bar. After he gave up some small-time pushers, he would get a few bucks and be cut loose. Mackey was well-known in Harlem. The Lenox Avenue people and all the cops knew him.

He served as an informant to both sides, and they both knew it. They both used him like that to get what they wanted, to give up people they didn't want pushing into their operations. The street people were smart. Mackey would make a few bucks, and the cops would do the work for the local mobsters and protect their actions.

Mackey was shuffled into a back room for questioning.

Palermo would get the word from The Gimp and I.D. Gatti in the same trip. The job wasn't always so easy. He squeezed a cup of water from the cooler. He looked tired. He was ready to call it a long day in "Paradise Gone Wrong." He could pass for a hood. He never had to wear a disguise like most cops in his Division. He just naturally fitted in with the street.

In 1936, at nine years old, he used to make his way to 114th Street on a Sunday afternoon. He would drag his shoeshine box and shine the shoes of wise guys. Those shoes of the armpit-holstered gunzels, the gamblers, the cowboys, the hoods. He had listened to them laugh and argue as he shined their shoes. He looked up to them and knew them by name. He wanted to be just like them. Instead, like they said, he went bad and became a cop.

Upstairs, he met Davis in the observation room and watched Gatti through the one-way mirror.

"That's him, for sure. Now let me get the hell out of here and get back to my family."

Gertrude Davis was gone.

Palermo stayed.

MICHAEL PALERMO, DETECTIVE, NARCOTICS

The poor bastard looks lost. He's not behind his eyes anymore. Lombardi and Croft beat the shit out of him. Resisted arrest. Bullshit. Sure they've got him on a direct sale but the guy's still human. A little respect for that. At least just for that. I watch through the two-way mirror.

LENNY LOMBARDI, DETECTIVE, NARCOTICS

Squat, powerful, swarthy, Mediterranean type. Temper often out of control. Reputation for walking the line, for abusing prisoners, especially Italian dope pushers. Often crossed the line. Cops knew, but nobody turned him in. They covered for him.

"Tommy, go get us some coffee."

Croft left Lombardi alone with Gatti. Dominic's head hung heavily over his chest, gently swaying from left to right with each labored breath.

"OK, you little shit. You half-ass junk pusher. You're not the big man on First Avenue now. Now you're on my turf and we can go one of two ways—either my way or yours. My way, we leave here and we both go to dinner. Your way, you end up in the hospital and I go to dinner with my partner.

"I'm talkin' to you!" He shoved Dominic, snapping back his head. Gatti's eyes looked at him but couldn't focus. His eyeballs rolled upward, burying themselves inside his head, which flopped over on his left shoulder.

Beads of sweat rolled over Gatti's furrowed forehead. The rivulets deflected down his high cheekbones. Lombardi's sack-like pants covered his tree-trunk legs. His rubber Cat's Paw heels were worn on the outer rear corners.

"Answer me, you guinea punk."

Gatti's eyes reappeared in their sockets, wobbled in the yellow sclera, and focused on the dark hulk before him. The corners of his mouth quivered and, in an eerie spasm, twitched a smile at Lombardi.

"You dirty bastard! This ain't no joke." Lombardi lunged at Gatti, grabbed his throat with his left hand and with his fist sent knuckles of granite crashing into Gatti's solar plexus. His diaphragm was paralyzed. He froze. His mouth and eyes locked wide open. He hunched forward as if hanging on a cross. He stopped breathing. Five seconds, ten, fifteen, twenty. His lips and tongue became blue. He was dying. Lombardi's anger was replaced by fear. He had killed him.

He began slapping Gatti's face. It was tight in spasm. "Come on, kid, snap out of it. What's the matter? Can't you take a punch?"

Gatti heard nothing. His mind registered nothing. Nature's gift for the unbearable pain. In thirty-five seconds his hands and legs began to convulse. Lombardi stepped back. In fifty seconds Gatti inspired a short, hollow rasping breath, followed by another and another. Lombardi grabbed his face. The convulsions stopped, and Gatti stopped breathing again. He hunched down in the chair and in a cracking instant retched forward, his mouth spewing a projectile of warm, lumpy, semi-digested vomit. It caught Lombardi in the chest and arms and sent him reeling into Palermo's mirror. Palermo leaped back. The glass held.

Croft came back into the room with the coffee and found a reeking mess. "What the hell happened?" he asked incredulously.

"One shot in the gut and the sonofabitch puked all over me. I read him the Riot Act, but I don't think he heard a word I said."

Croft took Gatti to the bathroom to clean him up. Lombardi showered and changed clothes. Palermo got the word from Jerry "The Gimp" Mackey and gave him a few bucks. Croft brought a cleaned-up Gatti back, took off his handcuffs, and gave him some soup. A sullen, shrinking Gatti sipped chicken soup.

"Feelin' better?" asked Croft.

"Wow, what the hell happened? I feel banged up."

"Don't you remember?"

"No."

"You fell down the stairs. You ought to be more careful. Listen, Lombardi will be back any minute. Make things easy on yourself. We'll give you a deal. A good deal. Just cop out to the sale and give up your connection. You'll walk out of here with two good friends looking after you."

Gatti finished his soup and bread and wiped his mouth with his shirt sleeve. "I'd like to thank you for dinner. The food was great. I hope I never have to come back to this sewer. As to your deal, I'll have to talk to my lawyer first because I think you're both full of shit. I didn't do nothin'. I don't know no junkie who says

I sold him coke, and I don't know what the hell a connection is. Your good-guy/bad-guy act ain't workin' on me."

Croft shrugged. "Remember, I tried."

Palermo returned to his window in a one-sided world. Lombardi returned and Gatti was handcuffed again.

"Look, scumbag. I want one thing. Just one thing. *Capisce?* I want your connection."

Gatti lifted his head. His skin was oily with a southern Mediterranean, tanned pigmentation. He had the face of a veteran boxer, nose flattened, skin taut and lightly scarred over prominent cheekbones. His hair was naturally curly and glistened under the glare of the hanging light. The pinnae of his ears were deftly carved, coiled cartilaginous ribbing. He whispered in frustration, "I don't know nothin'."

"Let's get the hell out of here," said Lombardi. The two cops left, shut off the light, and left Gatti in the dead dark.

After ten minutes, the door opened. The light stung Gatti's eyes. The door closed and it was black again. A flashlight shone brightly into Gatti's eyes. He jerked away from the pain and shut his eyes tight. There was a crackling in the air. It surrounded his head. He felt a feathery, gliding, slapping embrace of flakiness around his head and the back of his neck. He flinched and opened his eyes. There was nothing but dark. The light went on and he was still in the dark. Lombardi had put a paper bag over his head so he couldn't see the punches coming and set up for them. He shook his head to throw off the darkness, but a hand grabbed from above and seated the shroud more firmly.

"Last chance, snot nose! Who's your connection?" Lombardi screamed.

Loud and muffled, like a shrieking train whistle in a deep tunnel, Gatti screamed through the bag, "You ain't gettin' nothin' out of me, you big bastard!"

Croft shook his head in frustration. Lombardi ripped off Dominic's alligator belt and looped it over the bag around his neck, He tightened it until he heard a muffled gagging. He stepped back and clenched his right fist into a screaming cannonball. His knuckles tore through Dominic's white silk shirt on the right side and, with a hissing thud, splintered his ribs. The flesh tore away and bloodied the shirt.

Lombardi stepped back and cracked a steel left fist at Gatti's lower abdomen. Dominic was hurt but wouldn't black out. He writhed and fought to get his hands loose to throw off the bag. Lombardi moved to the right and pummeled the left kidney. Blood streamed into Gatti's bladder. His brain reeled with vertigo and madness.

Lombardi crashed the right kidney and yelled, "Where did you get the stuff? Who's the man, you guinea wop shit?"

Croft couldn't take anymore and grabbed Lombardi.

"Come on, Lenny. That's enough. Leave him alone for a while. Let me talk to him. You're gonna kill him. Go outside and cool off." He pushed Lombardi out the door.

Palermo raced out of his box seat and grabbed Lombardi in the hall. "Lenny, you stupid bastard. You're goin' to kill him. Lay off him. Or I swear you're gonna have to answer to me."

"That greasy guinea bastard. I'll kill that sonofabitch."

"No, you won't." Palermo pushed him down the hall.

"Look," said Lombardi, "I won't kill him. I just want him to give up some of his people. Let's head for the top for a change. You know what I mean. The big guys."

"We're never going to get the big guys, Lenny. Don't you know that by now? They've all got their asses covered by somebody bigger than we'll ever be. And what's with this guinea and wop shit?"

"That punk is making all Italians look bad. It doesn't mean a thing to that kid in there."

"Look, Lenny, I've got news for you. You ain't making Italians look any better. Lay off the kid. You hear me?"

"He's a nothing!" growled Lombardi as he took off to the showers again.

If nothing else, Palermo knew that Gatti would take everything that Lombardi threw at him and still wouldn't talk. He had guts. He was a stand-up guy. At least for that he earned, if not respect, then a little common decency. He was a criminal who should be tried and convicted but not punished by a sadistic bastard at the edge of insanity.

Palermo regretted ever bringing Lombardi into Narcotics. And to think, in the years to come, Lenny Lombardi would write a book and go on to movies and television as an expert police consultant.

But before, that he would falsify documents that stated that Dominic Gatti had given sworn testimony against some of the connections that Lenny Lombardi wanted to take down.

CHAPTER 3

Since the Lombardi interrogation, ten weeks of healing had passed and Dominic Gatti was out on bail awaiting trial.

At 2:00 AM, Pirelli's tavern held a bar full of customers. Dominic spent his time there quietly to himself. He had finished three glasses of scotch and was starting on his fourth. He was well-dressed in a $250 suit, highly shined shoes, and a two-carat diamond pinkie ring of yellow gold that sparkled when he raised his shot glass. Dominic Gatti was in the money now.

Dominic Gatti—an East Harlem kid who had come up through the streets running numbers and dumping stolen goods. He was heavily into selling heroin and cocaine. At twenty-eight years old, he was making money and spending it even faster. He had a well-stocked wardrobe, expensive jewelry and cars, and even more expensive girls. Dominic was still active in gambling but now was on the wrong side of the table and was heavily in debt from losses on slow horses and the wrong teams.

Three months ago he had borrowed $30,000 for a cocaine buy. He had completed the transaction and then lost the capital, the profit, and the loan-sharked usurious interest on a round-house of bad breaks. In a few minutes he would be meeting with Cheech

Scarmello in the Olive Grove to repay the loan with interest. Scarmello was getting more and more upset as Dominic kept putting off the payment. There had already been four postponements. This evening Dominic was going to ask for just two more days. He had told Cheech that the shipment had been delayed. He wasn't sure how he was going to raise the cash, but he had close calls before and there had always been a way out. Like that time out of nowhere, when, on the spur of the moment, he had taken down a payroll messenger and scored big. There was always a way out and he could always find it.

The Olive Grove was an Italian social club near Fordham Road and Third Avenue. The neighborhood old-timers had rented a storefront, furnished it, and used it as a place to listen to the music of Carlo Buti and Jimmy Sorelli while they played cards and enjoyed Chianti, cheese, and bread. Scarmello was at the Grove waiting for Dominic and his money. Six of the ten tables were filled with men playing briscola, rummy, and poker. Cheech Scarmello was listening to a record of Jimmy Sorelli singing *Mala Femina*. He was chatting with his associates and discussing Family business. He only spoke with his closest and most loyal soldiers about the making of button men for $40,000.

He belonged to the Valerio Fredoni Crime Family and shared a regime with Anthony Tremato, who was not involved in the button sales. If payments were slow, Scarmello preferred to use threats and an occasional broken leg to collect his money. He knew that dead or severely crippled men couldn't make payments. He also knew that payments must be made or he would be labeled a *fesso*—a fool. And a fool had no power, no strength. A fool was worthless, a piece of trash to be kicked aside. A fool was not entitled to respect but was to be ignored or laughed at. A fesso was like a *cornuto*—a man to be given the sign of the horns and be ridiculed because his wife was unfaithful. Scarmello sat in the

Olive Grove, waiting on a night that could not go without resolution, without satisfaction.

Dominic left Pirelli's and crossed the street, his steel-tapped heels tapping a steady cadence on the pavement. After four scotches, his head felt light. As Dominic entered the Olive Grove, Scarmello's face slowly tipped up. His eyes glowered through the dark streams of DiNobili cigar smoke and his left hand, with the open palm, offered Dominic the chair at his left. An overhanging lamp played a white circle on the green felt tabletop. It was a playing field and Dominic had the first move.

"Hello, Cheech. Well, I'm here. Like I said I'd be."

"You're damn right you're here," said Scarmello. "If you hadn't gotten your ass over here, I'm sure you woulda had a bad accident. You got the money this time?"

"Cheech, I need a little more time," strained Dominic.

"More time? You ain't got no more time, kid. You already used up more time than you had. You've been living on borrowed time for two weeks now," said Scarmello. He turned to a heavyset soldier on his right. "He wants more time, Lou. Take a look at your watch. Does he got any more time left?"

Dominic got up. Pallid and drained and tired. "Cheech, please, just another two days and I'll have it all. I swear. The shipment was delayed. I'll have it all in two days."

"Sit down," said Scarmello. Dominic sat. "I want it all now. I hear the shipment has come and gone and you're playin' me for a goddamn fool. Who the hell do you think you are?"

As Scarmello's voice grew louder, the players at the tables quietly rose and slowly left the club.

Dominic looked around him and panic filled his eyes. The Olive Grove was empty now and three of Scarmello's enforcers were approaching the table. The door had been locked and the shades and curtains drawn. Dominic Gatti, at that moment, knew that his life was over. As they approached, his mind flashed with the bitter memory of detective Lenny Lombardi crashing his fist into his gut and kidneys; a paper bag over his head; his mind in a celestial black hole; days of blood in his urine; weeks of aching, broken, healing bones; months of agonizing screaming within himself. And now he sat again in capture, but not for a moment so frightening, not for a pain so severe nor a convalescence so agonizingly morbid. On this night, at the Olive Grove, Dominic Gatti suffered not at all.

He was dead the moment the baseball bat crushed through his skull. He never felt the wooden sledge as it broke his arms and legs. The sweet moment of death had snatched him from Scarmello's revenge. The diamond pinkie ring slipped easily from Gatti's finger into Scarmello's pocket.

* * *

The rear bell rang, cracking the dead, early-morning silence, and an elderly silver-haired gentleman scurried down the rear staircase. He opened the back door to face two broad silhouettes framing a crumpled heap. One of the figures spoke.

"I want you to take this inside and I never want to see it again. *Capisce?*"

The old man nodded his head and the heap was brought into his house, down the basement stairs, and into the preparation room. The two visitors left, and Dominic Banducci gazed in deep sorrow at the crushed, bizarre shape of Dominic Gatti. He lay in rest finally and strangely in peace from this world. He laid on the preparation table but his remains would never be prepared. Dominic Banducci knew what he must do. He had done it twice before, not willingly of desire, but willingly of survival. To refuse would have been a serious mistake.

At ten o'clock the next morning, Father Tommaso Corelli had finished the final prayers of eternal resurrection and the weeping mourners of family, and friends had made their rounds by the open casket of Luigi Antonelli. They had paid their last respects to the man who had come from Naples to live, to raise his family, and finally to leave them for eternal life. The mourners were escorted out of the room and the doors locked so that the casket could be sealed before its trip to a Mass of the Resurrection.

Shuffling under a dead weight, Dominic Banducci and his son Thomas brushed against the rose and carnation floral displays. Flowers broke and fell and were crushed underfoot. The two men carried the twisted corpse of Dominic Gatti and laid him on the floor in front of the open casket. With expert hands they exhumed Antonelli, removed the cushions beneath him, placed Gatti on the floor of the coffin, replaced Antonelli, and sealed the casket, never more to be opened.

Hymns of angel choirs and peals of altar bells resounded throughout the church chapel. Mourners prayed, priests of God eulogized, children tired of impatience, and a casket of tandem corpses stood mutely before the Creator. The burial took place in St. Raymond's Cemetery. Only a handful of men knew what actually had happened. The lips of Dominic Banducci would be sealed forever.

Three weeks following the Antonelli funeral, Michael Palermo was dining with friends at the Half Moon Restaurant on Arthur Avenue. Peter the waiter whispered to him that Mr. Banducci would like to see him at his earliest convenience. The meeting took place on the next day.

MICHAEL PALERMO

I walked up the same steps that had brought me to Banducci when I was investigating the Groty beating. Banducci was a big help then and was now probably requesting some favor in return. I hate funeral homes. I don't accept death. It's something that will never happen. That's the way I am. I respect Banducci, the "impressario di pompe funebri." He is a respected mortician. I could never do that job myself. To each his own.

"Welcome, Michael. I'm glad you were able to visit with me so soon."

His eyes were bright but his drooping silver mustache told me that something was wrong. He looked like he was under a strain. He reminded me of how he had helped me when I was looking for the guy that beat up Jim Groty. Banducci gave up Vinnie Cannelli. He let me know that I owed him when he said, "I see Vincent Cannelli is back in the neighborhood. He's walking better every day."

"That's right, Mr. Banducci. I've seen him too. I want to thank you for all the help you gave us in that investigation. I think he'll be all right now. And how about yourself? Is everything OK?"

"That's why I wanted to speak to you, Michael. I have a lot of trouble. Things are happening that I know nothing about. I respect the dead, Michael." Banducci's voice cracked.

"I know that, Signore. Everybody knows you're a fine gentleman. They all entrust their families to your care. What's the problem? Let me help you."

"It's the police, Michael. They say people have told them that I desecrated the Antonelli funeral."

His voice broke and his bony fingers tapped the desk nervously.

"That's nonsense, Signore. I've known you for years. I know you'd never do such a thing. Who are these police? What do they say you've done?"

"Detective Howard Brenner asked all the questions. It is he who accuses me."

"What does he say?"

"He says I buried someone else along with Mr. Antonelli. Michael, I swear I would never do such a thing. Not for all the money in the world. This Detective Brenner wants to exhume poor Luigi and shame his family. Such dishonor to the dead I cannot allow. Let the dead lie in peace and await the Resurrection." Beads of perspiration broke out through his skin into the heavy rose-scented air.

"I'll speak to Detective Brenner and work to resolve this for you, my friend. I know you'd do the same for me."

Then Banducci got up, walked around the desk, and extended both his hands. I hate shaking hands with undertakers. They always seem to be taking my pulse as they grab my hand. Especially Banducci. He gave me a double grasp right up to the veins of my arms. His thumb pressed on the inside of my wrist. He looked at me like he was taking my pulse and measuring me for a casket. I swore to myself that the next time I had to talk with him I'd use the phone.

Brenner and I had gone to the academy together. He was in Homicide. The word from the street had reached Brenner that Gatti had been murdered at the Olive Grove and been buried with Antonelli. The Department and the D.A.'s office had repeatedly tried to have the casket exhumed and reopened, but the family had been dead set against it. The courts, fearing the charge of sacrilege in dishonoring the dead, would not order the exhumation in opposition to the family's wishes. Gatti would remain buried and forever a mystery. The chirping of all the birds in the world couldn't raise Gatti. I was convinced that the case was closed, so I called Banducci.

"Mr. Banducci, this is Michael. I just want to tell you that I talked with Detective Brenner and you have nothing to worry about. Everyone will rest in peace."

"Michael, I don't know how I can ever thank you. I appreciate everything you have done for me. I wish you were here. I would embrace you like a son."

I was glad I wasn't there. "It's my pleasure, Signore. Please stay well and give my best regards to your family. Ciao."

The Gatti investigation was terminated because of insufficient evidence. I returned a favor without doing a thing. But I knew that somewhere in St. Raymond's Cemetery there rested a casket with two men. And I knew that there had to be a lot more of them. The city's got to be filled with Banduccis.

* * *

CHAPTER 4

For me, life on Narcotics went on as usual. There were days of investigating, search, pursuit, and arrest. There were also days of deception. One of the master deceivers was Terry Fitzpatrick. I brought Terry into the new frontier, into the world of the Narcotics Squad when Harry Anderson was Captain.

"Mike, I need to replace Bowes and Kitel. Jimmy's put in his twenty-five and Abe is going to finish out his twenty on a precinct squad. Do you have anybody in mind?" asked Anderson.

Now I knew the ins and outs of the question. I knew what Anderson was really asking and what he meant. The new people would make a $500 donation to the Captain and they would get into Narcotics. They had to be men who could be trusted to work within the system—be good cops but not disturb the harmony within. I recommended Frank Catania, a good Italian cop who I knew would be good for the Bureau. Then I balanced him with Terry Fitzpatrick—a nice Irish name. I made the arrangements, passed on their "dues" fees to Anderson, and Catania and Fitzpatrick were brought into Narco. Nobody ever mentioned the dues. It never existed except in the minds of Catania and Fitzpatrick, and in Anderson's pocket.

From the minute he was brought in, Terry Fitzpatrick was a deceiver. He was kind of like me.

I got him in by omission. He was soot-black and named Terrell. His family had somehow in the past become black Irish. He became an outstanding detective.

Anderson met the new men, congratulated them, told them that they had come highly recommended and that he knew they had done and would continue to do the right thing. He then quietly whispered in my ear, "That was a cutie you pulled on me, smartass." Everybody was smiling that day.

The squad used deception in undercover activities on the street and in the lock-ups. In 1960, we used whatever we had to get the job done.

* * *

Calvin Green had been arrested on Lenox Avenue for dealing in heroin and was awaiting arraignment at the 32nd precinct. As he sat in the detention cage, his head buried in restless, groping fingers, he peered into the tiny puddle forming on the linoleum beneath his face. The sweat poured in drips from his nose and chin. He needed a fix bad. Outside the woven wire walls of his cell, a conversation faintly drifted to his ears. He looked up and saw a minister in black coat and white collar, a regal-looking black man who he thought might be helpful. Green recognized him from the neighborhood. For the past three months, Reverend George Culver had been seen frequently on the Lenox Avenue streets going about the work of the Lord.

"Say, Reverend, could I see you a minute?" Green's request was granted, and the two of them were led to a private room for privileged counsel. It was there, in that "safe" room, that Reverend Terry Fitzpatrick, in black coat with white collar, gave solace and advice and recorded every word of the baited conversation. The tapes were later used to put Green in Purgatory for seven years.

When Alfred Catone had been arrested for conspiracy to sell narcotics, an immediate conference with his attorney was arranged by his family. Seymour Kroll sported a luxurious mohair suit, diamond rings, and all the attire of the prosperous lawyer. His attaché case of burnt umber mellowed with the glow of Peruvian leather. Kroll was in his early forties and subtle bands of silver streaked his auburn hair and sideburns. His nails were manicured and polished with clear lacquer. A faint smile dwelt on his lips perpetually, a mask to hide what he was really thinking. He was to confer with his client to affect his speedy release.

"Good morning, Mr. Catone. I'm Seymour Kroll. Your family retained me to represent you."

"I don't know you. Where's Selkow?"

"We're associates and I've been briefed on your case. Harvey Selkow and I have been partners for many years. As far as I can determine at the present time, the case against you is weak. I'm sure we can refute all of it, but you must tell me exactly what happened. I'm sure you have no involvement in this whatever."

"Look, Kroll, or whatever your name is, I don't know a thing about this whole beef and I ain't talkin' to nobody but Selkow. Get him on the phone so I can find out what's goin' on and what I'm doin' here. I don't even know who the hell you are."

Catone stared into Kroll's eyes sternly and Seymour's perpetual smile stretched slowly into a Cheshire grin.

"Mr. Catone, we have to trust each other. If we can't operate on a feeling of mutual trust, we just can't continue this relationship and I can't help you."

"I gotta talk to Selkow."

Kroll was frustrated. He picked up his attaché case and called for the officer. He turned to Catone and his smile widened, "You're a smartass, Catone. There's nothing left for us to discuss. I'm afraid Harvey will have to handle your case personally."

"Yeah, that's right. Get him on the phone and get the hell out of here."

Milton Cohen, on this day also known as Seymour Kroll, quietly left the cell. He was a five-year veteran on the Narcotics Squad and had one year of law school behind him. That was Catone's day, but Cohen would try again and be successful with another "client."

MICHAEL PALERMO

Frank Catania became paired with Tommy Croft and Lenny Lombardi. Lenny had thrown a wrench into the departmental gears. He had been made aware of the $500 dues payment which was expected in order to become one of Anderson's people. After my recommendation, Anderson had requested Lombardi for the Narcotics Squad, and Lenny and I met to consummate the contract.

"OK, Lenny, everything's been taken care of and now it's time to pay your dues."

"Hey, Mike, you know, I've been thinking. Maybe this ain't the way to do this thing. In fact, I've made other arrangements."

"What the hell are you talking about? There are no other arrangements. What did you arrange? There's nothing to arrange except what we talked about."

"Well, the other day I took care of everything. Lieutenant Ryan says he has a strong hook and can get me and my papers in quick without any problems. You know this guy can even get people on the Force for 1,000 bucks. He guarantees it. This guy's well-connected."

"Look, Lenny, that's all bullshit. I knew Ryan when he was a sergeant. He's pullin' your chain. There aren't any papers. It's all done on the phone. His price used to be 500 bucks. He's playin' with your puddin'. He can't do a goddamn thing for you. I told you I made all the arrangements. You know the deal. I made the contract for you. You wanted in, now you have to come up with the bread. I started doing you a favor and now you're going to put me in the shithouse."

"I don't know, Mike. You see, Ryan said that for an outboard motor he'd get me on the Squad."

"I'm tellin' you Lenny, he's full of crap. Now fulfill your obligation or take a walk."

"I can't," whined Lombardi with his head hung over. "I already gave Ryan the motor. I put it in his car trunk last week and I already know that I'm in. Ryan definitely handled this contract."

"You stupid bastard. That was my contract that got you out of the bag. If you don't come up with the bread right now, I'm going to have to take it out of my own pocket." Man, was I pissed off.

"I'm sorry, Mike."

And then the sonofabitch just walked away and left me hanging there. When I told my partners, Richie Arculeo and John Amato, they both insisted on sharing Lombardi's dues to Anderson. We couldn't let the Captain know what happened or they would have laughed us out of the job. I had sponsored a zero. We had to calm Arculeo down. When I first told him, he blabbed so loud you could hear it all over the locker room, "You mean that Irish sonofabitch is taking outboard motors now!"

Lombardi got out of the bag and into the Bureau. Ryan chugged with his motor off City Island in the Long Island Sound, and me and my two partners steamed and avoided Lombardi. Captain Anderson congratulated Lenny and told him that he had done the right thing and that he was sure that he would continue to do the right thing. Lenny smiled and looked at me as if to say, "I told you so."

It took Lombardi six months to find out how contracts were really made. It was then that he finally paid his dues.

YEARS LATER

Captain Costello replaced Captain Anderson. I worked with my partners, making good arrests after thorough investigations and relentless stakeouts. We were especially active in Harlem, building cases and improving the quality of our work. Our team worked like a solid, sharply honed hatchet chopping away at illegal drug traffic. Richie Arculeo is muscle and brains. A thirty-two-year-old bachelor whose family came from Bologna. He's tall, dark, and handsome and always dressed like he's going to a formal affair. A serious athlete. The minute he enters Harlem, or any area where the team works, the streets always pick him out as "the man." He loves every minute of it. No matter where the job brings us, in the street or in the station house, people feel he's in charge. We put this to good use whenever necessary.

John Amato is patience and guts. Medium height and build, blonde, blue eyes, soft features, and a mellow guy. His family came out of Abruzzi in central Italy, east of Rome. He came into the Department not to be a cop but to play baseball. He's a great infielder but only an average hitter. A great scout for the Yankees once told him that his fielding was so spectacular that if he could only bat .250 he would get him Phil Rizzuto's job. He couldn't. His timing was off when he joined the Force too. While he was still in the Academy, the police, fire, and sanitation baseball teams were disbanded because of budget problems.

Richie and me usually plan the day or night work schedules. John's always on the job but it's like he's doing time, a twenty-year stretch. He's waiting for his twenty to be up so he can collect his pension. He wants no problems, only to be a good cop. Whenever we need him, he's there. He's the first one in the door when we break into an apartment. When the suspects run down the fire escape, John is right behind them. He plays the game well.

We're staking out a factory now. Near Amsterdam Avenue. It cuts heroin and packages it. They get it from the "Opium Road." From fields in Turkey, to Marseilles for refinement, to Canada, and then to New York. There are six workers in the plant. They cut the white powder with milk sugar and quinine and seal the exact amounts in clear glassine envelopes. The weights have to be deadly accurate because a person can get crippled or dead for coming up short, even if he didn't skim any off the top. These cutters work almost naked and wear facemasks like the doctors do. The air in the factory is heavy with a pungent bitterness. Heroin talc wafts imperceptibly as tiny, floating dust specks that can't be filtered. That's why cutters and packagers always become junkies. They breathe in the heroin every day. It's the same air that hooked Cantelopez who hooked Vito Genovese. The day that the factory workers stop working is the day that they start mainlining and make their arms and legs into pin cushions.

Jerry "The Gimp" Mackey had tipped us to this factory. On his regular marijuana sales route he overheard Rosalyn Jones in a Harlem bar. She talked about a factory. It was only that one loose, careless word that The Gimp had to hear. Lights went on inside his head. He followed her, unseen, with his shuffling, uneven gait, ducking into doorways or behind corners. He followed her to Amsterdam Avenue. He set up his own stakeout like he was a cop. Surveillance. His position with us gave him a little muscle. Some leverage. He could also make big bucks if he could come up with a big bust. This looks like the one that's going to make The Gimp rich. He caught a glimpse of Rosalyn in a street-view window. He figured out that the plant was on the top floor in apartment 5B. Smart guy. Could have been something or somebody big in another life.

We did our own surveillance and figured that now is the perfect time for a raid. We have to get in fast. The fire escape is too risky. If they see us coming up from the outside, they'll explode out in all directions and flush everything down the toilet or dump the bathtubs. Cutters usually work on boards over the bathwater. At the split second of an alarm, the heroin on the board is flipped over and the plug pulled from the drain. The evidence winds up in the sewers.

We could also get our asses shot off if we went up the escape route. We know they've got heavy weapons in there to protect million-dollar investments. We have to time the break-in perfectly. We need two points of entry. Richie came up with the plan. John is going up the dumbwaiter and The Gimp is doing the hoisting. He goes up to the fifth-floor apartment in the little elevator, gets in, and through surprise, busts out when Richie and me break down the door. Richie and me, we go up the inside of the building next door, get to the roof, over to the factory building and down the stairs, and break down the door.

Mackey's got this rotted yellow smile. I don't know if we can trust him. John says that The Gimp can taste the bucks he's going to get from this score, so he trusts him. That's OK with me because it's John's ass that's going to be swinging five floors overhead while Mackey is holding on to the end of the rope and pulling him up. I wouldn't trust him, but John says, "Go!" So we go. We send Mackey in first through the rear door to reconnoiter. He's quiet. The basement air is heavy and humid. He comes back with the all-clear sign. John Amato is the first to follow him back in.

The four of us make our way through the dark, dank, smelly bowels of the tenement, past the storage lockers, chained bicycles, and baby carriages. I pull the string hanging from a filthy light bulb on the ceiling. A dirty yellow glow filters through the clammy cellar. Richie opens the dumbwaiter door slowly. As we look in, six steely yellow eyes stare back at us. Then there's this loud, hissing squeal and three giant black rats jump out at us and almost knock us over. Their coats are shiny and bristling with grease, and their long tails snap like tiny whips. Mackey gets one stuck in his smelly, baggy overcoat. We help him get rid of it. In a second they disappear behind boxes and into the crannies of the broken walls. Everybody screams and curses and then everything quiets down. John sweeps out the rat droppings from the floor of the tiny lift, places some old newspapers down and curls up into the fetal crouch with his chin over his knees and his gun in his hand. Slowly he gets pulled up, with the bird, Mackey, heaving on the knotted hoist rope. He inches John up, carefully counting the knots on the rope so he can stop at the right apartment. John feels along the wall and counts the kitchen dumbwaiter doors.

Richie and me leave and get into the back alley and into the basement of the building next door. We race like crazy up the interior staircase. We have only two minutes from the alley, to the stairs, to the roof, to the factory, to break in. We run up the stairs mad and wild, taking three and four steps at a time, pulling on the steel railings with one hand, the other waving a .38 police revolver. Our feet dig into the loose pebbles that pock the tarred rooftop. We hurdle over the building edge walls to keep our appointment with an old friend in a dumbwaiter. The roofs and ceilings below pound with four feet fighting time. We race over beds of love and hate and over little children who'll soon enough be out on the street and playing cops-and-robbers with us with real guns. We stop and catch our breath at the factory rooftop door. I turn the knob. The door edges open a crack. I look down the stairwell straight into the back of a look-out polishing an automatic pistol. It's bigger and more powerful than my .38.

A minute and forty-nine, fifty. John must be counting too. I look back at Richie. Fifty-one, fifty-two. We can't wait. Fifty-three, fifty-four. With all our weight we ram the door into the sentry, knocking him down the stairs. He rolls and tumbles and cracks his head open on the railing post in front of apartment 5B.

Mackey pulls and strains, counting the knots, coiling and wrapping the rope around his sweaty black arms. Two knots, pull, heave; three knots, tight, heavy, pull, lean back, full weight, lean back; four knots, almost there. John's almost there. Five! We've got it. Now to hold and tie. Suddenly the door behind Mackey sweeps open, bathing the smelly dungeon with light as bright as the sun. In the doorway a startled black face with popping, yellow eyes stares in disbelief at a crouching Mackey. The Gimp's head snaps back to curse the light. Two black faces freeze and stare at each other in disbelief. The super had come for his brooms and dustpan.

Mackey holds on, encoiled by his knotted rope. He can't move. John is hanging five floors up. Five flights from death if Mackey lets go.

"What chew doin' there, man?" the super growls.

Mackey's thoughts race ahead at blinding split-second salvos. He's good at alibis. A good answer in the past has kept him alive many times when he should have been dead. His mind flashes: *I'm here for the garbage*; no, *I'm fixing the dumbwaiter*; no, *I'm an undercover cop*; he'll never believe that. *I'm the exterminator.* Yeah, that's it.

Fifty-five, fifty-six. John Amato counts.

Fifty-seven, fifty-eight. They should be at the apartment door now. Fifty-nine, sixty.

As his mind races, Mackey feels the weight on the rope disappear. John is gone. He lets go and the platform comes crashing down. A blast of smashing dust-smoke fills the basement covering The Gimp and the super. Through the debris cover of noise and clouds, Mackey shuffles out the back door, into the alley, and into the safety of the street where he lives and knows his way around.

Amato crashes through the little door, which hides him. He races through the kitchen, past the living room, and into panicked eyes frozen in paralyzed faces.

"Police! On the floor!"

Richie and me crash into the door but it doesn't move. It's bolted. The cutters have their coats on. Their pockets filled with heroin. We ram it again. It gives and breaks apart. We jump in with guns in the air. One guy tries to jump out the window on to the fire escape. John shoots him in the leg and he stops and falls down on the floor. John was ten seconds too quick for us and could have gotten his ass shot off. We were lucky. It was an important bust. A good, solid arrest. A good, solid unit. A good machine.

The next day I paid The Gimp off with a generous bag of heroin. He was in heaven. I could see retirement in his eyes. He said he was going to visit his brother in Georgia and disappear for a while. Maybe even retire.

CHAPTER 5

CHIEF COLLIN DEVLIN, RETIRED, MAY 1960

Michael and I are going to The Hole tonight. I'm waiting here for him at my place at 3 Metropolitan Oval, apartment 12F, high above the showering fountains and manicured lawns. He's bringing me my Nitroglycerin and Digitalis like he usually does. Too many years of late hours and rich foods and smoky restaurants with old friends have finally caught up with me and worn out the arteries, valves, and muscles of a tired old heart. I wonder what Heaven is like. Before I go, I want to bring Mike along, teach him to play chess, and help out some old friends. That's all. And God willing, I'll do it.

Ah, there's the brass chime at the door. He must be here.

His smile lights up the place.

NATALIE FITZPATRICK

It was Terry's thirty-fifth birthday, a sort of milestone in our lives. He never talked much about what went on in the job. But lately he was home more often and really got into the role of father and husband. Life was good for us in the Lenox Avenue apartments at 145th Street. Eleven-year-old Jackie and nine-year-old Alma had good friends and a safe playground. Terry and I grew up together and got married at eighteen. When Terry got back from Korea, we decided to have children.

On his birthday night, we had his favorite dinner. Baked Virginia ham with glazed pineapple and maraschino cherries. I served wells of syrupy brown gravy in puffs of whipped potatoes.

With a wide-eyed child on each leg of his lap and with me smiling over a nightcap of coffee, Terry told family stories about the cotton fields of the 1850s. He repeated the same tales that had been handed down to him through generations of Fitzpatricks. In his hands he held our futures. The kids listened to Terry like he was telling them fairy tales. They couldn't believe that all the slavery and black oppression had ever really happened. Little Jackie and Alma heard the living words of their great-grandparents. It was like being at a church sermon. And then we sang sacred hymns. It was a night I'll always remember.

And then the phone rang.

* * *

MABEL GREEN, NURSE

I've seen it all. The sea of sterile white uniforms and the pain and suffering. The tile-walled Emergency Ward sobbing and screaming with the torment of accidents, illnesses, slashings, beatings, and gunshot wounds. Sirens squealing in bouncing, dying echoes that soak into the walls, desks, and busy moving people. My ears have long since stopped hearing the background noises of people and machines. My mind carefully selects only the things that are essential for keeping people alive. I'm an Emergency Room nurse, a machine of cold efficiency racing against savage time. The howlings and wailings of the world must be concentrated in these walls tonight. At least when I go home tonight I'll have my paycheck and one week's vacation check in my hands. Right there in my tired hands. At ten o'clock tonight I'm taking a week off to spend some time with my daughter and my two grandchildren at my Roberts Avenue apartment.

STOKES AND CARVER, DRUG ADDICTS

The sweet nectar of honeysuckle vapors over the vest-pocket park. Clifford Stokes and Lionel Carver lie lifeless, minds floating in the cheating ambrosia of a heroin narcotic trance. They smell no honeysuckle. Their olfactory nerves have been burned useless from snorting cocaine. The two reek from weeks of body grime and urinous sweat. They float in a high that was soon to break, forcing them to grovel on the Harlem streets to get what they would need again and again, to get it any way at all. They lie behind the hedges, hidden from the sidewalk, away from the world, from the real. They had escaped.

* * *

COLLIN DEVLIN, CHIEF, RETIRED

At The Hole, Mike and I share a feast with Anthony Tremato and his lieutenant, Johnny Brescetti. Tremato is a capo in the Fredoni family that runs Fordham. He shares a regime with Cheech Scarmello. I know that Tremato met with the Commission the night before. A table had been called and a solution to the Scarmello sales of Family memberships had been arranged. Scarmello would be the last to know of the arrangement. I had talked to Tremato earlier in the evening when Mike and Johnny were at the bar. We took care of business.

"Tony, you understand the difficult situation this puts our people in. Soon we'll have to send street cleaners and garbage trucks out along with our radio cars to pick up bodies. It would be much better for all concerned if you people would dump your garbage a little here, a little there. Spread it around so that the Mayor and the PC don't get so upset. We realize you people have a business to operate, but we're in business too."

I wave a celery stalk in the air as I speak for effect. I don't have a cigar like Tony does. The "heat" came down from the top and we have to work out a solution to the acceleration of haphazard dumpings of underworld murder victims. The media are mounting a public opinion campaign, putting pressure on political and law enforcement leaders to put a stop to the mob violence. I had received a call from the Police Commissioner to see if things could be worked out. There were too many bodies turning up with holes behind the ears and between the eyes, morbid mutilations, victims locked and abandoned in car trunks, dead men floating in rivers, washed up on beaches and inside empty oil drums. I tell Tony that his people will have to start using restraint, selectivity of disposal, and organizational procedures. He agrees. He doesn't want trouble any more than I do. We lead our lives trying to keep out of trouble. Who needs trouble? Only a fool.

"Of course, Collin. Of course. It's no way to run a business. It's a damn shame. These young people today don't know how to control themselves, not their heads or their balls. Some of them think the world is there for them to rape. There's been a few problems in Fordham lately, but soon that'll be over. In the meantime some tolls on the bridges will be paid. That's no problem. We'll spread it out real good."

After that, the Jersey Meadowlands are used and Staten Island too. The other boroughs get their share, even Westchester and Putnam Counties and Connecticut are sprinkled.

* * *

NATALIE FITZPATRICK

Terry left the children and got up to answer the phone. I put the kids to bed. It was ten o'clock. I listened in on the extension. I wanted to see who had the nerve to call him out on his birthday. I was part cop, too.

"Hello."

"Fitz?"

"Yeah."

"Woezy. I got to see you tonight."

"Where?"

"Tinkers in two."

"OK."

I knew that Woezy was a code name for one of Terry's informants. He used to say that "The bird had a strong pipeline." He never said it to me but I overheard it when he was talking to his partners. A cop's wife has to be part cop herself. I knew that Tinkers was the old stone bell tower church. Terry often called it that. "In two" must have been code for eleven o'clock, I suppose because of the "two" ones in eleven. Anyway, Terry left the house at a quarter to eleven, right after he kissed the kids and me goodnight. They were asleep. I couldn't sleep all night. I never slept until he got back home from one of his "meets," as he called them. He gave too much to the job and not enough to his wife and children. But that's the way he was. He loved helping people and putting the bad guys away.

He must have walked right by that park near 138th Street.

* * *

STOKES AND CARVER, JUNKIES

Carver sat up. "Hey, man, you got any more 'shit' on you?"

Stokes still has his eyes closed. He is holding on and doesn't ever want to let go.

"You hear me, man? Gimme some more o' that good 'shit' o' yours." Carver persists.

With a groan of disdain, Stokes moans, "I ain't got no more, mother. How come you ain't never got your own 'shit,' man? Go get your own."

Carver rests his wet back against the hedge. Faint steamers mist off his shoulders in the cool spring air, like angel wings. He rolls his kinky black head in his hands like he wants to grab it tight, rip it off, and roll it away. His right jacket pocket sags as the butt of a rickety Brazilian .22 caliber revolver hangs out in the cool night air.

* * *

MABEL GREEN, TRAUMA NURSE

I'm wearing my sterile hospital-white uniform that is smeared by the blood of a night's work. I didn't change in the locker room because I don't want to waste any time getting home to my family. Time gets more and more precious every day. Here I am, a fifty-six-year-old, shuffling up Lenox Avenue with a large canvas bag suspended from my left shoulder. I grab the bottom of the bag real tight, like a vise, so that nobody can rip it out of my hands and run off with my pay. They call me tough and spunky. Got to be. What a terrible way to have to live. But if you don't live that way, you die. I've dealt with crime on the streets for the last ten years and I deal with it in the wards every night. I help to lift 200-pound dead weights from one table to another. One hard way to make a living, I'll tell you. I'm glad my momma isn't here to see me live like this. She was so happy and proud when I became a nurse. It's not all it's cracked up to be. Bed pans and blood and infection and disease.

Ever since I lost Herbert to a mugger's blade, I'm tougher than anybody I know. I'm no easy mark. If they try to mug me, I got a big heavy red brick in my bag. And I'll split their heads open with it if I have to. Kill 'em if I have to. Don't mess with Mabel Green.

* * *

"Shhh," said Stokes. "Listen! You hear that, man? Listen! That's a tired old scrape. Hear those shoes drag. It's easy bucks. That's yours, mother. There's your 'shit.' Go get it! Look here through the bottom of the bushes."

The two peered through the bare lower branches of the hedge, their eyes tensing to the swish of Mabel Green's baggy hospital dress. Her soft, white prescription shoes slid and dragged along the soil-powdered concrete sidewalk. She breathed in deeply as she passed the scent of honeysuckle flowers.

Sweat poured off Carver and Stokes and a shroud of steam mist sizzled off their backs. The hedge sliced open and apart and four black sweaty hands grabbed Mabel Green. They grabbed her head and arm, her neck and fleshy left breast. She was snatched, torn from the sidewalk, crashing through a hedge of brambles on to a wet, slippery crabgrass field.

"Gimme that bag, old lady!" screamed Carver as he reached for her purse. She pulled away and started to run. Stokes reached out for her left arm which was coiled around her bag. He spun her around and Carver grabbed her dress chest-high between her breasts. His tearing hands ripped out the front of the dress and tore off her white brassiere. She stood hunched over, stunned, looking at her two heavy black breasts, pendulously hanging over a field of lily white. Her mind crazed with a fever of disgrace, of bilious hate for the scum that had invaded her and had killed her Herbert. She was cornered and stood shivering. For an instant, the three of them froze, all glaring at this bare-breasted woman, crouched and entwined around her purse.

Carver's hands squeezed the handle of his .22 and he stuck the barrel into Mabel Green's face.

"Now, gimme that damn bag, you old bitch!"

Mabel said nothing. She sank lower, her eyes pinned on the ground. Suddenly, with the roar and force of an exploding sewer cover, she bolted up, and with spittle and tears streaming down her contorted face, she let loose a banshee scream of terror and revenge. Her bag-covered brick crashed out at the gun. It fired, sinking a bullet into the gnarled old oak tree that cowered behind her. Carver lost his grip, and the revolver skittled along the grass, landing in front of the bushes next to the sidewalk.

In a wild, whooshing arc, Mabel swung her bludgeon at her two muggers. She hit Stokes on the forehead, splitting the skin, exposing a grisly plate of chalkish bone. Blood streamed over his eyes, blinding him.

"She killed you, Stokes! The old bitch done killed you," yelled Carver as he turned and ran tearing through the bushes into the street. Stokes followed, wiping the blood from his eyes with his sleeves. In faltering gasps he screamed at Carver, "Help me, you mother. Help me. She's gonna kill me."

Mabel looked for the gun. This was not going to be over. For her, it would never be over. The memory of Herbert on a cold steel slab at the morgue for her to identify, with coagulated knife wounds all over his chest, under a cold white shroud; this would never be over for Mabel Green.

Carver and Stokes reached the street just as a small pickup truck was passing by. Carver jumped into the rear with the ladders, mops, and pails. Stokes chased after him.

Across the street, in front of the Angels of Heaven Church, stood Woezy, doing his nervous-in-place dance while he talked to Terry Fitzpatrick. At the crack of the gunshot, Fitzpatrick left Woezy and raced into Lenox Avenue in time to see Carver crashing out of the park hedge with a blood-spattered Stokes racing after him. In the corner of his eye, Terry Fitzpatrick could see a hysterical Mabel Green with the bushes chest-high before her. Fitzpatrick arched across the street, his short-barrel .38 caliber revolver flashing in his right hand. He was gaining on the truck. Carver was pulling on Stokes to get him into the pickup. Fitzpatrick's fingertips touched Stokes' smelly coat pocket. Terry's hand grabbed and pulled back.

Mabel Green stumbled out of the bushes with insanity in her glassy eyes, her left hand wrapped around her bag. Her long narrow, pendulous black breasts dangled over a bright white backdrop. She raised her right hand and squeezed the cold trigger of the Brazilian .22. An explosion! Acrid smoke—like firecrackers. The buildings echoed a hollowing blast through every alley and courtyard. Mabel Green collapsed from terror, madness, and exhaustion.

Terry Fitzpatrick's grip grew limp. His fingers hooked for a moment into Stokes' pocket and then Fitzpatrick's raggedy-doll body bounced on knees and shoe tops along the cobblestones. Stokes wrenched the detective's hand out of his pocket and threw it into the street. Fitzpatrick tumbled over and over, finally resting in a face-down spread-eagle. Stokes scurried up into the pickup with the mops and pails.

In the back of Terry Fitzpatrick's head was a small, round, red button hole that trickled blood out on to the boulevard.

Fitzpatrick died on the day he was born. Mabel Green didn't mean to kill him. She was just fighting back.

In ten minutes, night became day. Fitzpatrick's twisted corpse was ringed by bulb-popping newsmen, by police, medics, and gawkers. Mabel Green was wrapped in the dignity of a gray blanket. When asked what happened, she muttered in groggy coherence, "He tried to shoot me. He wanted my bag. She pointed to Detective Terry Fitzpatrick. Mabel was whisked away to the refuge of the emergency ward of her Havencrest Hospital. She would sleep in sedation.

A radio news station was the first to broadcast the shooting. A gawker's phone call had relayed Mabel's statement. On their way home from The Hole, Palermo and Devlin heard the special bulletin: "Informed sources report that a fatal shooting has just occurred at Lenox Avenue and 138th Street. Preliminary reports indicate that a New York City detective was gunned down as he attempted a mugging. We will cover this story in detail and will bring you exclusive on-the-scene coverage. We repeat: Informed sources indicate that a New York City detective was shot to death as he attempted a mugging."

Devlin stared in disbelief. Palermo veered the car to the right into a side street. They were only three blocks away. Beads of perspiration popped out from Michael's forehead.

"My God," said Devlin. "My God!"

"We'll be there in a minute, Chief," said Palermo as he slapped his flashing red light on the top of the car.

They arrived in time to see the police photographers and crime lab doing their job. Picture bulbs flashed like the lightning strikes of a small electrical storm. Men, bodies bent and stooped over, made a chalk outline of the body and gun. Detectives were questioning people in the growing mob, looking for witnesses.

CHIEF COLLIN DEVLIN, RETIRED

I moved slowly through the crowd with my hands on the back of Michael's shoulders. Each step became more painful as we neared the site we didn't want to see. Mike wedged the crowd away from in front of us, flipping his shield in time to his calls of "Police!" The words stuck in his throat like sawdust. I could tell. We reached the center circle. The body was being lifted onto a stretcher by two attendants. As we looked at Fitzpatrick, Mike's eyes locked on the icy stare in Terry's face, a face startled in unexpected death. With both arms outstretched, Mike grabbed Terry by the shoulders, refusing to believe what everyone else knew. The attendants stopped.

"Come on, Mike," I said. "Come on back here with me." My voice sounded thin and far away and lost in the buzzing of the crowd. I peeled Mike's fingers from Terry's arms. We moved to the side. Fitzpatrick went to the morgue.

"He was one of my people, Chief." Mike's eyes streamed with tears but he wasn't crying. The tears just ran free. Natural. "I brought him into the Bureau. Remember that fellow Fitzpatrick I told you about? That's him. If it weren't for me, he'd be alive today."

I tried to comfort him and told him that I understood. That he wasn't the only event in Fitzpatrick's life that placed him there on that spot that night. It was his whole life. That Mike was only a very small part of that life. It was his birth that placed him there that night. It was his youth, his schooling, all of the jobs he ever had, his family. It was where he wanted to be that night. It was what he wanted to accomplish for himself, for his people and for us that brought him there. It was his dream that killed him. Dreams have killed so many people. I told him all of this but I don't think he heard me or understood what I said. Maybe someday he'll remember and it will sink in.

We returned to the car and I told him to sit there for a while so that I could get the rest of the story. When I returned, his eyes had dried. The tensions released. The emotions exhausted.

Detectives from the Homicide Bureau were questioning a twenty-four-year-old Hispanic, Angel Rojas. I listened. Rojas had been riding past the Angels of Heaven Church. He was on his way to clean the floors of some local offices. He heard a shot from across the street and watched two men jump out of the bushes. One of them was bleeding from the head.

A woman raced after them screaming. Another man ran from the church waving a gun and yelling, "Police! Stop! Police!"

Through his rearview mirror he watched the two men from the park jump into his pickup truck. He got scared. Another shot was fired. He stopped his truck and ducked under the dashboard. When he heard the police siren, he got out. The two men in the back of his truck were gone but one of them had dropped a spoon and a needle syringe. He saw the dead police officer and the hysterical woman, who had fainted.

"That man was a hero, man. He wasn't trying to steal nothin'. All he was tryin' to do was to stop those two black guys. He didn't even shoot. He could have shot and stopped them, but he didn't. I guess he didn't want to hurt nobody who was clean. Instead he got shot and now it's all over for him, man. He should have shot." Rojas sighed and was asked to tell his story over and over again. Procedure.

I went back to the car and told Mike how it had gone down. We didn't talk on the way home. I don't think either one of us slept that night.

* * *

Terry Fitzpatrick was buried on a day of sun and flowers. He was given an inspector's funeral. Fifteen hundred policemen massed outside Christ the Redeemer Baptist Church. White-gloved police officers stood at attention. A groundcover of humanity flowed down the cathedral steps on to the concrete boulevard. Eight sullen police pallbearers lifted the casket and stepped slowly toward the church. They carried their friend up the stairs, down center aisle, and finally to rest in front of the altar. To the left of center, a magnificent oaken pulpit arched up and forward. A fan of polished black walnut capped the pastor's podium.

On 112th Street, the limousines and flower cars waited. Policemen who couldn't find room within the church listened from the steps. Fluted organ strains floated through the open doors and into neighborhood apartments. Harlem would know that Detective Terry Fitzpatrick was dead. The choir picked up the melody and 1,200 voices sang "Amazing Grace."

Reverend Wilbur Williams stood under the walnut fan, his head bowed in respect. The music ended and the voices of the gospel singers faded in a reluctant silence. From out of the church speakers' heavy breathing could be heard, a pastor's labored breath rising to a low moan. The pews carried their limit. Black and white sat together with heads bowed. Candles burned around the flag-draped coffin.

"We loved him, God." Reverend Williams' voice broke the silence. His face reached up past the painted ceiling into heaven itself. He was talking with Christ the Redeemer. "We loved our brother, Terrell Aloysius Fitzpatrick. We know that you loved him, too. We know that's why you took him, God. So he could be with you." The audience resounded, "Hallelujah! Amen."

"We know You have reasons, Jesus. And we know in time you will show all of us the light and the reason for our lives. You are our shepherd. You make us to lie in green pastures, beside still waters. You give us to eat and drink. You give us life." The pastor's voice gently swelled in volume and vibrato. The congregation responded with, "Hallelujah. Amen. Praise the Lord."

"And as you have done with our brother, Terrell, you will lead us into the Valley of the Shadow of Death. Give us strength, Lord, so that we are not afraid. You lead us and we shall all follow You. We shall share the glory of heaven." The reverend's hands reached toward the sky. With open palms, his fingers beat the air. With force and power he spoke to God for himself and for his people. And they responded, "Save us, Jesus."

"You took away our strength, oh Lord, when you took away our brother, Terrell. But we know you will renew us and him with new life so that we will both be stronger. In our love for you, we will be born again, reborn in strength and love and in understanding. Hallelujah!"

NATALIE FITZPATRICK

I sat in the front row, left of center aisle. Jackie and Alma were with me. I was so sorry for the children. Their father was gone forever. Only the memories remain. The dinners and family talk. The stories on their father's lap. The smile and wink they were yet to realize they would never see again. My strength was gone. I was empty except for my love for Terry and the children. No junkie or thief could ever steal that love from me. He was my man. This love will last until my last breath.

I cried myself into blindness last night. Blindness to the world and all its pain. Blindness to a life alone except for the children. My arms and face, my entire body feels like plastic. Unreal. Floating here. But not here. Not anywhere. Dizzy. Numb.

* * *

In the front row, right of center, sat Police Commissioner Kevin O'Hara, Judge Oscar Birnbaum, Borough Commander Sanford Garelick, Manhattan District Attorney Arnold Hunslinger, and Assistant D.A. Ross Simon. It would be Simon's job to prosecute Stokes and Carver and wring the maximum sentence and retribution from their carcasses. Police and prosecutors sat somber and at attention.

Tears dropped on the wooden pews. Tears, the salt of human grief, an ablution to cleanse the soul of those who can cry no more. In the last pew beside the entrance door, Mabel Green cried into a black handkerchief. She cried dry tears.

The services ended and the pallbearers lifted the casket on its way to the hearse. Natalie and her children exited first. In the entrance hall they passed a sobbing old lady dressed in black. Her dress was tear-soaked, and her head hung over her chest like the dead on the gallows. As the widow passed, she looked up and the two women locked eyes. One in the ultimate grief, the other in a plastic emptiness. Although they had never met, at the moment of sight they knew each other. Natalie approached and gently placed her hands on the old lady's shoulders. At her touch, the two women tensed and their bodies moved in shock, as if an electric field had been grounded and sent in relief deep into the earth.

"I'm sorry, Missus. I didn't mean to take your man. I didn't mean it." Mabel Green broke into hysterical contrition. "I haven't slept for days. I wish I were dead. I want the Lord to take me and give you back your man. I asked Him but He just won't do it. Forgive me. Please forgive me so that I can rest." She buried her face in her handkerchief.

Natalie raised her veil and looked deep into Mabel's eyes. "It wasn't your fault. I understand what happened. You mustn't blame yourself. It was God's will." With her black lace veil back in place, Natalie Fitzpatrick stepped down the cathedral steps into a black

limousine just like the one on her wedding day. She didn't hear
Mabel's lips whisper, "Thank you. Oh, God, thank you."

At the cemetery, a police honor guard attended the services.
Two hundred police officers cast a flower farewell into the grave-
site. A bugler blew "Taps." The widow was given the American
flag that had draped her husband's casket. The flag was folded
into a triangle and was presented by Terry's commanding officer,
Captain Costello.

"Mrs. Fitzpatrick, on behalf of the entire police department,
for myself and for all of Terry's friends, I want to extend our
deepest sympathy. He was one of the finest men on the Force."

As the crowd broke, Assistant District Attorney Ross Simon
turned to Commissioner O'Hara. "I'm going to prosecute those
two with headlines that will reach across the nation. We have to
show the street that they can't get away with this kind of thing. An
example has to be made and, by God, Commissioner, I'll see to it
that the criminal element never forgets this killing."

O'Hara nodded and shook Simon's hand. "That's the spirit,
lad. I'm sure we'll all be in good hands with you on the job." He
turned to District Attorney Hunslinger. "That Ross Simon is quite
a formidable fellow. Looks like he's going places. We'll have to
keep an eye on him."

Two detectives overheard the conversation as they walked
to their cars. Jim Groty whispered to Mike Palermo, "Yeah, you
better keep an eye on him or one morning you'll come to work
and he'll be sittin' in your chair. And it'll all be on Page One."

"Ah, he's not such a bad guy," said Palermo. "Give him a
chance. He's just doing his job."

"I don't like the bastard. He's doing a job on everybody,"
grumbled Groty.

CHAPTER 6

The night air was August, hot and sticky. It hung heavy as I walked from Amen's parking lot. I was the street kid from East Harlem, looking, always looking for the glint, the smile, the subtle nod that would give me the edge. Even relaxing off duty, playing cards or shooting craps, survival and success meant being smart, having the luck, and getting the edge, no matter how small.

Three weeks had passed since Terry Fitzpatrick's funeral. Jim Groty had asked for a meet at Amen's. I didn't know why, only that it was something important. After Groty had survived the beating in Ricco's by Vinnie Cannelli, he was never the same. The surgeon's knife couldn't repair the facial nerve damage that Cannelli had crushed with his heel. Vinnie's signature would be on Groty's face for the rest of his life. A reminder of a mistake once made, never cured. Jimmy had a drooped left lip. He had risen to the rank of Detective Lieutenant and now he wanted something from me.

A black Buick bounced reflections off its polished paint, and a face, framed in street lights under glass, watched me as I passed. The face was a woman with beady black eyes peering from the passenger seat. She was uncommonly unattractive, like something from a menagerie. The time, the words and the glance all jelled at once and a phrase stuck in my mind. Words I could never tell anyone. A little secret. A conglomerate phrase condensing from years of police work. The woman was ugly. Her eyes had a scavenging, hungry cast and she looked like she would copulate with a toad. As I passed the Buick, I began to itch.

The cool air behind Amen's front door felt good on my face, like a cold bed sheet on a hot summer night. The jukebox played a Jimmy Sorelli Neapolitan ballad and the whiff of whiskey and beer mingled with Italian food steaming from the oven. Later, at nine o'clock, I would have dinner with Buck, Johnny Nap, the Federal Treasury agent, and Jimmy Sorelli. It would be a routine evening. A chance to unwind over dinner with good friends and fine food. But first I would find out what Groty wanted. It had to be a favor. I was always doing favors for people. Either cops or hoods. Or maybe it was a lead or a contact that he wanted.

Groty was waiting for me at the bar. He was on time, and his eyes grabbed me as I entered. He was hot about something. A nod, a sign, and we sat at a small round table in the rear of the dining room.

"How you doin', Jimmy? What's happening?"

"I'm doing good, Mike. What's happening is that something's goin' down and you're in the middle. I'm gonna lay it out for you."

"What the hell are you talking about? I'm not in the middle of anything. Not now, anyway."

Groty laid it out.

"The feds got their hands out to this guy that they want to do business with, but he won't deal with them. They sent Lombardi to talk to him but the guy turns into a clam. He thinks everybody is wired. He says the only guy he'll talk with is Mike Palermo. He said to get him Palermo."

"Why the hell me? Where did he get my name? Do I know him? Who is he?"

I didn't want any part of the fed's "business." Those bastards got their hands out all over. They're in everybody's pocket. Selling information. Shaking down hoodlums. Now they were trying to shake a guy who was afraid of wires. Hell, maybe Lombardi was wired. What about Groty? Maybe he's wired now! The feds could be building a case against all of us.

"You know, Jim, I really don't want any part of this deal. I've got plenty of heat comin' down on the job right now and I don't need to play a connection for any feds. Let them get somebody else."

"There isn't anybody else. This guy asked for you personally. And I tell you, they can give him plenty of grief. I think you oughta talk to him. It'll be to everybody's advantage. The guy says he knows you from the old neighborhood. His name is Augie Coletti. They call him 'Little Augie.' Does that ring a bell?"

Groty was pressing. He must have a piece of this contract. He wants the deal to go down smoothly. The stronger he is at producing results, the larger are the bucks and favors he could ask for later.

"Coletti?" My mind searched back to place the name. Back through the walls of time. Back to East Harlem on 110th Street. Augie Coletti? Me, Augie, and Carmine Canicatti used to play stickball in the streets in the thirties. "Yeah. I used to play ball with a kid named Coletti. Yeah! Augie Coletti. I haven't seen him in over twenty-five years. Sure I remember him. What do they have? How strong do they have him?"

"They got him on a wire with Pasq Rosetti. He was lookin' to score. They can build a case with birds and circumstance and at the very least, they can give him a lot of heat."

Pasquale Rosetti was a small-time hood who would fence merchandise that fell off trucks or out of warehouses. He was in big demand. He could move anything from brassieres to diamonds.

"What are they looking for?"

"Ten large ones."

"Ten grand? And this Augie wants to see me? Let me ask you, does Coletti have to worry about any other wire? Like on you or under this goddamn table?"

"They just want the cash. To them he's nothing but a meal. Just another business deal. They had their ear to Rosetti's wire and this guy happened to call a few times and say the right things. He was a surprise. His mouth got him into trouble and he's playing it real careful from now on. I guess he feels he can trust you. What do you say?"

Groty waited while I thought it over and sipped my bourbon and water. I suppose I owed something to an old friend and forgotten times. Friends are hard to come by. Especially old friends. Trust was even harder. My old friend trusted me. I had no choice.

"I'll talk to him. I'll see what I can do. I can't promise anything, but I'll talk to him."

"Good, I knew you would. I told him to be outside at eight tonight. He should be here now. Finish your drink. I got a broad outside for some business of my own. Coletti said he would be in a gray Pontiac. Let me know how you make out." Groty got up to leave.

"Wait a minute." I downed my drink. "I'll leave with you. I want to check out your taste with broads anyway." I was playing a hunch. I wanted to see if I still had the instinct.

Outside Amen's I saw the gray Coletti Pontiac. I watched Groty drive away behind the wheel of a shiny black Buick, his arm around the woman with the beady black eyes. My hunch was right. Casper Nardino was right. You can't change a man's character. You can't change his nature. If you think you can, you're going to be hit by the sin of stupid generosity. It's nice to be generous, but not to be stupid. Groty will never change. Bars and broads are a part of his character, part of his blood. Nardino was right, except that Groty wasn't a frog. He was more of a toad.

I crossed under the elevated trains on Westchester Avenue. As I walked toward Augie, I remembered how Vito Genovese had been destroyed by the scorpion sting of stupid generosity. Was there a bug in the Coletti car? The feds could take us both down. Anything Augie, said could strengthen the case against him. And if they got me on the wire too, my stupid generosity could destroy me.

I stepped back into time when three kids, Augie, Carmine, and me, played in the gutter. Street fighters. Gutter guys. Back into the hot sweaty tenement days of rusty fire escapes and potted plants; when ball fields were measured by sewer covers and parked cars; when bonfires burned in the cobblestone streets on election night; when kids lugged refrigerators up on to the roof tops just to throw them off and watch them crash and explode five floors below. They were crazy days. So were we. And so are we now.

Coletti sat behind the wheel nervously tapping his fingers on the rim. His face bristled with a scruffy black beard. He looked like three days of restless neglect. The car was a junk heap, battered with rust, broken chrome, and missing hubcaps. Both taillights were smashed. His clothes rumpled with slept-in wrinkles. The face of a clear, vibrant youth had worn away like the eraser on a heavily used pencil correcting mistakes. I drew closer and Coletti's face glowed.

"Mike, it's good to see you. It's been a long time."

He opened the door and stepped out to shake hands. The blanket over the seat peeled back, exposing the bare coil springs of padding gouged by time worn heavy.

"It's been a lot of years, Augie." We shook hands. "Let's take a walk."

I had to get him away from the car which could be bugged. We walked past the closed storefronts, under the crash and quake of the electric trains overhead. We walked like two friends again talking about a ballgame, only this game was for higher stakes than beer and pretzels. It was for Augie Coletti's life.

"Mike, I'm sorry I had to bring you in on this. And I'm sorry we had to meet like this after all these years. But I got my ass in a fire and it's really starting to burn. They got me going crazy! They say they're going to bust me and put me away for ten years if I don't give them ten grand."

Augie's hands beat the air as he spoke, strong, fluid gestures. He had a muscular build, five-ten, black hair curled on his head, and hairy bared chest. Humidity beaded on his forehead. "I don't care about the dough. I'll pay them. But I sure as hell won't trust them."

"Wait a minute, Augie. Just what do they have? Were you doing business with Rosetti?"

"No, I never did any business with him. I swear! I did try, though. And that's what they got. A try on a phone tap. And it wasn't even his phone they tapped. It was the public phone down the corner from his house. They bugged the pay phone. But I never did any business with Pasq and I really didn't say much on the phone. But you know, Mike, these guys can be bad-asses who can give me a lot of problems. It's important right now that I stay on the street. I got big things happening and any trouble will tear the whole deal apart. I gotta have time. I want to pay them, but I want you to hold the money. I want you to talk to them for me."

Coletti's head instinctively snapped from side to side as he spoke, looking for a shadow that moved, a car that might bear down on him. He was walking on the edge of paranoia. A cat turned prey.

"Augie, the ball's in your court, but my advice to you is don't pay them a cent. Screw 'em. I don't think they got enough to make anything stick."

"I can't do that, Mike. I can't have any trouble, not now. I want to give them the ten grand. It's overhead. It'll pay off for me later. I want you to talk for me and to hold the money."

Augie put his hand in his pocket and pulled out a roll of bills. "Hold this for me. Every week I'll give you more."

"What the hell is this?"

"Two hundred bucks."

"What am I supposed to do with 200 bucks? They want ten large ones!"

"They'll get it. It'll take a while, but they'll get it."

The guy looked at me with eyes that couldn't be refused.

"All right. I'll talk to them. I'll see what I can do. I'll try to buy you some time. But I still think you ought to tell them to take a walk."

We shook hands and walked back to his car. Then he opened the trunk. It was filled with transistor radios. "Take all you want, Mike. I want you to have them."

"I don't want any, Augie. Just let me see what I can do." I turned to go back to Amen's but Coletti wouldn't be refused. He put a radio in my hand.

"Please. I want you to have it. Let me do this for you. "

I took it. When I got back inside the restaurant, Buck and Nap were at our table.

BUCK TRUCCOLINI

I love escarole and beans in garlic and oil. When I eat, the whole place fills with garlic. That's real Italian. Johnny is eating his usual fettucine puttanesca washed down with chilled Verdicchio. Puttanesca. That got its name from some of these women who spend the whole day whoring around and when they get home late they don't got time to make dinner for their old man, so they throw some fettuccine in oil and garlic real fast with some salt and pepper and maybe some black olives and that's Italian fast food. Mike usually loves that frutti di mare, the fruit of the sea, steamed in a seafood marinara sauce. Jimmy ain't here yet. He's late. He's always late for everything lately. And sometimes he don't show at all. It's that new broad he's got. He's with her all the time. I feel sorry for his wife and kids. A little screwin' around I can see, but Jimmy is overdoin' it. I think tonight I'm goin' to have to talk to the sonofabitch. Boy. This 'scarole and beans is great.

Mike's always running out on a good meal to go outside and have meetin's. Hell of a businessman. Helped a lot of good people. I wonder if it's goin' to rain tomorra.

* * *

"What'd you guys hear about the weather tomorra? We gonna get rain?"

"Nah, the sun's gonna be out all day," said Napolitano. "No mud around here, Buck. You gonna run Poppa's Pride?" Napolitano sipped some wine. "I might put a few bucks on her nose if you got inside information."

Palermo smiled. "Johnny, you should know by now that owners don't know anything. Trainers, jockeys, and the horses are the only ones in on the fix. Besides, feds aren't allowed to bet."

Buck looked up between spoonfuls. "Yeah, but if you were going to bet, you could clean up. We're going for a price. My baby's gonna burn up that track. The rest of the field'll be looking at her ass. But she don't like the rain. Don't like mud on her feet. If it rains, Johnny, put your dough in the bank. But if the sun's out, remember you still take your chances. I don't guarantee nothin."

* * *

I been lucky in business. I'm into numbers, horse parlors, sport betting, loan sharking, jukeboxes, night clubs, and protection services. I'm, like Mike says, diversified. I got nothin' to do with dope or broads. They hurt too many people. In what I do there ain't no victims. Every hand I play is a winner. I don't need no trouble with filth. I bought Poppa's Pride two months ago. They say she's a promising filly out of Mary's Pride by Poppa's Bet, both high-money winners. Sure, I'm in it for the bucks, but she's become kinda a pet to me, kinda like a daughter. Tarrytown Pete V. wanted a piece of her. He's the biggest book in Westchester. The word on the street is that the feds are goin' to take him down for taxes. Maybe Mike can help him. He already helped Gino, Count, and Pat. What an operation they got going. They used to bet the book with post bettin', setting the book's clock back two minutes by breaking in to the parlor in the middle of the night, and then usin' a guy with binoculars to give them the finger sign of the winner by a guy right at the tote board, and then call in the bet, get a time, and collect on a sure thing the next day. Now they gotta watch out for guys doing the same thing to them. Digital clocks are great for giving the exact time a race goes off. It makes post bettin' easier to pull off because the start time is so accurate and in the papers the next day.

I live with my mother and sister. That's why I got a filly. I respect women. Not all guys are like that. Not Sorelli. Whorin' around and missin' that Don's wedding when I promised that he would be there. He made me look like a fool. I gotta deal with him right.

* * *

"She'll murder 'em. If I were a bettin' man, I'd put five clams on her myself." As he spoke, Palermo pointed to the empty clam shells on his plate and Buck caught his smile.

"Hey, Mike, don't go crazy. Save some for her next time out. Don't blow your whole bankroll on one start."

Then Jimmy Sorelli made his entrance. When Buck saw him at the front door, his teeth clenched and his spoon crashed down and flattened on the table under his heavy palm. Blood flushed his face like a diaphanous red veil blocking the sun.

"That sonofabitch! It's about time the ungrateful bastard showed up!" seethed Buck in a low rasp.

MICHAEL PALERMO

Me and Nap were stunned. Buck was Sorelli's mentor. It was because of Buck that Jimmy was in jukeboxes across the country. It was Buck who opened the doors of nightclubs in New York and Las Vegas. He made Jimmy Sorelli. I never saw Buck so mad. Jimmy came over with a little shit-eating smile on his face.

"Hi, Buck. It's good to see you again. Mike. Johnny." He nodded. "Must be three weeks since we've been together."

Buck's hands became fists, like hammers poised to strike.

"Get that shit-eatin' grin off your face, you no-good punk. Get your ass on that chair."

Jimmy's jaw dropped. His eyes vibrated with fear. Not confusion. Just fear. He knew what it was all about. He must have gotten the word off the grapevine. He couldn't be invisible anymore. Nap and me didn't know anything.

"Where the hell you been? You too busy with that two-bit broad to do what's expected of you?" Buck's eyes popped.

"Buck, I . . ." Jimmy tried to answer.

"Keep your mouth shut 'til I tell you to open it. Where the hell were you when you were supposed to sing at the Marcante weddin'? You made a fool outta me. I promised them you'd be there. Where the fuck were you?"

"Buck, I had a sore throat," squealed Sorelli. His voice quavered and cracked like a little boy lying to his teacher.

"A sore throat, you ungrateful bastard. Was your throat sore all last week that you couldn't call me? You got a hair stuck in your throat? You want to eat pussy? Here, eat this!"

Like he was ripping a tree out of the ground, Buck's hands grabbed under the table and heaved it into the air on top of Sorelli. Pasta, tomato sauce, escarole, and beans, three full meals all fell tumbling over the singer, grazing me with red sauce. As Sorelli jerked away, Buck got up and reached over the table and cracked his open hand across Jimmy's left cheek, raising a welt, first white, then engorged in a red sea of stinging pain. He looked like he was going to cry.

"You ain't never gonna work no more! I asked you to show a little respect to the people who gave it all to you and you make me a fool. You slapped my face when you don't show up. Now you're finished. You ain't gonna be in nobody's boxes no more. You ain't gonna be on the radio or in no clubs. You ain't gonna be nowhere. You take your sore throat back to that broad and remember this night. Never forget it. If you remember anything at all, remember your wife and kids. That's all you got left. Don't be ungrateful to nobody ever again. Now get the hell outta here!"

Buck dropped into his chair and Nap and I tried to calm him down while Jimmy stumbled to the door, brushing food off his silk suit.

"Buck, take it easy. It's no good for you," I said.

"Look what you did to my dinner," said Nap.

Buck settled in. "I'm sorry. They'll bring more food. Sit down. I'm OK. It's just that that guy will never be no good. I'm through with him."

I brushed the tomato stains off my jacket and pants. He did a good job on me.

"Buck, I gotta change," I said. "I can't eat like this. I'll see you tomorrow. Good night, Johnny. Nap." I patted Buck on the shoulder. "Take care of yourself."

"OK, I'm sorry, Mike. You go clean up. I'll see you tomorrow."

As I left, I watched Napolitano searching under the table through the soggy cold rolls for a piece of celery. He was determined to finish eating no matter what happened.

Sorelli didn't know it but he had two guys at that table who hoped he would bounce back. Anybody could get knocked down. You just have to take the eight count, clear your head, and get back on your feet.

CHAPTER 7

Two weeks later, the 1:00 AM air is wet. It condenses in the hair and clothes of the Bronx street people on Paradise and Devane Avenues. A full moon glows like a cold sun, a mirror in the sky for the little people to look at and to find either romance or the madness of a werewolf. A full moon and its tides play strange tensions on people. Precinct phones and emergency wards work overtime on nights of lunar pressure. Bodies and buildings move in counteraction to the invisible pull of the round, pocked satellite's face. A time of violence, lunacy, and romance often intermingles on the street and in the alleys.

On Paradise and Devane, Carmine Canicatti and Johnny "Castle" Castlevetrano watch over their after-hours club, "The Rafters."

MICHAEL PALERMO

I got a meet set with Carmine at his place tonight. This is a final sit-down to put an end to the DeStefano affair. To build up his arrest record, Johnny D. is shaking down policy operations. If they don't put him on the pad, he busts them and closes up the shop. In setting up a shake he's been prying information from his brother,

Peter. His younger brother was brought into the organization by Joe Valachi. The trust between brothers had been stronger than the bonds between soldier and family.

Like Peter DeStefano, Joe Valachi couldn't keep his mouth shut. Valachi had been considered one of the most stand-up people on the street. Whenever anybody needed somebody for a tough job, Valachi would be called. Suddenly one day he turned informer and blew open the Family secrets. This stunned even law enforcement agencies. He said he wasn't getting the proper respect and his bosses had framed him into appearing disloyal. Vito Genovese put a contract out on him. So Valachi gave everybody up. He never mentioned anything to me about what was going down when I used to have a few drinks with him in his bar on Castle Hill Avenue in the Bronx near the RKO Castle Hill movie house.

So both Valachi and Genovese wind up in prison, and Valachi outlives him. Joe died like a rat, in maximum security, detested by everybody in the underworld. His revelations on Appalachin and Family operations throughout the country sent massive shock waves through organized crime. But, as always, after a while, things returned to business as usual.

I'm sitting with Carmine at a corner table in the back. A candle flickers in a glass vase. The flame laps at the red glass and plays streaks over our faces.

"Carmine, you remember Augie Coletti?"

"Sure, he's a good guy. We all used to play ball together. Hey, Mike, that was a long time ago. Those were good days. We were kids."

"Augie's got some heat coming down on him from the feds. I'm tryin' to square things for him. If it's all right with you, next time I see him I'd like to tell him that after things cool off he can come to see you and maybe you can find a place for him. Whadda you think?"

"No kiddin'. Whatta you know. There's gotta be a God, Mike. Augie's in my office now. He says he wants to talk to you. If he has any heat on him now, tell him to come see me when everything cools down."

"Augie's here? Tonight? I can't believe that. I'll talk to him later. Right now, about this DeStefano thing, I talked to him again, but I can't do a thing with him. I can't reason with him. He doesn't think there's anything wrong with what he's doing. I told him there were rules and he was making the wrong moves. He's got cement in his ears. He doesn't hear me when I talk."

"I understand, Mike. Thanks for trying to straighten him out. We wanted what was best for everybody. You don't have to bother anymore. You have a lot more important things to take care of. I know you did your best. Now I'm going to check out the tables. You talk to Augie and then we'll have a drink. Frascari has a run going. He says he's goin' to break the bank. Imagine that, Mike, in my joint, a bank heist? With the people I take care of around here, he'll never get out the door."

So Carmine leaves and Augie comes over from the bar. I feel like I'm playing musical chairs. Carmine and Augie pass with a nod.

"How's everything going, Augie?"

"I'm OK, Mike. Things are slowly getting better. What's happening with my friends, the feds?"

"I talked to their man and we have an agreement. I told them I'm sitting on the cash but first, before I deliver, I want to make sure you're out of it."

"Right now, I'm still in it. Wherever I go, I swear I got guys following me. It's like having a black cloud over my head. They're tying my hands, Mike. I can't operate with those people on my back. Look, here's fifteen hundred. Tell them they have to cut me loose or it's no deal. But be sure they understand, I want to pay."

"They know that, Augie. It's all in your head. There's nobody on you. We'll wait a few months after they round up Rosetti, then we'll give them the money and it'll be finished. I want to be sure I'm not in the middle of a double-bang. Now try to relax a little. I talked to Carmine, and he says that when things cool down, come to him and he'll find a place for you or give you a hand or something. OK?"

"OK, Mike, thanks."

"Come on, Augie, I'll buy you a drink."

"No, thanks, Mike, I gotta go. Take care of business. I've got a big nut to crack with those bastards on my back. You have a drink on me. Tell them to put it on my tab."

"Are you kidding? Your tab is already 8,300 bucks short."

Augie curls the corners of his mouth and his eyes twinkle in the flames.

"Well, then, what the hell's a few more bucks matter?"

"I'll tell you what, Augie. What do you say we let Carmine pick this one up?"

"In that case, I'll have a drink."

Augie and I drink and Carmine pays.

Augie leaves and I look up at the front door where there's an argument. Real loud. Johnny Castle is shouting at the top of his lungs at some guy with two girls hanging off his shoulders. He's dressed like a million dollars and so are the girls. I look again and I can't believe my eyes. It's Make-up Johnny DeStefano. He's tottering and ready to fall and starts pushing Castle. He's drunk and he's wearing a wig, make-up, and mascara on his eyelashes. Castle won't let him in. He and me are the only two cops let in "The Rafters." Johnny D. because of his brother, Peter, and me because I know Carmine. I get up to see what's going on and to see if I can make a peace. Under the hall lamp I see tiny cracks in the make-up on his forehead.

Castle turns him away. Two soldiers carefully escort him and his ladies down the stairs, past the private sanitation trucks in the garage under the club, and out into the parking lot.

Make-up Johnny will never see the inside of "The Rafters" or his brother Peter again. His greed and probes into his brother have finally spilled his own blood. But he'll never know it for sure.

I find out later from the grapevine that private sanitation truck #227 dumped the body of Peter DeStefano into an incinerator pile. Of the DeStefano brothers, one lost his life and the other lost his honor.

A week later, Johnny DeStefano makes his rounds at the Copacabana nightclub in New York. It's a chic supper club that features big-name performers. Its doors are open to anybody who can pay its premium prices.

DeStefano is with a flashy date in a sequined evening gown that looks like it's painted on her. He looks frightened and uncertain. Nobody on the street will talk to him when he asks if anybody has seen his brother, Peter. People shy away from him like he has leprosy. He asks me and some other cops if we've seen his brother and what's going on. Nobody knows anything. In addition to that, something else is wrong. I can't put my finger on it. The mood was set the minute we walked in. Jimmy Sorelli was supposed to be the headliner, but across his name and picture outside is a wide strip that says "CANCELED". Buck wasn't kidding when he told Jimmy he wouldn't be working any more. Jimmy was replaced by Italian singing star Carlo Cinqui. He's good, and after a while people forgot all about Jimmy Sorelli, like he had never existed.

By this time I had gotten married again. A wonderful girl named Laura. She's from California. She'd been a singer at some connected clubs in L.A. I got introduced when I went out on vacation. We hit it off just right. She sings me the sweetest songs when we're alone. Who needs Sorelli when you can have an angel?

But I don't want to talk about her. She's the private part of my life. This story is about me. My family privacy is too important for me to tell the whole world about it. Believe me, my life in the street and on the job is a lot more interesting. These days, who wants to hear about a perfect marriage?

Sid Burrell whisks us up front and puts a new table down for us. It's the size of a bar coaster. Little by little, the dance floor gets smaller and smaller as more tables are squeezed in. More and more special guests are accommodated until there's no more room to dance. It's a crazy kind of night. As I look around, I see the who's-who of organized crime sitting at tables next to cops from all over the city. Carmine Canicatti sits at a table with his boss, Casper Nardino. Augie Coletti with his business friends. Lenny Lombardi and his girl spend the evening with Jim Groty and Johnny Napolitano. There are T-men and F.B.I.

Cops and robbers. But the robbers are subdued, not wild and loud and crazy like they usually are. Their jackets hang tightly buttoned, highlighting chest and belly bulges. They're all packing heat. Everybody knows it. Their women are conspicuously absent. They huddle in secret conversations, like quarterbacks on a playing field. Something's going on, but the cops aren't in on it.

Cops are drinking and having a ball. Wine, women, and song. Whatever is in the air doesn't bother them at all. Carmine almost stiffs me when I go to talk to him. All I get is a fast hello. He brushes me off like he wants to have nothing to do with me.

Then I meet him in the men's room. We're alone and he's washing his hands.

"Carmine, what the hell's going on? Why's everybody so uptight?"

"It has nothing to do with you, Mike. Just leave it alone. I can't talk to you." He looks mean.

"What do you mean you can't talk to me?"

"Mike, get out of the way." He makes for the door. "Just leave it alone."

I push my hands on his waist and his jacket button unhooks, exposing a revolver under his belt.

"What the hell are you doing with that?"

He looks down at me and growls, "Mike, stay out of this one. Now get outta my way or you're gonna have big problems."

I let him pass. Now I have ten questions for everyone I wanted to ask him before.

For years the Copacabana was a nightspot for people on both sides of the law. There had never been any problem in the club except of guilt by association. Too often, me and a few other guys would be called on the carpet down to the Commissioner's office. Questions had to be answered. Why was I sitting, drinking, and eating with known members of the underworld? Why was I in so many photographs with known gangsters? It wasn't appropriate for a narcotics detective to be associated with reputed criminals.

Chief Devlin always calmed the waters for me. A call to one of his old friends vouching for my integrity by a man who had once been in the hot seat himself made miracles happen.

CHIEF COLLIN DEVLIN, RETIRED

"Look, Michael, if I told you once, I'm sure I told you a thousand times. I know you're not up to anything dishonest. I know that if anything shady was going down, you're not stupid enough to do it in broad daylight with everybody, including the Police Commissioner watching. You and me, we're too smart to be seen and get caught straining the law. We're so smart that sometimes we get caught in our own innocence. We get caught when we're doing nothing wrong. I know how hard it is to be in a place having a good time, and old friends happen to drop over to say hello. Sure, they'll pick up a check now and then. They'll sit with you for a while and that long-legged photographer will snap your picture together. You see, Mike, that's where the heat is coming from. You get your damn picture taken not when you're making arrests, but when you're sitting with hoodlums.

"It seems this long-stemmed beauty with the camera is Detective Eddie Silvestro's girlfriend. She's been giving Silvestro extra prints of all the pictures she takes. And he, like the good cop that he is, sends them down to the PC's office. And, my boy, your face is plastered all over their walls and is a permanent fixture down there. Now THAT is the problem, and it's time for some kind of a solution.

"I've told Sid Burrell and he was outraged when he found out that his club was compiling a Rogues' Gallery for the police. He never takes sides. Everybody is welcome. We're all his friends. His relationship is one of trust and respect as individuals. He knows from experience that there are times that the biggest hoodlum can be more honorable than the noblest cop. Sid has changed procedures. Silvestro's girl got another job as a waitress in a diner in Hoboken. All photographs taken in the club are presented immediately with the negative given to the patron at the table. Silvestro will spend his time at other establishments. There's no way in the world that your picture will ever get down to the PC's office again. That is, as long as you don't eat in that diner in Hoboken."

MICHAEL PALERMO

The next night I find out what was bothering Carmine and the boys. The Chief asks me to drive him to the Colonial Heights section of Yonkers. I know the area because at this time Laura and me are living in Yonkers. The Chief really opens up to me on the way up the Bronx River Parkway. He was a lot like me.

"Mike, I'm Irish and you're Italian. Sicilian-American, to be precise. Your folks come from the old country, Agrigento. That's fine. I know they're good people. In this country we all work together. It's a melting pot. And by helping each other, we all get by. Some people will condemn a man because of where his parents came from. We both know that's foolish."

"I always felt that way, Chief. I believe we have to look at the man, at the job he does and what kind of guy he really is."

"Ah, now that's the point I want to make. These people we're going to visit tonight aren't always wrong in the things they do. And in some of the wrong things they do, there's just no way to stop them. On the other hand, cops aren't always right. There's room for a great deal of improvement in the Department. You know that as well as I."

"That's true," I agree.

"People who make their living in the streets don't have it easy. They have families to support and they have feelings just like anyone else. Many of these people are as stand-up as cops in their own way, by their own values. In some cases, they're even more honorable, depending on how you look at things. Cops haven't been tested with jail terms. When that time comes, only then will we find out who has more honor. I hope I never see that day.

"These people we call wise guys, hoods, mobsters, gangsters, they have their own society, their own government, and their own little world that runs like currents under a lake, a world under ours.

"It's up to us to keep our house clean and for them to take care of theirs. Sometimes we have to work together to keep the peace. We have our problems and they have theirs, and when they cross we cooperate."

"I understand, Chief. I came up from the street like you did. I know just what you mean."

"Tonight, Mike, we're going to see a very important man. He's important because he's powerful. He has the power of life and death over many people, even over you and me if he wanted it. For that, if for no other reason, he's to be respected. Tonight we visit Albert Marcante."

The Chief pauses as if he has a great weight on his shoulders. I feel a chill and ice in my veins. Marcante is a legend. One of the most powerful men in the country. The Chief's right. He could have anyone whacked if he wanted to. Even the President. He controls Harlem and all of New York City. He took Genovese's place. Some people say that he had Vito put away with a frame. Hell, I was there. I know it was a frame.

A bet can't be made without Marcante's blessing. Every loan shark works from out of his pocket. Millions of dollars every day. He's got no direct involvement with drugs or prostitution, but I'm sure he gets a piece and they can't exist without his nod. He turns his head and pretends that the laundered money comes from other sources. In his mind he juggles honor with common sense. If he doesn't control everything, somebody else will come along and take a bite out of his loaf of bread. Then there'd be war. He lives by accommodations. He runs on a two-way street of accommodations with politicians, cops, and commerce.

"As I told you, Mike, Albert and I grew up together. We stole and fought and finally grew up in the Catholic Protectory. It was there that Brother Michael taught us to play chess. He said fight on the chess board and not on the street. Use your heads and not your hands and nobody gets hurt and you live a lot longer and God loves you for it. So we learned chess. Two armies facing each other in battle. Two gang fights, not on the street with chains and guns but on a chess board. A game played by strict rules which can't be broken. The battle strategy and advanced planning makes the winner. We were evenly matched. Tomorrow I'm going to show you my ivory chess set. Do you play?"

"No, Chief. But I'd love to learn."

"Good. Tomorrow you'll get your first lesson."

The car stops at a stone-pillared gate. Two heavyset bodyguards step out to meet us. A third stands to the side inside the grid work. The Chief is speaking with one of the guards. He gives the OK sign to the man inside. A switch is thrown and the gates open electronically. We ride up a long blacktop drive to a cobblestoned courtyard. Foot-high lanterns line the road with a golden glow. Two bodyguards meet us at the front of the house. Dogs bark in a kennel on the side. The front door is massive, of carved oak with a leaded stained-glass window gleaming above it. The entrance hall soars two stories high, framing a serpentine staircase and Italian tiled floors of brown and yellow. Outside the library stand two heavy weights that could be contenders for the crown. I see .44 Magnums in shoulder holsters. They can penetrate an engine block, so they say. I sit in the hall in a high winged-back chair opposite the two guards. No one speaks. No one smiles. I am uneasy. Feeling like I don't belong. I feel like I am sticking out like a blue thumb in somebody else's green garden. The library doors open and Giorgio Amadeo comes out to meet me. I know Giorgio through Carmine. He's a lieutenant under Casper Nardino. He and Carmine are Nardino's right and left arms. Amadeo is developing a ferocious reputation as a relentless enforcer. I see him at "The Rafters." His family operates a fleet of private sanitation trucks in New York City. In that fleet is truck #227.

"Mike, we want you to relax and make yourself at home. Come with me. I'll get you a drink and we can spend some time in the front drawing room."

I feel better already. Amadeo is direct and to the point. He's all business in everything he does. For relaxation he lifts weights regularly and has cast-iron muscles. He's called "The Bull" because he looks the part. He's more of a boulder that can't be budged if he doesn't want to move. He knows Kenpo, Chinese karate, and maintains absolute control of his temper. This control is what makes him a valuable part of the Marcante Family. Giorgio Amadeo follows orders to the letter. He never fails in what he sets out to accomplish. Marcante wanted me to spend some time with him. Why? My mind is trying to get into the library where the Chief is meeting with Marcante so I can find out what's going on. Will I ever find out?

"Collin, I'm glad you could come visit with me again." He and the Chief embrace. "You know, the years run past us and disappear like little boys stealing apples. First you see them and then suddenly—poof—they're gone."

"Albert, it's always a pleasure to see you and remember those days. A lot has changed since then. Where we live . . ."

Devlin looks up at the high-paneled ceiling, around at the plush carpets and opulent furniture. His eyes catch a figure near the fireplace. ". . . and how many old friends are still around us."

The figure approaches and Devlin's face opens wide like a flower at sunrise.

"Collin, if it hasn't been ten years. And you look the same." The figure approaches Devlin with outstretched arms.

"Angelo, old friend," bubbles Devlin for his second embrace of the night. "As to my looks, what you say is true. But then, you always were the diplomat."

Angelo Orabona is the don's consigliere, another face from Devlin's childhood grown old. Business dealings and orders come from the consigliere. He is a buffer between Marcante and his people. Next to the don, Orabona holds the reins of power. He is both counsel and business manager. His presence this evening forecasts a major activity for the Family. Important decisions have been made and Devlin's assistance is considered essential.

"And Casper, we almost see each other too much."

Casper and Devlin embrace.

"There can never be enough time for good food and good friends," says Nardino.

The four sit and sip brandy. Marcante slowly steers the conversation into the reason for the meeting.

"Collin, we've been having some trouble in the streets, and we don't know who's behind it."

Albert Marcante is in his late sixties. Heavy black-rimmed glasses cover his eyes. His sideburns shine the silver of age and wisdom. He sits at ease in a tan sport shirt with open collar. A diamond pinkie ring floats through the air as his hands gesture.

"Some of my people are disappearing. They're being snatched. One day they walk down to the store for a pack of cigarettes, or ride to their club for some business and like that—" the don snaps his fingers "—they're gone. It's not only my people. The other organizations have been hit the same way. The missing man's family then receives a phone call for money. Sometimes the wife gets the call."

Marcante's face twists in disdain. "You see, they even prey upon the women. *Disgraziata*! When the money is paid, the man is released."

Devlin's face is intense. "How long has this been going on?"

"Three weeks have passed since the first disappearance. Three of our people have already been taken. Onc a week. It seems we're ready for another target."

"Do you have any idea who's behind it?" asks Devlin.

The don nods to his consigliere. Orabona speaks with more determination than ease.

"We're not sure. Sometimes they flash a shield and act like cops. They know the procedures and they know our people. They pick the best opportunities and so far no one's been hurt. The money has always been paid.

"Our problem is twofold. First, we don't want anybody hurt. Second, as I'm sure you realize, it's a matter of honor for the Marcante family. Our people in the street are keeping their eyes open. Nobody goes anywhere alone. It won't be good for anybody if this continues. It can only lead to bloodshed."

The Chief is puzzled. "Do you think they're cops?"

"It's possible. And for that reason we ask for your cooperation. I'm sure none of your people want these things to happen. It can only lead to bitter confrontations up and down. We'd like your man, Palermo, to work with Giorgio to help end this before it ends in tragedy. It's a time for discretion."

"We'll do all we can," says Devlin. "If it's cops that are behind it, we'll deal with them ourselves. If it's people on the outside, they'll have to answer to you. There's no place for this kind of thing. Life is full of too many problems without this happening."

Orabona is troubled. "Collin, we've always worked out our differences together and found a fair solution. This matter is too important to be left in your people's hands. We must have complete control after they're caught."

"That can't be," says Devlin. "We have our own special people who'll deal with them if they're cops, to go all the way if necessary. It's been done before. It's a matter of keeping our own house in order."

Orabona grimaces in disagreement and seeks guidance from the don. Marcante's eyes signal no further discussion. Before the stew can be cooked, the rabbit must first be caught. He motions to Nardino. "Casper, bring Mike and Giorgio in here."

Giorgio has just finished explaining the kidnappings to me. We spoke freely and I sat on the edge of my seat. It was a fantastic story that tumbled from Giorgio's lips. It was a surprise. I had felt the tension in the air and sensed that something was wrong, but I never expected this. Nothing so bold. If cops are doing the job, they're keeping it under wraps. The capers are air-tight.

Nardino opens the drawing room door. "Hi, Mike. This time we meet with no pasta." He motions to Amadeo. "It's time. You and Mike come to the library."

Devlin makes the introductions. Orabona lays out the strategy.

"There are some things we'll be doing ourselves within our own organization. It's not necessary to discuss these now. While our own operations are going on, it would be good for Mike and Giorgio to work together, gather information, and develop their own leads. They should do whatever has to be done. Giorgio will report to Casper, and Mike to you, Collin. Working together like that, we'll have a better intelligence setup than Washington. Is that OK with you?"

Devlin answers quickly. "I have no problem with that. How about you, Mike?"

"Just one. I'm sure that Giorgio and I can work together fine, but with all due respect, I might be able to work with Carmine a little more smoothly. Carmine and I grew up together. We're from the same neighborhood. That is, if it's OK with Giorgio. But if it's necessary that we take it on ourselves, I'm sure we won't have any problems."

I know I can never work with Amadeo. I can't be comfortable with a guy I don't know. There would never be a betrayal between Carmine and me. How the hell can I confide in a Neanderthal enforcer? He might even think I was in on the kidnappings myself. If we caught the snatchers, how would they be handled if they were cops? Devlin would want them. Would Amadeo give them up? I would be in the middle again. I got a better chance with Carmine.

"That's all right with me, Angelo," says Amadeo. "I got a lot of things to take care of now anyway. Carmine is perfect for the job."

Orabona shakes hands with me and the Chief. "Good, then. It's settled. Arrangements will be made and this will be finished."

Marcante gives his approval and we start on our way back home.

Traffic on the parkway is light on the way back to Parkchester. Devlin seems to be upset by what he's heard.

"Mike, I've known Albert since we were kids and it's strange how things turn out. We used to talk about people and religion and people and cops. There are two ways to keep people in line,

he would say. First you have them follow their religion. That's
an honorable thing to do. What could be more honest than being
honorable? The Buddhists believe in reincarnation. They believe
that things will be better when they live again in the next life.
So the destitute crawl into the hovels of Asia and eat insects. If
they didn't believe in having a better chance the next time around,
provided they follow the rules this time, they would try to snatch
everything from those who live in the palaces with jewels and
banquets and there would be a revolution.

"Albert used to say that the morality set down by all religions
keeps people in line. He's a Catholic and his wife is an ardent
churchgoer, praying to a God she can never see, praying for a husband she can never know deep inside. She prays for heaven where
the good are rewarded. The irony of it is that Albert thinks he does
good. Good for his family and good for his people. He loves his
family and treasures loyalty. He says that religion delays the revolution of the poor. The threat to the strong comes from the weak,
not from the strong.

"He says that for those without religion as a constraint, we
have law enforcement. People without religion stay honest because
they fear getting caught. They suppress the bit of larceny that's
within us all. He respects the order of things and the order that
law offers. But when he sees how corrupt the law is, how people
can be bought right and left at the right price, then he knows how
weak the law is. It's only a tool for the right people who control
it. So he found a better law, his law. He keeps people in line with
some morality but mostly with enforcement.

"These kidnappings break his law and so they must stop.
I wonder how it'll turn out. If these people will be tried by him
or us."

I listen, completely absorbed, without interruption. I never
heard Devlin talk like this before.

Marcante has triggered something deep inside him. Who would have thought that people like Marcante wrestled with religion? Things in life always come back. When the tough street kids had been exposed to the religion of the Catholic Protectory, a cynicism grew from the common sense of the streets. Marcante is a realist, not a dreamer. He wants his now and not in another life. In the next life let him be poor. But in this life give it all to him.

"There are two more things that keep people in line, Chief," I say. "Drugs and alcohol. These people in the streets that we run after every day don't have anything but booze and drugs to make them feel good and satisfied. When they're feeling good, they don't want anything else. I think that maybe the worst thing we could do on the job is to get lucky and cut off their supplies. Then they wouldn't feel so good and they'll come after everybody who has something. They'll come after you and me and Marcante and the Rockefellers and Kennedys. The best thing might be to let everything flow the way it does. Don't make waves. Let them be happy and content. Keep them away from us. I could see a revolution if they were hurting. I think that it's opium more than religion that's the opiate of the masses."

"Well," says Devlin, "I suppose there are two sides to every story. It just depends what side of the window you're looking through." Devlin closes his eyes. "I've had enough for one night, my boy. I'm going to doze a bit."

I drive and think about how twisted life can be. Things can seem right depending on where you're standing. Who knows the difference between right and wrong?

The man who stands in the middle?

CHAPTER 8

Frank "Cheech" Scarmello sits in his private back room in the Olive Grove. A little more than three months have passed since Angelo Gatti has been bludgeoned to death at the same table where Cheech is playing cards tonight with his friends. Every Saturday night, he plays to get his mind off business. On other nights, he and Tony Tremato go over the day's collections. The two capos share a regime in the Fordham section of the Bronx. They control the loan sharking, horse parlors, and numbers operations. Pieces of twenty-eight legitimate businesses also belong to them. But this isn't enough for Scarmello. On his own he continues to sell buttons and "make" men for a price. He back-doors them for $40,000 each.

The Fordham territory belongs to the Valerio Fredoni Family. It was from Fredoni that Ricco Bodugno had sought help to deal with the Groty beating at his restaurant. Fredoni made the arrangements to get the cop's gun and shield back from Vinnie Cannelli.

Don Valerio has a Chief Inspector on the pad to keep the heat off his gambling operations in the Bronx. In selling buttons, Scarmello has just done some business. But he did it without his boss's knowledge.

Scarmello plays cards under the hanging lamp shining on green felt. Tonight he's away from business. But he can never be far enough away. Business always manages to intrude. His privacy will be disturbed tonight. The front room of the Olive Grove is heavily guarded. Undercurrents of kidnapping paranoia sweep the underworld. Scarmello is no exception. No one will get past his men in the front room.

* * *

While Cheech Scarmello plays cards in Fordham, Jerry "The Gimp" Mackey is back in town and is making his rounds of the Harlem bars selling marijuana and pills. He's back from the vacation that he took with the confiscated heroin that the cops gave him after the factory bust. The cops had been good to him. He turned his score into big bucks on the street. He went to Georgia for a few months to see his family. He saw some of his grandchildren for the first time. His sons wanted him to stay with them, but he told them that he has important business in New York. He's a business man. He can't stay off the streets. He needs the sweat and tears of the city. It's in his blood. To breathe, he needs the smoke of busy bars. The excitement of being where the action is. In Georgia he would have to go into retirement. If he does that, he's sure he'll die. He'd rather die on the streets of New York.

Mackey sits in Keno's Lounge on Seventh Avenue. His elbows flap over the bar rail. His toothless smile slobbers his words. He speaks juicy words with an oversize tongue that licks and tastes every sentence. He's mellow and he makes friends easily. Each new friend is a potential customer.

"Hey, Mackey!" A bald black man next to him calls out. "Where you been, man? I ain't seen you in months. I thought maybe you took a trip, real permanent-like."

"No way, Baldy. Nobody gonna put old Mackey away. I just been on a little business trip. And now I'm full up and my grass is as sweet as a bear in a honey tree. There'll be some sweet highin', some high flyin' now that Mackey's back in town. How much you want, brudder?" The Gimp's hands slip into his jacket pocket.

"Well, I don't know. Since you been gone, this guy Tatum's been movin' some pretty good stuff. You know you can't go off like that and leave the door to the store unlocked." Baldy baits the Gimp. He likes to play the spoiler. He keeps his shiny pate shaved to intimidate people. He's a big man with solid muscles that ripple under his tight shirt.

Mackey chuckles. "Baldy, I don't know this guy, Tatum. He may be peddlin' somethin', but I know that dude ain't never been up no honey tree. My grass is sweet. The best you ever had. How much you want, man?"

"OK, Mackey, I'll take a chance on you. Gimme an OZ for old times."

"All right, my man!" Mackey slaps his hands together. "And how 'bout the little lady? You ain't gonna leave her hangin', are you?" Mackey is bar-wise. He's been this route before. The girl next to Baldy smiles and takes a deep breath. Her bosom heaves and almost overflows her clinging red dress. Her cleavage jiggles like two water balloons. Baldy looks, grins and gulps. "Oh, hell, gimme twenty joints on top o' that."

Now it's Mackey's turn to grin. Tatum won't score tonight. He's got his old turf back. Tatum better find another neighborhood because Mackey's back in town.

* * *

Vinnie Cannelli's legs shake violently as he stands before Giorgio Amadeo. Giorgio is fuming. His temples bulge with blood vessels swollen in rage. The cowboy Cannelli has stepped out of line again. Amadeo's tongue whips into him, castrating his honor. Two floors up from the street, over the Villa Pietro Restaurant, Cannelli stands with his face flushed. Giorgio is screaming at him.

"You stupid bastard! How many times can you be wrong? Do you know what you did this time, you stupid piece of shit? This time, you slapped my face. Like this!" Amadeo's palm breaks the skin on Cannelli's left cheekbone. "How does that feel, you *cornuto?*"

"Giorgio, I don't know what you're talkin' about. I never hit you. What are you poppin' me for?"

"Shithead! You hit me today. At four o'clock. In Turcio's Grocery. You remember the grocery?"

Cannelli remembers. At four o'clock he moved in on Luigi Turcio at his store. Turcio runs numbers and Cannelli wanted a piece of his action in exchange for Cannelli protection. The grocer refused and told him he was with Patsy Vaccaro. Cannelli said he never heard of Vaccaro and began to wreck the store. Vaccaro happened to step in for a visit in the middle of the rampage. Cannelli picked up Vaccaro and threw him through the plate-glass window in front of the store, out on to the sidewalk. Vaccaro is in the hospital with his arms and face in shreds.

Cannelli's bowels turn to water at the mention of Turcio's.

"You asshole! You threw Patsy Vaccaro through a window?" Amadeo's left hand slaps Cannelli's right cheek. Blood drips from the corner of his mouth. The side of his tongue splits open.

"Don't hit me again, Giorgio," Cannelli screams.

Two of Amadeo's men step up behind Giorgio menacingly.

"Patsy Vaccaro is my uncle. Patsy Vaccaro is in the hospital because of you!" Amadeo whips his right hand across Cannelli's jaw. His ring tears a gash bone-deep.

"You ruin a kid with a bottle of ketchup in the Bronx!" A slap to Cannelli's face with his left hand. "You beat up a cop in Ricco's!" Another slap. "Don Valerio wants your ass for those things that you did in his territory. And now, you bastard, you throw my uncle through a window! Now I want you!"

Amadeo's left hand closes Cannelli's right eye.

"Giorgio, I said don't hit me again." Cannelli is defiant.

"You're tellin' me what to do now? You got three strikes against you. You don't tell nobody what to do. You just listen and take what you get."

The ring on Giorgio's right hand fractures one of Cannelli's front teeth. The piece of tooth bounces across the floor in front of his eyes. Partly out of anger and partly out of the intractable pain in his mouth, Cannelli swings at Amadeo. He won't take any more. His blow is blocked by a cast-iron arm that had expected and encouraged it. Cannelli is now dead. To strike a "made man" in the Family is a capital offense. That's one rule that can never be broken.

"You hit me?" Giorgio yells. He turns to his two men. "He hit me!"

Cannelli's eyes glare with black flames. He sees three faces glowering in revenge. He bolts out the door, tumbling down the stairs into the street. If he can make it to his car, he has a chance. As he runs, Amadeo moves to the window. He nods daggers to three men talking outside the Villa Pietro. Cannelli races past them, trying to get to his car. His body floats with fear. Leg muscles spear the air. Springing stronger and faster than ever before. Adrenalin pumps him into a frenzy.

* * *

Outside the Olive Grove, two black Lincoln Continentals pull up to the curb. The men who are gathered outside the club move aside, lining a path to the front door. Don Alberto's consigliere, Angelo Orabona, exits. His face is stern. He wears a black overcoat with a velvet-trimmed collar. His bowler hat nods as he passes through the line. Anthony Tremato, Scarmello's partner in the regime, follows next. Then Giorgio Amadeo steps out, followed by two of his men who witnessed the Cannelli problem a short time earlier. Six bodyguards leave the second car. They all enter the club.

Of the eleven, only three go into Scarmello's private back room. Orabona is the first to enter. Scarmello looks up in astonishment.

"Signore, welcome. I'm sorry I didn't know you'd be coming to visit me. We, Tony and me, would have prepared something nice for you."

Scarmello feels a surge of helplessness. First in his legs. Then his guts and finally his head. Tremato enters, followed by Amadeo. Cheech Scarmello has his own personal army outside. Protection against kidnappers. But no army can keep these guests out.

"Everything's just fine, Cheech," says Orabona. "We're here on important business."

"If it's the kidnappings and ransom, we have no trouble here." Scarmello looks at his partner, Tremato, for reassurance, but the capo's eyes are chained to the floor. Reassurance is out of his hands. Scarmello feels totally helpless, like Dominic Gatti must have felt just before he clubbed him to death with baseball bats in this very room. He waves his card-playing friends into the front room. His guests sit down.

Orabona speaks. "Some facts have been brought before the Commission. Some very damaging and serious facts. These have been examined by the Fredoni Family first. These are your people. Then the entire Commission heard the evidence. It was decided to test you. Don Alberto has sent me here personally to speak for him and tell you that you have failed that test."

Scarmello writhes uneasily in his chair. "With all respect, Signore, I've done nothing wrong. Nothing to hurt the Family."

"You have sold the Family honor when you sold the Fredoni name."

Orabona motions to Amadeo. Giorgio opens the door and nods. A young man enters the room. He is Frankie Faiella, one of the two men who were present at the Cannelli slapping. When

Scarmello sees Faiella's face, his lips and cheeks begin to twitch. His face pales, gripped in horror. On the day before, he had accepted $40,000 from Faiella and in return had brought him into the Fredoni Family. Frankie Faiella was his test and he had failed.

Scarmello says nothing. In his eyes is the surrender of despair. He knows there is nothing he can do. Faiella leaves the room.

The consigliere continues. "Your don has asked me to tell you a story. A man sits on his porch and he enjoys the sun. He hears the birds sing and smells the flowers in the air. Life's good and he's happy. While he sits in his chair, he notices that one of the boards in his porch is soft. He watches insects move in and out, rotting it a little more each day. The board is in a far end of the porch, outside the railing where no one walks. It presents no danger. The man decides to let the rotting board be. He puts it to use as an amusement. He sits and enjoys the sun and waits to see how long it takes for the board to fall away and drop to the ground. He knows that some day it will drop and return to the earth from which it once grew as a tree.

"While he sits and waits, he sees another board that's soft. With this board he cannot wait because it's in the middle of the porch. People are supported by it. This rotten board is dangerous. So he rips it out and replaces it with a new, strong board that he can trust. He acts quickly because one cannot have danger in an important place.

"Do you understand, Cheech? You are a very important man and you have had a fine life with honor. It is fitting that you be remembered that way."

Scarmello's face grows limp. "I understand. Is there anything I can say or do?"

"Nothing," says the consigliere. "It has all been said and done. Come, get your coat. Say good-bye to your friends. Tell them you'll be out of town on some important business for a few days."

Two black Lincoln Continentals quietly leave the Olive Grove.

* * *

Jerry Mackey makes the trip from the men's room to the bar many times. Each trip results in a sale. He has a good territory. Like a franchise. Who the hell does this guy Tatum think he is anyway? This is Mackey country.

A noisy party enters Keno's, three men and three young, buxom girls out for a good time. It's obvious that they're bouncing from one bar to another. Mackey's eyes stick on the older of the three men. He's seen him before. He's heard him before.

"What chew doin' there, man?" the man yells at the bartender.

Mackey's mind snaps. His feet want to run. His head wants to hide, but his eyes stay stuck on the big black man with the yellow eyes. He's the super from the heroin factory that he and the cops busted. And he was looking around to see if he could find any of his friends. He looks past The Gimp to a table in the rear and his face lights up. Mackey turns away and tries to crawl into the wall. The super and his party pass him by. He can touch them as they pass.

Mackey wastes no time. He's on his way out. Hell, maybe to Georgia. Retirement might not be too bad after all. With his uneven stride, he half-jogs and half-shuffles down 113th Street. Five blocks later, he slows down, trying to catch his breath. Cars pass him on the street and a pink Mark III Continental stops alongside him. The Gimp turns to ice. The super is driving. Two burly black men exit the car and pick Mackey up by his elbows. His legs run and kick in the air. The three disappear into an alley. Mackey tries to talk his way out. But a million words can't save him this time. A million cars can't whisk him away. A wagging tongue, spouting nonsense to ears that won't listen, stops as a cold blade pierces his chest. He feels the pain as the tip enters his heart. He knows he's dead. He shakes spasmodically as the blade probes inside him. Then, softly, he falls in a heap. His soul sees Jerry Mackey die in an alley, without friends, in the dark.

Tatum wipes the bloody knife on the dead man's jacket. He empties Mackey's pockets, and the pink Mark stops again back in front of Keno's.

* * *

Vinnie Cannelli tries to race his car through traffic, but it's too congested to make an escape as fast as he wants to. He wishes he were in a jet. That's right! That's what he needs now. A jet to shoot across the country. Far away from here. He can never come back to New York. He barely got off with his life this time. The pain in his broken tooth is killing him.

Damn the red lights! Damn the cars! Damn the truck in front of me! What the hell is a sanitation truck doing out at this time of night anyway? Cannelli nervously looks around him from side to side and into his rearview mirror. His arms shake, and sweat pours from his face. Fear turns into terror as he watches two of three men leave the car jammed up behind him. One of them carries a tire iron.

Cannelli blows his horn feverishly, pounding harder and harder on the steering rim. Skin gouges from his hands. He screams in hoarseness for the truck in front of him to move. One of the men from behind peers through the passenger-side window. He tugs at the door handle, trying to rip it off, rocking the car. Cannelli is in the middle lane. Cars on either side of him begin to move. He is bawling. Tears drip from his face, mixing with sweat.

"Come on, move! Move, you bastard!" He yells at the truck. He still has a chance. If the truck will only move. He can't see the traffic light but he knows it's changed to green. Traffic around him is moving. Why doesn't the damn truck move? The second man stands at Cannelli's side window. He pounds on the glass with the tire iron. The window caves in. Three, four, five blows. Splintered glass and dangling shards stick together with safety glue and shatter over Cannelli, tangling in his hair and splintering into his ears. He rams his car into the rear of the sanitation truck. It doesn't move. A hard left hand grabs his windpipe and tries to rip out his throat. A right hand opens the door and pushes Vinnie over. Traffic lets up and sanitation truck #227 finally moves. Vinnie Cannelli rides out of Harlem with an escort.

* * *

Frank Scarmello is planted on a beautiful grassy knoll with a view of the Mohawk River Valley just outside of Utica, New York. Vinnie Cannelli spends the night in the trunk of his car behind the grandstand at Pelham Bay Park. A bullet has split the center of his forehead and blown out the rear of his skull.

CHAPTER 9

Alfredo Morelli nestles in the soft sheen of blue satin sheets. Morelli is a capo in the Don Carlo Gianini Family, which controls the borough of Queens. Two bodyguards stand vigil in the hall alcove outside the second-floor apartment. Two more armed guards wait in the lobby. Alfredo smoothes his legs under the cool blue silkiness that floats over his chest and thighs. His lips suck warmly into the milk-sweet neck of his girlfriend, Maria. Two nude bodies caress, sensuously thirsting for orgasm. Maria's creamy young breasts heave with excitement. Her nipples are sweet red cherries and Alfredo's lips catch them in his teeth. Lightly, he presses as his hand strokes her thighs. He rolls over on top of her. She shimmers and throbs with desire. They are one. Maria trembles and screams.

The bedroom window softly opens and two men wearing ski masks enter. Like jungle cats springing from a tree, the two are on Morelli, stuffing a cloth in his mouth, tying up and gagging Maria. With lightning speed, the capo is wrapped in blankets and hustled down the fire escape into a waiting car. In less than a minute, from bed to backseat, he disappears.

In the car the gag is removed, and black impenetrable glasses are slipped over his eyes and taped to his head.

"What, the hell's goin' on?" screams Morelli. "You crazy or something? What's this all about? What the hella you want?"

A gravelly voice answers, "Quiet, Mr. Morelli. Be quiet and you won't get hurt. If you make trouble, you're dead. *Capisce?*"

"*Sì. Io capisco.* But just understand, you'll get what you want. I don't want no trouble." Morelli wants to cooperate. The Family strategy is "Pay Now And Whack 'em Later. It'll only be a matter of time before we get them. We don't want anybody hurt."

Morelli is driven inside the garage of a private house. No time is lost. "We want 100 Gs. Then you can go back to Maria," says a thinner voice.

"Gimme the phone," says Morelli. He is wasting no time. He wants out of there as fast as he can.

The gravelly voice answers, "In two hours, in the parking lot of Ferry Point Park. The money in a paper bag to the car with the right directional signal blinking. Dropped into the right passenger window. Nobody follows the car or you're dead. Your life is on the line. You follow the instructions and you're as free as a bird."

Morelli dials. "Leuco! Don't say nothin'. Just listen. Put 100 grand in a paper bag and do like I tell you . . ." He gives the directions perfectly.

At two o'clock that morning, a car with a blinking right directional signal pulls into the blackness of the Ferry Point Park parking lot next to the Whitestone Bridge. A brown paper bag containing $100,000 is dropped through its passenger window. The rear license plate light of the car shines brightly. The light will be of no help to anyone. The car and the plates are stolen. At 3:00 AM, Alfredo Morelli is dropped off unharmed at a diner in Jackson Heights.

* * *

MICHAEL PALERMO

I have a meet set with Carmine to talk about something he says is important. It better be. It's five in the morning.

"I know it's important, Carmine, but do you know that it's five in the morning? What the hell's goin' on? Who was snatched?"

"How'd you know about that, Mike?"

"I got a strong pipeline. And I didn't know, smart guy. But I figure why the hell else would you get me out of bed for a meet?"

"Big Al Morelli. They grabbed him outta bed with his girl, heisted 100 grand, and dropped him off in Queens. Everybody is uptight about this. The faster we finish it, the better everybody will feel. You got anything for me yet?"

"Carmine, it's only been a day. What the hell could I find out in a day? I need some help from your side of the street. I have to know all the people who've been grabbed."

"That's out of the question, Mike. That's Family business. Your job is to see if cops are involved. You guys in SIU have gotta have tons of files on everybody. You see how easy it would be for cops to be behind this?"

* * *

SIU (Special Investigation Unit, Division of the Narcotics Bureau)

MICHAEL PALERMO

I'm assigned to SIU. The elite of the Department. A lot of the guys in this unit dress and act like they're hoods in the dough. Me? I look like a guy straight out of Robert Hall. Carmine is right. We have voluminous files on mobsters involved in narcotics traffic. I've had a few important arrests in the last year and the new

District Attorney, Ross Simon, and me have sat down and gone over these files to build a strong case for court. Ross and I have become pretty close friends. We have lunch a few times a month to go over business. He asks how the family is, and pretty soon he and his wife are coming over for a barbecue. Good thing I moved to Yonkers. Imagine me and the D.A. eating franks and drinking beers and Carmine hops over the fence for a visit like he used to do when we lived side-by-side on the Neck. It boggles the mind.

We have information detailing residence addresses, family members, girlfriends, business associates, hobbies, automobiles, second apartments, bank accounts, phone numbers, doctors, and even pets. Everything you'd ever want to know about a hood. That's where I found out about the proctologist who the "boys" called "The Rear Admiral." Ross cracked up over that one. He went crazy when he saw how much detail we had. But still he wanted to reach higher up and nail some of the big boys. I told him we only went up so high. There's too much of a buffer between the guys at the top and the poor slobs who do all the work and get caught.

* * *

"Carmine, there's nothing I can do with the files unless I know who's been snatched. All I can do is get what I can off the street and see if I can get something off a wire."

"All right, do what you can because there are some heavy things going down right now and we can't afford any trouble." Carmine pinches his lips like he let something big slip.

I tell him I understand even though I don't. And then we call it a night. Or a morning. Or whatever.

The next day I check the conversations on the Canicatti phone tap that for weeks had been active in another team's unrelated investigation. Nah, I couldn't tell Carmine that his phone was wired. It's a matter of honor. He doesn't expect it. That would make me a stool. Besides, Carmine is a big boy. He knows how to handle himself.

The conversation is routine until I get to Carmine talking to Fat Tony, and him saying, "I understand. I'll pick up the boats at Arthur's tonight." Then I remember what Carmine said to me: ". . . something heavy was going down."

I say to myself, What the hell is Carmine doing with boats? Is he in the boat business too? And Arthur's? That's got to be Artie Locari's olive oil warehouse at the docks. What the hell would Artie be doing with boats? Philly? That could be Phil Esposito. He's a boss in the Marcante Family. He's heavy into heroin. I hear a buzzer go off inside my head. Phil Esposito must be taking a shipment of a big load of heroin. The boats are plastic bags. "Don't leak" must mean keep it quiet. Nobody is to know. The tape was made in the morning. The deal is for tonight. It's a long shot, but it could be a perfect chance for the kidnappers to bag a big drug shipment plus an enormous amount of cash, plus a ransom. After a hit like this, they could retire. How good was their pipeline?

I talk to the Chief and call the "Bandits" together. I don't bring Captain Costello in on the action because it's too sensitive. If he finds out, the Chief will cover for me.

Ferrara and me are in one car, and Dempsey and Goddard in the other. We arrive at Philly's warehouse at nine o'clock, just as it got dark. There's a black Lincoln Continental outside and one other car. We wait. The hours go by. Nothing goes in and nothing comes out. It's 1:00 AM. Nothing moves. We take turns sleeping. Suddenly at 4:00 AM, the doors of the warehouse open. This is it. After seven hours of waiting. It's going down. I draw my .38. Ferrara has the radio handset in his hands, ready to call for backup.

Four men exit. Two carry submachine guns. The others, shot-guns. I recognize them as Amadeo's soldiers. We sink under the dashboards. If they see us, they'll shoot first and ask questions later. They'll chop us up. We can't match that firepower. Where's Philly? Where are the cases for the money or drugs? Esposito can't be far behind. Where the hell are the kidnappers? Did they miss this one? This was the only lead I have.

We watch the four guns get into two cars and drive away. The warehouse is locked. The whole night is a waste.

*   *   *

While "The Bandits" are in stakeout, a big man is boarding a plane in Chicago's O'Hare Airport to New York City. He looks like any other routine passenger, except that he is bigger than most and uglier. His eyes penetrate everything. People turn away from his stare. He is missing the pinkie finger of his right hand. The finger had been chopped off ten years earlier. The victim of a madman's lust for the big man's pinkie ring while he slept. The madman was a soldier in the Chicago mob. The big man, his hand pouring blood, had strangled his assailant and torn out the man's eyes. He now wears the ring on his left hand. He is called Mostro and he is an executioner called upon for only the most ruthless killings. He is on his way to the East Coast and has been summoned by the New York Families. Mostro will fill a special role in an ingenious plan.

The day before the assassin leaves Chicago, the members of the New York Commission have a meeting in the executive cham-bers of the SYNCOM Company. SYNCOM, Syndicated Com-modities, is a legitimate major corporation listed on the New York Stock Exchange. Its principle business is foreign exchange transac-tions. Subsidiary companies that it controls deal heavily in foreign exports and imports. Mob money can be laundered clean by its own corporation.

Alberto Marcante has called this meeting and he presides. He unveils a bold plan to deal with the rash of mob kidnappings. After the customary amenities, he presents his proposal for approval.

"Gentlemen, our Families are healthy and our businesses successful. It's unfortunate that we have to meet on this matter that confronts us today. All of us have become targets of these kidnappings and we've all been forced to pay. We've all shared equally in the overall expenses. This, it was decided, would demonstrate our mutual and united effort to finish this matter.

"The approach I present to you, for your consideration and approval, is the following. We'll quietly let it be known in the proper sensitive circles that an influential member of our organization will purchase a large amount of merchandise for cash at a particular location. This information will discreetly be fed to those six circles which we think may be causing our present difficulties. The six locations will all be different and set in various parts of the city. The merchandise and the person of influence will vary as appropriate for the deception.

"Now, if we're right, and if we choose our suspects carefully, we can expect an appearance by these people at one of these sites. We'll be ready to deal with them at each of the six locations.

"My Family, through my consigliere, Angelo, will carefully feed a location to a prime suspect: The Special Investigations Unit of the New York City Narcotics Bureau.

"We have a good chance of finishing this quickly. I've already made arrangements to bring the gentleman from Chicago here for a visit. Are there any questions?"

Marcante's plan is approved with no questions.

At three o'clock in the morning of "The Bandits'" stakeout, Mike Palermo, a prime suspect of the syndicate, passed his test. Antonio Vecchiano was not so fortunate.

Four kidnappers with ski masks had walked into Don Alberto's surprise reception in a truck garage in east Harlem. One of them had a gravelly voice, another spoke thinly. Harry Grimes was a taxi driver. Andrew Beach, a liquor salesman. Paul Denisco and John Sentino worked in the construction trades. After a short period of questioning, they readily gave up the source of their information—Antonio Vecchiano, a soldier in Don Alberto's own Family.

The following morning, Mrs. Viola Denisco received a package in the mail. It was delivered by special messenger. Upon opening the box, Mrs. Denisco was thrown into convulsive shock. She subsequently lost her sanity. On a silver plate in the box was the head and bloody neck stump of her husband, Paul.

Dismembered body parts were fished out of the Harlem and East Rivers the following day. Identification was impossible, but Mike Palermo on that day knew that the kidnappers were not cops. On that afternoon, Carmine told him that it was all over. He also told him how close Palermo himself had come to being dumped.

The underworld rested easier. Four wild cowboys had been dealt with, and now all that remained was for Mostro, the "Gentleman from Chicago," to visit Antonio Vecchiano.

* * *

Saturday morning and the day is fun and song. Carlo Buti sings Neapolitan ballads on the radio. Twelve-year-old Salvatore feeds the pigeons that strut and sit on the kitchen windowsill. A metal gridwork protects pots, plants, and children from falling to the pavement three floors below. The family plans to soon move to more comfortable quarters. Papa Antonio has become more successful in business. The children and Mama will enjoy more of the luxuries that money can buy. Young Salvatore will grow up and go to college. He carries the name of his grandfather. He carries the seeds of Lucania. He is the oldest of three children and will pass on the family name.

Antonio Vecchiano and his son leave Mama and her two daughters to care for the house. They make their usual trip to Tullio's barber shop. Marco Tullio had arrived from Agrigento, Sicily, twenty years ago. His shop is on the Vecchiano block. He has worked in the same storefront for the last eighteen years. He cuts hair, shaves a face, and takes numbers action all at the same time. His business is comfortable. His customs and customers are old friends. Neighborhood blocks are self-contained worlds. People can find all of their daily needs within a few steps of their apartments.

Tullio flaps out the apron as Vecchiano enters. He takes his usual chair in front of the storefront window. The barber, as he always does, turns the chair so that Antonio can watch his son play on the sidewalk. In the sunshine, Salvatore flips baseball cards. He also is successful. In school he has won many times and filled shoeboxes with his winnings. They call him the banker at home because he sells the cards he won back to the losers for a price or a favor. One of the older children in school had tried to muscle in on his action. Salvatore organized with two of his friends and after school they beat and robbed the older bully. His mother reprimanded him, but his father just smiled as if to say, "You're learning what life is about, my son. If you don't take for yourself, somebody will take what is yours."

Tullio sings along with Buti and Caruso, and Antonio Vecchiano watches his son enjoy the sunshine in the street. As the time rings happy on First Avenue, the cold steel of a machine gun lies on the floor of a car just six blocks away. In a private garage a stolen black Chevy starts its engine. Teddy Schiavo is the wheel man. He arrived from Italy three months ago. He is imported from New Jersey for today's job. Schiavo has a special way with cars. In addition to having lightning reflexes, his eyes and ears are sharp and he can diagnose a sick motor and fix it at once.

The black Chevy pulls out of the garage. Schiavo is at the wheel and big, ugly Mostro from Chicago is in the backseat. The big man looks straight ahead. Not left and not right. There is no time for distractions. It is a time for business. For an execution. He has just one thing to do. Vecchiano must pay for his treason.

As of this moment, Vecchiano does not know that his four associates have been captured and butchered. If he did, he would not be sitting in Tullio's barber shop so complacently. Instead of running, he is dreaming of the big payoff this evening. Of the move to a better apartment. Of a fuller life.

The black car is four blocks away. Tullio has finished the haircut and now begins Antonio's shave. Salvatore flips cards and his friend, Tommy, loses and leaves sullenly. Antonio looks at his son and smiles. Mostro bends over and cocks the machine gun. The gun is supplied by the Brooklyn organization. The car is from Queens. Everybody has a piece of this verdict. Mostro cleaned and oiled the weapon on the night before. Test firing had gone smoothly in a basement range in Harlem. He is an expert. A professional. Executions are his life and he never makes a mistake. He can't afford to.

Powder talc puffs on Vecchiano's face as Tullio pats him in rhythm to the music. Salvatore stands in front of the window, flipping cards, his back to his father. Schiavo turns the corner of 111th Street and First Avenue. He is in Vecchiano's world. Mostro cradles the chopper in his lap and rolls down the rear window. A woman carrying a shopping bag filled with vegetables and a baccalà walks in front of the barber shop. Salvatore flips cards.

Tullio sharpens his razor on a strap.

Mostro's eyes burn into Vecchiano's. He raises the barrel of the machine gun and sticks it through the window. The lady with the groceries clears the barber shop. Antonio's eyes split with terror as he sees the muzzle sticking through the open glass. He jumps from the chair and yells, "No!"

Mostro opens fire, bouncing bullets off the pavement. Sparks shoot out between young Salvatore Vecchiano's legs. Bullets ricochet into the plate glass window and fly around Tullio's head. He hits the floor in panic. The machine gun muzzle explodes with fire and steel. Mostro walks the shells up from the sidewalk, into the crotch, belly, chest, and head of young Salvatore, cutting him in half.

His father races from the shop, screaming, "No!" But it is too late. With a bloody Salvatore in his arms, he cries tears into blood and despair. The Chevy stops. Vecchiano looks up into the smoking end of the gun. His eyes lock on the icy stare of the executioner. Mostro raises the weapon and aims. Antonio Vecchiano is resigned to die. He cannot live with this. "Shoot!" he screams. "You've already killed me. Shoot!" But the shots never come. The black Chevy bolts away. Its cannon rests on the floor in the rear. Its window is closed.

Antonio Vecchiano is left weeping, covered with the blood of his dreams, the blood of his own doing. Now he will die "The Double Death"—once for his son and later—for he is sure it will come later, for himself.

* * *

The shadows of the fountains grow longer in the waning afternoon sun. The big, still whale spouts spray with the other statues in the Parkchester Oval fountain. Two men sit before the casement window. A tiny square table built for chess stands between them. The chess pieces are of solid ivory. Hand-carved and polished. On the inlaid board are poised royal Kings of stern determination; statuesque Queens with a touch of soft silk on their faces; detached Bishops, aloof in a holy war; avenging Knights, slashing swords above the heads of their prancing stallions; mortared Castles, the keepers of wars and spoils; and, finally, Pawns, each side eight, the soldiers of destiny, the sweat and blood of battles, the expendables for the advantage, for the trap.

The two men sit in high-backed padded chairs. Chief Devlin with a snifter of brandy. Mike Palermo with a bourbon on the rocks.

"I can't believe it really happened, Mike. It's one of the most savage retaliations they've ever executed. To kill a young boy like that. To shoot him down for what his father did. I never thought they'd do such a thing."

Palermo nods. "They call it 'The Double Death.' The victim dies twice. First he watches his child die and wishes that he himself was dead. He goes through mourning with family and friends. He cries at the funeral. At the cemetery he wants to jump into the grave and be buried. And there's nothing he can do. After a while, they finally kill him too and end it all.

"'The Double Death,' Chief. They only use it in the most extreme cases. When they want to set an example of what can happen to people when they act like a finger and make targets of their own Family. I could never live with that kind of justice. There's nothing that could ever justify setting an example by killing an innocent child."

"This fellow Vecchiano, he was behind the kidnappings?" asks Devlin.

"No question about it. After the wasted Thursday-night stakeout, I got the word that the kidnapping problem was all over. Did you know those guys thought I might have been behind the setups? Can you imagine that, Chief? They almost dumped me too. God, here we both sat in the same room with those people. We thought we knew what was in their minds. Did you have any idea that they suspected me? They might have suspected us both."

Devlin looks up from the game board and into Palermo's eyes. "No, Michael, I had no idea at all. But there's a lesson to be learned from all this. There's always a lesson. In order to survive, you have to look hard for what you can learn. It's like going to school all over again.

"Did you ever ask someone for directions on how to get to a certain street? The people you ask are nice enough. They spend time and explain everything in detail. And you drive on following the details. You're going to an important meeting and you want to be on time. You ride and ride and finally come to the street they directed you to. But it's the wrong street. The name is similar but wrong. In fact you traveled in the exact opposite direction. You wasted a lot of time.

"The people you asked tried their best to help you but they couldn't. You trusted them but through their ignorance you were trapped in their weakness. To be strong, you must never be trapped in someone else's stupidity."

Devlin points to the small carved pawns, the little men with weapons.

"Vecchiano was a soldier, a pawn like these here. But he was a pawn of fools and that foolishness destroyed him, murdered his son, and ruined his entire family. It's all right to be a pawn, to be a soldier, a fighter, an aggressor. But be a soldier of the smart and the strong. There was no way Vecchiano could have won in what he did."

Palermo restlessly curls his lip over his lower teeth, gently biting it. "A pawn of fools. I never thought of it that way. But it's true. You have to be defensive 100 percent of the time."

Devlin's eyes twinkle. "And now I'm going to show you something else you never thought of. Here's an opening move you should know. It's called 'The Sicilian Defense.'" Devlin smiles like a father watching his son dig into the cookie jar.

"'The Sicilian Defense,'" repeats Devlin. "This move is for Black after White has opened. Now you are Black and you move your pawn to Queen's Bishop Four, like this."

Palermo is puzzled. "That's all. That's all there is to it?"

"That's all," says Devlin.

"Why is it called 'The Sicilian Defense'?"

"Because the move does more than accept the inevitable. It goes beyond trying to be equal and fights back immediately. 'The Sicilian Defense' enables Black to counteract on the Queen's flank. Usually, White then attempts to break through on the King's flank. When that happens, the result is a fierce battle. The side that gets to the battleground with the most pieces in the shortest time is usually the winner."

Devlin sinks back into his chair. A little weary, he sips his brandy and continues.

"And always remember what I taught you. Concentrate your power and control in the center of the board. He who controls the center, controls the game. The closer you are to the center, the more squares your pieces control."

MICHAEL PALERMO

Chief Devlin taught me a lot about the strategy of the game. It was his gift to me. He passed it on. He used to say, "We never really own anything. Real estate, cars, jewelry, money. These things we use for a while and then pass on to someone else."

And with his knowledge of the game of chess he did the same thing. He passed it on to me. This gift of his to me was to change my life forever.

Without it, I would be dead today.

CHAPTER 10

Patrolmen Arnold Stern and Steven Richards make their routine patrol rounds. 3:00 AM this Tuesday morning finds them in Pelham Bay Park in the parking lot behind the grandstand. There are just the lovers in parked cars. They scatter the young people who make love not war. Engines rumble. Clouds of exhaust fumes and dust powder in the muted brilliance of burning headlamps. Pebbles pop and bounce along the blacktop and moving cars. The whirling red lighthouse atop the squad car plays a merry-go-round of red and brilliant white lights over the lovers' exit.

The lot is cleared out except for a Pontiac Bonneville with a broken left rear tail light. The driver's window has been smashed through and glass nuggets cover the seat and floor. The keys are in the ignition. Stern and Richards open the trunk and find a body. It is the remains of Vinnie Cannelli. The back of his head is missing and a hole clogged with dry blood is stuck in his forehead.

They call for the Sergeant on Patrol and Sergeant Ralph Sanders responds.

"Douse your lights. Let's not wake up the whole neighborhood. Get Leavitt and Boggs down here. We got one body too many down here. The Cap's got heat coming from the PC about having a clean sector. This guy's takin' a trip over the bridge. Things have slowed down in Queens. Let's give them some excitement and then we won't have to spend the night filling out reports."

Howard Leavitt and Bill Boggs arrive with Mike Palermo who had sacked out in the four-five overnight because of an early court appearance with his partners on Tuesday morning. They had finished duty late on Monday.

The car is registered to a Vincent Cannelli. Leavitt had bumped into Palermo and knew Palermo knew Cannelli, so he invited him along for the I.D. When the detectives arrive, Sanders has already sent the two patrolmen back to cruising their sector.

"Sure don't need any more dumpings in this sector, Sarge," says Leavitt.

"That's for sure. We're already up to our asses in paperwork."

As they talk, Palermo examines Cannelli. He lays broken and contorted. His arms and legs are broken. The "Bandits" could have "gone all the way" with more mercy. Flashes of Cannelli's wife and baby light up Palermo's mind. Groty's smashed face on the floor of Ricco's. Young Martin Robbins' head split open with a ketchup bottle. *What a waste is lying in this trunk*, he thinks.

"Is that Cannelli?" asks Leavitt.

"Yeah, that's him," says Palermo glumly. "He finally got his ass kicked in and his head blown off. He sure worked hard to get here."

Leavitt closes the trunk. "Mike, the Sarge will take you back to the house. Billy and me are going to give this guy a ride over the bridge." Leavitt winks. "We got too many stiffs around here lately. We're going to share the wealth, spread it around and give our boys in Queens a little work."

Palermo goes back to the Precinct House and Bill Boggs follows Leavitt and Cannelli over the Bronx Whitestone Bridge into Queens.

At 4:15 A.M. Abe Coster is walking his dog, Maxie, in the side street off Francis Lewis Boulevard. Coster is a retired accountant. Poor Maxie has indigestion and has to go out for relief. Coster watches Leavitt park the black Pontiac with the broken window. As he and Boggs drive by, he remembers the license plate of the unmarked car. He is good with numbers.

At ten o'clock that morning, Leavitt is in the office of Chief of Detectives, Ed Sperry.

"Look, what did I ever do to you?" asks Sperry. "No matter where I put you, you keep popping up like a bad penny. It's not enough that you develop a reputation as a hard-sleeping cop who coops out on an air mattress. I took you out of the bag so you'd be less obvious to people and get in less trouble. Now you get caught moving dead bodies around town, and you get caught by an old man and a dog with diarrhea." Sperry paces his office, flailing his hands in the air as he speaks. Leavitt stands stiff at attention.

"So help me," continues Sperry, "if you weren't my sister's kid, I'd skin you alive!" He walks in front of Leavitt and stares at him face to face. Spittle flies from his lips as he yells, "If you're going to do something, do it right goddammit, or don't do it at all. Change the fuckin' plates on your car before you dump a body. Now you got the PC's office on your back. When they're on your back, they're on my back. I don't know what the hell I'm going to do with you." Sperry sits down behind his heavy mahogany desk. "What am I going to do with you? You tell me!" he yells as his fists pound the desktop. Papers jump up and fly off into the air.

Leavitt stands stiff, his eyes riveted blankly on the wall. He croaks, "I was just trying to do the right thing."

"You did the right thing," barks Sperry. "Only you did the right thing wrong."

"It won't happen again, Sir."

"You're damn right it won't happen again. One more fuck up and you're going to find yourself working in the laundry down the street. Now get the hell out of here!"

* * *

A few nights later the action rolls heavy in the back room of "The Rafters." Johnny Castle has just given the OK to raise the house credit limit for the man who stands at the end of the craps table. He sways uneasily with tinges of panic in his eyes. Two black and white dice hide in his hands. He rolls them between his open palms and then shakes them in a sweaty cupped fist. All eyes around the table hang on his hands as if he was throwing their fate out at them. He is a prophet unfolding destiny. He is Charlie Rosen, and his accumulated debt to "The Rafters" last month totals $85,000. It is through the special intercession of Carmine Canicatti that his credit has been allowed to rise this high. Rosen has been a good customer over the years and has always paid his debts. This last month, however, holds Charlie Rosen gripped in fear. He is determined to hit the big point, to walk off with the big odds. All he wants is to hit once and to hit high. If he can do that, then his world, his life, his business, and family will all come together and everything will be all right again. For if he can have that one big roll, Charlie Rosen will be even.

His right fist rattles and sweat pours off his chin. No one speaks. No one moves except Rosen. His point is four. Three chances in thirty for everything to be fixed right in his life. The dice fly out of his hand and tumble down the alley. Three and one stand on top. Rosen wins. He is the only one cheering. Everyone else has bet against him. He is even, and he is hot.

Castle smiles and pats him on the back. "Nice roll, Charlie. You got magic in those hands tonight."

Rosen's chest heaves. His shirt soaks tight with sweat. The stub of a dark chewed cigar pokes through his lips. "Magic. I've been waitin' a long time for this night. I knew if I waited long enough, I'd have it."

Card games play in tables around the room. Blackjack and poker. "The Rafters" is New York's unsung Las Vegas. Carmine Canicatti sits at the bar in the outer room and Johnny Castle joins him. He tells Carmine about Rosen's big roll.

"He finally hit! Eighty-five big ones. Tonight he's got magic in those hands."

Canicatti smiles. "Is that what you told him? I'm glad for him. He's a nice guy. I know he can use the bread. I hope he plays all night, the bastard."

"It's in his eyes," says Castle. "He's gonna be with us for a long time."

The evening passes quickly. The time for Charlie Rosen's payoff approaches. He speaks with Carmine and Castle in their private office.

"You did good tonight, Charlie," say Carmine. "You did good, but you tried to do better. Nobody could stop you. I know you had to roll while you were hot."

Rosen stares sheepishly at the floor. "But I tell you, I had it tonight. I had it all."

"Yeah, you had it," smiled Castle. "So where is it now? I tried to tell you, Charlie. You should have taken it while you had it. Now you're in deeper than before."

"How much?" asks Rosen. "How much of me do you own now? Do you own my hands, my arms, my legs, my guts? Tell me!" he screams. "How much of me do you own?"

"One hundred and twenty-five grand." Canicatti waves a handful of Rosen's markers. "How much of you is that worth? Is that your hands, your guts, or your head? We don't want you, Charlie. We just want the money. How soon can you have it?"

Rosen stiffens. In the past they always gave him time. Don't worry about it, Charlie. We'll put it on the tab, Charlie. We know you're good for it. You've got a good business. You're a respectable business man. We trust you. And now they want 125 grand right away.

"Are you kidding?" says Rosen. "It's gonna take me time to raise that much."

"You don't have any time, Charlie," whispers Canicatti.

"What are you telling me? What am I supposed to do, rob a bank for you?"

Castle smiled. "Well, either that or Carmine and me, we're goin' into the meat packing business."

"Never!" screams Rosen. "You'll never get your greasy hands on my business. I know about you. You ruined Fortas. You used his credit, dumped his merchandise, and bankrupted him. You two guineas will never do that to me. Never!"

Canicatti leans back in his swivel chair behind his desk. "I'm sorry you feel that way, Charlie. If that's your last word, you better go rob a bank. Mr. Castle will see you out."

* * *

Giorgio Amadeo receives a phone call at three o'clock this morning. He has just finished a Bud's Morelli special feast at "The Hole" with Casper Nardino. After his phone conversation, Amadeo speaks briefly with his boss and Nardino gently nods.

At 5:00 AM the bedside phone rings next to Charlie Rosen's head. He is groggy but he listens and remembers every word clearly. "Think it over, Charlie. Think it over. We've decided to give you some more time."

The line goes dead. Rosen goes back to sleep. Puzzled, but a little more relaxed.

At the first light of dawn Rosen awakes, exhausted but unable to sleep anymore. He slips out of the house without waking his wife and reaches his office in the building of Rosen's Meat Packing, Inc. He walks into a flurry of unusual activity. He is directed immediately to the large refrigerator room down the hall. People jabber at him as he walks. His mind races with 100 contingencies and he hears nothing they say. His pace quickens to a shuffling trot. Butchers in clean white aprons follow and lead him on, finally swinging open the steel door in the meat locker and framing before his eyes the bloody barbarism of "The Double Death."

Impaled on a meat hook, hangs the nude body of Antonio Vecchiano. His chest and abdomen are raked with the razor slices of a butcher knife. The final slash has severed his genitals and they are stuffed into his mouth. Like a slaughtered chicken, Vecchiano had bled to death before his killers, fully conscious.

Rosen freezes and his stomach jumps into his chest. He turns and races back to his office, holding his mouth. He brushes past two uniformed police officers and stumbles into his toilet where his insides explode. Rosen, the butcher who thought he had seen everything, vomits over the floor and the walls.

Thirty minutes later, during questioning by the police, Charlie Rosen's phone rings. A voice on the other end asks simply, "Will eleven o'clock be convenient for you to sign those papers, Charlie?"

"Eleven o'clock will be just fine," says Rosen without hesitation or expression. He hangs up and tries his best but is unable to shed any light on the Vecchiano killing.

The Marcante family adds a wholesale meat supply house to its string of legitimate businesses. Johnny Castle controls a laundry chain. Giorgio Amadeo runs garbage pickups. Carmine Canicatti has an interest in a restaurant supply company. All of these concerns are important in operating restaurants and after-hours night spots. The profits and skim from these businesses are extraordinary.

When a legitimate business is acquired because of gambling or loan shark debts, it is integrated into the Family establishment to strengthen itself and others.

If there are no synergistic opportunities, the company's good credit rating is extended to the limit, and vast amounts of merchandise is ordered and immediately dumped at below wholesale prices. Sometimes an apron fire will bring insurance money into the company and it will never be reopened but declare bankruptcy.

If fires are too common at a particular time, the company simply seeks a debtor's protection from the Courts under Chapter 11 of the Bankruptcy Code, reorganizes, and either pays a few cents on the dollar of debt and reopens or simply throws up its hands and goes out of business.

This is the way of legitimate business and it is sanctioned by Court justice. It's a way of American life. From the old days of the Terranova control of the artichoke trade imported from Sicily, the immigrants with power exercised firm control over essential commodities. Artichokes were a staple of the Italian diet. Through control of their food, Terranova had controlled the Italian community, the vegetable dealers, wholesale and retail, truckers, dock workers, and, indirectly, the mothers, fathers, and children. Terranova was a master of power. It was because of respect for this power that he was called "The Artichoke King." It is curious that the commodity that gave him power had in its name the symbolization of the strangler. The artichoke. Terranova choked free trade and set an example for people like Marcante to follow.

* * *

CHAPTER 11

MICHAEL PALERMO

This afternoon we're celebrating the christening of my new daughter, Michele. Laura and I are so happy that we've been blessed by God with such a beautiful baby. I wonder what she's going to be like when she grows up. I love them both so much. They say she looks just like me but I think she looks like her mother. Let's hope so anyway because I shudder when I think of any girl looking like me.

We're at The Chateau Pelham and the place is jumping. This has got to be a scene that'll never be again. My mother and my aunts and uncles are here. Cousins and nephews. Even my two boys that Rosey and I had, Michael and Paulie, are here. I ask them how their mother is and they say she's happy with her new husband. An accountant. I tell the boys they can "count on me" for anything they need and we have to always stay in touch. They miss the joke and say "yeah" and then shake hands with me. I figured maybe I'd get a hug but I guess they're too old for hugging. Hell, even old "wise guys" hug. They even kiss before they execute each other. "The Kiss Of Death."

Mike and Paulie are in high school now. They're growing up fine and we keep in touch. I try to be the best father I can be to them but the job takes up so much time.

That's always been the problem. We have a quota of five arrests per month that we have to meet. After that, it's time for fun and games and parties. But you have to understand I work a twenty-four-hour day.

I spend a lot of time doing research on the organized crime families. Whenever somebody needs information on some wise guy's address or girlfriend or what car he's driving, I got it at my fingertips. Even if it's a guy I know. The job comes first. Everybody understands that. What I don't give up is anything I learn about guys that has nothing to do with business. Things told to me as a friend and of a personal nature. If I'm too close to a guy who's being investigated for a bust, I tell the Cap to put somebody else on the case. That way, there's no conflict.

Baby Michele is in Tony Amendola's private office in her bassinet with a friend of the family, Mrs. Mugovera, watching over her. All my friends are here. The place is filled with cops and robbers. Cops on one side of the room and robbers on the other. I've been seeing a lot of D.A. Ross Simon lately. Not only on the job but also socially. He's at a big fund-raising party that the Rockefeller's are having in the next room for some charity. He said he's going to drop in and say hello later.

* * *

The Chateau Pelham does a heavy catering business in the Pelham Bay section of the Bronx across the street from Amen's Restaurant. Casper Nardino and his wife sit at a table in the Raindrop Room. He's flanked by Giorgio Amadeo and Carmine Canicatti and their wives. From the stage, Buster Long's quartet plays Italian ballads and pop music. At their half of the table, the three men are engaged in serious conversation. They discuss matters quietly and out of earshot of the wives. A day's receipts from the numbers take; an overdue loan shark debt; a restaurant's bar operation; a new race horse acquisition; boxing matches and basketball games. With the delicate deftness of a tightrope walker, they discuss business.

The women talk about cocktail dresses, never going out for a night's dinner with their husbands, the bums their daughters are going out with. "He's in the same business as my husband is. Why can't she go out with a nice guy who's going to be a doctor or lawyer?"

Tables down the same side of the dance floor hold more "wise guys"… people who make their living on the street, families who survive the hard way with uncertainty and violence. At every table the men talk business and the women talk of life.

In the background, Buster Long's music plays.

Across the parquet floor on the opposite side of the room, tables talk a different way and the music beats to a different drum. Seats are filled with New York cops, federal agents, assistant district attorneys, and their wives or sweethearts. The women's conversations are about the same as the other side of the room. The men talk about the job and the major arrests or prosecutions they handled. Knives become longer and sharper, guns loom larger and louder, car chases speed faster around more and more curves.

Lenny Lombardi complains in disbelief. "Can you believe it? There's Baroli. I've been trying to lay my hands on him for a week now but he's been on the lam. And there he is sitting right across from me. I thought he got swallowed up for good and now I sit here and watch the guy drink champagne with a smile on his face and a broad on his arm."

"Forget him," says Captain Costello. "Tonight's not the night. Remember what I told you, Lenny. Timing's everything in life. Eat your ravioli."

At the dais sits Monsignor Gian Torrone. He is on the staff of the New York Archdiocese. He attends this evening at the invitation and as the guest of Mike Palermo and Casper Nardino and

Collin Devlin. Torrone, Nardino, and Devlin, who as children spent punitive time together at the Catholic Protectory. They break bread this night, a monsignor, a retired police chief inspector, and a syndicate boss—an alumni reunion.

Alongside Monsignor Torrone sits Father Vincent Baldini, the parish priest who had baptized tiny Michele earlier this afternoon. Antoinette Mugavera, an old family friend, gently rocks the baby and knits a black woollen shawl in the back office.

Mike and Laura beam from the dais. They wave to their friends throughout the room. Buck Truccolini comes up to talk to them.

"Mike, I got a surprise for you and Laura tonight," he whispers as he leans over the table. He waves at the front door and a handsome young man dressed in a tuxedo comes up to the bandstand. He is Carlo Cinqui, Buck's new protégé to replace Jimmy Sorelli. Buster Long makes the introduction and the room bursts into applause and cheers. Buck is walking on clouds. He gives his friend a gift that nobody else could give.

Cinqui's voice is soft like the finest silk and as rich as the finest red wine. He sings to the dais and to both sides of the dance floor. When his songs end, Tony Amendola is so impressed that he personally thanks Carlo and announces that he is so inspired by his performance and by the excitement of the evening that he wants to personally present Michele with a gift.

"For the little girl who sleeps here tonight, I want you all to know that when she is married her reception at The Chateau Pelham will be the gift of the Amendola family."

Everybody applauds, especially the Palermos.

In the room next to the Palermo party, a reception fund-raiser for New York City orphans and abandoned children is in progress. It is an expiation for the moneyed. Politicians, public servants, and the very rich mingle together for the common cause.

Laurence Fredricks has descended from a line of old money. His bank vaults are lined with the gold and deceit of the robber barons of another age. Years ago, oil and land speculation, larceny, and political bribery had built a financial base for the Fredricks family. It is this fortune that had helped Laurence's father, Phillip, exploit the bootleg alcohol business during Prohibition. Canadian distilleries under the family control smuggled scotch and bourbon over the border. Payoffs in the right places insured delivery to local organized Crime Families. It was nothing more than one family helping another.

Alberto Marcante and his wife are also at the fund-raiser. He and the Fredricks family continue an active business relationship using the Fredricks family banking empire to launder and legitimately invest Marcante money. Both sides are content. Police Commissioner James O'Hara and Chief of Detectives Edward Sperry share a table with Bronx District Attorney Ross Simon.

In the lobby, people from the Palermo and Rockefeller parties shake hands and discuss business. They all get along well together. Jimmy Colucino, from the Rockefeller party, speaks with fervor to everyone about the cause he is spearheading. It's time, he says, that people come to realize that all Italians are not criminals. Too often the Italian heritage is linked to terms like "Mafia." The Jews have their Anti-Defamation League and now Colucino has organized the Italian Heritage Association. In reality he is organizing a political base to control votes of the Italian community. Jimmy is the son and underboss of Don Francesco Colucino, whose Family runs the Brooklyn waterfront.

When Laurence Fredricks hears that Carlo Cinqui sang at the Palermo christening, he wants him to sing next door. His request is made to Commissioner O'Hara, who passes it on to District Attorney Ross Simon. Simon and his wife visit the Palermos and give the baby a $100 savings bond as a christening gift.

"God bless both of you," says Simon. "I looked in on the baby and she's beautiful. Why don't you ladies talk about baby stuff while I talk to Mike a while?"

Mike and Simon move to the side.

"Mike, where'd you ever find all these 'wise guys'? This place is like the who's-who of organized crime. I see guys here that I put away years ago. And on the other side of the room is half of the law enforcement department of the City. This is like a little Appalachia and a police racket at the same time."

"They're all my friends, Ross. Just like you. Thanks for the thoughtful gift for the baby. I know you couldn't be here because of that big Fredricks benefit."

"To tell you the truth, Mike, I'd rather be here any day. But I have to show the proper respect. Those are all important people in there who make and lose millions in hours."

"Hey. If you got some people who want to lose millions, bring them into the back room. We got a hot craps game going on all afternoon. Come on, I'll show you."

They walk to a back room and enter. Inside, kneel men of all ages and mixed occupations. Some are bent over and others stand. They all yell in a frenzy.

Captain Costello rolls the dice with the luck of the Irish. Bets are covered and payoffs go back and forth to cops to hoods, from federal agents to prosecutors on the D.A.'s staff and back again. Bad money covers good. Nobody can tell who's who, what's what, who's good, and who's bad, and nobody cares.

"You want to make a few passes, Ross?" asks Palermo.

"I'll take a rain check, Mike. You've got half my staff here and half of the guys they prosecute. If I make one pass, they'll blackmail me out of office for the rest of my life."

They return to the banquet hall and Simon asks, "Mike, Larry Fredricks would like to have Carlo Cinqui sing at our function. Do you think you can get him for us? Larry's prepared to make a big donation to the Orphan Fund in Cinqui's name."

"Let me check with a friend, Ross."

Palermo speaks with Buck. Buck thinks it over and agrees, with one stipulation. Mike returns to Simon.

"Carlo will sing for your people but the donation has to go down as contributed by Carlo Cinqui and Buck Truccolini."

"No problem. I thought you were going to say Genovese."

"Nah. He's away."

"Thanks. Look, I'll meet you for lunch on Tuesday. I want to go over some new cases. I want to nail some of the guys at the top for a change."

"See you Tuesday."

Buck granted the favor because he knew that some day it would come back to him. The exposure at the Rockefeller party would also help Carlo's career.

During a break in the music, Mike's eyes catch a man in the doorway.

He is a dark-skinned African-American with black glasses. He is flanked by two heavyset black bodyguards. The three of them enter the room and approach the head table. Mike's mind races back to two years ago when he had first met Tommy Favors in a rundown Harlem hotel.

* * *

John Amato and I responded to a tip that a drug buy was set for 9:00 PM in Room 301 of the Washington Hotel. Richie Arculeo was checking some wires that we had running. You see, the difference between a narcotics detective and a squad detective in a precinct is that a Precinct Squad detective responds to complaints or calls by patrolmen, and a Narcotics Bureau detective goes out looking for trouble, following tips, wire tapping, and following leads. We were out looking for trouble to make our quota of five narcotics arrests per month. We got to the third floor and Amato went into action.

"Open up, Police!" Amato kicks down the door.

In front of us sits a blind Tommy Favors. His face is dripping with sweat. A rubber hose chokes his right arm, bulging the veins.

Alongside him sits a mousey Willie Sims, heating a spoon of water over a flame, dissolving heroin. He sits thirty seconds from sucking it up into a syringe and shooting it into Favors' swollen arm. Tommy Favors sits like a rag doll, no movement, no expression on his face. He speaks first.

"Come on in, man. Have a seat. This won't take but a minute. This is one minute I gotta have."

We're surprised and lower our guns. Amato checks the closet. It has no door. Not even a curtain. The place is empty except for Favors and Sims. I walk to the table. Favors senses our every move.

"Sit down, friend. Both of you. We can both use the time. A few more minutes ain't gonna matter one way or the other."

Sims fills the syringe. It cools to blood-warm and the needle sinks into the black bulge pounding inside Favors' arm. Dark glasses hide his eyes. A smile of relief slowly spreads over his lips. I see myself reflected right and left in the shiny black lenses.

"Tommy Favors? It was only six months ago I saw you on TV. What the hell is this all about?" I can't believe this. This is not a "broker," a down-and-outer in the street. This guy is a well-known international star.

Amato approaches, keeping a careful eye on Sims.

"Have a seat, friend. It's a long story and maybe it's about time it got told."

I send Sims down to the liquor store for a bottle of bourbon and two glasses. John and I listen as Tommy Favors peels off the layers of his life. Up until four months ago he had been working, appearing in nightclubs and on television, a favorite of both the black and the white audiences.

"I fought this monkey on my back through my whole career. I started with marijuana with the old jazz bands of the forties. It was accepted, then, among musicians. It was easy to get and easy to smoke. Then over the years I moved on to pills, cocaine, hashish, and then heroin. I beat the needle once before. It was the hardest thing I ever had to do in my life.

"I felt good bein' clean. I won the impossible dream, the impossible fight. My career took off again. One night I lost somebody dear to me and I started all over again. I know I'm in the gutter again. I can't go down any lower. I can't get a job. Nobody wants me anymore. And I can't blame them.

"You don't have to tell me, man. I know." The sweat turns to tears, falling from behind black glasses as Favors speaks. "I can't see, but I know how bad I look. I know there's only one step left for me and that's under the ground. There ain't no place else to go."

I shrug my shoulders. "Look, Tommy, they've got places that can bring you around again and give you another shot. You beat it once. You can beat it again."

"They've got some new rehab clinics and some new drugs they're working with now," says Amato.

"I know, friends. I know. And I been thinkin' about it. About stoppin' this shit. But I just ain't never been up against it so bad as this time, But I tell you, and I swear to you, that if I had another chance, I'd take it. I'm gonna get this mother offa my back this time for the last time. What do you say, friend? Do I get another chance or do I go down the sewer?"

Johnny and I look at each other and nod. We always seem to know what the other is thinking. "You get another chance," I say. "But this time you better make it work, because if you don't you ain't never gonna get another one."

The three of us sit and drink and talk about show business, celebrities, and the street. We let Mousey Sims go. We can always find him if we want him. If we take him down for this, we have to bust Favors. We find out that the world is full of closet junkies, people hooked on one thing or another.

Two cops leave a blind Tommy Favors sitting at a dusty old wooden table under a shining lamp that he doesn't need to see the light.

* * *

And now Tommy Favors and his two bodyguards are walking toward me. Across the dance floor to the dais. People around the room look up, and whispers fill the air. Tommy stands in front of me and extends his hand. We shake.

"Friend, I heard your little girl was baptized today and that she's having a party this evening. It would be my pleasure to sing her a little song."

"Friend," I say, "it will be our pleasure and you'll be our guest. I'd like you to meet my wife, Laura."

"I'm honored, sweet mother. May your daughter live in love and find a man as good as your husband."

I introduce Tommy all around the room. He sings his gift and I remember the last time we met.

It's one year earlier. I am in charge of organizing a racket for the Police Department to be held at The Chateau Pelham. I need a big-name performer and Tommy Favors is back on top of the charts. By coincidence, I drop into The Coals Lounge in Midtown Manhattan. In the far corner I see the black glasses and Tommy's familiar face. He is relaxing with a cigarette. I walk over to talk with him and walk into a wall of heavy black muscle.

"Can I help you?" says his bodyguard politely. He is bovine. But nice bovine.

"I just want to say hello to Tommy," I tell him.

"Mr. Favors is resting. He can't be bothered now."

Favors' ears prick up at the sound of my voice and I see his head snap in my direction. I know he remembers me.

"Let him pass, Billy. That man is a friend of mine."

I step up to the table.

"Have a seat, friend. It's good to hear your voice again."

"It's good to sit with you again, Tommy. Do you remember the last time we met?"

"I sure do. I'll never forget it. How's life treating you, Mike?"

He remembers my name. He inhales a cigarette and taps the ashes squarely in the center of the ashtray before him.

We talk a while and then I ask him.

"Tommy, could you make an appearance at a racket I'm putting on at The Chateau Pelham on April 16th?"

"Billy, where we gonna be on April 16th?"

Billy checks the booking schedule in his inside pocket. "We gonna be in L.A., Tommy. You're gonna do a week at the Surf Club."

"I'm sorry, Mike. My schedule's real tight now. I can't get out of that date. Let me take a rain check. It'll be my pleasure."

"I understand, Tommy. You have a good tour and take care of yourself."

"And you too, my friend."

We shake hands and I leave.

* * *

One year later, Tommy Favors steps down from the stage amid the cheers of the room. He waves to the dais and leaves with his two associates. He passes through the lobby, past the high society fund-raiser next door, and past District Attorney Ross Simon, who peers into the Palermo banquet room to see if there are any more big-name celebrities he can get to sing for Larry Fredricks. Simon has decided to run for Governor and he needs all the big money backing he can get. He also needs some big-time drug busts. Some big-time Italian mobsters. Something that his friend Palermo isn't giving him.

* * *

Buster's band sounds great and everybody is either dancing or shooting craps in the back room. Everybody's having a good time so I figure it's time to take care of the business I have to do with my cousin, Aldo. He's seventeen and thinks he knows it all. He's named after his mother's father, my uncle, Aldo Rancolo. I used to play in Zio Aldo's store in east Harlem back in the thirties. I was the little *Procione*, the robber raccoon, with my black mask and wooden gun. I used to hold my uncle up for some candy. I always got what I wanted.

Uncle Aldo is now in his late seventies and he has discreetly asked me to talk with his grandson. The old man has the wisdom and gut feeling to know that something is not right in his daughter's house. This feeling hurts him very badly.

I bring my cousin into Tony Amendola's office while baby Michele is sleeping with Mrs. Mugavera watching her. The old lady smiles and nods as she rocks.

"Signora," I say, "you've been so kind to us this evening. I'd like you to enjoy some of Michele's cake. Please see my wife, relax, and listen to the music outside. Aldo and I will watch over the baby."

"*Grazie, mio riguardoso ragazzo,*" she answers as she folds her knitting. With a last look at the baby, she adjusts the blanket before she leaves.

"Isn't she beautiful, Aldo? You know some day you're going to have one just like her."

"Nah, Cuz! I ain't gonna have no kids. Kids are nothin' but trouble."

"What are you talking about? Where'd you pick up that kind of stuff?"

"Ehh, my father says who needs kids? You feed 'em, give 'em clothes and a roof over their heads, and where does it get you? What do they do? They grow up and kick you in the ass when they get big. I ain't never gettin' married. Where does it get you? Marriage ain't nothin' but a dead end. Look at my father. He don't care about nobody. Not my mother. Not me. He spends all his time at the track runnin' around with a lot of cheap broads."

I can see that Aldo is upset. He's nervous, moving from side to side, snapping his head to whip the long, black hair from his forehead.

"Aldo, I know that I've been out of touch with the family for a while, but there's one thing I do know. I know your father and mother both love you very much. We go back a long time, your father and me, and I know how excited he was when you were born. He and I both wanted our first child to be a son. You should have seen his face light up when you were born and he held you in his arms. You were his whole life. I know he always wanted the best for you.

"You see that bassinet? My third child sleeps in it. That's not just an ordinary basket. It's been in the family for over fifty years, brought over from Agrigento. It was handmade by your grandfather, my uncle, for whom you were named. And I know personally that he loves you very much.

"That basket was your cradle and mine, too. Michele sleeps safely in the love of her family. And we all stick together. We all move on together. That's the way it always was and the way it'll always be.

"I held you in my arms when you were baptized. I speak to you now as your godfather. I want you to remember what I tell you. It was on my sacred oath that I swore to look after you if your parents couldn't. If you need me, I'm here."

"Ahh, you don't have to worry about your oath, Cuz. I release you from it. I gotta go now. I got things to do."

I can feel the veins in my neck pop out, and my face grows hot with the fire of blood.

"Listen, you smartass, maybe you can pull that bullshit at home and get away with it, but don't pull any of that crap on me." Aldo backsteps. "I know you're messin' around with drugs and you're giving your family a lot of grief. If you keep it up, you're as good as dead. And don't try to bullshit me, pal, because I'm the biggest bullshitter there ever was. I deal with it every day. That's my job. That's all I do.

"Now, if you need help, my hand is out. Grab it or I can guarantee you're going under. I see young punks like you every day. They're dead from an overdose. Just some rotting flesh on cots soaked with urine, with maggots and flies running through their eyeballs. You're racing down a dead end, kid, into a meat grinder.

"Now if you're as smart as you think you are," I poke a stiff finger into Aldo's solar plexus, "and if you're as tough as you talk, then you'll straighten yourself out and make your family proud of you again."

Aldo loses control. The shell he keeps around himself shatters and cracks wide open. He begins to cry.

"Mike, I've tried." Tears drip from his eyes. "It's not that damn easy. I can't do it. Nobody can do it. Once the needle's in, you can't never get it out."

"Do you want it out, Aldo? Only you can take it out. But I can help you. Did you see that blind man who sang for Michele tonight? He had the needle in his arm. He was a dead man but he ripped it out. And now he's alive. I helped him a little. But that man. That blind man ripped it out himself. Why do you think he came here tonight? He didn't have to come. He's an international star. He's on network television. He came to thank me for helping get him off drugs. And I ended up by thanking him. I can help you, too, Aldo, but you have to grab my hand."

I extend my open palm to him, and a weeping, scared young man grasps it with both hands and squeezes tight. He holds on for dear life. Together we stand, arms wrapped tightly around each other, tears in our eyes, while baby Michele sleeps.

I wonder what twenty years will bring for Aldo or for his own children. It is the future that is better left unknown. We stand together for a long time, until the tears dry. Cousin and cousin. Godfather and godson. Blood and tradition.

Aldo makes his way to the washroom and I return to the party. I see guys coming out of the back room. The craps game is over. The ladies want to dance. The room fills up with dancers. Everybody's a winner this night. They all have a good time. Finally Laura and I stand at the door to say good night to our guests. Envelopes with cash fill the white satin bag suspended from the bassinet.

I can see Ross Simon watching from the lobby as I exchange handshakes and hugs with reputed criminals, cops, prosecutors, and federal agents. He looks puzzled. Like he's got a problem.

And I'm it.

As Johnny Napolitano leaves with his wife, he whispers in my ear to remind me of our meeting on Wednesday afternoon. I nod. We'll meet at the Sunshine Diner on Bronxdale and Tremont Avenues.

Chief Devlin leaves with Monsignor Torrone and Father Vincent Baldini. They take a cab.

We get home at 3 AM and put the baby in her crib.

* * *

The next morning at seven, the phone rings next to my head.

"Hello, Michael. This is Father Vincent Baldini."

"Yes, Father, I'm here. What is it?"

"Chief Devlin is in the hospital. He was stricken last night as he rode with the Monsignor and me. It's his heart, Michael. He's here in Parkchester Hospital. He asked for you."

"I'll be right over, Father. Tell him I'll be right there. How bad is he?"

"We're not sure. He seems to be improving. Monsignor and I have been here all night. The people in the hospital have really worked their hearts out for him. Monsignor Torrone has heard his confession and given him the last rites."

"Father, I'll be right there. Please tell him I'm on my way."

As I enter the private room, the two priests rise from the bed-side. Collin Devlin lies propped up, his head and chest slightly raised. He's breathing from an oxygen machine. Clear tubing carries an intravenous drip into his arm.

"Hello, Chief. This is a fine way to wake me on a Sunday morning. Hello, Monsignor, Father."

Devlin smiles and calls me over. The two priests excuse themselves and leave the room. I clasp the Chief's hand. It is pure white, cold, and bony.

"Michael, I knew it would have to come some day."

Devlin's breathing is labored. His words are slow, a total effort.

"I'm glad I saw the little girl. She's beautiful. Take good care of her. Little girls are the smile of God, you know."

"I will, Chief. But don't talk any more. Save your strength. You've earned a rest."

Devlin persists. "Michael, I want you to do one last thing for me. Monsignor Torrone has the key to my apartment. I want you to have that ivory chess set. Use it and keep it in your family. When you play, think of me. Remember, be careful and think everything out before you make a move."

"Thanks, Chief. Now get some rest. When you get out of here, you'll give me the set yourself." Devlin nods weakly and his eyes close. He falls into a deep sleep of fatigue and medication. Monsignor Torrone returns and stays by his side. He waits for Casper Nardino. I drive Father Baldini to the parish rectory.

At 10:00 AM that Sunday morning, with two childhood friends at his side, Chief Collin Devlin dies in his sleep.

On Tuesday, I attend the Devlin wake. Mourners spill out of the Ryan Funeral Home and line the sidewalk across from St. Raymond's Church. I sit with my Uncle Aldo. Flower wreaths hang on the walls all around us.

"Michael, thank you for speaking with the young man. He has a hard time. It's not for me to judge his father. That's up to

God. I only want my daughter to be happy. If there's no happiness for her with her husband, then let her be happy with her son.

"Little Aldo came to me yesterday for the first time. And we talked. We talked like you and I used to speak. Do you remember, Michael?"

"I remember, Uncle."

"And when you were sixteen and you ran on the streets, do you remember that I told you that the days of the *procione* were over?" The old man taps his fingers on his knees and gently rocks back and forth. "As your godfather spoke to you then, you've spoken to your godson and my grandson. I'm proud of you. I'm glad our time was well spent." Turning his head to me, he purses his lips like he's going to cry. "You know, the boy told me he loved me. Then we hugged each other. All of us together, we'll save him. And his mother will be happy.

"Mr. Devlin lies there before us where I'll soon be. He and I spent much time together at Michele's celebration. We broke bread and he spoke of you at every chance. In some ways, my son, you're very fortunate. You never had a father who you could know well, but you had three fathers who loved you very much—your father, Mr. Devlin, and myself."

Tears well up in the old man's eyes and I squeeze his arm. Aldo Rancolo sits with his life all around him. There is nothing he can change except directions for the future.

* * *

The informant: The testimony of Joe Valachi (1904–1971) against the Cosa Nostra before the U.S. Senate Committee on Government Operations provided federal authorities with the first proof of the mafia's existence. Among those whose activities he described were Vito Genovese, Carlo Gambino, Tommy Lucchese, Joseph Bonanno, and Joseph Colombo.

The Don: Vito "Don Vito" Genovese (1897–1969) was head of the Genovese crime family.

Top brass: Tommy Lucchese (1899–1967) was identified as a leading member by Valachi in his testimony.

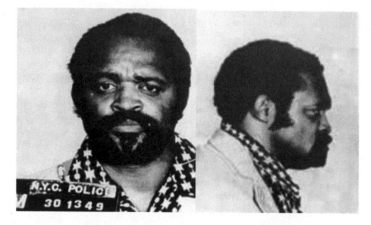

The king: Nicky Barnes (b. 1933), Harlem drug kingpin.

Meredith Hunter (1951–1969) at the Rolling Stones' 1969 Altamont, California, concert, 1969. Hells Angels in foreground. Hells Angels member Alan David Passaro (d. 1985) was tried for the stabbing death of Hunter but later acquitted. The case was reopened in 2005 but closed soon after.

CHAPTER 12

SUNSHINE DINER

"Mike, do you remember discussing the major conspiracy case with Tommy St. John about five years ago?" asks Treasury Agent Johnny Napolitano.

"Yeah, I remember it, Johnny. The damn list he had looked like something out of the National Crime Archives. He wanted me to give him everybody on that list whether they were guilty or not."

"Yeah, and you said something about it looking like a wedding invitation for some Don's daughter."

"Why are we talking about that now, Nap? That was a long time ago."

"That was my case, Mike. St. John was working with me and I asked him to sit with you. I know you have a lot of input and a lot of files on these people. I know some of these guys are friends of yours but I know that with you the job always comes first. And I know you keep private matters private. All the time we sit with Buck and break bread, we never talk business. This is different. This *is* business. I've always respected your judgment."

I sit up stiffly. "You mean to sit here now and tell me, after five years, that you were the guy who made up that phony list? After all the times we sat together, over food and over cases, you didn't come to me direct."

"It couldn't go down any other way, Mike," says Napolitano with an empty grin. "I had to stay in the background. I had my bird to protect and I wasn't going near anybody at the time."

I nod. "Yeah, I guess I wouldn't of had the balls either, Johnny, but not because of the bird. That case never smelled right. It was bad. Every damned one of those guys was framed. St. John knew it. You knew it. Everybody knew it. Mickey Mouse could have been on that hit list and he would have been indicted."

"What's the difference how they went, Mike? They were all dirty at one time or another. How else are we going to get these bastards off the street?"

"Yeah, but you knew they weren't dealing in junk. But I guess that's your problem, Johnny. You have to live with it. Now tell me what's on your mind."

* * *

MICHAEL PALERMO

Five years ago, Tommy St. John comes to me with a list. We meet in a luncheonette on Boston Road. St. John unfolds a white sheet of paper with a list of handwritten names. There are over forty names. Almost everybody I know in the whole underworld is on this list.

"Mike, I'm working on this case and my information is that these people are all part of a big heroin operation. Before we move on them, I'd like you to tell me how many of these names you recognize as to moving drugs."

I look. I know most of the names. What the hell is St. John up to? How did he put this list together? His bird can't be that strong or he wouldn't be sitting with me. I know that the people I know that are on the list aren't into drugs. They wouldn't be caught dead with their hands in drugs. It's too dirty and there's too much heat.

They're into gambling, loan sharking, protection. Stuff like that. St. John's looking for me to make his case.

"I'll tell you, Johnny, I can't tell you how many of these people are into drugs, but I can tell you how many that I know wouldn't be found dead with their hands in drugs. It's too dirty and too hot. These are quiet people who don't like any heat."

"Here's a pencil, Mike. Scratch out the names of the people who aren't involved." St. John stands over the table like a vulture over pigeon meat.

"Let me see. I know this guy wouldn't go near drugs." I scratch out Carmine Canicatti's name. "Here are some more." I scratch out Nardino, Tony Tremato, Patsy Vaccaro, Johnny Castlevetrano, Johnny Brescetti, Buck Truccolini. I remove the names of my friends. After two minutes, the list is down to twenty-five names.

"These other guys, I don't know anything about them."

"What about this guy, Rosetti?"

"Nah, I don't know him."

"How about this guy, Guido Gambelli?"

"I heard of him. The word is out that he's into numbers and artichokes. But I don't know him either. He'd a real old-timer. He was a very powerful man years ago. Hey, Johnny, let me ask you, just how strong is your pipeline? I mean, you got some people on there who don't belong. How can you be sure the others do?"

"It's a strong line, Mike. It's from the inside. We have testimony that will put these people away for a long time. But it doesn't really matter too much how dirty they are now. All of these guys got a little dirt on their hands and under the rug. It doesn't really matter what we get them on as long as we get them."

"Looks to me like a goddamn wedding invitation for some don," I say, shaking my head. "But I tell you this, those guys aren't going to like the reception."

"They don't have to like it. Nobody likes getting caught."

"Yeah, Tommy, but what these guys aren't going to like worse is getting caught for something they didn't do. I don't want to be in your shoes, man, when they get out and find out who put them away. Of course, my lips are sealed forever."

* * *

In five years, St. John dies from lung cancer. Rosetti squirms off the list. Some of my friends are put back on the list, and Guido Gambelli and nineteen other guys are convicted and are serving long terms in federal prisons across the country. And now this sonofabitch tells me that this was his case all along. When is it ever going to sink in about this guy? When am I ever going to stop trusting him?

Napolitano leans forward. "Just listen. Now we got a chance to set things straight. Those twenty guys were put away by the testimony of Joe Bops."

"Joe Bop. That's Joe Abruzzi. I remember him. On the streets they call him a scumbag."

"Well, he ain't such a bad guy. His people caught him skimming and they put out a contract on him. He had no choice. It was either him or them. So he put them in the slammer and we put him in our witness protection program. Now Joe feels he's not getting everything he was promised. He says he's a prisoner."

"Yeah, but at least he's alive. But he's got to live with himself. The poor bastard. What did he expect? The minute he puts his head out on the street, they're going to chop it off. He went into this thing with his eyes open. Did he think he was going to come out smelling like a rose?"

"I'm sure he was just looking to stay alive. But now he says he's ready to change his story and swear that he was forced to say what he did. He was scared and threatened. He said what he did under duress. Anyway, that's going to be his new story. Now he just wants to help those guys."

"Just like that, Johnny? Just out of the blue like that?"

"Just like that, Mike—for 250,000 bucks."

"Two hundred and fifty grand? What are you, nuts? Where do I fit into this? What am I supposed to do for you and that rat?"

"Look at it his way. This is a chance for twenty guys to walk. They can cut it up twenty ways. Twelve five apiece. And there's nothing in it for me. It all goes to Joe and his family. He's got a wife and kids. If you can handle the contract, ten grand off the top is yours."

"Look, Johnny, I don't want any part of this. Those guys all went down on a bad rap. This whole deal stinks. If this bird wants to cleanse his soul, all he's got to do is sing an encore."

"Mike, you know as well as me that he's not gonna last ten minutes on the street when these guys are out. They already had a contract out on him before he sang. What are they going to do now, kill him 100 times? Once will still do the job. He needs the cash to get lost, to get out of the country, to take care of his family, and to stay alive."

I wave my finger at Nap. "I can't promise anything. But I'll reach out and see if there's any interest. As far as I'm concerned, we never met. But I'll be in touch with you either way. Just sit on it."

"That's the way I want it. There'll be plenty of interest. Keep me out of it. You handle it."

* * *

The Merritt Parkway snakes through the black Connecticut countryside. Buck Truccolini chews on a long Havana cigar as we drive. Smoke from his mouth blows across the dashboard, hitting the windshield, swirling back in brown clouds and floating up into my face.

"I tell ya, Mike, you come to me with this thing and I gotta tell ya I ain't heard nothin' like it before. It's way outta my league. Are you sure you ain't gettin' double-banged?" Buck screws his ahead around toward me.

"I hope to hell I ain't, Buck. I told this guy I don't want any part of this deal. But we gotta do what's right. Those guys all took a bad fall. The feds never had them right. Who the hell knows what can be done? We'll give it a shot and see what your people say."

"Yeah," snorts Buck, "and remember what I told ya, get in, bring them together, and get out. Ain't nobody gonna look after you if later on people start gettin' burned."

The car pulls off the parkway and rolls down a country road into Greenwich. Stone walls slip by the windows. House and field lights brighten the lawns of manicured estates. The neighborhood is money, respectable, and secure. Buck makes a right turn into a private drive and stops at a black iron gate that drapes across two stone pillars. He gets out of the car and speaks into an intercom that is set into stonework. The gates open, activated by a control in the main building.

We ride up a tree-lined drive. Buck says his last words for the evening. "Like I said, I hope you remember how to get here because after tonight we won't ever be comin' back here together."

"I remember."

"And don't be surprised if they ask for your piece. Give it to 'em. You got nothin' to worry about tonight. Tonight you're with me. I brought you here. Later on, you're gonna be on your own."

As the car reaches the front of the fieldstone mansion, the entrance door opens. Anthony Tremato stands in the doorway. He is a caporegime in the Valerio Fredoni Family of Fordham. I'm brought into the library where the don is waiting for me. He's sipping brandy with his consigliere, Gaetano Carini. I know that Tremato has now assumed full control of his district after Cheech Scarmello took his permanent vacation.

Buck didn't know that Fredoni would never ask for my gun. There was no need. The don and I have known each other for over fifteen years, ever since Commander Hecter had me on wiretap duty in the basement of the haberdashery store tapping the phones of the United Cigar store opposite the Yankee Stadium where I destroyed all the gambling operations in the Bronx, all this while I didn't even know what the hell I was doing. Fredoni was the one who had the Bronx Borough Commander Deputy Chief Inspector Hecter on the pad. When I came out of the basement one day, two guys escorted me to the candy store on the corner where Fredoni bought me a malted and told me the facts of life personally. I never had much to do with him but from time to time our paths crossed.

"Mike. Welcome. You're looking fine."

"Thanks, Valerio. It's good to see you again. It's been a lot of years."

"I want you to meet Tani Carini. He'll join us tonight so we can get to the bottom of this. First, let's have some brandy." Fredoni pours three glasses. "It was quite a time we had together, Mike. Old Chief Hecter and you destroyed the Bronx. I told Tani about it. Imagine a green cop in a basement killing everybody's action. But that soon passed, as it always does. Now tell me, what's this all about that you talked to Buck about? I was told that for 250 grand, twenty of our people can walk out of federal prisons when this Joe Bops changes his testimony. Is that right?"

"That's what this Fed told me."

"Who's the fed?" asks Carini.

"At this stage, he doesn't want his name known."

Fredoni looks at me intensely. "You understand, Mike, we have to know who we're doing business with. If you're the only one we sit with, then we regard you as the man in charge. As for me, we sit with, then we regard you as the man in charge. As for me, I can accept that. But if something goes wrong, can you accept the responsibility?"

"No, I can't and I don't want it. What I want is to get your people together and you take it from there."

Fredoni's eyes turn to his consigliere and a message passes in the air. "OK, Mike. I'll talk to the right people and tomorrow night I'll meet with you here and give you our answer. But remember one thing, my friend. We put our lives and honor in each other's hands. Be careful. *Ciao!* I'll have somebody drive you back to the city."

The next night I find my way through Greenwich and sit again in the Fredoni library. There is another man with us. He is Guido Gambelli. The man in federal prison.

He is on a medical furlough so that he can receive treatment for cancer. He sits next to the don and assumes the reins of power. He is still a don and a man of great influence. After the introductions and greetings, I sit opposite three very intent men.

Gambelli is first. "What can you tell us about the man who made this proposal to you?"

"I can tell you this, Guido, I personally don't trust him and if I were you I would walk away from this whole deal. I'm just bringing you together. Now you do what you feel is right. I don't want any part of it."

"We can't walk away from it. There are too many families who have been hurt by this and suffer more every day. We have to go with it. But I have to see this federal agent face to face. I have to look into his eyes. Tell him that you have made the arrangements, and he has to meet with the people who make the decisions. Tell him we want assurances, and then we'll make the payment."

As Gambelli speaks, a gray cast draws over his face, a sickly shade of a man who has slept with ghosts.

"I'll tell him what you said, Guido. I don't know if he'll go for it. I think he's a little worried himself how big this thing is. There are guys in six federal prisons around the country. The federal government is involved. Personally, I don't know how the hell this is going to work."

Gambelli's eyes glint with a spark of life.

"Worried men are weak men. Let's see how strong he is with his offer made man-to-man. For your safety and ours, there can't be any other way. We have to deal with strength or his contract isn't worth his word." Gambelli moves his hand palm down from his chest to me, signifying that the meeting is over. We have coffee and cake and talk of other things, of the old days, of Hecter and wires, and of cigar stores.

The next day, Napolitano squeals when I tell him that he has to make a personal appearance or there's no deal.

"You handle it, Mike. You don't need me. I can't meet with those people. I put them away."

"They're not interested in you, Johnny. They just want to get their people out and make sure you're on the level. And that everything is handled the right way." I was after his ass.

"Gambelli is already out and I talked to him myself."

"Gambelli is out? And YOU TALKED TO HIM? How the hell can he be out?"

"He's out on a medical furlough. He says he wants to look into your eyes. And Johnny, when he looks, I hope for your sake everything he sees is clean."

"I ain't goin', Mike. You think I'm crazy? That guy remembers me. I testified against him! Joe Bops is my bird!"

"Nothing is going to be discussed except this business deal. These people are from the old values. They act by instinct. You'll go in there with me and you'll come out with me. It's strictly business. When you leave, you might have a deal. Gambelli will keep his word. I give you mine. This is your deal, and if you want it to go down, you gotta be there."

"All right," says Nap staring at me wildly. "I trust you, Mike. Remember that. Pick me up at eight. You're in the driver's seat."

"No, Johnny, you're in the driver's seat tomorrow."

That evening, five men sit in the Fredoni library. I can see Nap's legs shaking under the table. I know his gut is light and itchy. I sit next to him on a small sofa, a fireplace on our left. Fredoni and Gambelli sit across from us and Carini is in a chair to the right. The three of them can watch Napolitano's face from all sides. No gesture or movement will be missed. Johnny Nap is on trial. He has walked into the wolf's den with his eyes wide open. It was easy for him to find trouble. To get free is the art. He passes his first test when he lets Tony Tremato search him in the sitting room where he finds no wires or transmitters. I felt this was no insult to me because even I didn't trust the bastard.

Gambelli is in charge again.

"And now, Mr. Federal Agent, you come to us with a plan you say can bring some people out of prison. This is important to us because we all have families who have been hurt by this thing. And you say Mr. Abruzzi will say that his testimony against us was false. That is quite true, you know. You say we have to pay $250,000 and you will give this all to Abruzzi. That's a very fine thing for you to do. A very unselfish gesture. I'm sure you're a man of your word."

Napolitano can't stay quiet. "Guido, what you say is true, but I do have some expenses that have to come off the top."

"That's understandable," says Gambelli. "I'm glad you're being honest with us. You understand we can only do business if we're all honest with each other."

"Of course," assures Napolitano. "That's the only way I work. Ask Mike here. He'll tell you."

"You're here tonight only because Mike brought you. And that's the only reason you're going to leave here tonight, because he brought you. He's already told us all about you."

Johnny relaxes a little and sits back in the sofa. He doesn't know that I told them that he can't be trusted.

Gambelli, sensing that Johnny is disarmed for the moment, leans forward, his eyes burning into Napolitano's, and says, "I will give you $500,000 for Mr. Abruzzi if you will give Mr. Abruzzi to me."

A dead silence blankets the room. There is no sound. No breathing. No movement. Napolitano's face blanks for a moment while he thinks it over. I know what is going through his mind. He's got a chance to make a cool half-million all for himself. Nobody knows. No taxes. No years of hard work to make that much. His eyes dart from don to don to Carini. He turns to me like I betrayed him. Like if he doesn't give up Abruzzi to these guys, he doesn't walk out of here tonight. I meet his eyes head on and gently raise my forehead as if to say, "So what do you do now, Johnny?"

Nap breaks into a nervous, empty laugh like a man caught in bed with another man's wife. "No, no, no. I can't do that. That's not the deal. Mike told you how it's got to go down."

The smart sonofabitch knows that if he makes the double-bang on Abruzzi, then these guys here can't trust him and he'll never live to spend the money. And if they can't trust him they won't even make the deal and then this night is a total waste. He sure thought fast. Imagine that. He turned down a half-mill.

Gambelli squints and his gray lips curl over his teeth as he speaks. "It'll be worth it for both of us, Johnny." He speaks softly, as if he accepts Napolitano as one of the Family. A spider's allure into the web. "And then you'll leave here with a lot of strong new friends."

Johnny sits on the edge of the sofa. "Guido, you say we have to be honest with each other. I can't give you Abruzzi. If I did, I could never look at myself in the mirror again. I have to live with myself after all this is over. It's no good for anybody the way things are now. Not for you, Abruzzi, or all the others. I'm just trying to help you all out. For twelve and a half grand each, you and them can all walk.

"When Abruzzi took you all down, I believed him. So did the judge and the jury. I was just doing my job. Now Mike tells me that it was a bum rap and I'm just trying to do the right thing."

Gambelli sits back in his chair, exhausted. The strain of the evening has drained him. He snaps the back of his right hand at Fredoni, giving him the floor. With no emotion, no expression on his face, he lays out the contract.

Fredoni takes over. "The money will be paid. It will be my money. There will be no negotiations on the price. You'll receive $250,000 for which we'll receive Abruzzi's deposition and the release of our people. We'll arrange for a lawyer to meet with Abruzzi and take his statement. There will be every legal protection for both sides. When our people are out, you'll receive the money."

"Valerio," says Johnny, "it can't work that way. You know Joe Abruzzi has a contract out on him, and it wouldn't make any sense for anybody to know where he is. I'll make all the arrangements and when everything is completed and when your people are out, I'll take payment and give it to Joe."

"As you wish," says Fredoni. "It's important that this be done right away."

"Certainly. I understand," says Napolitano. "I'll get right on it tonight."

Two weeks later, Joe Bops Abruzzi gives a revised sworn statement in a Supreme Court closed-door hearing. The federal government does not risk exposure or embarrassment by opening up a new trial. The presiding judge orders the twenty prisoners released for time served. Federal agent Johnny Napolitano receives $250,000, of which, I find out later, he passes $150,000 to Joe Abruzzi. Nap has personal operating expenses which he has to cover, so he says. Only the five people in the Fredoni library and Joe Bops Abruzzi ever know that the Gambelli package of freedom has been bought. Joe Abruzzi remains in hiding today under a fictitious name. His contract remains open.

I never receive the $10,000 that Nap promised me, and I never ask for it until I sit with Jim Groty a month later.

We sit in a rear booth. A sizzling hot pizza steams between us. We wait for the oil to cool and talk business. I hand Jimmy over a fat envelope of money.

"Jimmy, here's the ten grand that Augie Coletti gave me. I just want to go over it again so that there are no misunderstandings. He's cut clean from the case against Rosetti and the matter is dead. No more tails. No more surveillance."

"That's right, Mike. I'll pass this on to those people today and as long as he doesn't walk into anything else, he's clean. As far as everybody is concerned, the case is closed."

"The kid had to scrape up everything he had to come up with this. I even had to put 800 bucks of my own money into it. They're really hurting him." I pour my beer and loosen a large piece of pizza strung with gooey cheese. The tip flops over as I lift it out and the oil runs off. The first bite is always the best. Tangy, hot, and smooth. Strings of mozzarella stretch from mouth to hand. "This is fantastic, Jim."

Groty agrees. We clink beer glasses, sealing the Coletti contract and begin a new point of business. I chew and swallow and ask, "Jim, let me ask you out of curiosity, who's taking the bag on this one?"

Groty is puzzled. "You mean you don't know, Mike?"

"No, I don't know."

He hesitates. "Well, I thought you knew. I think we ought to drop it. What's the difference?"

"No, no. Who's the man behind this contract? We go back a long way, Jimmy and this is no big deal."

"Mike, you sit with the guy almost every day."

"I sit with him?"

"For Chrissakes, don't you guys even talk to each other over dinner?"

My mind clicks picture frames, ten a second. Like a machine, I edit my life. The film stops at Amen's, Buck and me at dinner with . . . Johnny Napolitano. The camera of my mind closes in for a close-up of Johnny's face with an empty grin, a nervous laugh. Goddammit! Does he have his fingers in everything? Doesn't anything go down without him knowing or having a piece of it?

Groty sips some beer and grins. "He's like Jesus Christ. He travels in mysterious ways."

I shake my head. "No, he's more like bullshit. He's all over the place."

Groty makes a face. "Come on, Mike. I'm eating."

"I'm sorry." I take another slice of pizza. "Jim, let's forget about Nap. I want to thank you and Dempsey for what you did for my cousin Aldo. Tell me, how'd that go down?"

"Dempsey, Coltrane, and me were staking out Donny Dixon's candy store on 123rd Street. Dixon runs a nickel bag operation for Albie Simmons. Simmons is one of Nicky Barnes' key men."

"I know Barnes. He's the only black guy who can deal direct with the Italians. The stuff he gets is close to pure."

"Right. So Dempsey and me sit on Dixon's action while Coltrane walks the streets. He blends in like one of them. I don't know how the bastard does it. He's gonna get his ass busted someday either by one of them or by one of our guys who don't know him. Anyway, this kid ain't too smart. No offense, Mike."

I wave him on. "He ain't too smart to be sticking needles into his arms either, Jimmy."

"Right. So this white kid pulls up in front of Dixon's and goes into the store. We wait and we watch. The kid pulls away and we grab him on 140th street just when he's clear but not close enough for us to burn our surveillance. We question him and he says he was lookin' to shack up with one of those broads down there. Under his seat we find three nickel bags of junk. He says he don't know how they got there. Dempsey rolls up the kid's sleeves and he's got tracks running up both arms.

"I tell you, Mike, he would have taken a fall right there but he dropped your name. I told him he was lucky and that this one was on us. I made it clear that I was going to talk to you about it. Dempsey told him he better straighten himself out and that if we catch him in this neighborhood again, we're going to break his ass. The kid shit and we ain't seen him since."

I nod. "Thanks, Jimmy. Pass it on to Dempsey if you see him before I do."

I walk away with the check. Jim Groty leaves with $10,000 in his pocket in an envelope earmarked for Johnny Napolitano and the federal agents who set Coletti free.

* * *

MICHAEL PALERMO

My cousin was used to doing business as one of the buyers of Nicky Barnes' heroin operation. Barnes runs the smoothest drug business ever in existence. It's virtually foolproof. The buys and payoffs go down without a risk. He has a million-dollar business from a nickel bag operation. Barnes sells his wholesalers $15 bags for $45. They resell them for $75.

At four o'clock in the morning, one of Barnes' many black cars cruises Harlem. Inside are five black experienced killers—bombers. They stop at certain street corners and collect money from the buyers. At ten in the morning, they cruise again. This time they write out and hand out slips of paper. From corner to corner, drop points have been memorized, distributed, and forgotten. Beforehand, between four and ten, package drops of heroin have been deposited under stairwells, on rooftops, taped under counters, in telephone booths, in garbage cans, under cars, behind loose bricks in building walls, under washroom sinks, and in a thousand other hiding places. After they receive their sheets of paper with the drop addresses, the wholesalers score and go retail.

The riders in the black cars have very limited vulnerability. If they're stopped and searched, the only thing found is cash. At times they carry over $200,000. The word on the street is that they carry shotguns and automatic weapons. Even cops and neighborhood cowboys don't want to tangle with them.

Nicky Barnes sends five black killers in a black car and runs the Harlem nickel bag operation. He's too smart to get caught. Little guys like Donny Dixon are busted from time to time. The Barneses and the Simmonses are too smart and too well protected to get caught.

* * *

After discovering that Johnny Napolitano was collecting from both the Gambelli and Coletti payoffs, I decide that the time is right for me to collect the ten grand that Nap had promised me for Gambelli. It's only right. I figure I'll give the money back to Augie minus my 800 bucks, of course. I corner the bastard at the bar at The Grotto Restaurant on Mott and Hester Streets.

"Johnny, a lot of time has passed since the Gambelli deal. I know the money went down."

"Sure, Mike, it did. And I want to thank you. I couldn't have done it without you. You did a great job and did right by those people."

"Good, I'm glad it went so well. I'm still waiting for my ten grand."

"Hey, Mike, yeah! I know we talked about it, but I had big expenses. I had a lotta hands to grease to fill that contract. There's nothin' left." He shrugs. "I didn't even get a piece for myself. But look at it this way, at least we helped a lot of people."

"Bullshit, Johnny. That'll be the day when you walk away with nothing. You guys made ten grand on Coletti alone. How much money did you lose on that deal?" I'm fuming.

"Hey, OK. I made a few bucks on that one, but it had nothing to do with Gambelli."

"Look, all I can tell you is I'm supposed to get ten grand for that contract and I want it. So go get yourself something else working and come up with it. The way you operate, every contract in New York must go through your hands. I expect it, Johnny."

"Mike, you got me wrong."

He is weaseling. I hate it when he weasels.

"If you hold me to it, I'm gonna have to dig into my own pocket."

"Then dig, Johnny. Start digging now!"

"Give me some time. Give yourself some time to think it over."

"I ain't thinking it over. I expect it."

I am mad and I leave the bar. I only met Nap there today by coincidence. I am on Mott Street to keep an appointment with Carmine Canicatti for lunch. Carmine is sitting at a table in the rear with his back to the wall. We meet from time to time as friends. No business. We eat lunch and Ross Simon comes in. I find out later that he's downtown for a Federal Crime Task Force meeting in Foley Square. I see him talking to Johnny Nap at the bar. He's worked with him before. Simon looks around and sees me in the back with Carmine and he ignores me.

The next morning, Captain Harry Jacobs calls me down to the Police Commissioner's Office. He's blunt.

"Palermo, this is the last straw. There's nobody who's gonna pull your ass out of the fire now. We got a reliable source who says he saw you yesterday consorting with a known criminal and Mafia member at The Grotto Restaurant on Mott Street. What do you have to say?"

"Captain, I was there and I had lunch with a friend. We never discussed business. It was just a social meeting. There was nothing wrong with it. I'm fed up with all this crap going down. All this guilt by association. Look, I've had fifteen years in Narco and every time I turn around there's more bullshit flying through the air around my head. I've had enough of it."

"Well, you won't have to put up with it anymore," says Jacobs. "The word is you're gonna be transferred to a squad. Talk to Captain Costello tomorrow and you two make arrangements for whatever you think is best for you and the Department. You're on your own now, Palermo."

The next morning, Captain Costello and I talk.

"Mike, I'm going to put your papers through for a transfer request. It won't be the same here without you."

"Thanks, Cap. That means a lot to me. It just seems that after Chief Devlin died, everything around me fell apart. The Chief could always patch things up and keep everything together."

"Yeah. We all miss him. I'm not going to put you in a country club assignment, Mike. Nothing like the four-five on Barkley Avenue. I think you want an active house. What do you say?"

"Absolutely, Cap. I gotta be out on the street. Put me in a busy house."

My orders come through a few days later. I'm assigned to the four-two under Captain Jake Squibb. The four-two is under the command of District Commander Inspector John O'Hagan. O'Hagan maintains his command offices in the building of the four-two. It's a stroke of fate that throws me and O'Hagan together again. We became good friends at the two-three. O'Hagan had been a Squad Commander at the East Harlem precinct house. It was in the two-three that Lenny Lombardi almost killed Dominic Gatti with a bag over his head.

While at the four-two, I keep my dinner meetings with Buck at Amen's Restaurant in Pelham Bay. After a few weeks of squad work, we have a big dinner together.

"Buck, this guy Napolitano is nothing but a two-faced snake. You know you never really know people. Today you think you know them and tomorrow they're a stranger and you're left holding the bag."

"What's the matter, Mike? What's your beef with Johnny?"

"That double-banging weasel owes me ten grand for the Gambelli contract and now he's giving me some bullshit about high overhead."

"Is that so important to you, Mike?"

"I'll tell you why it is, Buck. This bastard also just finished shaking down a friend of mine for ten grand. I wound up going down with part of the bread to somebody in the middle, and I don't find out until later that Napolitano is the man. I've got to find out second hand like I'm the fool."

I'm really upset and Buck tries to calm me down.

"I understand how you feel, Mike, but take it easy. We don't want nothin' to queer that Gambelli deal. It's important to a lot of people. We don't want nothin' to come back to cause any problems. Do you understand?"

I nod. "Yeah. I understand, Buck. But I can't see lettin' this guy walk away with a loaf of bread under each arm and him bullshittin' that he's in the poor house. We had a deal, Buck, and I want to see the bastard keep his part of the contract."

"Mike, I'll give you the ten grand. Just let it be. I tell you, we don't want any trouble." Buck stops eating and stares at me intensely.

"I understand, Buck, but I just can't let him get away with it."

Buck frowns. "Shut up and eat. Don't ruin a good meal. We'll talk later."

The next time I see Napolitano is two nights later at Amen's. We meet before Buck arrives. Nap passes me a fat white envelope.

"Here you are, Mike. I want you to know this is like taking a pound of flesh. I had to dig into my savings for this. But a deal is a deal."

"OK, Johnny. How much is in here?"

"Ten grand, like we agreed."

"Do I have to count it?"

"Are you kidding? After all we've been through?" The sonofabitch smiles and I feel like counting it.

"It's all there, Mike. If it ain't, your dinner's on me tonight."

Later that evening, I count out $10,000.

At the Rafters I return $9,200 to Augie and get my 800 back. Augie is working with Carmine and he's doing real good. He's moving up. I feel good. Maybe some day I'll need friends in high places.

CHAPTER 13

I'm a squad detective in the four-two precinct now and District Commander Inspector John O'Hagan and I are eating Irish sourdough bread with raisins and sipping coffee. O'Hagan has earned the reputation throughout his career as being impeccably honest. Everything he does, he's done by the book. It's refreshing being under his command.

"Mike, it's been a long time since we crossed paths in the two-three. What are you doing in a squad? You were one of the hottest narcs in the Bureau."

"I'll tell you, Inspector, after fifteen years, I felt I needed a change of scenery. I want to stay active and it looks like I pulled a good house to work in."

"I'm glad you're with us. We need people who can do the job, but more importantly we need people who have a little humanity in them. If it hadn't been for the way you talked to Lombardi back in the two-three, that Gatti kid would be a cripple today. Whatever happened to Gatti anyway?"

"I haven't seen him around. Nobody has. He disappeared. I think somebody dumped him. He just never turned up."

"Mike, I sent for you today because I want to put you to work for me on a special assignment. You have priceless years of street experience. I want you to work on a precinct level on a case that nobody has been able to crack. Every time we get close to this guy, he takes off. He's like a jungle cat. He senses everything that's going on.

"As you know, my district consists of four precincts. The four-oh, two, four, and eight. This case involves all of Harlem.

"You also know that the bulk of the Harlem drug traffic is controlled by Nicky Barnes. One of his two underbosses is Albie Simmons. Simmons is running his junk through my district like a sewer rat and I want it stopped. Now I'm not an overly religious man, but I feel it was the Man upstairs who sent you here to me. I want this Simmons and I want him right."

As soon as I hear the name "Simmons," the fires go on inside my head. They burn as I hear Jim Groty say once again, "Dixon runs a nickel bag operation for Albie Simmons. Dixon, Simmons, the guys who hooked needles into my cousin Aldo's arms. I inhale deeply, trying to relax. O'Hagan can't know. If he thinks I have a personal vendetta against Simmons, he won't put me on the case. O'Hagan won't know.

"OK. Inspector. I'm your man and I'm looking forward to it."

"Good. Now you can pick the men you want on your team, but I know you'll be more comfortable with the men I think would be best for you."

"Whatever you say, Inspector."

"I've called a briefing in my office this morning and I'll fill you in on all the details later when we're all together. You'll be working with Eddie Williams and Arturo Gomez. Williams has been on the Force for two years. He's eager, young, and inconspicuous in the black community. But he lacks street experience. Gomez' family is from Spain. He's an expert interpreter and excellent with reports."

At the briefing O'Hagan gives us a dossier of Albie Simmons. We study the pictures, his rap sheet, current address, and apartment and phone number. He's bedded down on Lee Avenue, in the five-two. According to regulations, we notify the Borough Commander that we'll be conducting surveillance in a district outside our own.

On the first evening, we wait for hours and finally Simmons makes an appearance. He pulls up to the front of the building in a sleek Lincoln Continental. The car sparkles, well waxed, with a special two-tone paint of light champagne tan and dark champagne brown. In the roof is a motorized moon roof. The car is elegant like something the Liberian ambassador would drive. Simmons doesn't want to be mistaken for a "petty pink pimp" as he calls them. Albie Simmons takes no chances with his life. All the glass, the cockpit walls, roof, and floors are bullet proof. He's in a dangerous business, one in which friends can turn on him overnight.

Every day Gomez fills out the reports that O'Hagan wants submitted on a daily basis.

Simmons lives with his wife and daughter in an apartment rented in his wife's maiden name. Every morning Simmons routinely comes home like any loving husband after a tiring night's work. He's got more regular hours than a cop has. The superintendent of the apartment house is very cooperative with our team. He doesn't know that the occupant of apartment 4G is a drug dealer killer. He even gives us an empty flat in the same building and a layout of the Simmons' lair.

We decide we need a search warrant and wiretap from the District Attorney. A meeting takes place in the conference room of Senior Assistant District Attorney Robert Scott, who is the chief of the Narcotics Bureau. Scott is a light-skinned black man who, no matter how he tries, can never pass for white. He works closely with his boss, District Attorney Ross Simon. Scott always personally processes and finalizes any request for search warrants or phone taps. He wants to be on top of every narcotics case. He's a graduate of New York University Law School, and after ten years has worked his way up to Bureau Chief, Narcotics Section.

I sit in the conference room with Gomez, Williams, District Commander O'Hagan, Scott, his assistant James Adams, and a staff clerk. Scott is complaining.

"I don't know why you guys are jumping over precinct lines with this case. It's a narcotics case. I don't see why you don't leave it to Narco and us. What are you tryin' to be? Some kind of hot shots looking for glory? Why wasn't I informed about this investigation?"

And then Scott stares at me like I'm making some kind of trouble in Paradise. O'Hagan gets his hackles up.

"Just a minute, Scott." The fur stands up of the nape of O'Hagan's neck. His lower jaw juts forward like a lance in battle. "We're looking to work and coordinate with all appropriate agencies. You're being notified right now. That's why we're here today. To do a job in my district that needs to be done. We're here and these men are on the case because I assigned them to it. You're not about to tell me how to run my office, are you?"

Scott backs down. "No, of course not, Inspector. What do you guys have and what do you want?"

I push the paperwork in front of him. Everything's in order. Scott is still hesitant.

"Look, Mr. Scott," I say, "this guy Simmons is dealing junk all over Harlem. You know it and we know it. Everybody knows it. We got him right. On the stakeout we see packages going in and out of that apartment in the hands of known drug dealers who have been observed entering and leaving the premises. Nobody's been able to nail this guy so far. And nobody knows why. He's more slippery than greased pig and chitlins. Get us the warrant and the phone tap and we'll put Simmons in your pocket."

Scott looks at me funny. Like he doesn't like my remark about the pig and chitlins. Screw him. It's the truth.

"OK. I'm convinced. You got it. Laurie, call Judge Bolton and tell him we'll be right over for him to sign some papers. Mike, how soon will it be before you get the tap in?"

"Well, I don't know. I guess it'll take about a day to get GIB to get the job done. Probably tomorrow some time."

After the papers are signed, Inspector O'Hagan pulls some strings and speeds things up. He calls the right people in GIB, people who had worked under his command when he had served in that Bureau. The wire goes in early and the tap is hooked into Madeline Jones' phone, apartment 4G—Simmons' home. We go home for a good night's rest. We plan to resume surveillance of the building and phone tomorrow. While we sleep, the tape machine will activate and record whenever the Jones' phone is used.

Albie Simmons never returns home that morning. He is working cops' hours. His heroin factory cuts and processes the drug after it's shipped from Nicky Barnes' plant. Barnes' Italian contact, the man he does business with, is Vincent Gennaro. Gennaro belongs to the Colucino Family, which controls the Brooklyn waterfront. Gennaro is directly responsible to the Don's son, Jimmy Colucino.

The bulk heroin packages received from Gennaro are cut into smaller packages in Barnes' plant and then sent to factories throughout the city, factories controlled by Barnes' two underbosses, Monroe Benson and Albie Simmons. At the factory the heroin is cut with quinine, dextrimaltose milk sugar, or mannite. It's then packed in $5 bags and wrapped fifteen to a package and distributed to the retailers. Most of these small businessmen are addicts themselves and sell only as much as they have to in order to support their habits. They use the rest themselves. It's not unusual for them to re-cut and dilute nickel bags with more milk sugar. Skim is the name of the game. It's a dangerous game that often ends in murder. Hundreds of new young addicts wait in doorways to take the nickel hawkers' places. The street corner nickel-and-dime-baggers surround themselves with their own protection and small armies dressed in rags control street slices of each district. Territorial control is sacrosanct and well-guarded.

Before I go home this evening, I have dinner with Buck and Johnny Nap at Amen's. Johnny and me healed our wounds and now we talk about the big Italian-American rally that's going to take place in the city this weekend. It's organized by Jimmy Colucino.

"It's about time somebody did something like this," says Buck. "They been smearin' our names every chance they get. People oughta know there are a lot of other people in the business. I mean, look at the arsenal gang. Those Irish guys would cut your throat for a dime. You can't walk down in Hell's Kitchen no more."

Napolitano looks up. "Everybody's got a piece of the action. The Jews, the blacks, the blues, the greens, and the reds." He grins and slurps a spaghetti string between his lips.

"Hey, what the hell's he talkin' about, Mike?"

"Buck, you know Johnny's always good for a laugh."

"What do you say, Mike? You gonna go down with us Saturday? I got twenty buses rented. People are coming from all over with flags and banners. Thousands of 'em. There's gonna be a big mob down there. Afterwards you'll go to a private party with me. There are gonna be a lot of politicians and big people there. It's gonna be the social event of the year." Buck laughs and digs into his lasagna with both hands.

"I got business, Buck. It's gonna keep me tied up. But if I can make it, I'll let you know."

"How 'bout you, Johnny?"

"Sure, I'm gonna go. I'll do anything to help the Italians. What the hell are friends for, anyway?"

The next morning we beat the sun up. A large moving van is parked in front of the Simmons' building. Furniture is rolling out the door. There's a big move going on. Gomez checks the phone machine in the basement. The tape has run out and the reel is spinning, flapping a loose tail of tape. It had to take hours of phone time to use all that tape. There must be a lot of heavy conversation. And the machine is still going. Gomez slips on the earphones. Simmons' teenage daughter, Aretha, is talking freely, nonstop.

"Yeah, Shirley. Ain't that a shame? Here we go again. We finally settled down for a bit and now we gotta move again. Those damn cops are after my father again. I don't know why they don't just leave my poor daddy alone. They ain't give us nothin' but grief. They suppose to put a tap on this phone later today. My poor mama is packin' up all the junk around here and we gonna get out fast. We goin' to my Grandma Hattie's. I don't know the address or the phone number, but I'll call you when I get there.

"Now tell me how ya hittin' it off with Lionel? Did you let him score yet?"

Gomez drops the ear set and scoops up the tape reel. He races out to the stakeout car. I sit in the rear seat. Williams enters the building and watches men and furniture zip by him. People are moving like the place is on fire. He peers into the apartment. A teenage girl is attacking the phone receiver, her lips flapping like a flag in a windstorm. Simmons' wife is scurrying around, filling a carton with brown packages. The timing is right but Simmons isn't around. We can't hit without nailing Albie Simmons.

The furniture is loaded, and the truck begins to pull away. "You guys follow the truck and don't lose it," I say. "I'm going back to the office and listening to the tape. Call me as soon as you get the location."

Back at the precinct house I listen to the conversations on the tape with Inspector O'Hagan. The reel is filled with Simmons' daughter's conversations to her friends. An underlying theme in every call is that the cops are after her father and her phone is going to be tapped.

"They made us, Mike," says O'Hagan. "They were tipped. Somebody blew the whistle."

"Look, Inspector, nobody knew about the wire or the warrant except our people and the D.A.'s office. We got an inside rat."

I run the tape machine back and stop at the dialing clicks before a selected conversation. "This is a call to the kid's grandmother where they're supposed to be moving to. I want to get the number. I run the machine at slow speed, count the click digits and write down grandma's phone number. "I'll have Watson take this and give us the address."

O'Hagan nods. "Start getting papers ready. We're going to pay Mr. Scott another visit. I want another warrant on Simmons while Judge Bolton's pen is still warm."

I prepare the papers and return to O'Hagan's office. The phone rings. Williams is being patched through to us. "Hello, Eddie. I got the phone number and address off the tape. It's 7914 Holly Avenue."

"The hell it is," says Williams. "It's 593 Ember Street, apartment 5B. Mrs. Simmons' mother's pad. Hattie Jones."

"Well, what the hell do I have?" I look at the name on the sheet Watson gave me. "Albert Simmons. The kid must have been calling her other grandmother. OK, stay with it, Eddie. I'll be right over with another warrant."

O'Hagan leaves the room to talk with his clerical man. I take the moment to whisper to Williams, "I want you to get a wire on that line right now. This is one wire that nobody's going to know about. Use the equipment from Lee Avenue." Within minutes, Williams is on his way.

O'Hagan returns. "Mike, I had a call put through to the D.A.'s office. Scott is expecting you. I have to be gone the whole day for a meeting with the brass downtown. They're making preparations for that Italian Heritage rally Saturday at Columbus Circle. Scott's boss, Simon, is going to be at the meeting so he can coordinate things with our people. I'll tell him that he can expect some activity up here soon. I want you to call me here or at home as soon as you have something. Good luck." We shake hands. I change the address on the search warrant and proceed to meet with Scott.

"Hey, Palermo. What the hell is happening around here? You and your warrants are like vitamins, one a day. Do you have everything right this time?"

"We had everything right the last time. We're going to have Simmons right this time."

"When do you expect to hit the place?"

"That's top secret."

"Yeah, but I got a right to know. When?"

"Not until tomorrow some time. The Inspector will be gone all day and I want him in on it."

"OK, Mike. I want Simmons' ass worse than you do. Let's go visit Judge Bolton one more time."

I leave the Supreme Court building with a warrant in my pocket, a license to search the premises of 593 Ember Street, apartment 5B. The warrant reads: ". . . because of information received from an informant . . . reliable in securing three past convictions . . . saw narcotics in the apartment . . . probable cause."

Williams is on the roof inside the landing where he can keep an eye on the Hattie Jones apartment. There's no sign of Simmons. Gomez is on the phone tap in the basement. The line hasn't been used. I join Williams on the roof. "What's happening, Eddie?"

"It's quiet, Mike. No sign of Simmons. The movers left an hour ago. I haven't heard anything from Art."

In the basement the tape recorder clicks and the reels begin to spin. Art Gomez listens.

"Hey, Mrs. S. You got more stuff layin' around here, if you know what I mean?" says a man's voice.

"Bring it on over. Don't waste no time. Get it out of there fast and get it over here. Hold on."

A man's raspy voice replaces Mrs. S. "Hey, Benny. Get your ass and all that shit out o' there, man. Now! You understand me, man? Now move it!"

"I got you, Albie."

The machine stops. Gomez purrs softly, "I got you, Albie."

He arches up the stairs of a building three doors away and skirts over the rooftops to join his two partners.

"Simmons is in the apartment," says Gomez. "I just had him on the phone. What do we do now, Mike? Did you get everything we need?"

I tap my jacket over my heart.

"I was hoping we'd have O'Hagan in on this with us but this is too good to lose. Do you guys realize that nobody at all knows we're here and that Simmons is in there surrounded by his junk? Nobody knows but us."

"Shh," whispers Williams. "Somebody's coming up the stairs."

A teenage black girl knocks on the door of apartment 5B.

"Who's there?" asks a woman's voice from inside.

"It's me, Mama. It's Retha."

Bolts and bars clang and the door opens, still bound by a chain. "OK, child. Just a minute." The door closes again. The chain is removed. The door opens.

I whisper, "Go!" to my two guys. The three of us race down the stairs, pushing the girl into the apartment, smashing the door against the wall. The woman screams. I crash into the bedroom. There in the bed, bare-chested and on his way out from under the sheets, is Albie Simmons.

He looks up at me and down the barrel of my .38 and lies back down, propped up by two pillows, his hands in the air. He speaks with a face full of surprise. "Hey, man, this don't have to go down this way. There's no reason for this. Everybody can have a piece. There's enough here for everybody."

"Is that right?" I say. Williams enters the room. Gomez listens in the doorway, keeping an eye on the two women. They are sobbing on the sofa.

"That's right," says Simmons. "I'll have forty grand here for you in ten minutes. What do you say? You can go home with a big paycheck. Just one phone call is all I need."

"We can't do that, Albie."

"Why not? You know as well as I do that shit like this goes down every day."

"Not this day."

Gomez and Williams look at each other. A look of surprise laced with admiration. Before my eyes flash the needle tracks on my cousin Aldo's arms.

"Well, then, if we can't do business, at least do right by my ladies. I hear them bawling outside." Simmons puts his arms down, resting them on his legs.

"We're not looking to give your women any trouble. We just want Albie Simmons."

"Then you got him and there's no way out. There ain't nothin' this man Simmons is gonna do but go along with you and do anything you say. You be nice to those ladies there and we gonna have an easy time with no trouble. You hear?"

"Get dressed, Albie."

* * *

Ross Simon returns to the Supreme Court building from the combined services briefing that planned the strategy and intelligence gathering for the Italian Heritage rally on that coming weekend. He goes straight for Robert Scott's office.

"Bob, O'Hagan told me there's heavy activity coming down in his district. He says he's got a former narc who's going to deliver us a big man."

"That's right, Chief. O'Hagan was in here with a hot shot team, some glory boys. They wanted a warrant, the second in two days. Mike Palermo says he's going to put Albie Simmons in my pocket."

"Palermo?" screams Simon. "That sonofabitch has got hands dirtier than Simmons. Every time I turn around, this guy is hugging some guinea hood. I try cases in court and Palermo's walking by in the hall. The guy I put away runs after him and shakes his hand like he's his godfather or something.

"I don't understand the guy, Bob. Just a few weeks ago, the PC caught him with some dago mobster at The Grotto. I go to a charity fundraiser and the guy is next door shaking hands with wise guys, narcs, and feds all at the same time. I know his hands are dirty. It's just a matter of time before we get him right."

Simon pauses. "Maybe he's doing us a favor running after dope dealers right after they threw him out of Narco. Maybe that's the way he makes his money. Can't keep away from the payoffs. Maybe he's squeezing somebody and doing a favor for one of his guinea friends. Maybe he needs the money. Maybe he wants to move up and is trying to impress O'Hagan. Who the hell knows? But somehow I feel it's almost more important for us to nail Palermo than it is for us to get Simmons.

"I want you to stay on top of this case and keep me informed of everything that goes down. Palermo has lost his rabbi. Now he's on his own. There's no one who's going to bail him out this time."

The two prosecutors, at that moment, don't know that Albie Simmons has been arrested.

* * *

On the evening of the Simmons' arrest, a special dinner is being served at the Perugia Restaurant on Mulberry Street. At a round table in the private back room sit three men who head the most powerful of the New York Families.

Alberto Marcante of Harlem, Valerio Fredoni of Fordham, and Francesco Colucino of Brooklyn. Three Dons sit to conduct business. Marcante speaks first.

"Francesco, we sit with you this evening and break bread because we're friends. We've always been able to settle problems in a reasonable way."

Colucino nods.

"You have a fine son in Jimmy. He's grown up to be a strong and intelligent young man. You and Evangelina are to be complimented."

Colucino nods and smiles.

"Jimmy's working hard to protect and gain respect for our Italian Heritage. We all understand his motives and we're simpatico. But Francesco, I know you realize that every good has an evil. Take these black Sicilian olives. They're soft and ripe. But inside there's a hard pit. The man who's unaware of the pit and who bites hard through the olive meat will break a tooth and be in great pain.

"So often the young aren't aware of the pitfalls of what they do, of what the dangers are of their enthusiasm."

Colucino listens intently. It is not yet his turn to speak. He can sense that Marcante is speaking for himself and others.

"The Families of New York feel that Jimmy should end his activity in this Italian Heritage thing. We know ourselves who we are. We know our names and we respect each other. That's enough. We don't need the recognition of anybody else. You see, Francesco, this recognition is not good. This exposure to the public eye at Columbus Circle, with senators, congressmen, judges, and policemen, makes our Italian community stand out even more.

When something stands out, it becomes a target. Sooner or later a target will be shot. Shot right between the eyes, Francesco. For that is its nature.

"I know you as well as we don't want any of our people shot. The Families wish to be quiet. To conduct business in the background and not on television or the front pages of newspapers."

Marcante stops to slake a dusty throat with Chianti. He swallows, licks his lips, and points to Colucino with his jeweled pinkie.

"Do you understand what I've said, my old friend?" Marcante is finished. It is now Colucino's turn.

"Thank you, Alberto. I understand. And I have talked with my son about this very matter. You say he is strong and that's true and for that I'm slightly sad. You know the youth of today. They want everything at once, and at once they want everything. Jimmy is beyond the age of reason and I can't reason with him anymore.

"I find it difficult to hold him back. He's no longer a young child who listens to his father.

"He takes this Italian movement very seriously, like Garibaldi, Count di Cavour, and Mazzini and those of the Risorgimento. He wants to set his people free."

Fredoni has been tasting the antipasto while his two friends speak. His role is to listen and then to convince. Colucino faces two men this evening. Two can be more persuasive than one.

"Francesco," says Fredoni, "there is an old saying that when a calf has become too large to suckle, the calf must be cut free and left to graze in the fields. The same is true of sons, my friend. When a son has become too strong and too smart to obey his father, then he has become too strong and too smart to stay in his father's house."

Colucino nods with a frown. "I will speak with him again."

Marcante looks him straight in the eyes. "We want no more Italian rallies. Finito."

"*Sì,*" says Colucino. "*Io capisco.*"

The Italian Heritage rally is held at Columbus Circle on a beautiful sunny afternoon. Federal, state, and city politicians, lawyers, doctors, engineers, and policemen, all of Italian descent, speak in praise of their heritage. It is a time of pride, a time to step up and be counted, to speak of positive action, to move ahead as a united people.

Jimmy Colucino takes the microphone and unfurls an Italian flag. People cheer, reporters record, photographers snap photos, and the television cameras roll. Colucino proudly proclaims that he will lead another rally bigger than this outpouring in another three months.

The United States will know who the Italians are, he says.

* * *

CHAPTER 14

PRECINCT LOCK-UP

"Mike, Albie Simmons wants to talk to you before you go uptown."

"Thanks, Murphy. That's just what I need."

I go to the holding cell where Albie Simmons is waiting for me. He looks wrinkled, both skin and clothes. Can't take slumming. The bum. Cops do it every day on stakeouts. What does this zero want now? Another bribe?

"What do you want, Simmons? Bed too hard for you? Want some special treatment? An air mattress?"

"Hey, no. I just wanted to say I'm sorry for the way that went down yesterday. You're a gentleman. You were good to the ladies. I appreciate that. I heard about you. We both come up from the street. We both know how to handle ourselves."

"Whatta you want, Simmons? What are you reachin' for? You want to try to buy me again? There's nothin' I can do for you now."

"There's always something you can do. You *can* do for me. And I *can* do for you. I can do big for you. So big you'll never have to work again. You can retire from this nothing job tomorrow. I know I made a mistake discussing business with those other two cops around. A hundred large for you if you make a loophole for me to squeeze through. It's easy. They do it every day. The lawyers. The judges. The cops. I pay good. I ain't cheap, man. And I know you ain't either. A hundred large. This afternoon if you get me back on the street. I got big things going down. You can't believe how big."

I whisper and look around. "Maybe we can make a deal."

"There. I knew that you and me, we'd get along. I'll have it here at four o'clock."

"You can walk today. Back on the street to take care of business. You just have to do one small thing for me."

"Anything, man. Anything. You name it."

"I'll put you back in business if you give me Nicky Barnes and Monroe Benson."

Simmons' smile turns to disgust. "Anything but that, Palermo. Don't make no rat outta me. That I can't do. Anything else and we deal."

"There's nothing else that you have to trade. It's easy. It won't cost you a cent. And then you can take over the whole racket and you got strong friends behind you. There's nothing to it. And nobody but you and me will ever know. I'll tell them I forgot to read you your rights before questioning. Everything will be inadmissible."

"Fuck you, Palermo. I ain't no rat and you ain't gonna live to see the day that I give up nobody. But I'm gonna give you something anyway. I'm gonna give you a contract and put it out on the street to all the brudders. I'm gonna put out a contract on you like all the wop Mafiosi do. And I'm gonna get your ass shot off. The 100 grand I offered you is the contract for your ass. Forget we ever talked. Now you're a dead man. You ain't never gonna testify against me. You blew it, Palermo. Now your ass is mine.

"My lawyer says that my bail will be fifty grand. That's pocket money. I'll be back out on the street tonight takin' care of business before you even get out of this dump. And I'll be lookin' for you."

"Fuck you, Simmons. Bullets fly two ways. I'll be lookin' for you too."

Albie Simmons is back on the street before I finish with my day-long testimony in court. He walks out of the revolving doors of Justice, laughing, to take care of business and I go home exhausted.

CHAPTER 15

MICHAEL PALERMO

After Simmons walked and I got home, I started to wonder how serious he really was about putting a contract out on me. Why not? A hit's a hit. Everybody dies. Nobody's immortal. Guys have threatened cops before. The guy's gotta be crazy. Maybe he's crazy. He's got the weapons and the army and the will to do it. It's very possible. What's there to stop him? He makes an example out of me and there are no more narcotics busts, only a lot of would-be arresting officers.

Let's see. There are guns, knives, clubs, stranglings, falls, poisons, and accidents. An accident's the best because then nobody would ever know he did it. Only the people he wanted to know. A quiet whisper through the streets and the station houses. No evidence. No crime. No investigation. Only some 100 grand rich black guy who becomes a hero in the streets. More contracts and there are no more cops, only rich street people. Then there's peace in the city. All because of one cop who turned down a hun-dred grand bribe. I gotta be crazy. But that's the job. You gotta be crazy to do this job.

Hell, this feels good. I haven't been home in four days. Laura's great. She understands. The baby's great. I hold her in my lap.

She's growing more every day. This is what life's all about. Great dinner Laura made. One of my favorites. Lasagna. Beats eating with Buck and Johnny Nap. I oughta come home more often to eat and hang around. It's crazy to have a twenty-four-hour-a-day job. Now that I'm on a precinct squad, things will be easier. I'll have more time to spend with Laura and Michele. And I can take Mikey and Paulie out. One big happy family.

I ain't leaving this chair tonight even if there's an earthquake.

The phone rings. "I'll get it, Laur."

For an earthquake, no. For a phone ring, yes. Part of all the years on the job, I guess.

"Mike, listen, a bunch of the guys are down here at the Briar Inn on Central Avenue. Everybody has been talking about the Simmons case and they want you to come down. They say you ought to join the Westchester Shields."

"Joey. I'm tired and just relaxing here with my wife and daughter. Tonight's a bad night. I'm trying to unwind."

"Come on down. So you just stay for a few minutes. The guys all want to meet you. Come on. I'll buy you a drink."

"Go ahead, Mike," says Laura on the extension phone. She's part cop by now. She's got a wire on my phone. "I'll wait up for you. Go ahead." What a woman.

"OK, Joey. But just for a few minutes. And get the drink ready."

So I go. The Briar Inn sits on Central Avenue not far from the Westchester County Center. I arrive in a sweat suit and slippers. I'm introduced, pay my $5 membership fee and stand at the bar. Joey introduces me all around. I meet everybody. The crowd rings around us. My back aches from the pats of congratulations. In no time Joey has me talking about the stories that cops always tell on the job. I say, OK, one drink, one story, and then I got to go. So I tell the "fingerprint" story, which is true, like all job stories are.

It goes like this. This sergeant responds to a call on a burg-lary in an apartment in the city. He looks around, makes the lady happy. She sees he's really interested in finding whoever ripped her off. He looks all over the floor. Takes dust samples from under the sofa and puts them in an envelope. Sweeps dirt up from the front hall that might be from the perp's footprints. Then she says to him, "And I found a fingerprint on the window."

So he looks very interested. Walks over to the window, takes out his handkerchief, and wipes the print off the window. Then he folds up the hankie very neat and careful and puts it in his inside jacket pocket. Then he pats his chest over the hankie with the fingerprint and says, "I'll take this fingerprint down to the lab right away and have it identified." She thanks him and he leaves.

Her husband comes home after work and asks her how the investigation went by the police. She says, just fine. They took dust and dirt samples from under the sofa and in the hall and, oh yes, I found a fingerprint on the window, so I told the sergeant and he took it back to the lab for identification.

Now, when the husband hears this, he gets very excited and interested. Maybe he'll get his television and watch back after all.

He asks her what they used to get the print. Did they dust it or take a picture?

She says that the sergeant just rubbed it off with his handker-chief and folded it up and put it into his pocket.

Now, this doesn't sound right because it turns out that the husband is an FBI agent and he knows that something is rotten in the precinct, so he makes a call to the CO who puts him through to the sergeant who feels like his ass is in a hot sling and is now in a lot of trouble with the boss. But the Sarge is smart. He goes to the FBI agent and tells him that he was just trying to look good for the lady so she'd be confident that everything possible is being done. The FBI agent is a good Joe and laughs and lets the Sarge off the hook. Of course, he never sees his TV or his watch again, but his wife is still confident that some day they'll catch the guy from the fingerprint she found.

End of story. I'm out of here. I try to leave and Jerry Marshall grabs my arm.

"Mike, I haven't seen you since Terry Fitzpatrick's funeral. How've you been? You're looking great. Hey, let me buy you a drink."

I get a drink.

"Say, I want to tell you, that was a great arrest on Simmons today. You did a great job. They're going to put that badass away for a 100 years."

I shrug and talk into my drink like I'm embarrassed. "He's already walking the street."

"Is that right?" says Marshall, surprised. "He must have juice somewhere. A strong rabbi."

"Yeah, I guess so. Birnbaum put him back on the street for fifty grand. That was ten grand more than Simmons offered me to look the other way."

"Hell, man, you should have taken it."

"Yeah, after all the crap that goes down, maybe I should have. It sure as hell was easy enough to get him back on the street again. He's probably laughing at me right now."

I couldn't tell him about the 100 grand Simmons offered me and I turned down. He'd think I was a raving lunatic or a damn liar. I don't really know how many cops would have turned down $100,000. Like Chief Devlin said, "Cops haven't been tested yet." There are a lot of tests. I passed one of them today. And then there was the time the Internal Affairs guys planted a thousand bucks in my car to see if I would turn it in. I turned it in. I passed that test too. Those guys are always setting guys up like that. That's why the guys hate the IA guys.

Maybe Simmons is IA? That would be a pisser. No, I can't even picture that. I'd wet my pants.

And I can't tell Marshall about the contract Simmons said he was going to put out on me. I gotta have more proof than just my word. No corroboration. The guy's probably just pulling my chain anyway.

"Listen, Mike, that D.A. Scott is a good friend of mine. We're like family. Both our families go away on vacations together, kids and all. Would you mind if I talk to him about the Simmons' case?"

"Me mind? Hell no. What the hell do I care? It's out of my hands. I made the arrest. Now it's Scott's ball. He can do whatever the hell he wants with it. It's all right with me."

"Well, you did a great job, Mike." Marshall pats me on the back. "Everybody tried to nail him and you got him."

"Hey, there were more people involved than just me. There were my partners, Williams and Gomez. And we couldn't have done it without O'Hagan."

Marshall says good-bye and I finally get to go back home to Laura and the baby. I never should have left home in the first place.

* * *

A week later, I get a call at the squad office during day duty. Robert Scott calls me personally and tells me he'd like to see me in the District Attorney's office that afternoon. Two o'clock is fine.

His office is small but he has a view of the Yankee Stadium.

"Hi, Mike. Come on in. Sorry to keep you waiting. That Simmons case is coming up soon and I thought we'd prepare for the Grand Jury."

"Aren't Williams and Gomez going to join us?"

Scott leans forward, taking a cigar from a box in front of him. He closes his desk draw and continues. "No, I don't think they're necessary right now. By the way, Marshall stopped up to see me the other day. He said he bumped into you last week at a racket. I think it was just after you busted Simmons."

"Yeah, that was after a Westchester Shields meeting."

"He must have told you he was up to see me since then."

"No, that's the last time I saw him."

"How long do you know him, Mike?"

"It must be over ten years. He was in Narco when I was there."

"Well, he and I go back farther than that. We're very close. Did you ever work with him?"

"No, I never did."

"He's a great guy."

"Yeah, I like him. He's a good cop. Made some great collars while he was there. We called him 'the panther.' He moved like a cat. We left Narco at about the same time."

"Marshall told me you discussed the Simmons case."

"The subject came up."

"He tells me you'd like to help him."

"Are you kidding? I don't remember our talking about that. Why would I want to help him? I arrested the bastard. If I wanted to help him, I never would have arrested him."

"That's what I figured. I was curious about that. Didn't you ask him to come up to see me to see what could be done for Simmons?"

"No, I didn't. And I resent that."

"Then what did you tell him?"

"I didn't tell him anything. What is this, the third degree? What are you fishing for?"

"Nothing. Just tell me what happened so we can make our case."

"Marshall told me you two were close and so were your wives. You two had a personal relationship. He asked me if I had any objections to him coming to see you and see what could be done for Simmons. I told him it was out of my hands. It was your baby now."

"That's not what he told me."

"What the hell did he tell you?"

"Let's take it easy, Mike. We're all friends here. Now tell me what did Marshall and you want me to do? Let's knock it around."

"Scott, if you and Marshall got something going, that's your business."

"What do you mean, if Jerry and I have something going?" snaps Scott.

"Look, I don't know what you two guys talked about but it's not the same thing that Marshall and I talked about. Something doesn't smell right here and I don't want any part of it."

"Look, what did you tell Marshall about the way you thought Simmons ought to be handled?"

"I told him it was out of my hands. That it was up to you now."

"Did you tell him you didn't care what I did with Simmons? That anything I did would be OK with you?"

"Yeah. But I don't have any say in how you handle him. You're the prosecutor. It's your job to see that he doesn't squeeze through any loopholes in the law."

"Loopholes in the law? Funny you should say that, Mike. Those are the exact words Marshall used, about finding loopholes in the law. How come you two talk the same language?"

"Look, I don't have any say in the way you prosecute Simmons or how you handle the prosecution."

"But you do have a say, Mike. You have to testify, don't you?"

"Of course I have to testify. I nailed him and now we have to convict him."

"Did Albie Simmons offer you money to let him go?"

"Yes, he did."

"How much?"

"Forty thousand dollars."

"Did you take it or any part of it?"

"No. I didn't."

"Didn't you tell Scott you wished you had taken it?"

"What the hell are you trying to pull? That guy tried to straighten me out when I busted him. I told him to take a walk."

"He tried to bribe you?'

"Yeah, he tried."

"Did you put that in your report? Did you include in the report a charge of attempting to bribe a police officer?"

"No."

"Why not? You know that bribery is a serious offense, don't you?"

"I know. But there were no witnesses."

"Weren't your partners there with you during the bust?"

"Yeah, but they were in the other room. They didn't hear anything. Look, we had this guy dead to rights on a major heroin bust. Why the hell would I want to throw in an uncorroborated charge of bribery with no witnesses? It would look like I was throwing all kinds of crappy charges at him with no evidence to back them up. It would have weakened our case."

"You say your partners didn't hear the bribery attempt?"

"That's right. Because if they heard it and didn't report it, then you'd go after two more good cops like you're going after me. They didn't hear a thing. You got nothin' on them and nothin' on me."

"What did you mean when you said anything I did with the Simmons case would be all right with you?"

"Nothin'. Look, I told you. I did my job and now it's time for you to do yours. So far, all you did was put Simmons back out on the street. If Simmons is back on the street, he should be back on the street working for us."

"Look, Palermo. Let's get one thing straight. I had nothing to do with putting Simmons back on the street. I wasn't even at the arraignment. I'm sure the D.A.'s office tried to get the highest bail possible.

"Marshall discussed taking it easy on Simmons in the Grand Jury and leaving him an out where it could be of help to him at the trial. You discussed that with him, didn't you? He even told me he'd get back to you after he spoke to me."

"I never discussed the Grand Jury or the trial with Marshall."

"Didn't he get back to you?"

"I told you, I haven't seen or talked to him since that Shields meeting."

"Well, let me lay it out for you. Simmons says that he has nothing to do with drugs. That you and your team broke into his place and planted twenty keys on him. His wife and daughter are witnesses against you. He says you tried to shake him down for $100,000 and told him that if he opened his mouth and didn't come up with the money, that you were going to kill him. His wife and daughter have corroborated this.

"I think we got a big problem here. I talked with his attorney, Marcus Brown. He's one sharp guy. We went to school together. He's on his way up. He knows every inch of the Penal Code to get his clients off. He does it all the time. Now you have charges hanging over your head. And I just have to see how much is here. Maybe we'll have to play ball with him. See if he'll cop a plea."

"Cop a plea? Are you out of your mind, you stupid bastard? We got him dirty. He's a sewer rat running drugs all through Harlem. Everybody knows that. You can't be that stupid. Marcus Brown represents every fuckin' black drug dealer in the city. Can't you see through all this crap they're throwing at you? Are you fuckin' blind?"

"Hey, Mike, take it easy. Calm down. You're crossing the line. I'm going to have to call the guys with those funny white jackets if you don't calm down. Take it easy. Let's give it a few more days and see what turns up. Then we'll get together again."

"Just as long as you put that bastard Simmons away for life."

"Sure, Mike. Sure. You know I'll do everything I can."

I leave Scott's office and know that I'm being set up for something big-time. Simmons has a contract out on my life and now the D.A. wants to get me for bribery and a 100 other felony charges. Eighteen years on the Force, busting my balls, ruining my marriage, getting shot at, dealing with the scum on the street every day, twenty-four-hour workdays, and now these bastards are going to go after my ass and my pension, with just a few years to go before I make my twenty.

I should have been a hood. Like Carmine. It would have been easier. The guy's loaded; I got pennies. He doesn't have to worry about his pension. He doesn't need one.

Like Rosey used to say, "Carmine went bad and he did good. And you, Mike. You went good and you did bad."

Now I have to cover my back from Simmons and my front from the D.A. I only got two sides left. The guys on the Force and the guys on the street. Where'm I gonna turn?

To the good or the bad? To the right or to the left? Or maybe to both?

Why the hell is this bastard Scott doing this to me? He should know better. No drug dealer's testimony is going to stand up in court against the cop who busted him. And Simon. Why is Simon letting this happen? What the hell has he got against me? What did I ever do to him? We were good friends. We used to eat together. He'd come over to the house for a barbecue. The women got along. All of a sudden one day, he looks at me funny. I don't know why. Then he doesn't talk to me. Looks at me strange, like I'm some kind of jerk that he doesn't want to have anything to do with. Like a leper. An outcast. A pariah. Like he's talking behind my back. *Why don't you ever bring me any of your big Italian friends?* he starts asking me. Maybe that's it. Maybe he's trying to turn me into a rat. I do the job. If my friends are involved in the investigation, I close my mouth and tell the Cap to put somebody else on the case. I'm too close to it. It happens all the time. Not just with me. The Department doesn't want you working on a case that you're too close to. It's for the good of the Department. Simon's got to know that.

* * *

ROSS SIMON

This Palermo's one smart sonofabitch. Playing kissy-kissy-huggy-huggy with every hood in town. He never gives me anybody big. None of his big Italian friends. That night at The Chateau Pelham was the last straw. The guy was like a mafia Pope. Everybody in and out of law and order was shaking his hands, trying to kiss his ring. Cops and hoods. A good cop can't conduct himself like that. It's not for the good of the Department. He's a disgrace to the uniform. Good thing he never wears one, except at funerals and awards.

I don't know how he does it. So far, he's got six commendations, three meritorious awards, and participated in more than 2,000 arrests. He's an expert witness in drug cases but still doesn't give me anybody big. Except this last case. This Simmons thing. And according to Scott, he thinks Palermo has blown this case for us because of poor police procedure and maybe even planting the drugs and trying to shake Simmons down for forty grand. What an idiot. He shouldn't be on the Force. I'm gonna get him and I'm gonna get him right.

And it won't look bad on my record against crime when I run for governor. You don't think I want to be a stinking District Attorney all my life, do you? Maybe a Supreme Court judge, if I'm not strong enough for governor.

I see Palermo leave Scott's office so I walk in to see my Narcotics Chief.

"Well, how did it go, Bob?"

Scott smiles and gestures me over. He opens the desk drawer. A tape recorder stands motionless. "It's all on here. He's a fox, Chief, but I'd say we got him, and we got him right. The bug's in the phone. When I close the drawer, it activates the machine. I used the same thing on Marshall. Now for Palermo's two partners, Williams and Gomez. We'll have indictments on a gang of crooked cops and clean up the police department."

I'm impressed. I nod and smile. "Bob, this case is going to put us on the big board. The timing is perfect. It's going to put me in the governor's chair and you're coming along with me. You're going to be the first black Attorney General in New York's history."

* * *

MICHAEL PALERMO

I go back to my squad and I start to get a headache. All day long, all I can think about is the Scott meeting. It's like a bomb is going to explode and I can't stop it. I call up my old Narco partners for a meet at the Sunshine Diner at eleven o'clock. I get there early. I wait and the hands of the clock don't move. It's like they're chained still. They move a minute an hour. Finally, Richie and John break the doorway and come over to the table.

"What's the trouble, Mike? What's the jam?" asks John.

"I got bad problems. I think I just smelled a rat and I'm being set up."

"What happened?" asks Richie.

I explain every detail, every word. It is all fresh and clear in my mind. From the take-down in Simmons' pad to his sweating face on the bed to Scott's haughty hypocrisy.

John Amato becomes incensed. "Look, the first thing you got to do is get back to that bastard and clear the air. He's got to have a bug in that room. Everything you and he said has got to be on that tape."

Richie Arculeo agrees. "Johnny and I will reach out for Marshall and pull his coat. But you stay away from him. Scott wants you to go after him. He's probably got you tailed right now. You can bet he has Marshall and now he wants you. Did you see a tail?"

"No. Nothing. And I was looking. Look, talk to my partners, Williams and Gomez. They're good cops. The best. Scott is trying to implicate them in this frame too. I told Scott that Williams and Gomez were in the other room and never heard Simmons attempt to bribe me. They gotta say that because if they don't the sonofabitch is going to charge them with failing to report an attempted bribe."

Arculeo puffs. "That stupid bastard. He knows that buy-offs go down every day. If we reported every one, we'd be doing paper work thirty hours a day. Scott's acting funny, like he's got a personal interest in this. Something don't smell right."

"That's what I think," I say. "I think the bastard is in bed with somebody. I don't know who. But I'm gonna find out."

Amato is grim. "You call Scott tomorrow. Tell him you have to talk with him again. Give him the time to set up his machine. Make it super-clear that you don't have or want any part of the Simmons bullshit. We'll meet you here tomorrow night same time. Meanwhile, we'll tip Marshall, Williams, and Gomez."

"Thanks," I say. "That means a lot to me. We've been through a lot in Narco and nobody needs this crap that's going down. You know what I think? I think that tomorrow I'm going to wear a wire and nail Scott on the other end. Just a tape recorder in my pocket for a hammer."

"Shit," says Richie. "Why the hell didn't I think of that? Do you need a warrant?" he jokes.

"The only warrant I need is right here." I pat my .38 in my shoulder holster.

"If the sonofabitch gets me mad enough, I'm gonna put one in his head. He's just screwing around to move himself up in his job. He ain't goin' to walk over my body to do it. He's messin' with the wrong guy."

The next morning I set up another meeting in Scott's office. I know I have a problem by just admitting that I discussed the case with Marshall and by telling him he could go to Scott. I wish I could swallow the words when I said that if Scott and Marshall had anything going that was their business. I felt like I was digging my own grave. But I still had my tape recorder so I could set things straight. But then Scott would say that I said what I said because I was taping the meeting and said whatever I could to make myself look good. But then again, I might also catch Scott in something that might incriminate him. And if I had a tape, I could use it to show that Scott altered the tapes, if he does alter them. I don't trust the guy no way.

I have to cut this thing off before I lose control and shoot the sonofabitch.

I switch on my tape recorder and walk into Scott's office. He greets me and closes his desk drawer. That must be where he has the machine. Where's the mic? I want to speak into it loud and clear. Maybe I should ask him where it is.

"Mike, I left a message for Marshall to get in touch with me. Have you heard from him yet?

"No, I haven't and I don't expect to. I told you I don't speak with the guy or see him. I haven't seen him but three times in the past year."

"Well, you two have got to get together on this Simmons case."

"Why? Marshall's not an arresting officer. What the hell does he have to do with the Simmons case? It's my case. Me and Williams' and Gomez' and Chief O'Hagan's. Where the hell does Marshall come in?"

"Well, you discussed the case with him over a drink in a bar. You told him to come see me to see what could be done for Simmons."

"That's bullshit, Scott! What the hell are you trying to do? The last time I was here you had my head spinning. I'm trying to keep my cool, but you keep talking about some kind of a fix between Marshall and me and you. I told you before I don't want anything to do with this."

"Palermo, you know damn well what's going down here. You sent Marshall up here for a deal on the Simmons case. Now what's the deal?"

"You must be nuts! The only person talking about a deal is you. I never discussed a deal with Marshall. Marshall was the one talking about Simmons and you the last time I saw him. You know what I think? I think you got a deal to cut Simmons loose and you're looking for a way to compromise the evidence and the case. I think you got your hands out for forty grand or maybe more."

Scott tries to interrupt.

"Let me finish. I listened because I like him. The conversation couldn't have lasted over thirty seconds. I haven't seen him since, and after this bullshit, I don't expect ever to talk with him again. We ought to take this whole thing to the District Attorney now. I don't want to sit on this. I was willing to let this wash but now you're pushing me."

Scott can't hold back any longer.

"Palermo, you're full of shit! You were trying to make a deal and you couldn't do it with me."

"Deal?" I scream. "The only deal I'll make with you on Simmons is if he wants to work for us and give up Nicky Barnes. If he doesn't, he can spend the rest of his life in the can. Unless he can make a better deal with you. But that's out of my hands and in yours. Whatever happens to Simmons next is on your head."

Scott stands up and is enraged. "Get out of this office, you slick sonofabitch! I'm not through with you yet. Simmons will go, but you'll be holding his hand. Your famous Sicilian Defense ain't gonna help you this time."

As I leave, I lose control. "You can blow this bullshit out of both of your ears. And I'll tell you again, pal, I don't give a damn what you do with Simmons. I did my job, now you do yours."

I shouldn't have lost control, but I did and there's nothing I can do about it now. At least I feel better. Just let Scott bring that tape into Simon. I've got my own tape and he doesn't even know it. What the hell did he mean when he said that my "Sicilian Defense" isn't going to help me now? That's a chess move. The move Chief Devlin taught me. Is this nothing but a game to the bastard? A game with my life hanging in the balance?

AMEN'S RESTAURANT

Buck Truccolini reaches over for some bread. "Mike, did Johnny take care of his obligation?"

"Yeah, Buck, the guy coughed it up a couple of weeks ago. I forgot to tell you. It was like ripping his heart out. He said it was like giving up one of his kids."

"Ehh, he's a good actor, Mike. You know all you cops gotta be good actors. You know, you guys oughta be in the movies. You want me to set up a screen test? I can do it, you know."

"I'm sure you could, pal, but nobody would pay to see this puss of mine. I'd rather have Robby Benson play me in the movie. I wouldn't have the strength anyway. What I need now is a vacation."

"Come on, Mike. What's got you? Have a rough day?"

"I'm OK. Say, I meant to tell you, I've got some more free time now. The next time you go to that Italian Heritage rally, let me know. I'd like to go down with you."

"There ain't gonna be no more, Mike."

"What are you talking about? There's supposed to be another one in a month or so."

"We ain't going to that one, Mike. None of the boys are going. Say, you want a piece of a racehorse? I can get you a good deal on a sweet little filly."

* * *

I go back to squad duty at the four-two. District Commander O'Hagan doesn't need me on special duty anymore, so I pull my regular duty under Commander Jake Squibb. I still have my partners, Williams and Gomez. We respond to a disturbance at a bar on 116th Street.

The outside is quiet enough so we go to walk in the door, when all of a sudden from out of nowhere, I feel a whizzing go by my head and the big plate glass window in front of the bar shatters and sends splinters of glass over me and my partners. We hit the ground and crawl along the curb protected by the cars. Nothing. Quiet. And then a guy comes staggering out of the bar wearing a white apron and a blood-red shirt. The blood is real. The guy's got a hole in his chest that is pouring blood all over the sidewalk. He's the bartender. He falls down, gurgles something we can't understand, and dies.

We get on the horn and call for backup and a meat wagon. It was a phony call. A set up. There was no disturbance except for this dead guy who was minding his own business and didn't have an enemy in the world. We can't figure it out. We figure it's just a street corner hit and they got the wrong guy. I don't put two and two together until the next night when I go to get into my car and go home and find that the four tires on my car are slashed. I call AAA, and they fix me up with a tow to a gas station where the guy gives me a new set of wheels.

While I wait and smoke a half-pack of Lucky Strikes. I get to feeling that maybe the target of the hit at the bar was me. The damn bullet gave me a shave as it zipped by. The tires are a warning to scare me. There's only one enemy I have in Harlem who would have the balls for such a hit, and he's back on the streets, compliments of the judge. Judge Birnbaum let him out on a pocket-money fifty grand bail.

Albie Simmons. The guy who says I framed him with twenty keys of heroin and who told me that he was putting a contract out on me in Harlem. I work in Harlem. He lives here. He has an army. He's got big weapons and tons of cash. I got pennies and a D.A. who wants to put me away holding hands with Albie Simmons like we're buddies.

I think I've got big trouble.

I can't bring my old partners, Richie and Johnny, in on this. They've already got plenty to do with this Scott thing. Besides, it's too dangerous for these two white guys to go up against a top black Harlem kingpin out on a personal private vendetta to whack a cop who wouldn't take 100-grand bribe to turn him loose. Instead, he's contracted for 100-grand killer to be the first black bastard to make me into a pin cushion.

I can't go to the cops and the D.A. because they'll say I'm full of crap and that I'm trying to make it look like I'm lily white and that Simmons is out to get me to stop me from testifying against him. Which is true, but I can't prove it.

There's only one place for me to turn.

* * *

THE GROTTO

"Carmine, I hate to bring this to you. We never talk business, and I don't want any favors from you because I don't want to have to pay anything back. But this is different."

"Don't be silly, Mike. We've been friends all our lives. Your problems are my problems. No strings attached. Tell me the problem and I'll see what I can do."

The Grotto Restaurant in Little Italy is Carmine's place. We sit in the rear and I have my back to the wall. I'm in the gunfighter's seat. I'm safe here because Albie Simmons would have to be crazy to try a hit in here. The Italians would make eggplant parmigiana out of him.

"I got two problems and maybe you can help with one of them."

"Maybe I can help with both of them. Mike, this is no bullshit, you're like a brother to me. We go way back into the old-time streets. Anything I can do, I'll do. And I'll do it right and then we can forget about it. I know if the noose was around my neck you'd do the same for me."

I nod. "That's right. I would." I touch his hand lightly. I don't think I've touched him in over thirty years. Guys don't touch enough. Dolls touch all over the damn place.

"You don't look good. What's happenin', Mike?"

"I took down Albie Simmons on a twenty key heroin bust. He offered me 100 grand to open some doors for him. I told him to go to hell. He told me he was puttin' out 100 grand contract on me with his brothers in Harlem."

"He's full of crap, Mike. He'd never hit a cop. All hell would break loose. He's a lot of hot air. He's pulling your chain."

"That's what I figured, but the other day me and my partners go to a phony call at this Harlem bar and a bullet zips by my head, busts a plate glass window, and kills the bartender that everybody says is a saint."

"Bad hit. Everybody's got something to hide. There are no saints, Mike. Saints only live in heaven."

"Then the next night the four tires on my car are slashed. I figure they're lookin' to make me sweat."

"Ehh, could be a coincidence. But I'll tell you what, let me look into it. In the meantime, let me give you some advice. Like a friend."

"I'm listening."

"You got to remember I'm a businessman. Business first. Your mistake was you should have taken the 100 grand. Now don't interrupt me. I'm goin' to give you my opinion. We're just talkin' and I'm not goin' to pull any punches with you. This is the fact of life today. There's no more honor on the job. Not on mine and not on yours. The old days are all gone and the sooner you realize that, the smoother things will run. And if you don't believe me, you better go into another business because what you're doing now is going to get yourself clipped some day. And if Simmons has a contract out on you, this may be your lucky day.

"I don't have to tell you but we got so many people on the pad we got a bigger payroll than General Motors. Now, what's your other problem? Broads?"

Carmine smiles and puffs on his cigar. I sip my bourbon and water and feel like a little kid in confession with a priest, looking for help.

"The D.A. wants to put my ass in jail for some two-bit procedure shit. Simmons offered me forty grand to cut him loose and I turned him down."

"He can't put you away for that. You didn't take the bread. Or did you? I thought you said it was 100 grand."

"Albie upped it later in the lock-up. I turned it down again. Now a hotshot assistant D.A. named Robert Scott, who may be dirty himself, is trying to give me grief because I didn't write up Simmons on a bribery rap. I couldn't. I didn't have any evidence. Then this idiot cop who I talked to for thirty seconds thinks he's going into business on his own with the Simmons case and tells Scott that I'm looking to make a deal to let Simmons walk. He's full of shit.

"I think he and the D.A. Ross Simon are in this together and that Simon is after my ass because I keep seeing my old friends."

"You don't make it easy, Mike. Trouble is trouble, but you got yourself into a fuckin' earthquake. Still, let me reach out and look into things. You never know what can turn up. Everybody's got their hands in everybody else's pocket. Who knows? Just the other day, we bought a judge we thought we could never touch."

CARMINE CANICATTI

I was surprised when Mike came to me. He was always a private guy and we never talked business. But this was more than that. This was his life we were talkin' about. I figure what if one of my boys came to me with a bum rap over his head? I would help the guy. I know Mike longer than any of my boys and Mike is like family, so I got to help him. It's only right.

So I talk to Casper Nardino and he sets up a meet with me and Don Alberto's consigliere, Angelo Orabona. Angelo is very interested. He says that Mike is a stand-up guy and that Don Alberto knows him and likes him. I was surprised. I didn't know Mike had reached out that far. He always kept his mouth shut about everything he did. I was later to find out that Mike had a lot of friends on the street. He was a popular guy because he kept his word and never double-banged anybody.

I meet with Angelo and the don, and Don Alberto asks Angelo to set up a meet at my place, The Grotto, with Valerio Fredoni and Francesco Colucino and their consiglieres. The Colucino

Family deals direct with Nicky Barnes in the junk business. Don Francesco's son, Jimmy, runs that whenever he's not running Italian Heritage rallies. He's close to the blacks and works well with them. I guess they trust each other ever since Jimmy was in the joint and he took a lot of them under his wing. He taught them a lot about the business. I think that was a mistake. When he got out, he had a lot of new strong black friends. Personally, I think he's crazy. You can never trust those guys. They always stick together and in a show own they're gonna go with their own people against us. Then Jimmy's ass is gonna be wide open and he's gonna get a bullet in the back. Some of those bastards are crazy. Like animals. No honor. I guess you got good and bad all over.

Meanwhile, before the meet, Don Alberto says that I should put a man on Mike's tail, kind of like a guardian angel. Frankie Faiella gets the job. He calls me every few hours to keep me up to date. He tells me Mike's got two guys tailing him. A white guy and a black guy behind him and they're not together. With Frankie, Mike's got three guys tailing him. He's gotta know something's up but he never lets on. Frankie uses the shield number and name of one of the cops on our pad and makes the white guy through his license plate and the grapevine. The guy is a detective who works for the Bronx D.A. Ben Burns. He don't know that he's got a black killer on his ass. Frankie makes the black guy the same way and finds out he's a hit man for Albie Simmons. He's looking to collect on Albie's contract on Mike. So with this I go into our meet in the back room of The Grotto in Little Italy. I sit with three dons and their consiglieres.

"Carmine tells me that the blacks have a contract out on this cop, Mike Palermo."

Don Alberto starts the meeting. There's no food on the big, round table. The tablecloth is empty except for water glasses and ashtrays. This is only business, like a Cosa Nostra sit-down to work out problems. Everybody says the old days are over and we got to talk and not whack guys for small things. Maybe they're right. But a bullet always talks fast and strong.

"For some stupid thing, if you can believe it—that he wouldn't take 100 grand to let this Albie Simmons walk. He's an underboss of this Nicky Barnes. Is that right, Francesco?"

"Yeah. Jimmy has Vinnie Gennaro deal with him. We have to control the junk business. We let the blacks run it. Without us they'd be whackin' each other right and left. We're like the police, we keep the peace. Law and order in the streets."

"You can keep them in line?" asks Don Valerio.

"Yeah," says Francesco. "They give us the respect due. If they don't, we cut off their supply and get somebody else to move it for us. So far, they listen to us. But tell me, why are we so interested in a cop? Since when are we looking out for cops?"

Don Alberto motions for me to answer.

"Francesco, Mike Palermo and me are old friends from when we were kids. We grew up together. He's good people and he's done a lot to keep the peace. He's a good cop and he's also a good friend to our people. He's not a rat to either side. He's a *uomo rispetato*. A man of respect.

"He's gettin' heat from this black street punk, Simmons, who's lookin' to take over not only Barnes' operation but the whole junk business on the East Coast and cut us out. He's no good for anybody. And now he's playin' God and puts out a contract on a guy who's my personal friend and who's a friend of the Family."

"I can speak on that," says Valerio. "It was Mike Palermo who put together that Gambelli deal so that twenty of our people could walk out of the federal prisons where they took the fall on a bad rap. I know him for years back to when he was a green beat cop in a basement putting all the books in the Bronx out of business. He's honorable. This Simmons has no business hittin' him. We should act on this and act right. When they start hittin' cops, they're gonna bring all the cops in the city down on everybody, including us. We don't need this kind of heat. We pay plenty to keep everything running smooth. We grease a lot of doors to keep things quiet. But more important than taking care of business, this cop has helped us keep the peace and we have an obligation to see he's not hit by some black cowboy with a personal vendetta. Business is business and Mike Palermo is our business. He's done nothin' wrong."

"I see," says Colucino. "If you want, I'll talk to Jimmy and he'll talk to Gennaro and he'll tell Nicky Barnes to call off the contract."

"What if he refuses?" asks Valerio.

"Well, then we'll know just how strong we are with these people. If Barnes refuses, then there'll be a lot of accidents out on the streets and we go look for somebody else to do business with."

"Meanwhile," says Valerio, "I have Carmine looking out for Mike now to do whatever he has to, see that nobody whacks him."

Everybody agrees, and I have the food brought out and we all eat like Nero while Rome burns. The hell with the world. I'm hungry. Let's eat.

* * *

CHAPTER 16

MICHAEL PALERMO

Two weeks after the interrogation in Scott's office, I'm called to appear at the District Attorney's office for a hearing to investigate the conduct of the officers in the Albie Simmons case.

I'm sitting at the conference table with a Detective Endowment Association attorney, Nelson Andrews, District Attorney Ross Simon, Assistant District Attorney Robert Scott, Inspector O'Hagan, and a stenographer.

Simon begins.

"Detective Michael Palermo, you are here today to answer some allegations made against you by Senior Assistant District Attorney Robert Scott, in which he alleges that you tried to bribe him in regard to the disposition of the Albie Simmons case. Do you have any objections to answering this charge?"

"I have no objections to answering any questions about the Simmons case. The only objection I have is that the man who is making the allegations shouldn't be present in this room."

I surprise them.

Simon tries to justify Scott's presence.

"Mr. Scott is involved in the prosecution of this case. Even though it's true that he's the key witness against you, he has the right of the prosecution to hear your defense. He'll be reading the transcript anyway in order to weigh the evidence. What you say now in his presence may persuade him to re-evaluate his testimony and perhaps withdraw the allegations."

Detective Andrews comes to my defense. "Mr. Simon, Detective Palermo has a very valid point here. I'm sure you're going to question Mr. Scott after Detective Palermo gives his testimony. I'm sure you wouldn't want Mr. Scott to rely on Detective Palermo's testimony to support his own."

The clerk takes down every word. Simon accedes.

"Bob, would you please wait in your office so that we can get on with this?"

Scott leaves.

"Now, Detective Palermo, what is your answer to this charge of attempting to bribe an Assistant District Attorney?"

"I deny the charge completely and most emphatically. I've never tried to bribe Mr. Scott or any District Attorney or anyone else for that matter. I did my job and arrested Albie Simmons. I want to see Mr. Scott do his job and have Simmons sentenced under the full weight of the law."

"Are you willing to appear before the Grand Jury under oath and repeat these statements?"

"Detective Andrews has informed me that it is my right to refuse to testify before the Grand Jury. But, Mr. Simon, I have nothing to hide. I want to testify. I'm not guilty. I want the Grand Jury to hear the truth and not just a bunch of twisted lies. My reputation is important to me and to my family. This is my life we're talking about. If I don't set this thing straight now, I may never get another chance."

"Then you will sign a waiver of your rights and you agree to testify before the Grand Jury?"

"I will."

Inspector O'Hagan speaks up. "Mike, give yourself a little more time to think this out. It may be the most important decision in your whole life."

"Inspector, it's something I have to do."

* * *

I spent one of the most grueling times of my life before the Grand Jury and I don't recommend that anyone ever do it. I wasn't allowed to have an attorney present. I waited outside the Grand Jury room for a long time to testify and finally the doors opened. Out walked Scott. He had just given his testimony. As he brushed by me, he stopped and said, "I got your ass, pal."

I just stared at him for a long, hard time and his smirk turned into a phony smile, like he had just eaten a porcupine and was afraid to swallow. I entered the Grand Jury room.

My recollection of those proceedings is cloudy, like I was never really there. Like someone else was speaking and answering for me. Some details stick painfully in my mind. I'll never forget them.

The District Attorney was speaking. Ross Simon made sure he handled my case personally. He addressed the Grand Jury.

"Ladies and gentlemen, our next witness will be Detective Michael Palermo. Detective Palermo has waived his constitutional rights against self-incrimination and as a peace officer and has agreed to testify before this Grand Jury. Detective Palermo understands that anything he says can and will be used as evidence against him in a court of law."

Then he started to hammer on me. "Detective Palermo, did you arrest a suspected narcotics dealer named Albie Simmons?"

"Yes, I arrested Simmons."

"Did Mr. Simmons offer you a bribe to set him free?"

"Yes."

"How much was it?"

"Forty thousand dollars."

"Did you accept the money?"

"No, I did not."

"Did you arrange a meeting with Detective Jerry Marshall?"

"I didn't arrange a meeting with Marshall. It was just a coincidence that we met."

"Did you know that Detective Marshall was a personal friend of Assistant District Attorney Robert Scott?"

"I didn't know of Marshall's relationship with Scott until he told me that night at the Briar Inn."

"Did you discuss the Simmons case with Marshall?"

"Yes, I discussed the Simmons case insofar as I said that Simmons was already back on the street and that he had offered me money, which I had turned down."

"Did you know that it is against Departmental policy to discuss any pending case in a barroom?"

"Yes, it's against Department policy, but I didn't say anything important."

"When Mr. Simmons tried to bribe you, what did you say?"

"I told him no. No bribe was ever going to get him off today."

"Did you tell Detective Marshall that you wished you had taken the bribe?"

"Marshall told me I should have taken the money. He was joking. We were drinking. I told him maybe he was right. I was joking too."

"Did you include bribery on Mr. Simmons' arrest report?"

"No."

"Why not?"

"It wasn't important. It was a narcotics arrest. Every day, these people offer cops money to let them go. Besides, I had no corroborating witnesses."

"Weren't your partners there to hear the bribe attempt?"

"No, they were in the other room. They didn't hear a thing."

"In the other room? They didn't hear a thing? Suppose I told you that they have testified that they heard the bribe attempt? What would you say then? Would you like to re-evaluate your testimony given under oath just now?"

"They couldn't have overheard Simmons, because if they did and didn't put it in the arrest report, you'd be after them for failing to report a bribe."

"Not if they were given immunity from prosecution for testifying against you, I wouldn't be after them, would I?"

"I don't know. That's your business. I can only testify to the facts as I know them."

"Would you say that bribes to arresting officers in narcotics arrests are commonplace?"

"No. Bribe attempts are common-place. Not bribes."

"If that's true, why aren't there more bribery attempt charges on these arrest reports?"

"I don't know. Maybe because the arresting officers don't pay much attention to things that aren't going to change the outcome of an arrest."

"Did you blame Mr. Scott for the fact that Mr. Simmons was released on bail?"

"Yes. Scott got me upset. He was baiting me. I had to strike out at him."

"How much more was the bail over the amount of your bribe with Mr. Simmons?"

"Ten thousand dollars."

"Did you say that Mr. Simmons would be laughing at you?"

"Yes."

"Why is that?"

"Because if I had taken him up on his offer, I'd be a lot richer and wouldn't be having this aggravation."

"Since you agreed that you should have taken the bribe, are you now considering diluting your testimony against Mr. Simmons and taking his money?"

"No. I would never take a bribe. I will testify against Simmons. I'll do my job. Just like I've been doing for the last seventeen years."

"Did you say that you didn't care what Scott did with the Simmons case?"

"Yes. I wasn't involved any more. The case was in Scott's hands."

"Did you say that anything Scott did would be OK with you?"

"I said that it would be all right with me if Marshall talked to Scott. Anything Scott did would be all right with me if he sought the full punishment of the law."

* * *

I was dead tired after the first day of testimony. Art Gomez and Eddie Williams visited me at home.

"The whole thing's crazy, Mike," says Gomez. "We had a perfect arrest, and now the D.A.'s going to blow the whole case. Look at this. Art has something interesting for you to read. We got a thirty-page transcript of the wire. I know there's something here but I can't put my finger on it. See what you can make of it."

"The wire we had on Simmons when we busted him was still operating that night until we got back the next day," says Williams. "This is what was on it. It's mostly that kid Aretha again. But here on the last page is a call to Simmons' wife from an attorney named Marcus Brown. Read what it says."

I read.

> *"Your husband will be well represented. Of course, a retainer will be necessary."*

"I understand, Mr. Brown."

"Now I want you to get King for the money and drop it at my office tomorrow."

"I will, Mr. Brown. I'll be there at nine tomorrow."

"What the hell does all that mean, Mike?" asks Gomez.

"I don't know, guys. Do you really think there's something here?"

"I feel it, Mike," says Williams.

I think as hard as I can. My mind is working like there's sawdust in the gears. There's too much happening in my life. Everywhere I walk or drive, I feel I have a tail on me. First a white guy and then a black guy. Every time I turn around and see somebody looking at me strange, I look for the bullets to zip by my head. Simmons' strategy is working. So is Scott's and Simon's. I look at the transcript and think harder than any time in my life. My whole life is on the line. I have to get these bastards off my back.

"Let's see. They didn't know we had a wire in there. We know they got a bird somewhere that's been tipping them off. Who the hell is this guy King?"

"We're trying to check it out," says Gomez. "There's nobody in the precinct or the D.A.'s office by that name. We've got the word on the streets. So far nothing's turned up."

"Maybe it's a code name. Hoods always talk in code. These guys who are doing this to me are nothing more than hoods."

"I never heard of any KING, Mike," says Williams.

"Get King for the money and drop it in my office tomorrow," I repeat it out loud.

"Get King for the money."

* * *

I am drained after two days of testimony and intensive gril-
ling by the D.A. and his research staff. Scott has already testified.
Marshall has not been dragged in to tell his version because he
didn't waive his rights. They must have the stupid, ignorant, bastard right. He must have laid his dreams for retirement out in plain
English on Scott's wire. He's terrified that we'll both be indicted.
I'm the only one waging a defense. A Sicilian Defense like Devlin
taught me. I'm the only one fighting back.

I have one more day of testimony to come. I have to clear my
mind. If I could only talk to Chief Devlin, then I'd know what to
do. But I can't talk to the Chief, so I do the next best thing. I set
up Devlin's ivory chess set. I'll play both sides, move for the Chief
and move for me. I'm Black. Black is the underdog. I hold each
chessman in my hands and feel the warmth of friendship soothe
my mind. My head is clearing. I'm getting relaxed. I can see things
through the veil.

Devlin moves his Knight to Queen's Bishop Three.

I move my pawn to Queen's Bishop Four.

THE SICILIAN DEFENSE—The move that does more than
accept the inevitable. A bold thrust out on to the center of the
board. Isn't that what the Chief said? Devlin moves his Pawn to
King Four. He retaliates, not prepared to relinquish control of the
center squares. The pulpit of power.

I move my pawn to King Four. I fight for control of the middle.

And at that moment, I suddenly know who the man in the
middle is. Who the contact is that has been feeding Albie Simmons with information about search warrants and wire taps. It all
comes together like the pieces of a jigsaw puzzle. The man in the
middle. The man in control through whom everything must pass
is King Four.

Marcus Brown was telling Madeline Simmons to get *King
Four* the money, not to get *King for* the money. I know who the
man in the middle of the *Palermo Frame* is.

I can't finish the game. I can't sleep. I get out of the house and walk the streets, trying to think of what to do. Looking over my shoulder to see if I still have salt and pepper tailing me. Who would believe me? Only Gomez and Williams, and they would think I'm crazy. Maybe Inspector O'Hagan. No. This is too big. He's got his own career to take care of. There's nobody except maybe Amato and Arculeo.

No, I can't bring them in on this. The D.A. will find some way to bring them in as accessories.

*   *   *

On the third and final day of testimony I hear Scott's tapes of our conversation for the first time. . . .

"Did Albie Simmons offer you money to let him go?"

"Yes, he did."

"Did you include in your report a charge of attempting to bribe a police officer?"

"No."

"Why not? You know that bribery is a serious offense."

"I know."

"What did you mean when you said that anything I did with the Simmons case would be all right with you?"

"Look, Scott, you can blow this bullshit out of both your ears."

I only remember the barbs that stick out sharp and tear at my insides.

The District Attorney states that part of the tape of a second meeting is inaudible and Mr. Scott has provided a transcript of that part of the tape to the best of his recollection. My outright denials are either not recorded or erased. My tape of that meeting is useless because a wire connection to the battery broke during recording and my machine stopped. One goddamn little solder connection broke, and because of that my life is now in the dumper.

At least I got part of the conversation. The true conversation that took place will never be heard by the Grand Jury.

After the third day of testimony, after hearing all the lies, I completely lose control. I go straight to Scott's office and throw open the door. Scott is alone. It is closing time and the secretaries have left for the day. The office is empty except for Scott and me.

"I know who the man is, Scott. The man behind the whole fuckin' frame. The man who's got his hand in Albie Simmons' pocket. The man who's been tipping him off about warrants and wiretaps."

Scott closes his desk drawer to record me. "What the hell are you doing here, Palermo? You're not supposed to be up here."

"You see, Scott, there was a tap on the Simmons' phone when we busted him. A call came in that evening and we have it recorded. It's got your name on it. Marcus Brown, your old law school buddy, fingered you. I got you right."

"What the hell are you talking about?"

"Brown said, 'Get "KING FOUR" the money.'"

Scott's eyes chill. "So what?"

"I'll tell you what, Mr. Scott. I know that YOU are KING FOUR. And that you're in Simmons' pocket. You must have laughed like hell inside when I told you I was going to put Simmons in your pocket. You're the only person with motive, method, opportunity, and money. Method was your access to Simmons' lawyer, Brown, to set up the shake. And opportunity was your job that gives you access to all the vital, sensitive information that goes down on a drug surveillance. You're the fuckin' Chief of the District Attorney's Narcotics Section. Everything in Narco goes through you.

"And you play chess and know about the SICILIAN DEFENSE. Remember when you told me, my SICILIAN DEFENSE wasn't going to help me now? You know the game and you know that the Black Pawn controls the board from the center of the board, from the KING FOUR squares. You're KING FOUR, Scott, and it's checkmate. That comes from the Persian where the game originated. It comes from the Persian words *Shah Mat* which means 'The King Is Dead.' And it ain't the white King, pal, and this ain't no game. It's my life we're fighting over. If I go down, you go down too. Either in the courts or on the streets."

"Palermo, you're full of shit again. I don't know what the hell you're talking about. Now get the hell out of here before I call the cops."

"I am the cops, Scott. You don't have my gun and shield yet. And you're never going to get them. If you do, it'll be over my dead body."

"That can be arranged. Now look, I already told you, Palermo. Get out of here."

I throw my hands up in the air, pull my gun, and step behind Scott's desk. His face drains and almost turns white. I open the drawer to his desk. I watch the tape recorder and reel stop. I rip the recorder out of the drawer and smash it against the wall and take the tape and put it in my pocket. I put the gun to his head and say, "This one's for me, pal."

I think he messed in his pants because he started to stink. I holstered my gun and stomped out. I left the bastard cringing in the corner. He made me into a monster, and now I'm out of control.

* * *

On the next day, the Grand Jury delivers its decision. I'm indicted on a charge of attempting to bribe an Assistant District Attorney. A warrant is issued for my arrest.

* * *

RICHIE ARCULEO

The deal was made. Mike would surrender himself to John Amato and me. We had a lot of time together in Narcotics as a team. Made some good, solid arrests. Mike used to kid me and say that all the streets knew I was "the man" and that I looked like I was in charge. Maybe that's so, but it was a team effort and we planned and executed every arrest as a team. We all covered each other's asses.

John and me couldn't believe this was happening. It was worse than the blackest nightmare I ever had. And it was for real. That was the unbelievable part. John and me picked Mike up at his house. No handcuffs. Fuck regulations. Put me away for that, Simon.

John sat in the back of my car with Mike. I was the chauffeur. I felt like an executioner. Nobody spoke. The air was like super-cooled icy despair. There was an impotence and frustration spawned by the hollow accusations of a District Attorney who was fabricating and grabbing for headlines to move himself up the political staircase into the governor's mansion.

The three of us walk silently into the four-four, past the high-seated nodding lieutenant, in between desks sheaved with reports, quickly by detectives watching and speaking in muted whispers stealing a glance at us. We're straight-backed with gritty bands of steeled cheek muscles popping defiance to the rest of the world.

With routine detachment, with no emotion, like I was a wooden robot, I fill out the fingerprint card and another robotized John Amato rolls Mike's fingerprints over the black-inked glass slab, and again over the white card; the card that was reserved for the accused; the innocent until proven guilty; the always-anonymous never-personal wooden robot prisoner; the man on the bad side of the good-bad line. We're all made of wood.

All Mike has left after eighteen years on the Force is ten black fingertips and a flood of tears flowing within him, dusty tears drying before they reach his eyes. He's the ultimate disgrace.

A cop being booked before an audience of equals, all of whom could be here in his shoes tomorrow because of a selective prosecution and bum rap frame by a D.A. A cop just arrested by his superior officer, stripped of his gun and shield.

John wouldn't let anyone else do the printing, not even me. Pictures flash next, front view, side view.

"Thank you. I'm sorry."

Down the hall, more reports, now to the arraignment.

* * *

District Attorney Ross Simon stays up half the night until the early morning hours. His eyes are red, baggy medallions. Beside his desk stands a half-empty bottle of scotch, a cloudy fingerprint smeared glass, and his private phone directory of the media. He has spent the evening and early morning hours personally apprising radio, television, and newspaper reporters that he is about to blow open the biggest case of his career. He will personally prosecute and expose mob-connected corruption within the Police Department. He is a fearless champion of the law. A fighting District Attorney. A man who will not tolerate corruption. He is saving the identity of the prosecution target until the arraignment the next morning. Like a Hollywood film director-producer, he makes arrangements for TV cameras, microphones, podium, studio lights, news releases, and a diatribe of silver-throated demagoguery. He charges that he is going to bury corruption and impale a decorated narcotics detective for conspiring to bribe an Assistant District Attorney in order to secure the release of a major Harlem heroin trafficker.

JOHN AMATO

The three of us march in step quickly from the car, Mike in the middle, up the courthouse steps, past the TV cameras and reporters, acknowledging greetings, stepping smartly past the confusion and electricity, past the people who don't know yet that the target is Mike Palermo. Like a prisoner in a police uniform, like a military spy, we slip by them into a private office, a wood-paneled cell of justice, to rest for a moment until the gates of the arena open for the spectacle of the gladiators against the lions.

It is five minutes before the court clerk calls Mike for the arraignment. Before he meets Simon and his mace of chains of hate. Mike is nervous and trembling in a chair by the door. His fingers fidget with a medal of St. Jude on a silver chain. A silver medal of a saint of protection, a symbol of his hope and his faith that his innocence will somehow swell and rise up triumphantly above the massive publicity and mob-control propaganda of a man who is using the D.A.'s office and its awesome power for his own interests. He strokes St. Jude, the patron saint of lost causes. Mike says that saints only live in heaven. I hope that if St. Jude is watching that he'll come down and give Mike a hand today.

No one speaks. There's nothing to say that we haven't said before. I pace in front of the rain-streaked window. A knock on the door. Richie gets the word.

"OK, Mike. They're all ready. Let's go"

I put my arms around my five-foot-eight-inch buddy. I hug him. I got tears in my eyes.

"Now, listen. We're all behind you. You've got the whole world on your side. You go in there head up and look them in the eyes. Show them the truth. Let them see it in your eyes. You'll be done in a few minutes, and Richie and me will get you out of here in nothing flat."

Mike nods. He can't speak. He's swallowed his voice. He slips across the hall, past the melee of the media hounds, and in seconds stands before Judge Oscar Birnbaum. His attorneys stand with him. Now he's in their hands and in the grace of God.

* * *

A team of attorneys stand with Mike Palermo. They are from the Washington, D.C., law firm of Edward Bennett Williams. They are supplied by a Friend of the Family.

Allen Hopkins, fifty-eight years old, silver-haired, aristocratic, yet his suit is rumpled. Gerald Yates, thirty-six, auburn close-cut hair, manicured nails, Georgetown graduate, impeccably dressed, the equalizer. Both barristers belong to one of the most prestigious law firms in the Capitol.

"Michael Palermo," says Judge Birnbaum, "you are charged with conspiracy to bribe an Assistant District Attorney. How do you plead?"

Hopkins answers without hesitation, "Not guilty, Your Honor." The response is routine and automatic. He hasn't yet had time to examine the case. "We ask that bail be waived and that our client be released in his own recognizance. As the records show, Your Honor, Detective Palermo is a highly decorated police officer who has made outstanding arrests in the narcotics field. He is also a decorated combat veteran, having served his country in World War II and in Korea. After eighteen years of life service to the Police Department of the City of New York, Detective Palermo asks nothing more than the opportunity to clear himself of these charges. He is a family man with responsibilities to be discharged at home."

The judge leans forward on his forearms, his flowing black robe swallowing all of his body except for his head, neck, and hands. His forehead holds pellets of perspiration in its deep creases. Oscar Birnbaum has been around for a long time and has seen everything. He has been an Assistant District Attorney, a job he acquired after graduating from law school at New York University. Eight years of private practice, political involvement, favors, and then a judgeship. Eventually he became the mentor and rabbi of Ross Simon and was supporting his political ambition to become governor.

When he first met Simon, he was a young Assistant District Attorney. Birnbaum took him under his wing. Their relationship began in Harlem at the Inspector's funeral that was held for Detective Terry Fitzpatrick who had been killed on the job on a hot East Harlem summer night. Simon was given that case and it started his career moving. It got him attention. Birnbaum was the presiding judge and had eased judicial conduct aside and had briefed and tutored the green Assistant D.A. along every inch of the case as it proceeded to its inevitable guilty verdict. It was important that the people responsible for the killing of the policeman were caught, that Simon was victorious, and that Birnbaum had done his job to the applause of the electorate.

Oscar Birnbaum peers down over the round wire-rimmed glasses perched on the tip of his nose. He turns to the prosecution. "Do you have any objections, Mr. Simon?" He speaks like a recording in a mannequin, like he had never met Simon before.

The producer-director now has the spotlight. He wears a dark-blue pin-striped suit, the elegance of Madison Avenue coterie. A blue-stoned pinkie ring sparkles on his right hand. He gestures abundantly as he speaks.

"Your Honor, Detective Palermo is indeed a police officer with an outstanding police record behind him. It's true that he's had a distinguished military career and has made important contributions to the war against crime. In fact, I've always had the greatest admiration for Detective Palermo."

Palermo listens as Simon speaks. Mike had made the arrest of Simon's first prosecution as an Assistant District Attorney. It was Judge Birnbaum who had called a recess during the trial because Simon had not been using his witnesses thoroughly enough. Simon, in fact, had been losing the battle on points.

As Palermo and Amato had sat in Simon's office during that recess, they listened as Judge Birnbaum called, berated, and advised Simon of what his next moves should be. Through a coalition of cop, D.A., and judge, the defendant was neatly collared, conned, and convicted.

Palermo now listens as the other two parts of that old coalition conspiracy take his life in their hands. Simon pauses. He waits for dramatic effect, curls his right hand into a fist, and holds it before his eyes.

"The first case that I prosecuted was brought to a successful end because of the fine police work of this very man. But. . ." he hesitates and spins around to face the gallery in the courtroom, raises both his arms high in the air, and booms, "but I cannot tolerate, I will not permit a crime to go unpunished. Regardless of my personal feelings for the defendant, I must, and by God, I will strip this friendship and admiration from me. I will see that justice is done for the honor of my office as District Attorney and for the good of the People of the State of New York. There is no place in our society for men who would betray a public trust. Let the criminal element beware and let them take careful note of the disgrace that this man has brought upon his Police Department, his family, his friends, and himself."

Michael Palermo stands, his muscles frozen in a time warp of fear and bewilderment. His appearance from the rear, as seen by the gallery of newspapers, radio, and television people, is the portrait of a little guy flanked by two well-dressed attorneys. How bad can the little guy be?

"Mr. Simon," says the judge as he taps his gavel on the wood clapper. "Do you have any objections to the waiving of bail?"

"No, Your Honor. No objection," answers Simon, somewhat annoyed at having been cut short in his oratory.

Although fifteen minutes have passed, it seems like only seconds to Palermo. He feels like he's on a roller coaster. The reporters and TV cameras amass in the hallway outside the courtroom.

Ross Simon steps out into the lights, drinking in the glamour and notoriety. He has scheduled a press conference in the hall and is now going to smear little Mike Palermo all over the front pages and home television screens. And he's going to paste Ross Simon right up there in front, a hard-hitting, gut-honest, fighting District Attorney.

RICHIE ARCULEO

John and me just couldn't let Simon drag Mike through the cameras. We hustle him out through a rear door in the courtroom, down a side stairway, and into a waiting car. Simon is disappointed. There's not going to be any Mike Palermo on stage to dance for him.

"That guy is the biggest sonofabitch that was ever born," I say. "Don't listen to anything he said. We're going to my place for a drink." I weave in and out of traffic. We don't want to leave Mike alone at a time like this. We don't know what he'll do. The pressure of the job. A cop without his gun and shield. The family hardship. The newspapers and television and an upcoming trial. Some guys in a situation like this have blown their brains out.

"Take me home, Richie," says Mike painfully. His voice is hoarse and scratchy, and I know he hasn't swallowed in hours.

MICHAEL PALERMO

After the arraignment, John and Richie took me home and I spoke to no one. I retreated into a shell of private solitary refuge. At night I had to fight to fall asleep. It was then that the nightmares began.

My mind is midnight. I run through a jungle of lamp posts hung with syringes and glassine bags of white powder. A laughing voice resounds through the alleys.

"It's never as dark as midnight. Ha, ha, ha! Get him! There he goes."

Two shots crack.

"Stop! I'm the District Attorney. Stop or I'll shoot."

The hot steel pierces the runner's chest. It burns in my gut. But still I run on.

A giant, round tube looms before me. A glass tube. A place to hide. Inside, it is flame and red and as bright as the sun. I pace foot over foot, heel over toe. The tube disappears behind me. It narrows into a steel shaft, the hollow needle of a giant syringe. I run, and the walls turn over and over like the rolling barrel of a horror house amusement. Up the spinning walls I race, with the voice of a madman echoing behind me.

"I got him. Call the papers. I'm the D.A. Stop or I'll shoot!"

I snap around. Ross Simon's teeth are sharp nails, flashing and spitting at me. I find an opening and race out of the shaft, exhausted and out of breath. Simon is gone.

I walk the streets of Harlem. Empty tenement stoops flicker past. They pass in whispers and giggles. My eyes search the stone steps to find the gawkers, but they're gone, whispers now only in my mind. I pass Fleischer's Chicken Market, and Morris stands in the doorway.

"Take a chicken. Everybody takes one. "

"Are you sure it's kosher?"

"I'm sure. Look, I'll give you this nice big chicken."

Fleischer's hand strangles a headless bird. Blood squirts from its neck. Wings flap and feet claw in the air. Suddenly the bird is free, running around in circles, screaming without a head. Blood sprays high in the air and falls back in red rain. It soaks the streets.

I run again. The chicken's cries fade back into time. My heels strike the pavement with the staccato tattoo of machine gun bullets. Through the clatter, flashbulbs pop and Simon's voice bellows, "I cannot tolerate, I will not permit a crime to go unpunished." I run harder.

"I will see that justice is done . . . for the honor of my office as District Attorney . . . for the good of the People."

An abyss opens in the sidewalk, and the runner falls into a swirling black hole. Strobe lights flash twisted rainbows on the rock walls. Down deeper and faster I fall into a well of relentless hate. I can feel it tear at my flesh. A bottomless fall into a room with a bed and brown bags stacked on the floor. Voices of sobbing women peel from the walls. The bedcovers are stitched with $100 bills. A black man with white powdered skin lies cushioned on the blankets of cash and beckons with his hands full of crisp new $1,000 bills. Forty of them.

"There's enough here for everybody. You can go home with a big paycheck. Deals like this go down every day."

The white powder turns red. Flames leap from the mattress and the heat drives me back. Through the fire, a face with horns laughs in scorn. A face of contempt and ridicule.

"Cornuto! Stupido!"

Needles of stinging fire prick my brain. Butcher knives slice through my head. And then the room turns to smoke.

Simon's voice booms, "Palermo, when are you going to stop bringing me all these fuckin' niggers and spics to try? Bring me some big Italians for a change. Some real big Italians!"

"Hey, Mike, you're doing such a great job. Why don't you come and work for my office? The D.A. and a hot cop. We'll go right to the top."

"Sorry, Ross. I can do more in the streets. I can do more in the streets."

"You're a bastard, Palermo. I offered you a job and you turned me down. I'm the District Attorney. You and your guinea friends, you're all bastards. I'll get every last one of you."

"That Simon's a saint, or at least he should be. Because then he'd be dead."

"Saints only live in heaven, Mike."

I run again.

"Gotta see the Chief."

"The Chief is dead."

"I don't care. I gotta see the Chief."

"When you find your friends, Michael, be sure you know them. Wish your friends fortune and success. You want your friends to be strong and your enemies weak."

"Simon's my friend. I helped him become strong. Now my friend wants to ruin me. He's trying to kill me. I don't understand. I'll never understand."

"You can't change a man's character. The scorpion played the friend, and now the frog is dead. You're gonna take a hit by the sin of stupid generosity."

"Vito Genovese is dead. The don is dead."

"If they can nail Genovese on a frame, they can get anybody. Anybody at all. Even you and me, Mike."

The black smoke thins into a rainbow spray on a rainy night. Sergeant Halloran's voice booms, "Fuck 'em. Nail 'em. It'll make up for all the red lights he's run through before. He needs to be taught a lesson. This'll be his penance for all his past sins. For all his past red lights or whatever the hell else he's done that was wrong."

"I'm Simon, Commissioner. I'm going to prosecute this guy with headlines that will reach across the nation. We have to show the street they can't get away with this sort of thing. An example has to be made, and, by God, Commissioner, I'll see that the criminal element never runs a red light again."

"That's the spirit, Simon. I'm sure we'll all be on the front page with you around."

Detective Groty turns to the Commissioner. "I don't like that Simon bastard. He's doing a job on everybody."

"Yes, he's quite a formidable fellow. We'll have to keep an eye on him."

My dream snaps. My mind is midnight. I'm running through a jungle of lamp posts hung with syringes and glassine bags of white powder. A laughing voice resounds through the alleys.

"It's never as dark as midnight. Ha, ha, ha. Get him! There he goes!"

Two shots crack. "Stop or I'll shoot!"

The hot steel pierces the runner's chest. It burns in my gut. But still I run on. The runner runs and bursts through sleep. Sitting up in my bed, my clothes are soaked in sweat and my head aches. My dream is gone, except for the needles and knives. It's past midnight and getting darker.

* * *

CHAPTER 17

The pains started the first day after the arraignment. Knives began slicing into my brain, cutting my head in half.

The window shades are drawn. Alongside the bed, a radio plays classical music. Chopin, Tchaikovsky, Rachmaninoff. I never listened to them before, but now they are relaxing and help me think. I lie on the bed, my head propped up on two pillows, half-sitting, I watch the shadows of street reflections through the shades. Cars leave patterns on the walls and ceilings. They move, stop, and change shape. I don't shave.

On the second day I squat down on the floor alongside my bed. With two hands, using index fingers and thumbs, I grab the wall molding near the floor and pull. It comes off with a snap, exposing a small, dark, cavernous hole. A trap hole like the kind made to hide important things. This trap is a Palermo special. It holds an equalizer. My hand trembles as I reach into the hole. My fingers shake as they curl around the handle of a loaded throw away .38 caliber revolver. They took my gun away but that won't stop me from doing what has to be done.

I watch the shadow patterns move on the walls. My fingers toy with the cylinder, spinning it like a roulette wheel. I hold the gun against my temple and squeeze the trigger. The hammer moves back. I've pulled the trigger many times before. There have been shootings. I've seen the blood, the agony, the guts, and brains on the clothes and walls. Wives and kids left behind.

My finger relaxes. The hammer slides back gently. It's not worth it. Simon's not worth it. The job's not worth it. The whole damn Department's a waste. People on the pad left and right. Nobody cares or does anything about it. Scott's a stool and nobody will believe it. It's a waste. Why blow my brains out for a waste? Got to think some more. Rest some more. I put the gun back and replace the molding and listen to Debussy and fall asleep. I sleep but don't rest. Simon and the rolling steel shaft won't let me. The slicing pains won't let me sleep and rest.

On the third day, my unshaven face is covered with a sooty scruffiness. I take out the revolver again. From my dresser I take out a spent empty cartridge from my jewelry box. The bullet from the casing was shot from John Amato's gun three years ago. It broke the right arm of a junkie who was about to blow my face off with a shotgun. It was only a matter of seconds. Everything in life, it seems, is only a matter of seconds. Seconds from Amato's gun, a squeeze of his trigger into Vasquez' right forearm, a shotgun blast wild into the wall. The empty cartridge is an amulet to me. A protector, like St. Jude.

In my right hand I hold the shell casing that saved my life. In my left is the gun that can take it away. I am a second from eternity.

I remove one of the six bullets from the gun and replace it with the empty shell case. One empty shell case and five live rounds. I spin the cylinder like in Russian roulette and let it stop wherever God wants it to stop. I hold the gun muzzle to my right temple and squeeze the trigger. The hammer draws back slowly. If God wants me to live, He'll put the empty cartridge under the firing pin. If not, then let God's will be done.

One chance in six if I'm to live. Not bad odds for a miracle to happen. My hand trembles and my trigger finger shakes and feels weak. The hammer goes back slowly, inexorably, taking a thousand years to travel one millimeter. I feel the final resistance. The final release is just one second away. Then the resistance is gone and the hammer snaps forward and crashes against the firing pin and against an empty cartridge, and there is no explosion, only a metallic click.

God wants me to live.

The phone rings.

"Mike, Augie Coletti is on the phone. Will you pick up in there?"

"Sure, Laur. I'll pick up in here."

Augie's worried about me. He wants to sit with me and go over a few things. He says he's doing good now and that now is his chance to help me. He knows about the trouble I'm in. All the boys want to help out. So I should come on over to his mother's place in the Bronx for lunch and we can talk about it.

God is good.

* * *

Augie Coletti sits in a soft armchair in the living room of his mother's house in the northeast Bronx. He wears brown silk pants, diamond rings, shoes shined to glass, and a white summer undershirt with narrow shoulder straps. Across his chest hangs a St. Jude gold medal encrusted with diamonds and suspended from a gold chain. Augie's mother brings out espresso coffee and homemade ricotta-filled cannolis.

"Mama, that's just what we needed. Thank you, *cara*. I can't resist your pastries." Augie smiles and squeezes his mother's hand. She pats him on the head and then pours two cups of coffee.

"Mrs. Coletti, I can't wait to try your cannolis again. It's been a long time." I sit in the chair opposite Augie.

"It's been too long, Michael. It's too many years since we see you. When you were little boys, I would see you all the time. You were good boys. I remember. But now you're all grown up. You don't eat much sweets anymore? You must be watching your figure."

She pats me on the shoulder and goes back to the kitchen to make pasta.

"She's something, ain't she, Mike? Eighty-two years old and she wants to do everything herself. I want to get her a maid or a cook and she says no. She just wants things to stay as they are. To never change. She'd keep us little kids forever if she had her way."

Augie twists a slice of lemon peel and slips it into his coffee. "How's your mom feeling, Mike? I bet she's just like mine."

"She's fine, Augie. I found her a nice little apartment up in Yonkers. She's happy. I see her a few times a week." I bite into the pastry. "These are the best cannolis I ever ate. Remember how Sal Attari used to flip over your mom's cooking when we had those block parties in the old neighborhood? We couldn't get him away from her table."

"Sal Attari. He's away now, up in Ossining. Remember how crazy he was? Stealing everything out of Woolworth's that wasn't nailed down. Sal's problem was that he didn't know when to stop. Like that day when we ran interference for him and set up a diversion so he could fill up his pockets. He was the only one who got caught. You'd think the dummy would have realized that you can't hide a cash register under your coat."

Coletti settles more comfortably in his chair. I know he didn't set up this meeting to talk about his mother's cooking and the old days.

"Yeah," I say, "but you can't always call the shots, though. Take Eddie Pavia. I'll never forget the day when we were swimming in the East River off 116th Street. Poor Eddie. Everybody was diving into the water. Remember that water, Augie, deep brown, the oil slick, floating garbage, white eels, and pieces of turd? How the hell did we ever go in? Poor Eddie. He dove and never came up. You and me jumped in to find him. It made me sick. When I got back on the dock, I puked my guts out. I wonder if he felt anything? If he knew what happened to him? His head stuck in one of those old milk cans. He scraped his face off with the dive. His legs just floated there in the garbage straight up."

"I remember," says Augie. "It took the police divers two hours to raise him. They pulled him out with his head still stuck in the can. You see Mike, Sal and Eddie were losers. Sal because he was stupid, and Eddie because he didn't have the luck. It's not enough to be smart. You gotta be lucky too. And you gotta have friends. Friends in the right places. That's the edge you gotta have. I'll never forget what you did for me. We go up and we go down in this life. Now I'm up. And I'm gonna bring you up with me.

"You're facin' a bad rap. This guy Simon wants to use you to get his ass up to Albany. Forget about him for now. Put your head together and let the lawyers handle it. They're pros.

"I've got a friend in the William Morris Agency who's connected with a rock group from England. They're called The Rolling Stones. He's bringing them into the country and he needs somebody to see that they stay out of trouble. A security deal. *Capisce?*"

"I understand," I answer.

"I've told them I've got the man for the job. It's yours if you want it. You'll go all over the country on the Rock circuit. If you want it, it's yours. You'll be representing me. It's important that they avoid trouble. I have other investments with these people and this can lead to bigger arrangements. You'll be paid by The Rolling Stones and you'll draw from me. You'll be my right arm looking after them. It'll give you a chance to get away and clear your mind. When you get back, the lawyers will handle everything. What do you say?"

Augie holds out his hand and I grab it right away. It's a sweet deal. One I never expected. A handshake. A deal. A new job and maybe a new life.

"Before you leave, Mike, I have something for you." Augie takes his hand out of his pants pocket. In his palm is a gold St. Jude medal encrusted with diamonds on a gold chain just like the one around his neck. "When I was low and really down so bad, you helped me. And so did he. He still does. They say this fellow helps those who need it the most. Now it's my pleasure to help you too. Take the Saint with you. I know he'll be a great help to you too."

Augie drops the medal into my hands, and I immediately put it on over my silver St. Jude medal. Two's gotta be better than one. It won't hurt.

"Remember what I said, you gotta not only be smart, not only be lucky, but you gotta also have the edge. Have a good trip, and keep in touch. The boys are looking out for you too."

* * *

BROOKLYN DOCK WAREHOUSE

"Look, Nicky, this is no bullshit," says Vincent Gennaro. "It comes straight from the top. Not from just my Family, but from the whole Commission. I never seen these guys so mad. They're gonna cut your balls off and hang 'em from the flag pole if you don't stop this contract. You gotta control your people. You can't afford to have shitheads like Albie Simmons ruin your business. If you want to do business with us, you gotta keep the peace. You can't have your people goin' around and putting a hit on a cop. And this guy's no ordinary cop. He's a personal friend of the Family, if you know what I mean. He's got two dons asking every day how he is. I got orders to have your fuckin' head blown off if he gets a scratch on his ass.

"Do you understand what I'm sayin'?"

"Yeah, Vinnie, I get the message. I'll talk to Albie first thing. I'll set him straight. I don't want nothin' to burn our business. We got too much to lose if we go at each other's throats." Nicky Barnes lights a cigarette and blows smoke rings in the air.

"No, Nicky, you still don't understand, do you? We ain't talkin' about going at each other's throats. I'm talkin' about blowin' your fuckin' head off if this cop gets a cold. Do you understand me now? You ain't gonna have a chance to do nothin' except get buried."

"I gotta to talk my boys."

"Didn't you used to have a 'boy' named Ernie Chubbs?"

"What do you mean 'used to'? He's Albie's right hand."

"Well, not any more. He just took a vacation. Permanent, if you know what I mean?"

"Oh. I understand. I'll talk to Albie now."

"Good. Because if we hear any more talk about contract, or if anybody I know's got bullets flyin' around his head, there ain't gonna be no more Albie, or Monroe, or Nicky. We're gonna find a new crew to do business with. *Capisce?*"

"Yeah, I understand. Now can I get the hell out of here?"

"Sure, as long as you take care of business—now."

* * *

Frankie Faiella watched Ernie Chubbs as he got into his car at 125th street and Third Avenue. Chubbs lit a cigarette. Faiella had followed Chubbs as he had tailed Mike Palermo. Chubbs turned on the ignition switch just as his new Cadillac Coupe Deville exploded and turned cartwheels up the avenue, coming to rest in a shoe repair shop window. Faiella went home. The detective tail from the D.A.'s office, himself tailed by Chubbs, had lost interest in Palermo days ago. The Italians sent a message loud and clear. There would be no more contracts on any Family friends by the Barnes' organization. Albie Simmons saved 100 grand and a life— his own.

CHAPTER 18

MICHAEL PALERMO

The next morning I drive down the Harlem streets, and flashes of yesterday light up my mind so clearly I can touch them. I smell the foods and enjoy the wine in my mind. I relive my whole life as I drive to The Hole to meet with Carmine for lunch. I know my job with The Rolling Stones is finished. I'll probably never see them again up close. But that's OK. It's time to move on to other things.

Tenement buildings sweep by and little people walk and talk through life as if nothing has ever happened for the last seventeen years. It's like time hasn't moved. Nothing has changed. Time running on has brought nothing but the same.

Children play in the street. Drug dealers deal their hands. Protection and numbers action quietly creeps in the background. Loan sharks cut deeper into the poor and the weak. Cops do their jobs and the hoods do theirs. After eighteen years on the Police Force, it's hard to see any improvement. It seems that after the war is fought or left unstarted, when enough years have passed, the outcome is the same.

I meet Carmine Canicatti in a quiet rear table. He leaves the gunfighter seat open for me. He knows I'm going to need it. I'm under fire. I look forward to seeing him.

"Mike, how was the trip? I hear everything went smooth out on the Coast except that you almost got killed at Altamont." He smiles.

"It was a piece of cake." We shake hands. "And how's everything going in New York while I was away?"

"The same. We ain't had no complaints. Just a minute, Mike." Carmine has been waiting for the cook, Buds Morelli, to come to the table. "Here, Buds, your brother Fredo sent this over." Canicatti passes a fat envelope to Morelli. "He says to tell you that the Family sends their best regards and that they're behind you all the way. He wants you to tell little Fredo that his uncle will be over to see him tomorrow."

I know that Buds's brother is Alfredo Morelli, a capo in the Carlo Gianini Family of Queens. Fredo was the one kidnapped by Vecchiano's boys. That was the case where Carmine almost had me whacked because the "boys" thought I might be behind the kidnappings.

Fredo just sent $15,000 to his brother for the hospital expenses for Buds's son, little Fredo. The boy's got a brain tumor. Buds had taken the week off and only came to The Hole to meet Carmine and oversee the preparation of our lunch. Carmine looks proud as he tells me the story.

"How are the guys?" I ask.

"You heard what happened to Augie Coletti?" asks Carmine.

"Augie? No, I was just with him last night. What the hell happened?"

"Well, it must have happened right after you left him. The feds busted him on the Coast last night on an old rap. It's a damn shame. He finally had things going right for him. He was movin' up good. They got him on an old wire with Pasq Rosetti. He says he paid those bastards ten grand years ago to cut him loose. Now on this beef he figures the best he can do is cop a plea and do a year."

NAPOLITANO! I think. That bastard. He don't know what the hell he's doing. He must be a complete idiot. He sits at a table, accepts a contract, and then doesn't deliver. And he puts me in the middle. And of all people, why Augie Coletti? He was good to me. The guy trusted me. Put up his money and now he's gonna do time. That stupid bastard Johnny Napolitano. What the hell went wrong? It was nothing but a caper.

"And Buck," continues Carmine, "he's been bitchin' about having to put up ten grand of his own money to cover a contract that he didn't even have a piece of. But that's Buck for you. He'd give the shirt off his back if it'd keep people happy."

So the ten grand that Napolitano cried over, that he had to take out of his savings account, that was like giving up one of his children, that was Buck's money. And nobody said a word to me about it. Johnny played the poor goat.

I change the subject. I don't want to hear any more about what happened while I went away. I'm liable to find out that I'm already dead and that Ross Simon has been dancing on my grave.

"I hear that Jimmy Colucino is running another Italian Heritage thing next weekend. You gonna be there?"

"No, Mike. Me and the boys are going to pass on this one. I'd stay away from that if I were you. Last time, everybody was snapping pictures like crazy. It was like being in the movies.

"Look, I want to talk to you about the heat you got. Everybody knows you're taking a fall on a bum rap. We're all behind you. A hand was put out, but nobody can reach Simon. He thinks he's some kind of superhero who thinks he's God. It may not mean anything to you now, but I want you to know that my people are behind you. You were always there for us. It's a two-way street. You did the right thing with us, and we want to do the right thing for you. Now it's our turn. You do what the lawyers tell you. They know what they're doing. They're pros and they're working for us."

I'm moved. Simon and Scott, the people I work for, want my shield, my pension, and my life, while Carmine and his people are backing me all the way.

"Thanks, Carmine. Just hearing you talk like that means a lot to me. But I don't want anything. Whatever I did in the past was done because it was the right thing to do."

"I understand, Mike. But if you need us, we're here for you."

Carmine extends his open right palm and we shake hands.

"And Casper says to tell you that now that Devlin is gone you can expect people to come out of the woodwork and come at you from all sides to try to knock you down. He wants you to know that he'll do whatever he can. All you gotta do is ask.

"One final thing. There was a big meeting and a decision has been made on how to handle the D.A."

"What's that?"

"Well, this guy, in addition to giving you heat, has been after our people lately like never before. The word is that he wants to bring down our people at the top. The dons. We can't let that happen. You understand we have no choice with this bastard. He thinks he's a savior. Meanwhile, everything he's doing, what he says about us on the TV and radio and newspapers, is said to help him move to Albany. The decision has been made to make sure he gets his wish and gets to Albany—now. He's gonna be our guest. We're gonna bury him there."

"Carmine, you can't do that. He's the D.A. They'll hound your people until they get them. They'll never forget. They'll have to make an example of you. They can't let this ride. You'll have every cop in the state after your asses."

"Mike, there are ways to do this so that they'll never know who did it. We even got permission to clip Simon from another guy who wants to be governor. They can think they know who did it, but that's not enough for them to do anything about it.

I told you, it's a whole new world out there. I think a lot of people are gonna become targets in this new world, including cops and D.A.s.

"By the way, Mike? You might want to know you got nothing to worry about anymore with this Albie Simmons thing. It's all been taken care of. There's no more contract out on you. I had some people talk to him the way he understands."

"Thanks, Carmine. I appreciate it. So you see I wasn't wrong. The bastard was out gunning for me. See, you said he wouldn't do that. You were wrong. And you're wrong again on this Simon thing. You can't hit the a District Attorney."

"Well, Mike, the only other way is to have somebody talk to him. Can you take that contract?"

"Shit, Carmine. I feel like I'm walking in shit now. Give me some time to think this out."

"Take all the time you want, Mike. Just don't stand in front of the bastard. I don't want to lose a good friend. You know, Mike, if Simon is out of the picture, all your troubles are over. The word is out that Scott will take his place as acting D.A. and Scott's in our pocket. He wants to dump this whole case he started with you but the D.A. won't let him. Simon is on some kind of a personal crusade to get you. When Scott's the D.A., the charges will be dropped. Take my word for it. See what you can do, Mike. If Simon lets up on us and cuts you loose, he can live. If he wants to be a fuckin' saint, we'll give him his wish, but he's gonna have to go to heaven first. I told you saints only live in heaven. In the meantime, like I say, don't stand in front of him."

I leave the meeting with five faces in my mind. Augie Coletti, who got burned; Buck Truccolini, who got ripped; Johnny Napolitano, who double-banged them both; the D.A., who's going to get whacked; and me, the guy who got himself in the goddamn middle again.

CHAPTER 19

The day of the Italian Heritage rally is sunny and crisp. People slowly trickle in. The crowd is not as large as the first meeting. The politicians and other guest speakers are few. Jimmy Colucino will have to carry this event on his own. Banners are missing and the air is flat.

A black man with a camera meanders through the crowd and makes his way to the speaker's platform. He is Buster Moore and he is breaking his way into an alliance with the Marcante Family to start a new wholesale drug operation in Harlem. He stands in front of Jimmy Colucino and looks at his future, at his life on easy street with pink Continentals and flashy women and diamond rings. He puts his hand over a .45 caliber automatic pistol that is tucked under his belt. From left to right he snaps his head, examining faces. Jimmy Colucino needs protection.

Frankie Faiella has moved up in Giorgio Amadeo's private army. Frankie stands behind Buster Moore. Moore has been promised the same kind of operation that Nicky Barnes has. After today, Moore will be dealing directly with the Italians and his merchandise will be the closest thing there is to pure. While Barnes deals with Colucino, Moore will deal directly with the Marcante Family. He will work with Giorgio Amadeo. But first there is one favor he has to do. Jimmy Colucino speaks with enthusiasm about Italian contributions to the United States and to the world. He speaks of da Vinci, Donizetti, and the Pope. About hard working Italian immigrants and Ellis Island.

A quick glance from side to side and Buster Moore rips out his .45, aims it at Colucino, and blows a hole through his forehead. Paralysis grips the crowd. Blood splashes down from the stage over the spectators. Guest speakers next to Colucino are splattered. They catch the dead man as he falls into them.

Frankie Faiella grabs Buster Moore's arm and spins him around face to face. A sawed-off shotgun springs out of Faiella's coat. With the barrel in Moore's mouth, he pulls the trigger. The blast shatters Moore's head and sprays it over the front stage. He is out of the drug business. Permanently.

The scattergun jumps from Faiella's hand into the throng behind him. It runs through the hands of ten men and is finally swallowed into a sewer cover slightly ajar. The cover is quickly sealed by the feet of a frightened crowd.

Frankie Faiella lowers the brim of his hat, turns, and walks away.

On the television screen that evening, Francesco Colucino watches the newscast as his son is murdered. He grows limp. The words of Alberto Marcante echo through his brain like a bad dream.

"When something stands out, it becomes a target. Sooner or later, a target will be shot. Shot right between the eyes, Francesco. For that is its nature."

Don Colucino cannot cry. He will mourn his son but not with tears. Life has left him dry.

CHAPTER 20

MICHAEL PALERMO

The trial is coming up, and I have to go over the case with my lawyers. I go back to Parkchester to see the fountains and ride around them like I did with Chief Devlin. I don't know what to do. The "boys" have a contract out on the D.A. Scott's ready to take his place and drop the case he brought against me. Scott's dirty and I'm clean. He's going to be the D.A. after the hit on his boss that he knows is going down. His boss, Ross Simon, wants to take me off the street and ruin my life. Carmine wants to clip him. What's the problem? Why am I so stupid? It's that goddamn line that I can't cross. Do I have to be stupid? No. For a change I'm gonna be smart, go bad, and keep my mouth shut. Say nothing. Congratulate Scott, the new D.A., and dance on Simon's grave.

I ride on nervous energy capped with frustration. At St. Raymond's Church I make a left turn onto Bronxdale Avenue. The Ryan funeral home and Sunshine Diner are on my right. I try to touch the past and crawl back into it. Only I don't fit anymore. Pearce Avenue is on my right just past the train bridge. I remember the little foreign car that had crashed two years ago into the bridge abutment, killing both passengers. The car hit it head-on and the backseat ended up touching the abutment wall. The guy made a mistake of only a few inches. A second too late to turn away from the bridge.

Sometimes all we get is a second to change our lives forever. What a waste that crushed car was.

I turn on Pearce Avenue. Two blocks to Radcliffe. There's the house on the corner. A two-story, one-family frame house with two kitchens, one on the first floor and one in the basement. In the back yard is a grape arbor. A wooden table and benches sit empty under the vines. They are Alfonso Palermo's vines. It is my Uncle Alfonso's house. I have to talk with blood.

I enter through the side gate into the vineyard pavilion. There in the corner is Alfonso Palermo pruning vines, already preparing for the next year's harvest. It is almost Christmastime and Alfonso knows the importance of planning ahead. This holiday, as always, he will have homemade wine, wine like he used to make back in Agrigento with his brother, my father, Pasquale. That time was a thousand years ago, and its memory must be growing dim in the old man's mind.

He hears the gate latch clink. He turns and smiles. Under the arbor and sleeping vines we embrace. I am his link and picture of the past and he is mine. He says I remind him of my father. We sit in the December chill and talk Sicilian.

"You look tired, Michael. It's good that you've come. I don't know how, but somehow I sensed that you would be coming to see me."

"I was riding, Uncle, and the car had its own way and just took me here. It stopped outside and here I am."

Alfonso smiles, "Like the young goat who walks away and goes out on his own. Sooner or later he returns to his old pasture."

I nod. "I feel more like one of those fish, those salmon, fighting to get upstream, to get back home, into the quiet water where everything is peaceful. And then the fish dies."

"I see. Come, let's go inside where it's warm and we can sit by the fire and have some vino."

We enter through the back door into the kitchen. Aunt Maria is glad to see me. We kiss, speak a while, and then Uncle and I take the stairs down to the basement.

"Tell me what the trouble is," says my Uncle. "I can see the trouble on your face."

"It's a long, long story, Zio, and everything seems to be falling down on me at once. I can't begin to explain."

"Michael, there are no new troubles. They've all happened before, only they come back with different faces. The Palermos have never had the easy way. In the old days we had to fight and steal just to have food and a fire like the one we sit before today."

The fire burns in an old black iron stove and we drink dark red wine, the color of blood.

"Your father and I came to this country together from Agrigento. We left our wives and families behind. We came to find the better life. The big ship that carried us across the great ocean was called THE FATHER. Over the years it earned its name. That voyage was not easy. The ship lost a propeller and it took us sixty days to make a crossing that should have only taken thirty.

"Many people got sick, some in their stomachs and blood, and others in their minds. Many died and we buried them at sea.

"It was wintertime when Pasquale and I finally arrived at Ellis Island. We wore summer clothes, for that was all we had. Sicily was warm and there was no need for the things of winter.

"We had very little money, but when we saw the Lady in the harbor with the torch in her hand, we felt proud and strong, like we were welcome. But . . . as with many things, we were wrong.

"Together, side by side, in the summer clothes of Agrigento, your father and I shoveled snow for the City of New York. I'll never forget how cold it was. We had never before felt the bony coldness of winter or the loneliness. Your father got a job on the docks and worked unloading ships. I built houses, brick by brick, hand by hand. Soon we had enough money saved so that we could bring our wives and children over.

"We remembered how on Ellis Island people had been herded like cattle. Many became sick from the voyage. Your father thought it would be best for our families to come here directly and not be part of the crowd. Some people, because of illnesses, were sent back to Italy. Your father would take no chances with his family's future. He was a strong man who did what he thought was right. He was like you, Michael. He had made a decision like a king for his people. Little did we think then that even the greatest king is a subject of destiny and death."

Uncle Alfonso's face grows sad, weighted for a moment with the dusty memories of the past. He pauses, inspires deeply and continues. He talks now with the heart of a proud young man filled with anticipation.

"I remember the day. Your mother and Aunt Maria and their little ones huddled on the deck of the big ship. Together Pasquale and I rowed out to meet them. We looked up. The women were crying, and the children were laughing. Nervously, your father tied a rope tightly around a small package of money. His poor fingers could not work fast enough. The ship's captain pulled the money up, counted it, and released our families. Down the ladder they came and climbed into our little row-boat. For us it was summer.

"We rowed back and sang, all of us together. The white seagulls flew all around us and they sang too. I'll never forget that day, Michael. I haven't thought of it for years. I almost lost the memory. It's good you've come today. I'm glad."

I am sitting perfectly still. Afraid to move and break the spell of vision in the old man's eyes.

"You've made me glad too, Uncle. Please tell me more of those days and of my father. No one's ever told me these things before. I want to know about my father."

"It wasn't easy, Nephew. No, it wasn't easy. We all worked hard then in different ways than people work today. Our families each had their own apartment on the fourth floor of the same building. We had no heat. They called it a cold-water flat. We used the kitchen stove to keep warm and to cook our food. We burned coal and wood. Your brother, Salvatore, would do his job selling paper bags and clothespins. Quietly, like a fox, he would steal pieces of coal that had broken loose from the bags in the coal truck. One at a time, he would take the black rocks home to burn, to keep his family and the new baby warm. For you were born at this time. Pasquale had left you inside your mother in Sicily. So you see, my boy, you have roots in that country. It's your home, your other family.

"Carmella, your mother, would wrap the blocks of ice in newspapers to make them last longer before putting them in the icebox. Salvatore got a job working after school and on Saturdays. He made $2.50 a week. And that was a lot of money.

"I remember bonfires on the streets. They kept people warm. They were bad times but they were good times because we were all together. But there were some crazy people in those days just like there are today. One day I stopped some boys from starting a fire. They were going to burn a wagon, horse and all. And the boy I stopped, and I remember him well, became a fighter. And, if you can believe this, Michael, he became the middleweight champion of the world. But at that time he was not too strong, so I stopped him." Alfonso tilted his head from side to side, smiling.

"Your father was pleased with Salvatore. The young boy was allowed to bring home all the rotten fruit that was not sold in the store. But he was too smart for the Barese that owned the store.

Salvatore would put good fruit in the bottom of the box and cover it with the rotten. On his way home he would throw the bad fruit to the dogs. They were so hungry that they would eat anything. They would eat what the Barese had intended for us. And so everybody was happy. Your mother, because she had nice fresh fruit for her family; your father, because Salvatore had told him of his plans; the Barese, because he could feel that he was better than the Sicilians. And you, Michael, you were happy because you were a baby and your family loved you. And they took good care of the littlest *bambino* on Mott Street.

"And then later things became very bad."

Tears formed in the old man's eyes. I could see the pain that was not healed by time. But he continued.

"Then your father became sick, and he died, leaving you and everyone else who loved him. He didn't want to go to the hospital. People said the hospital was a place where people went to die. Many times, that was true. And Pasquale waited too long, and the people were right.

"Enough about the past. Let me get you some cheese."

Uncle Alfonso gets up carefully and goes into the kitchen wiping his eyes. I watch the fire dance in the open stove. I see shapes that jump and drop and swirl around. Fingers of fire waving at me, laughing and happy. The wood hisses and crackles as it burns. It is warm. It's good to be with family. My uncle returns with the cheese.

"Uncle Alfonso, we haven't spent as much time together as we should have. My life has kept us apart. Today, instead of coming to you with a gift, I come to you with problems."

"What's the matter, Michael?"

"Uncle, my thoughts are still not clear and I have headaches that won't stop. I feel like the world is crumbling around me. My enemies are getting stronger and my friends weaker.

"Like everyone else, I'm not an angel. But I'm being accused of the wrong things. As a young cop, the job was all a game. As I grew older, what I thought was fun became a serious business. People's lives were at stake. A wrong decision could have destroyed a family or a life. Maybe that's where I went wrong? At times I became too personally involved and I wasn't sure which side I was on. And then I became a target of the ambitious. I became a man of influence and some people became jealous.

"Today I feel like a wounded fox being attacked by jackals thirsting for blood. Even the dogs nipping at me have the faces of people I have mistaken for friends."

"I see, Michael. Perhaps together we can find an answer."

Uncle Alfonso sits back in his chair and gazes into the fire. With his mind he reaches back into time to find values and answers for me for today. He senses my desperation and shares my torment. It is that one special time in his life, for an old uncle to be strong and to be wise, to give a gift that only he could give.

"You haven't told me exactly what your problems are, Michael, but I'm sure that it isn't something that hasn't happened to many people before you. Over the years I've learned many things. Let me tell you the story of Santo Merola."

"There was a man in our neighborhood named Santo Merola. He was a mechanic and he was the best mechanic in New York. At least, that's what people said. Santo worked in a garage uptown. One day the garage owner received a car to fix. It was a Rolls-Royce. You know how expensive they are. This car had been in a very bad accident and everyone said it could never be fixed. Santo Merola asked the garage owner if he could have the car, since it would never work again. The man gave him this as a present. The garage owner felt good that he was giving to peasants and that he would not have the trouble of disposing of the wreck himself.

Santo was happy because he had faith in himself and because he believed in miracles.

"Every day for months, on his own time, Santo Merola worked on the broken Rolls-Royce. Part by part, gear by gear, he fixed it and it finally ran and looked like new. His friends were happy for him, and his enemies hated him even more. His family was proud. The garage owner slept with regret that this peasant did what he could not do. He hid this regret, praised Santo, and in the eyes of the people he slept with honor.

"The Merola family would ride through the streets of New York in a shiny Rolls-Royce. They sat on a false fortune and played the part the car demanded. And they were happy.

"One day Santo Merola received a letter in his mailbox. It said, 'If you want to see your son again, you will give us $100,000.' The note had directions for poor Santo to follow. He could not raise 100 pennies, much less $100,000. His wife cried and he cursed his big, shiny car.

"In two days, he received a package in the mail. In it were his son's two bloody ears. His wife almost died from the shock. Santo offered the thieves his Rolls-Royce but they refused the car that they could never hide or sell.

"Santo Merola's boy was found dead, floating in the East River."

Uncle Alfonso, with the love of a stern father, looks me in the eyes and says, "Michael, don't try to be something you are not. Be yourself and you'll always be right. If at the time you believe what you have done is right, then there's no sin, no crime.

"I'm sure you realize by now that no one cares for you more than your family. Beware. Many strangers lie under the skin of friendship.

"Tell me, Michael, how can I help you? Is it money that you need? So often money becomes a nuisance in people's lives."

"No, *Zio,* what I needed you just gave me. I can never thank you enough for being my uncle."

"Michael, whether a man is on top of the world or on the bottom, he still has the same dignity. Remember that no matter what you are or what you may become, you will never be anything more than the seeds of two families. One is made of clay, the other of honor."

CHAPTER 21

The Washington, D.C., law firm of Edward Bennett Williams maintains a luxurious Park Avenue apartment. Allen Hopkins and Gerald Yates have been regular but intermittent residents for the past few months. They commute from Washington to New York for the defense of Michael Palermo.

The apartment overlooks Central Park and the steel pillars of the New York City skyline. Palermo's feet sink into the thick velvet carpet. He feels like he's walking on live chinchillas. Hopkins and Yates join him in the living room and they talk in front of a large picture window. The two lawyers are expensive and they are being paid by one of Palermo's Friends. They discuss the meeting that will be held later this day in Ross Simon's office.

* * *

Simon is behind his desk. His phone rings and his secretary answers. Then she buzzes Simon and says, "Assemblyman Simonetti would like to speak to you, Mr. Simon."

"Hello, Tom. How are you?"

"I'm OK. Listen, I want to make this short and sweet and off the record. I'm getting phone calls from a lot of people. These are my constituents. Without them, I wouldn't be where I am today."

"All right, Tom. What's this all about?"

"I'm calling for the sake of common decency and justice. I know I don't have to say this, but I want you to be sure Mike Palermo doesn't get railroaded. You know how people can get chopped up in bureaucratic machinery and politics sometimes. I want you to be sure he gets a fair shake and doesn't get the shaft. If you feel that there isn't enough evidence, then drop the case. But that's up to you. It's in your hands and on your head. You make the decision. Don't let anything cloud your judgment.

"The way this case is going now, you must be getting a lot of pressure from somebody to convict this guy. I want you to know that there are a lot of people who want to see him get a fair deal."

"I understand, Tom. I wouldn't handle it any other way. If anybody tried to influence me one way or the other, I'd throw the book at them."

Simon hangs up the phone and takes Palermo's case folder off the top of the pile before him. Maybe the sonofabitch will cop a plea and then the whole thing will go away and be out of his hands and Palermo will admit he's dirty. Nobody can say anything about persecution then. Yeah. Maybe he'll cop a plea. That's right, a cop copping a plea.

* * *

Palermo sits uncomfortably in the soft sofa that swallows him. Hopkins is fifty-eight years old, silver-haired and aristocratic, yet his suit still rumples with a spurious sackiness. He waves some papers in the air.

"Your first mistake, Mike, was to testify before the Grand Jury. That was a dumb thing to do. Didn't anybody warn you? Advise you against testifying?"

"Yeah, they all did. But I figured I had to deny the charges and clear myself."

"Without your testimony, they could never have come back with an indictment. That smart S.O.B. D.A. tricked you into waiving your rights. I bet he goaded you so bad that you jumped at the chance to jump into the fire. He had you on the stand for three days of testimony. He must have grilled your ass good."

"Yeah. He did that all right. I can't even remember all the things I said or what he asked. It was like I was in dream."

"Why the hell did you do it?"

"There were too many lies being thrown around. I wanted to set the record straight."

Hopkins continues. "Look, this Simon guy is a real prick. We've had motions on his desk for months now and he keeps delaying everything. I can't even get a copy of the Grand Jury transcript. We're entitled to it, you know. I'm sure that some day we'll get it, but right now his strategy is to drag this thing out and wear us down. And he's doing it."

Gerald Yates interrupts. He is younger, brighter, and more polished than his partner. His auburn hair is close-cut, nails manicured and polished clear, a Georgetown graduate, impeccably dressed and well-connected in Washington political circles.

"Look, let's relax a little. Would you like some coffee, Mike?"

"Yeah, Jerry, thanks. I could use some. I'm getting real nervous about this thing. It's messing up my whole life. I just want to get it over with."

Yates serves coffee and Hopkins pours himself a scotch on the rocks.

* * *

Ross Simon examines his Palermo file. Carefully he checks every line, every crack in the face in the photo. Years ago, he remembers a much younger Mike Palermo. He remembers his first prosecution case as a young Assistant D.A. The defendant had been arrested by Detective Palermo. Simon had been less than effective in the prosecution of an open and shut case.

Ross Simon remembers how he had to play the obsequious sycophant to Judge Birnbaum when he had been phoned by him during a recess.

"Yes, Your Honor. No, Your Honor."

He had watched Palermo's eyes. He thought he had detected an aloofness. Those black eyes seemed to scoff and mock his inexperience. But the cop never said a word. The derision was only in Simon's mind.

After the recess, Simon asked the right questions, followed the right strategy, and played the jury like a Broadway actor. He won the case and invited Palermo back to his office. Simon wanted to celebrate so they decided to go out on the town that evening. The Copacabana would be just the place. They listened to Jimmy Sorelli sing. Tough-looking people kept coming over to the table to say hello to Palermo. He introduced them to Simon, who would later ask Palermo who they were.

"Just some old friends," he would answer.

The cop and the lawyer ate and drank and talked about how they had gotten to the present point in their careers. Palermo introduced Simon to some show girls and he danced with them.

"Ross, do you want to take one of them home tonight?"

"Maybe, Mike. We'll talk."

Simon drank and loosened up. He was no longer the staid, reserved Assistant District Attorney. He let himself go, and deep fantasies perched on his lips.

"I'll tell you what I would like, Mike."

"What's that?"

"Some dark meat. I never had any."

"Well, I tell you, Ross, I think that can be arranged. There's this dynamite black chick who has a pad on Park Avenue. She's expensive and exotic but she owes me and it won't cost you a thing. She's got Oriental blood in her. Let me make a call and see if I can arrange it. You sure you want to go?"

"Yeah, I'm sure. I can't wait."

Lainie Kwan, with almond eyes, was indeed exotic. Part Malaysian and part Harlem. Her long black hair swept over Simon's chest as he lay in her bed. Silken white sheets backgrounded her black skin in stark silhouette. Her flesh was honey with flowery oils. Her lips scarlet red, moist, and hot like a vulva in heat. She leaned over and pressed her mouth to Simon's. He tasted the sweetness of raspberry candy. Her breasts bobbed and dangled over him. She gently rested her nipples on his.

Simon was in ecstasy. She left him on the edge of orgasm and finally fulfilled him.

Ross Simon remembers that evening fourteen years later. He had succumbed to a fantasy. He had sullied his pride and been unfaithful to his wife. A forbidden delight that his religion and culture abhorred. It was Palermo who made me do it. Palermo will always have something on me. Simon's tryst left its indelible mark of guilt on his soul and mind from the day after it happened and he had carried it ever since.

Ross Simon's phone rings. His secretary says, "Congressman Hamill would like to speak to you, Mr. Simon."

* * *

Hopkins is on his third scotch. The morning rolls on, and Yates is speaking.

"If you go to trial, I don't think they have enough for a conviction count. However, there's no guarantee. Anything can happen when a case goes to the jury. That's a chance we may have to take. We may be able to plea bargain. How would you feel about that, Mike?'

"I don't like it. I can't lose my pension. I worked hard for it. I need that for my wife and kids. They won't go for a deal on the pension."

"We could try to bargain the pension. Now, I don't want to try to push you into anything, Mike. We're with you all the way, all through this, the trial, appeals, everything."

"What do you two guys think?" asks Palermo.

Hopkins swirls his drink. "I think we ought to break for lunch and go over some options."

* * *

Ross Simon's phone rings. His secretary says, "Judge Birnbaum would like to speak with you, Mr. Simon."

"Hello, Oscar. How are you?"

"Not too good, Ross. Look, this Palermo case is snowballing more every day. Are you sure you have to go on with this thing the way you're doing it?"

"Just what is the problem, Your Honor?"

"Look, my boy, don't give me any of that 'Your Honor' crap. Save it for the courtroom when people are listening. I brought you along in this club. Don't be a wiseass. Everywhere I go I bump into people, big people, who tell me they hope the right thing is going to be done for this decorated, brave, and loyal New York City detective who seems to be on somebody's shit list."

Simon says nothing. He just listens.

"You've opened up a hornet's nest, Ross. I hope you know what you're doing. There's been talk around about putting you up for governor next November. And the people who have talked about that are now talking to me about this Palermo thing. If you think you're going to make a big name for yourself with this case, just remember that it's not so much the man but the opportunity that determines who wins an election."

"I thank you for calling, Oscar. My phone hasn't stopped ringing all morning about this case. I've been talking to people I never thought knew that Palermo even existed."

Birnbaum answers.

"They may not have known until their friends and their political and business associates and their big-money backers told them. Just handle this the right way and don't make any mistakes. Be fair to everybody. Fair to you, fair to me, and fair to Palermo.

"Good-bye."

Simon hangs up, and Robert Scott walks into his office.

"You sent for me, Chief?"

"Yes, Bob, sit down. I've been getting a lot of interest in the Palermo case. What are your feelings?"

"Well, Chief, maybe we ought to take another look at what we've got. I went over all the transcripts and there's really not much there. Some procedural irregularities, but you know as well as I that these things happen every day on the job. His defense is going to cry, 'Selective Prosecution.'"

Scott is uneasy. He doesn't want to go to trial. A lot of embarrassing things might surface, including his own involvement with Simmons.

* * *

Palermo and his two lawyers eat lunch in The Golden Horn Restaurant. Hopkins has a double scotch. He drinks like he has plastic guts.

"Allen," says Yates, "I have that Grant case that's coming up back home tomorrow and I'd like to get back for it. I want to put everything together on Mike's case before I leave. I want to make sure he knows what's happening; how it affects his future and his reputation; and what the chances of success are with all the options."

Gerald Yates is scheduled to appear in court in Washington, D.C., tomorrow morning to defend William Grant, the son of United States Senator Hiram Grant. The young man has been swept up in the Washington cocktail circuit. At these affairs it is not unusual for a back room to be used for hashish and cocaine.

William Grant has been arrested for the possession of heroin. He had been caught after he left a candy store in a black section of Washington. Detectives found five bags of heroin under his front seat. He had two armfuls of needle tracks. He dropped his father's name and the police added another charge to his arrest record: "attempting to bribe and intimidate a police officer." Yates had postponed this trial too many times in the past and the newspapers are screaming: PREFERENTIAL TREATMENT. Sensationalism has its own insidious way of trying a person in the media.

* * *

At 2:00 PM, Allen Hopkins and Gerald Yates enter District Attorney Ross Simon's conference room. Michael Palermo remains at the Park Avenue apartment and rests from the strain. Ross Simon greets the defense attorneys.

"Good afternoon, gentlemen. Have a seat."

"It isn't such a good afternoon, Ross," says Hopkins curtly.

"What's the problem?"

"Look, why don't we stop playing cat-and-mouse. We've had motions before your office for over seven months now and almost everything hasn't been answered or has been refused. We don't even have a copy of the Grand Jury minutes. How the hell did you manage to get him to appear anyway? You must have felt real good about throwing him to the lions."

"That was your client's decision, Mr. Hopkins. My department advised him of his rights," says Simon, pointing his finger.

"We're ready to go to trial right now. This has been delayed too long. What are you trying to do, torture him? Why haven't our motions been answered? Why hasn't this gone to trial yet? You know you don't have a damn thing to convict him on."

"Mr. Hopkins, I can assure you we have a solid case. But there may be another way to handle this without putting Palermo and the Department on trial. We may have a solution before us that will be fair to everybody."

"What do you have in mind?"

"If your client would agree to cooperate with our office in an investigation of corruption within the Police Department, we'll drop all charges when the investigation is complete."

"You want him to be a rat, a stool?" thundered Hopkins. "Forget it. That's out of the question. I know he'll never go for it."

"Try him," suggests Simon.

"Forget it!" repeats Hopkins sternly.

"Well, then, we have nothing to discuss, do we, gentlemen? . . . unless . . ." Simon hesitates.

"Unless what?" asks Hopkins.

"Unless he takes a plea."

"What did you have in mind?"

"If he pleads to the lowest felony charge, a Class E felony, we might be able to arrange a short prison term. Almost like a token sentence."

"A felony? Forget it. That's impossible. The man is innocent. But, understand, we're reasonable people. He might agree to pleading to an offense," says Hopkins.

"An offense? That's a parking ticket! What do you think this is, a game? You're sitting here in the District Attorney's office in the Supreme Court Building with a client who's going to be put away for a long time on a major felony conviction and you're talking about an offense?"

Simon feigns amazement. He's just negotiating. He doesn't want to go to trial. He wants a piece of Palermo and wants to get the pressure off his own back at the same time.

"I'll tell you what," he says after examining the papers in his hand. "Suppose he pleads to a misdemeanor?"

Hopkins asks, "What would the charge be?"

Simon thinks. "Well, it has to relate to the case. Something simple like 'obstructing governmental administration.' That's almost like spitting on the sidewalk."

"Spitting on the sidewalk?" asks Hopkins.

"Well, a little more serious than that," says Simon.

Yates speaks for the first time. "What are the implications of that charge?"

"He'll take a short sentence and it'll be over," replies Simon.

Yates answers immediately. "You know as well as we do that a cop wouldn't last a week in prison. He'll wind up at the end of a shiv. Mr. Simon, there's only one way we can present a compromise like this to our client.

"Number one, he won't serve any time in prison. And number two, he gets his pension."

"Are you crazy?" yells Simon. "A dirty cop getting his pension intact?"

"Mr. Simon, have you convicted him already?" asks Yates coldly.

"Look, there's no way this guy's going to walk away from this with his pension. It's unheard of. The Department will never go for that."

"Well, then, we go to trial, and we want all our motions acted on immediately or we'll file a malfeasance and obstruction of justice charge against you!"

Yates becomes the aggressor.

"Don't threaten me, Mr. Yates, or I'll have you thrown the hell out of here!"

"Gentlemen, take it easy," says Hopkins. "Look, Mr. Simon, why don't you think it over? We'll discuss this with our client and you see what you can do?"

"All right," says Simon. "But one last thing. Your man must agree to testify at the Simmons trial after this is settled. And if the pension deal can be arranged, which I doubt it can, first he pleads guilty and then the pension is approved. Do you understand that?"

Yates shakes his head. "Impossible. Too many things can go wrong. Things outside your control. You could die or get killed before you can carry out the contract. First he gets his pension and then he takes the plea."

"You know, you guys drive a hard bargain," says Simon. "Talk to your client and we'll meet here tomorrow to see what we have."

Hopkins and Yates return to the apartment. They present the compromise to Palermo.

"Look, Mike, you don't have to decide now. I think we should all sleep on it," says Hopkins.

"No, I want to decide now. I have to put this thing to rest. I have to get it over with. Now, you say I get my pension and I don't go away and I testify against Simmons?"

"That's right," says Yates. "It's a misdemeanor, and you'll have a record."

"Imagine that," groans Palermo. He hesitates, looks up, and says, "Take it! I'll take it and it'll be finished."

"Now, Mike, Simon's still going to check out the pension. Nobody's ever gotten his pension in a case with a plea like this. You'll be the first one," says Yates. "And if he comes back with no pension?"

Palermo interrupts, "Then tell him to shove his plea up his ass, and we go to trial, and we go all the way."

"OK," says Hopkins. "Now let's have a drink."

"You two go ahead," says Yates. "I have to catch the plane back home for tomorrow morning's case."

Hopkins drinks alone after Palermo leaves. He drinks into the early morning until he collapses. He is handling his marital problems with alcohol. His wife has won a separation. His alcoholism has severed a twenty-year marriage. Hopkins knows she's been dating and the alcohol that ruined him is now his refuge.

On the next morning Allen Hopkins finishes the negotiations with a splitting hangover.

"Your boy must have a hook somewhere," says Simon. "I got him his pension. This is unprecedented. I really had to reach a lot of people."

Hopkins' head pounds. "You got some coffee around here?" he asks.

"Sure," says Simon. He orders coffee. Hopkins wants to wind things up quickly.

"Look, about this misdemeanor, 'obstructing governmental administration,' is that the bottom of the list in terms of penalty?"

"It's like spitting on the sidewalk."

"Look, it carries a prison term. People don't go to prison for spitting on the sidewalk."

"It's only an expression."

"Is this the bottom line then? If we don't take this, we go to trial?"

"We go to trial," says Simon.

"We'll take it."

* * *

Michael Palermo's pension application for early retirement after eighteen years of service is processed and approved. He becomes the only police officer in the history of the New York City Police Department ever to receive a pension while under indictment. His case serves as a precedent for others.

While waiting for his pleading before the court, he testifies as the arresting officer in narcotics cases and other cases before the Court. At the end of one such day of testimony, he steps out of the building on to the top steps of the concrete stairway leading to the street.

He lights a cigarette and inhales deeply. He hears talking behind him and recognizes the voice of Ross Simon. He is talking business with one of his assistants.

MICHAEL PALERMO

I can't believe it when I hear Simon's voice behind me. I don't want to have a confrontation. I don't want to blow the plea deal. I need my pension and I've agreed to lie to a false charge to get it. I can't take any more pressure. There's too much. Then I remember the words of my Uncle Alfonso.

"Be yourself, Michael, and you'll always be right. Don't try to be something you're not. If at the time you believe that what you do is right, then there is no sin, no crime."

How can I take a plea and deal with this bastard behind me? My life's a lie then. How do I live with myself? I wish the sonofabitch was dead. He deserves to be dead for what he's doing to me. Carmine was right. I should have taken him up on whacking Simon. The bastard deserves it more than anybody I know. I believe that's the right thing to do. Then, like my uncle said, there's no sin, no crime.

"Don't stand in front of Simon."

That's what Carmine said.

"I don't want to lose a good friend."

I wouldn't be found dead within 100 miles of Simon. Pass me, you bastard, and walk down those steps into your department car with your bodyguard cop chauffeur waiting for you at the bottom of the steps. He brushes by me, alone. Carrying a case. My file is probably in there. Tomorrow's the pleading before Judge Birnbaum. His friend, "the friendly to D.A.s" Judge Oscar Birnbaum.

Simon's going to laugh his ass off when I cop to a plea. Maybe I won't. Maybe I'll surprise the bastards. I'd love to see the expression on Simon's face when I change my mind. No, I can't do that. If I back out, I'll never get my pension again in 100 years. Then I'll blow everything. And if I go to trial on the felony charge, I lose my pension and do time. I won't last a week in jail. Gotta think. I wish Simon was dead. Then Scott's the D.A. and he drops the case and I have no more problems.

As I watch Ross Simon walk down the Supreme Court Building steps, I see two familiar faces across the street watching him make his way to his car. Frankie Faiella and Giorgio Amadeo sit in a black Buick. Simon's chauffeur-driven car waits for him, and the driver gets out to greet the D.A. I see a car, a brown Chevy, parked a few car lengths behind Simon's car. I don't know the driver. The man in the back is big and ugly. My mind trips over the frames of organized crime figures that I examine every chance I can on the job to get to know every mob guy who might be a potential enemy. The picture stops. The guy is a "bomber" from Chicago. His name is Mostro. He's a suspect in the Vecchiano "Double Death" killing. He's disappeared. He's got a warrant out on him. He's my ticket out of here if he's here to whack Simon. The D.A. stops to talk to a judge. I testified before him. He likes me. Mostro rolls down his window. I walk toward Simon. The judge leaves and Simon walks down the steps. I follow. Giorgio and Frankie wave me off. I shake my head. I have to get between the D.A. and the Bomber. It can't go down like this. It's too much to ask me to cross over the line. The Chevy moves forward.

"Ross!" Can I see you a minute?"

Simon turns around, startled by an old familiar friend's voice. His face looks puzzled as he looks at me.

"Palermo, you know I can't talk to you. What are you doing here?"

I place my body between Simon and the Bomber who's gotta have a machine gun with what I know from the Vecchiano killing. These guys always stick to the same M.O.

"You here to beg, Palermo? I already gave you your pension even though you don't deserve it. How the hell did you ever get on the Force, you with all your guinea mobster friends?"

I think maybe I'm making a bad mistake. I turn sideways, about to leave and let fate take Simon to an early grave. But he keeps talking and I have to stay and listen. Not run away from the bastard. I can't have him think I'm scared of him. I see Mostro look across the street at Giorgio as if to ask, "What do I do? Do I take both of them down?"

"Fuck you, Simon. You can go to hell!" I scream at the D.A. and make a sharp left turn down the street and away from the hail of bullets I know is coming any second.

They never come. I see the Chevy bolt down the street. Giorgio must have waved him off while I was standing in front of Simon. Giorgio didn't want Carmine to lose a good friend. Carmine must have put out the order.

Simon's still alive and I have to face him in Court in the morning. He drives away with my old partner, Richie Arculeo, behind the wheel. He's got taxi duty today. Good thing Simon didn't get whacked. Richie would be dead by now for sure.

* * *

SUPREME COURT COUNTY OF THE BRONX
THE HONORABLE OSCAR BIRNBAUM PRESIDING
"Michael Palermo, you are charged with obstructing governmental administration. How do you plead?"

I stand before Judge Oscar Birnbaum with my attorneys. The deal is I will answer the charge personally.

There is a pause. A dead time in space in which hearts stop beating and breaths stop. It is a pause of no return. The moment is not recapturable. It is a moment of deadly silence in which tiny, disinterested specks of dust float imperceptibly in the muted shaft of sunlight sprayed in spotlight on the Judge's desk. Larger specks of dust stand around the wooden desk waiting for the accused to answer. From dust to dust, my answer will be final, a breath, a voice which once cast on its way, will instantly pass the point of no return.

In that pause of seconds, the thoughts of a lifetime race through my brain and are swallowed in the tempest of a neural electronic storm, an explosive dynamism of nuclear fusion. In that final moment of the greatest crisis of my life, an answer is forged of pure-crystal clarity, a response tempered from war, from honor, and from love; a voice of a life fighting for survival from Sicily to Harlem. A voice rings out uncontrolled, unfettered, and unchained, a spontaneous flow of incorruptible, simplistic truth thunders through the courtroom, ricocheting off the desks and walls and people. My throat swells in sound.

"NOT GUILTY, YOUR HONOR!"

It is my voice, the voice from within that cannot be repressed, cannot be caged for a lifetime behind bars of fabrication. It is a voice that needs fresh air; a voice that will wither and die if it is created from the breath of a liar.

The accused will stand behind the voice from within, and I will stand trial.

Rustling whispers shake and crinkle among the spectators, gently rising to the level of plain speech, and finally breaking into the trumpet of a crowd gone wild with surprise; a Coliseum of Christians crashing into applause because the lions have lost. A peopled courtroom pokes and shoves and crowds the railing separating the arena from the spectators.

Ross Simon's head snaps around, glaring at me. A tremble trips from his lips, and his voice cracks in a high pitch above the gossipy roar of the crowd.

"I object, Your Honor. He can't do that. We had a deal!" Simon waves papers in the air in front of Birnbaum. "You can't back out of this deal, Palermo! You've been squirming out of things for years. Well, not this time! We got you right this time!"

Judge Birnbaum's face registers a blank page. His mouth dangles from his face, speechless. Hopkins and Yates ring around me. Yates is the first to speak. "Mike, do you know what you're doing? Do you realize what you did?"

"Sure, I know. I'm fighting the bastard back. I'm not going to lie down for that bum and that two-bit lackey stoolie he's got working for him. They think they've got Palermo counted out? Well, tell them they better start counting again. Tell 'em I haven't even thrown the first punch yet." My right hand slowly curls into the sign of the horns—the *cornuto,* and I point them at Ross Simon.

"Order! Order!" demands Birnbaum as he whacks his gavel on the clapper. "I want order in this Court!" He restores decorum from disaster. He has never seen a District Attorney come so close to physical embattlement in a court of law. "Mr. Simon, what is this you said about a deal?"

"Your Honor, certain pretrial understandings and accommodations were determined before this appearance, and they have been repudiated and not carried out as expected."

"You mean to say, Mr. Simon, that certain understandings have become misunderstandings?"

"Yes, Your Honor, apparently."

"Well, then, I suggest we take a short recess at which time I will confer with the attorneys for the defense and the prosecution in my chambers."

The gavel so rules.

Hopkins puts his arm around me and leads me off to a holding room across the hall.

"You're some helluva surprise, Mike! You've got a magnificent pair of balls. And I'll tell you something else, I'm glad you pulled the rug out from under them. Now we'll see what the hell they're made of."

"Ross, what the hell's going on here?" rasps Birnbaum as he pours ice water into a glass.

"I thought you said this case was cut-and-dried. That he copped a plea."

"He did. That was the agreement."

"Did anyone tell him that was the agreement?"

"His lawyers did. They were supposed to. I'm sure they did. Now he's trying to pull a fast one to make us all look bad." Simon is badly shaken.

"Your Honor, I object to the District Attorney's attempt to prejudice you against our client by irresponsible and unfounded accusations," Yates pipes in.

"Well, Mr. Yates, was there a plea bargaining agreement or not?" asks Birnbaum.

"My client and only my client can be the judge of that, Your Honor. The only agreement that binds is that which he makes in his heart and with his conscience. The only answer he gives to the charge against him is the answer he gave to your question. Morning brings clear answers to muddy questions of the night before. It is obvious, Your Honor, that our client is not guilty and has given the District Attorney the opportunity to prove him otherwise. We will go to trial."

* * *

That evening is the scene of one of the wildest, unbridled parties of sheer joy and celebration in the histories of the police department and organized crime. The city is a party. Mike Palermo's health is toasted in after-hours clubs, gambling parlors, precinct locker rooms, country clubs, and church rectories. It is from these sources that favors and friends will be called in for the title defense of a street kid from Harlem who wouldn't kneel before lions.

Tony Amendola hosts a small private party at his Chateau Pelham. Michael Palermo is the guest of honor and is his old self again. He sits and breaks bread with friends, with cops, and wise guys, in one room, in one mind. He sits with his attorneys, with his partners, and with his bodyguards, with people who wouldn't let him and wouldn't want him to go down without a fight. He sits with his two families: one of blood, the other of honor.

MICHAEL PALERMO

A warm confidence trickles over me, and I get up to speak with friends. A hint of tears glisten in my eyes. My throat is dusted with the sands of overwhelming gratitude. I sip some wine to clear the web of time and memories.

"I want to thank all you guys for sticking with me." My voice cracks. "There's nobody who wants to take a fall on a bad rap. We've seen a lot of things go down in our time, things that were rotten. Together we all worked hard and made a lot of those things right. I don't know how this is going to turn out but I can tell you one thing. I ain't goin' down without a fight."

All my friends stand up and applaud. Fists punch high in the air. Cigars jiggle as tough, rough faces cheer: "You tell 'em, Mike! Attaboy, Mike! We'll murder the bum, Mike!" And they're for real.

"Thanks, but I'm going to do this myself, and I'm going to do it the right way. I'm going to pick him apart, piece by piece. But first, I'm going to wipe the slate clean." I take a piece of folded paper out of my jacket pocket. With one hand holding it, I flick my lighter and set the paper on fire. Orange flames snap at my fingers and white smoke veils my face. Through the smoke, I speak. "This is my pension going up in smoke. If I'm not good enough to have earned it, then Simon can have it. I don't want it unless I get it the right way." I cup my hands and let the flames burn and die in my palms.

"This Cosa Mia is mine alone. Thanks for your help, fellas, but in the end there'll only be two people in the ring. Me and him. And he's the one who's going to take the fall."

From the doorway, an elderly, ruddy-faced, silver-haired man watches me speak. I look up from the ashes in my hands and my head turns towards the doorway to see the warmth and empathy glow in the face of Chief Collin Devlin.

"Stay in the center of the ring, my boy!" he calls. And then the face and the words disappear. No one else hears. No one else sees. But now I know I have everyone I need on my side.

The day of the trial explodes with reporters and flashbulbs in the halls of the courthouse. The media becomes permanent fixtures.

The courtroom overflows into the halls. In row upon row sit witnesses, character witnesses; leaders in law enforcement, leaders in crime, leaders in faith. The centrifuge of life separates the defense artillery across opposite sides of the room. It is a scene from my daughter's christening. Cops and robbers. Good money and bad. All the same. And Monsignor Torrone and Father Baldini in the front row with Casper Nardino. And Judge Oscar Birnbaum presides. Politicians, prosecutors, and priests come to testify. They are all there, and they won't let me stand alone. It is a time for favors and for dues to be paid.

Hopkins and Yates flank me. I know District Attorney Ross Simon feels feathers in his gut as he thinks: *Maybe this isn't the way to the governor's mansion. Maybe I should drop the case. Withdraw the charges. Make the whole world happy. Be happy so they'll leave me alone.*

I'm ready. Let him come at me!

* * *

The pause of private fantasy is shattered by the Judge's gavel. "Perhaps you didn't hear me. I will repeat it again. Michael Palermo, you are charged with obstructing governmental administration. How do you plead?"

There is no pause now. No longer the luxury of time. No more freedom of fantasy of what might be. No longer the time to indulge in "what if." There is time only to answer, not to question. Only to answer, not answers forged by others. But I can't answer for others, only for myself. I can't smother the fire that burns at me from deep inside. I can't throw away everything in my life that I hold most sacred. I can't give the jackal my honor to maul and tear apart in bloody victory on the streets of New York, the streets that are my life. My family will not live the words manipulated by others, the words of the puppeteers who seek to use me as a cobblestone in the march to Albany.

My head snaps around as Birnbaum waits impatiently. Disbelieving reality, I scan the faces of the crowd watching me. All my character witnesses have disappeared back into my mind. They're all gone. I stand alone. But I stand strong. The crowd begins to whisper and snicker. Seconds become hours.

I look back at the judge, at my attorneys, face to face, at Ross Simon's smug aloofness of victory, back to Birnbaum. There will be no second chance, no second answers. My voice booms through the courtroom, ricocheting off the walls and desks and people.

"NOT GUILTY, YOUR HONOR!"

Ross Simon's head whips around, glaring at me. I glare back, cold steel wrapped in the horns of the *cornuto*. The victim will live to fight another day and Ross Simon will stand trial and fight for Mike Palermo's life. Fight to steal it from Lady Justice.

CHAPTER 22

MICHAEL PALERMO

There's a lot of preparation work to do before trial. My Washington, D.C., law firm sends up attorney Mary Larkin. She's an expert in jury selection. She examines the backgrounds of prospective jurors and either accepts or rejects them. She looks at their ethnic heritage, sex, age, job, education, economic class, past history with the police, religious beliefs, and things like that. She can win or lose a case depending on how sharp she is on picking the right people to be on the jury for our side. The lawyers and witnesses play to the jury.

Hopkins tells me, "Everybody lies in Court. The plaintiff lies, the prosecution lies, the defendant lies, the witness lies, the defense attorney lies, the judge lies, and sometimes the jury doesn't know its ass from a hole in the wall."

I tell him, "Yeah, well, the only thing I know is that I'm not lying. I'm telling the truth. And if I don't walk after telling the truth, then the system's not fair."

He tells me that President Kennedy once said, "Who ever said that life is fair?"

The jury is six men and six women, six white, three black, two Hispanic, and one Chinese.

We're going to let Simon present his case, his evidence, and his witnesses and then we're going to parade in our own army of character witnesses. Yates says that people have been calling nonstop to testify for me. He's got to be careful and pick the right people because Simon's one sharp and mean sonofabitch. He says that the bastard would even put a Monsignor away. I go over our witness list with him and we agree.

Simon gives us a list of his witnesses and the evidence he's got. Jerry Marshall and Robert Scott are his star witnesses and he's got tape recordings of our meetings and Scott's transcript recollection of part of a tape that was inaudible. One thing that he doesn't have is the truth. And the truth is going to set me free. I'm nervous but I'm confident. Laura is at my side and my family is behind me 100 percent.

On the day of the trial, the courthouse is packed again with the media. I brush by TV cameras, reporters, and photographers. This time I let them snap my picture because I know I'm going to win. I give them something to remember me by. And even if I lose, I'm going down fighting. If you put up a good fight, there's nothing to be ashamed of.

In the courtroom, the gallery is filled with my law enforcement buddies. Detectives Groty, Ferrara, Dempsey, Goddard, Lombardi, Amato, Arculeo, Napolitano, and lots more. My other friends are there too. Buck, Carmine, Coletti (who's out on bail), Faiella, Amadeo. And the brass, Captain Costello, Inspector Anderson, Inspector O'Hagan, Assemblyman Simonetti, Congressman Hamill. My mother, and Augie Coletti's mother. In the front row are Monsignor Torrone, Father Baldini, and Casper Nardino. This is no fantasy. It's the real thing.

It's family.

The bailiff calls: "THE SUPREME COURT OF THE STATE OF NEW YORK SECOND DEPARTMENT IS NOW

IN SESSION. ALL RISE FOR THE HONORABLE JUSTICE OSCAR P. BIRNBAUM."

We all stand as Judge Oscar Birnbaum walks in and takes his high seat above us.

The bailiff reads the docket: "THE PEOPLE OF THE STATE OF NEW YORK AGAINST MICHAEL A. PALERMO."

I get a sick feeling in my stomach, like I'm going to throw up.

Judge Birnbaum asks, "Michael A. Palermo, you are charged with a Class E felony count of conspiracy in attempting to bribe an Assistant District Attorney. Do you understand the charge against you?"

"The defendant understands the charge against him, Your Honor," says Gerald Yates.

"How does the defendant plead to this charge?"

"Not guilty, Your Honor."

"Are the Prosecution and the Defense attorneys ready to proceed in the case of The People of The State of New York Against Michael A. Palermo?"

"The Prosecution is ready, Your Honor," says Ross Simon. He has Robert Scott and another assistant with him at the table on the right.

"The Defense is ready, Your Honor," says Gerald Yates. He is the Defense attorney of record. Allen Hopkins is associate counsel of record.

"Does the Prosecution wish to make an opening statement?" asks the Judge.

"Yes, Your Honor. The People will make an opening statement," says Simon.

He approaches the jury, lithesome as a leopard in his Brooks Brothers black pin striped suit.

"Ladies and gentlemen of the jury. You are here today not only to hear the evidence and to hear the witnesses for the Prosecution against the defendant, Michael Palermo. You are here also to help your law enforcement agencies root out corruption in the police force, a corruption that has grown into a cancer that threatens your safety and that of your wives, husbands, children, and friends. Oh, believe me, there is a strong case against the defendant.

"You will hear the Defense tell you that the defendant is a decorated war veteran and a decorated police officer. And this is true. But this is not the issue in this case. This is not relevant to the charge against this defendant. The Facts of Evidence, and that is all that you are charged to consider, and only this must you consider when you deliberate over the evidence—The Facts of Evidence will prove beyond a reasonable doubt that Michael Palermo is guilty of corrupting the sacred trust of his office as a New York City Policeman, and that he willfully and deliberately engaged in a conspiracy and attempted to bribe Assistant District Attorney Robert Scott, who sits here at my side."

Simon gestures at Scott and pauses.

"It's not an easy thing to prosecute your friend. That's right. Detective Palermo was my friend. We worked together. He was a good cop. Made a lot of good arrests. Took criminals off the streets. I respected him then. But that's not the point in this case. Not the issue before you today. All of his past accomplishments and all of his character witnesses that his Defense attorneys will parade before you, are not the point and not the issue. Not the Facts of Evidence you must restrict to your consideration.

"Because after Michael Palermo did all those good things, after he did all those things which he was paid to do, he went bad and tried to go into business for himself with a major heroin dealer in Harlem. He was looking for the big payoff from the man he arrested. The man who sells heroin to school children and ruins the lives of families throughout the city. Families like yours. Michael Palermo is as guilty as the dope pushers if he helps the dope pushers get back on the street.

"It's for this reason that you must help us rip out corruptors in the Police Department like Detective Michael A. Palermo, and I know that after you hear the evidence you will agree with the Prosecution and find him guilty as charged.

"Thank you."

Simon returns to his seat in the center of the Prosecutor's table. Scott and Bowman are at his side. He sits back to await the salvo from our side. But it never comes.

"Does the Defense wish to make an opening statement?"

Yates stands up. "Your Honor, the Defense will waive its right to an opening statement at this time but will reserve the right to make an opening statement after the Prosecution has presented its case."

"If there is no objection, I will allow the waiving of right and the reservation."

There is no objection. Yates has discussed this strategy with me. He figures to let Simon make his best case and then refute it in the opening statement, and then again when we call our witnesses and present what little evidence we have. It's hard to get evidence to prove you're innocent. I'm not supposed to have to prove that anyway. It's the other way around. The Prosecution has to prove I'm guilty beyond a reasonable doubt. Or I walk.

"The Prosecution may call its first witness," announces Judge Birnbaum.

"The Prosecution calls Detective Gerald Marshall," says Simon.

He's prosecuting this case himself. He's in the spotlight all alone. And he's got a New York City cop as his first witness against me. My friend Jerry Marshall.

Marshall puts his left hand over the Bible and raises his right hand, bent at the elbow, upper arm parallel with the floor that I feel like decking him on.

"Do you swear to tell the truth, the whole truth, and nothing but the truth so help you God?"

"I do."

I bet he doesn't, I think to myself.

Simon walks slowly up to the witness stand. Birnbaum looks down at him through his wire-rimmed glasses. All the cops in the gallery are waiting to hear what this cop, this star witness for the Prosecution, has to say.

"Please state your name," says Simon.

"Detective Gerald Marshall."

"Detective Marshall, you are a Detective First Grade and presently employed with The New York City Police Department. Is that correct?"

"Yes, that's correct."

Marshall swallows dryly. He won't look at me. He knows I'll spit in his face, the stupid bastard. He's the one who made up the whole story and put me where I am today.

"How many years have you been with the New York City Police Department?"

"Eighteen."

"Were you a detective in the Narcotics Bureau with Detective Michael Palermo?"

"Yes, I was."

"For how many years?"

"Twelve years."

"What kind of police officer was Detective Palermo when you worked alongside him?"

"He was a good cop. Made a lot of good, solid arrests."

"Did you meet him at The Briar Inn on Central Avenue in Yonkers, New York, on the evening of November 13, 1969?"

"Yes, I did."

"Did you talk with him?"

"Yes, I did."

"Did you talk about the arrest that day of Albie Simmons by Detective Palermo on drug-related charges?"

"Yes, I did."

"Is it against Police Department regulations to talk about pending cases over a bar as idle conversation?"

"Yes, it is."

"Then you and Detective Palermo broke the Police Department regulations. Is that correct?"

"Well, strictly speaking, yes."

"Strictly speaking? Is there any other way to enforce Police Department regulations?"

"No. No other way."

"Do you recall that conversation?"

"Yes, I do."

"Please tell the Court the substance of that conversation in your own words and to the best of your recollection."

"Well, it was about nine o'clock and Mike, that's Detective Palermo, came down and all the guys in the Westchester Shields were patting him on the back because of the big arrest he had made that afternoon. The Albie Simmons arrest."

"The Westchester Shields? Please tell the Court what that organization is."

"It's a society of cops who either live or work in Westchester County."

"And then what did you say?"

"I told him I knew Assistant District Attorney Robert Scott and that Scott and I were good friends."

"And are you good friends with the Assistant District Attorney?"

"Yeah, or at least I was. I don't know about now."

"I see. Please go on."

"I asked Detective Palermo if he would mind if I went up to see Scott to talk to him about the Simmons case. He said, 'No. Go see him. I don't care what he does with the Simmons case. It's in Scott's hands now.' He was mad that the D.A. and Judge Birnbaum put Simmons back on the street for such a low bail."

Judge Birnbaum loosens the white collar of his shirt that peeks out from under the top of his black robe. He twists and shakes his neck nervously. He's not looking too good to the law enforcement community right now.

"And then Mike went home and that's all there is to it."

"And did you go to see Assistant District Attorney Scott?"

"Yes, I did."

"What did you talk to him about?"

"I told him about my meeting with Mike and asked him if there was something that could be done for Simmons. Something to give him an out."

"Why did you ask that?"

"I wanted to see if there was a strong case against Simmons."

"Didn't you tell Assistant District Attorney Scott that Simmons could make you all rich if there was a loophole in the law that he could slip through?"

"Yes, I did."

"Why?"

"Well, no cop's ever going to get rich just doing his job. What Simmons makes in one week we have to work a lifetime for. Why shouldn't I look for the easy buck? I gave my life to the Police Department, and what did it get me?"

"Was your offer made to Mr. Scott with Detective Palermo's knowledge and complicity?"

"He knew I was going up there to talk to Scott. He said he didn't mind. What the hell did he think I was going up to talk to him about? The weather? He had to know what was going down. He's no dummy."

"So then it's your opinion, your expert opinion as a police officer with eighteen years of experience of the Police Force, and after having worked with Detective Palermo, that he knew that you were going to see Mr. Scott to try to find a loophole in the law that Albie Simmons could slip through, so that you and Mr. Scott and Mr. Palermo could get rich from bribes from Albie Simmons? Is that your expert opinion?"

Yates jumps to his feet. "Objection, Your Honor. Compound questions, leading the witness, calls for a conclusion."

Birnbaum looks at Simon.

"Your Honor, Detective Marshall, as a police officer, is an expert witness and as such can give his opinions and conclusions from the facts stated in his testimony. The facts contained in the question have already been stated in testimony and are not leading the witness, and while the facts may be compound, the question is not."

"Your Honor," says Yates, "the Defense accepts Detective Marshall as an expert witness on police procedures, but he cannot make judgments or draw conclusions that are outside his area of expertise. Clearly, Detective Marshall can only speculate what was in Detective Palermo's mind or what facts Detective Palermo understood relating to Detective Marshall's admitted attempt to bribe Mr. Scott. Detective Marshall's opinion is pure speculation and calls for a conclusion relating to facts outside his area of expertise."

Birnbaum sits back in his chair, looks up at the ceiling, rolls his eyes, and says, "Objection overruled."

Yates says, "Exception."

Birnbaum says, "Noted."

I don't know what all this mumbo-jumbo means, but I think I'm getting the shaft.

Birnbaum instructs the witness. "You may answer the question, Detective Marshall."

Marshall says, "What was the question?"

Simon picks up without losing a beat. "Let me rephrase the question. Is it your opinion that Detective Palermo knew and approved and expected to share in the bribe attempt you made to Mr. Scott to find a loophole in the law to have the charges against Albie Simmons dropped?"

Yates jumps up again. "Same objection, Your Honor, to a different question."

"Overruled."

"Exception."

"Noted."

Same shaft.

"Well, Detective Marshall?"

"Yeah, it's my opinion that Detective Palermo knew I was
going up to see Scott to make a deal to get Simmons a walk
and that Palermo was going to share in the payoff. That's my
opinion."

"No further questions of this witness," says Simon as he walks
by my table and smiles at Yates. "Your witness, Counselor."

Now it's our turn to cross-examine. I'm glad I got a lawyer
who knows what he's doing. I hope he knows what he's doing
because my head is spinning and I'm feeling dizzy from all this
stuff. This is all outside of my area of expertise. And besides, I'm
too close to it. It's starting to suffocate me.

"Detective Marshall, in all the years that you knew Detective Palermo did you ever once know him to take a bribe of any
sort?"

Simon jumps up. "Objection, lack of foundation."

Yates answers. "Your Honor, the People have elicited testimony from this witness implying that Detective Palermo was
engaged in a bribe attempt. The foundation of my question is
based in bribery. Before a bribe can be consummated, an attempt
must be made. Such attempt need be only the acceptance of the
bribe. The question seeks to establish if the defendant has a history
of attempting or taking bribes in the opinion or knowledge of this
expert witness."

"Objection overruled. The witness may answer the question."
Judge Birnbaum overrules.

We won one.

"I never knew Detective Palermo to take a bribe or to solicit a bribe in all the years I knew him."

"Did YOU ever take or solicit a bribe?"

"Objection," says Simon. "Self-incrimination."

"Sustained."

"I withdraw the question," says Yates. But he's got Marshall jittery now.

"Detective Marshall, did you ever know Assistant District Attorney Scott to take a bribe?"

"Objection!" cries Simon. "Mr. Scott is not on trial here."

"Your Honor," says Yates, "I am trying to establish the credibility of the evidentiary material presented by Assistant District Attorney Robert Scott. If Detective Marshall testifies that he knows that Mr. Scott took a bribe, this compromises the evidence of Mr. Scott and any testimony he may give. Mr. Scott's credibility is a relevant issue."

"Objection sustained. Mr. Yates, change the subject of your questioning, please."

"I withdraw the question."

"Detective Marshall, what were your exact words to Mr. Scott when you attempted to bribe him?"

"I don't remember."

"Is there a record of that conversation?"

"Yes, there is."

"Where is it?"

"Mr. Scott has it. He secretly taped the conversation."

Yates steps back. "Your Honor, at this time I ask the Court to instruct the Prosecution to present the tape of this conversation and have it marked as Prosecution Exhibit One."

"Very well," says Birnbaum. "Mr. Simon, will you please present that tape recording to the clerk to be marked as Prosecution Exhibit One."

Yates has them on the run. I can feel it. The momentum's moving our way. He forced Simon to present the tape before he wanted to. He stole his thunder. The tape is marked and played.

"Is this the conversation which took place in Mr. Scott's office between you and him on the day at issue?"

"Yes, it is."

"The tape is clear and complete, is it not?"

"Yes, it is."

"Mr. Marshall, were you given immunity from prosecution if you testified against Detective Palermo today?"

Simon jumps up. "Objection. That is confidential information between the witness and the District Attorney's office."

"Your Honor," says Yates, "if this witness has been granted immunity from prosecution for testifying against the defendant, this can constitute a motive for the testimony he gives. This defendant admits that he attempted to bribe an Assistant District Attorney. If he has made a deal and been granted immunity from prosecution, this provides motive enough for a perjured testimony to be given in order to save himself from conviction and a jail sentence. It is vital to the Defense that full disclosure of immunity from prosecution be revealed so that the Defense can attack the credibility of the witness. If he makes a false statement about the defendant, he gets off scot-free."

Birnbaum inspires deeply. "Objection overruled. The witness will answer the question."

"Yes, I was granted immunity from prosecution in this matter if I testified against Detective Palermo today. What else could I do? They had me cold."

"What does 'immunity from prosecution' mean?"

"It means, like you said, I get off scot-free if I testify, which I did, and now they can't touch me. I said what they wanted me to say."

"What they wanted you to say? I see. No further questions. Thank you, Detective Marshall."

I think we won that round. Now for round two. All we gotta do now is knock Scott out on his ass. Simon calls his next witness.

"The Prosecution calls Senior Assistant District Attorney Robert Scott to the stand," announces Simon.

Scott is sworn in and sits down easily. He's relaxed. This is like a chess game to him. He's used to the pressure. So am I. He doesn't get many chances to sit in the witness stand. He's usually on the other side of the railing.

"Please state your name and position."

"Robert Scott. Senior Assistant District Attorney. Chief, Narcotics Section, Bronx County."

"How long have you been with the District Attorney's office?"

"Eighteen years."

"As Chief of the Narcotics Section, do you have many prosecutions in which you have participated over the years?"

"A vast amount of prosecutions with a high conviction rate."

"A high conviction rate? How high?"

"Ninety-six percent."

"How do you account for such a high percent of convictions?"

"That's because before we bring a case to trial we are very thorough with our Facts of Evidence and our testifying witnesses. We make sure we have a solid case before we go to Court."

Yates interrupts. "Objection, Your Honor. The District Attorney has embarked on a self-praise oration on how good his department is. This has no relevance whatsoever to this case."

"Sustained," says Birnbaum. "Mr. Simon, will you please get on with it."

"Yes, Your Honor. Mr. Scott, did Detective Michael Palermo, the defendant, come to you for a meeting in your office on the morning of November 18, 1969?"

"Yes, he did."

"What was the substance of that meeting?"

"Mr. Palermo said he didn't care what I did with the Albie Simmons case."

"Mr. Simmons was arrested for trafficking in heroin, is that correct?"

"Yes, that's correct. He's a big fish in the Harlem drug trade, according to our evidence."

"Did Detective Palermo admit that he broke Police Department regulations and discussed the pending Simmons case over a bar with Detective Gerald Marshall?"

"Yes, he did. He said they talked about the Simmons case at a Shields meeting at The Briar Inn in Yonkers."

"Did Detective Palermo admit that he knew that Detective Marshall was coming to meet with you and that he told Marshall that it was OK with him?"

"Yes, he did."

"What did Detective Marshall talk to you about?"

"He wanted to know how strong the case was against Albie Simmons and if anything could be done to help him walk through a loophole in the law. He said this could make a lot of people rich, including me."

"Is it your opinion as a Senior Assistant District Attorney with eighteen years of service in the District Attorney's Office and with vast amounts of experience in prosecutions, is there any doubt in your mind that Detective Marshall was speaking not only for himself but also for Detective Palermo to get a deal for Simmons?"

"Objection, Your Honor," pipes up Yates. "Calls for a conclusion, speculation, compound question, and leading the witness."

"Mr. Yates," says Birnbaum, "we've gone over this before and I've over ruled you."

"With an exception, Your Honor. With due respect to the Court, Your Honor, this is a different question to a different witness about a different matter, and my objection stands."

"Very well. Mr. Simon, do you have an argument in opposition to the objection?"

"Your Honor, Mr. Scott is an expert witness as an Assistant District Attorney. His expertise has a foundation developed over years of evaluations of vast amounts of testimony in which he makes conclusions about the meaning of testimony and statements made in regard to criminal activities. He has the expertise to interpret not only words but nuances in conversations that implicate co-conspirators. The question asked of Mr. Scott is exactly that type of question that falls within his area of expertise. Is Detective Palermo, in Mr. Scott's opinion, based on the conversation he had with Detective Marshall — is Detective Palermo a co-conspirator in this bribe attempt?"

Simon says, "The witness is not being led but only testifying about previous testimony given to this Court. And finally, the evidence cited in the question may be compound, but the question itself is not. The question simply is, 'Was Detective Palermo involved with Detective Marshall in attempting to get a deal for Albie Simmons as part of a bribe attempt?'"

"Well, why don't you ask it that way? Objection sustained."

"Mr. Scott, is it your opinion that Detective Palermo was involved with Detective Marshall in attempting to get a deal for Albie Simmons as part of a bribe attempt?"

Yates jumps up again. "Objection, Your Honor. Speculation. Calls for a conclusion."

"I'm going to allow it this time, Mr. Yates. Over ruled."

"Exception."

"Noted. The witness may answer the question."

"There was no doubt in my mind that Detectives Marshall and Palermo were in this bribe attempt together. I wasn't born yesterday."

"Do you have a tape recording and transcripts of your meetings with Detective Palermo?"

"Yes, I do."

"Your Honor, at this time I would like to enter into evidence the tape recordings and transcripts of Mr. Scott's meetings with Detective Palermo on November 18 and 19, 1969, and I would like to have them marked as Prosecution Exhibits numbers two, three, four, and five."

"The clerk will so mark and enter," says the Judge.

Simon plays the tapes that Scott made with the so-called inaudible sections in which I denied everything. And then that's all they had. Now it's Yates' turn to tear Scott apart.

"I have no further questions," says Simon. He turns to Yates. "Your witness, Counselor."

Yates stands up at our table and projects his voice across the room to Scott.

"Mr. Scott, in the interest of Justice, let's go over the so-called evidence you have presented to this Court and this jury. You say that the tapes of yours that were just played for this Court had certain inaudible parts in them. Do you know why certain sections were inaudible?"

"No, I don't."

"Your tapes from the Marshall meeting were perfectly clear and very audible. How do you explain that?"

"I can't."

"Did you have a weak battery in the Palermo tapes?"

"I don't know."

"Was there a loose connection in the tape recorder?"

"I don't know."

"Was the tape bad?"

"I don't know."

"Was there a defect in the tape recorder?"

"I don't know."

"You don't know very much, do you Mr. Scott?"

"Objection!" yells Simon as he jumps to his feet. "The witness has already answered the questions and said he doesn't know what the problem was with his tape recorder."

"Sustained," declares Birnbaum. "Mr. Yates, will you please get on with another subject."

Yates leaves our table and approaches the witness stand. He looks at Scott intensely.

"Mr. Scott, the Defense will prove that the inaudible parts of your tape are audible in Detective Palermo's tape of the same meeting. If I told you that this tape of his will be entered into evidence, will this jog your memory about what Detective Palermo said in those inaudible parts on your tape? Or would you like to hear the Palermo tapes now?"

"Palermo made a tape?" asks Scott.

"Yes, he did."

"Then why wasn't it put into the evidence list?"

"We just came across it."

"Objection!" yells Simon. "That tape is inadmissible. It was not declared. The Prosecution hasn't had a chance to authenticate it."

Judge Birnbaum asks, "Will you be entering that tape into evidence, Mr. Yates?"

"Not at this time, Your Honor."

"In that case, Mr. Simon, we shall take up your objection when it becomes relevant. Please proceed, Mr. Yates."

"Now then, Mr. Scott. Do you remember that on the tape sections that were inaudible on your tape, do you remember what Detective Palermo said about his involvement in any bribe attempt for Albie Simmons?"

"Yes. I do. He denied being involved in any bribe attempt."

"And did Detective Palermo tell you then that he wanted to take this whole matter to the District Attorney, Ross Simon, right then and there?"

"Yes, he did. But if he was taping the meeting himself, he said what he wanted to be heard on the tape recorder to show that he was lily-white."

"Lily-white? Mr. Scott. That's a street term used by the drug pushers of Harlem, isn't it? Hardly a term to be used by a Senior Assistant District Attorney and Chief of the Narcotics Section, is it?"

"I guess that some of the job rubbed off on me," says Scott.

"Do you have a close relationship with the drug pushers of Harlem?"

"Objection!" yells Simon. "Mr. Scott is not on trial here."

"Sustained."

"I withdraw the question. So, Mr. Scott, let me get this straight. Mr. Palermo denied taking a bribe and denied having anything to do with bribing you. Is that correct?"

"Yes."

"And in your testimony and transcript evidence you never included his denials. Is that correct?"

"Yes."

"Now, let's take the testimony of Detective Marshall. Detective Marshall has admitted that he committed a felony when he attempted to bribe you on behalf of reputed Harlem drug dealer, Albie Simmons. Is that correct?"

"Yes."

"Therefore you have brought charges against Detective Palermo on the testimony of an admitted felon. Is that correct?"

Scott begins to squirm in his hot seat.

"Well, Mr. Scott? Will you answer the question?"

"Yes."

"Yes, what?"

"Yes, I brought these charges based on the testimony of an admitted felon."

"You took the word of an admitted felon over the word of a highly decorated war veteran and highly decorated police department veteran with participation in more than 2,000 arrests in his eighteen years of service. Is that correct, Mr. Scott?"

"Yes," says Scott meekly.

"And you call this good, solid evidence and a good, solid case?"

Scott pauses and looks at Simon with a blank stare on his face.

"Well, Mr. Scott. What's your answer? Do you call this good, solid evidence and a good, solid case?"

"Yes," says Scott in a whisper.

"Mr. Scott, I have gone over your tapes of your meetings with Detective Palermo, and I have yet to find one single instance where he attempted to bribe you. In how many instances can you show this Court and this jury the exact places in which Detective Palermo tried to bribe you?"

"It was more his attitude than anything he actually said. The way he looked at me. His body language. The nuances of the conversation."

"The way I'm looking at you now, Mr. Scott? Can you read my nuances and my body language?"

Yates looks like he's going to shoot Scott's ass off.

"I withdraw the question. No further questions of this witness."

Yates returns to our table with a wink. Another one for our side.

"We will adjourn until one o'clock this afternoon," says Judge Birnbaum.

Yates looks at me and asks, "How'd I do?"

"I think you blew him to hell," I say smiling. "But what do I know? How do YOU think you did?"

"I think I blew them all to hell."

Monsignor Torrone comes over to wish me luck and gives Gerald Yates a letter in an envelope. He says it's important. We break for lunch.

It's one o'clock and Judge Birnbaum bangs his gavel. "All right, let's begin. Mr. Yates, the Prosecution has rested its case. Is the Defense ready?"

"Yes, Your Honor. The Defense moves for a dismissal of all charges against the defendant because the Prosecution has not produced one piece of evidence to support the charges against Michael A. Palermo."

Birnbaum stiffens his neck, curls his hands into fists, and says, "The Court has reviewed the testimony of this morning and finds sufficient evidence to continue this trial in the interest of justice. The Defense motion is denied. Please proceed with your defense."

"With the Court's permission, the Defense will now make its opening statement," says Yates as he approaches the jury box.

"Ladies and gentlemen. You have heard the evidence and heard the witnesses for the Prosecution and I am sure you're puzzled. You're confused as to why this case was ever allowed to be brought to trial in the first place by the District Attorney. I agree with you. You should never have been brought here to spend your valuable time deliberating on a case where there has been no believable evidence presented, in fact, no evidence at all. The Assistant District Attorney, Robert Scott, has stated under oath that Detective Michael Palermo never tried to bribe him with words. He said, in fact, that Detective Palermo told him that he wanted the District Attorney to investigate this whole matter, while only Mr. Scott was talking about a bribe. Mr. Scott stated that it is his opinion that Detective Palermo tried to bribe him with body language and nuances. What is a nuance? A smile? A wink? A come-hither glance? A nuance is for a seduction! For a love affair."

Yates raises his voice.

"Not for a BRIBE to set a drug dealer free!"

"Detective Marshall admits that he tried to bribe Mr. Scott. And what did Mr. Scott do about it? Why, he's setting Detective Marshall free! That's right. The one admitted felon in this case is being set free by the District Attorney's office if . . . if that felon testifies against Detective Palermo. He testified and what did he say? He said that Detective Michael Palermo was an outstanding police officer. A good cop who never took a bribe or attempted to take a bribe in all the eighteen years that he has known him. But he says that it is his opinion that Detective Palermo knew what he, Detective Marshall, was going to talk to Mr. Scott about even though he never told Detective Palermo what he was going to talk to Mr. Scott about.

"You know what I think? I think that Detective Marshall told the District Attorney what he wanted to hear so that he would be granted immunity from prosecution and be set free. He told them what they wanted hear, whether it was true or not. His testimony has the weight of an admitted felon, and that's not worth anything. He's just out to save his own neck while he strangles his brother officer who is a highly decorated veteran of World War II and a highly decorated veteran of the New York City Police Department.

"Let me tell you something about Detective Palermo. Did you know that he volunteered and enlisted in the Marine Corps in 1944 when he was just eighteen years old? You know the Marines are always the first to take a beach. He was wounded in Okinawa where he was awarded a Purple Heart. He saw more action in the Pacific Theater where he was awarded a Bronze Star, a Silver Star, three Campaign Stars for Asiatic Action, and a China-Burma-India Patch. He was one of 200 marines in Peking, China, who were entrusted with the mission of protecting Chiang Kai-shek during his strategic withdrawal from the mainland to Taiwan. He emerged from World War II as a Master Sergeant. And that's not all. Then he went to Korea and worked in Marine Intelligence during the Korean Conflict and was Honorably Discharged from the Marines as a First Lieutenant.

"And that's not all. Then he devoted eighteen years of his life to the Police Department of The City of New York and became a Detective Lieutenant. He was awarded six Commendations, three Meritorious Awards, and participated in over two THOUSAND arrests. He was appointed to the elite SIU-Special Investigation Unit, where he waged a war on international drug smuggling. He repeatedly testified as an expert witness in drug prosecutions, many times for this same District Attorney who is now PERSE-CUTING—I mean, prosecuting him. This is no ordinary man you see sitting here quietly today. But that's the way he is. Quiet. He does his job and gets it done right. And he doesn't blow his own horn and tell the world about it. And one other thing he doesn't do—HE DOESN'T CONSPIRE TO TAKE BRIBES, as the District Attorney has charged with no evidence to support this charge. But don't take my word for it.

"You want to know about this man's character? Well, we're going to let the people who know him best tell you about him. These are his character witnesses. You'll hear from his fellow policemen; his bosses in the Department; a Congressman; an Assemblyman; a Monsignor and a parish priest; the wife of a man he arrested; and some of his old friends that he grew up with on the streets of East Harlem in the 1930s. His mother's in the courtroom watching what you're going to do to her son. But she won't testify because we all know what she's going to say. Don't take my word for it. Listen to the people who know him best.

"And now I would like to call the first witness for the Defense, Detective Lieutenant John Amato."

The parade of my character witnesses takes two days of testimony, and I'm starting to feel like a saint. My partners testify and so does Lenny Lombardi. Inspectors O'Hagan and Andrews, Captain Costello. Laura Cannelli tells them I left her a $20 bill of my own money when she had no food for her baby. Even Carmine Canicatti goes on the stand with Casper Nardino. They say their occupations are "investors." Then Father Baldini. Congressman Hamill and Assemblyman Simonetti. They're all there and more.

But there are two that make the biggest impact. The first is Monsignor Torrone.

Gerald Yates questions the Monsignor.

"Tell us about the character of Detective Palermo, Monsignor, please."

"I first met Michael at his daughter's christening. I was with my old friend, retired Police Chief Inspector Collin Devlin, who has since passed away. I think Chief Devlin expressed my feelings about Michael better than I can. I'll tell you what he said."

"Objection! Hearsay," bellows Ross Simon.

"Your Honor, the words of Chief Collin that the Monsignor was referring to are not hearsay. They are contained in this notarized affidavit which I now enter as Defense Exhibit One. This affidavit was just given to the Defense by Monsignor Torrone at twelve o'clock noon today. I have had the signature and handwriting of Chief Devlin authenticated by the Police Department of The City of New York and there is an official certification and seal attached and affixed. I ask that this be marked as evidence for the Defense."

Simon storms up to Judge Birnbaum and examines the documents and finally agrees to accept them into evidence.

"Please read the affidavit from Chief Collin Devlin, Monsignor," says Yates.

The Monsignor sits forward in the witness stand and adjusts his black horn-rimmed glasses firmly on his nose, clears his throat, and begins.

To whom it may concern:

I, Collin Devlin, Chief Inspector, Police Department of The City of New York, Retired, do hereby solemnly swear that this statement that I give as a character witness for Michael A. Palermo, Detective, Police Department of The City of New York, is the truth, the whole truth, and nothing but the truth, so help me God.

Michael Palermo first came to my attention in my official capacity in 1960. He was recommended to me by his commanding officer at that time, Inspector John Phillips, and by his Supervisor, Captain Harold Anderson. Detective Palermo, over the years, has carried out top secret assignments for the Police Department of The City of New York in a superior fashion. He has worked in a special capacity for me and with me personally to coordinate police procedures so that peace and harmony were preserved in the City and the public welfare was served and protected. He did this at times with bravery and complete disregard for his personal safety. He exposed himself unselfishly to danger and mortal injury for the good of the Police Department. All this he did while carrying on his official duties on the Force in an exemplary manner that brought good will and respect to the Department.

I know that when I am gone, people may come out of every crack and crevice and attack him. This always happens to men of value. I have always known him to do the right thing. He is, as they say on the street, a 'stand-up guy,' and I am proud to have worked with him. He is a credit to the Police Department and to his brother officers. He is one of the finest men on the Force."

So sworn before God,
Collin Devlin
Chief Inspector, Retired.
Date—May 14, 1968

"That is all that Chief Devlin wrote," says Monsignor Torrone.

There is no cross-examination. He leaves the stand.

When the Monsignor gave us the letter at lunchtime, he said that he had just come across it in the Chief's papers which he had just happened to be going over the night before. Tears filled my eyes. Even from the grave, the Chief came back to help me. He knew how the nature of some men completely overwhelms them sometimes and turns them into monsters. I think we have this thing beat.

And I know we're going to have it won after we call our last witness.

Yates guides the Monsignor from the witness stand and calls, "The Defense calls Aldo Rancolo to the stand."

My cousin Aldo walks proudly by me and pats me on the shoulder. His hair is shorter. He is well-dressed in a business suit. From the stand he nods to me and our eyes reach out in embrace. After the preliminaries, Yates begins.

"Aldo Rancolo, what is your relationship to Detective Michael Palermo?"

"He's my cousin and my godfather." Aldo tips his head toward me and smiles.

"Aldo would you mind removing your jacket and your shirt?"

"No, sure. I'll take them right off."

"Objection, Your Honor. The witness is here to give testimony. The Defense is trying to make a circus of these proceedings with irrelevant histrionics."

Judge Birnbaum glances at Yates for his retort. "Mr. Yates?"

"Your Honor, I can assure the Court that this avenue of approach and questioning has the highest relevance related to the motivation of Detective Palermo's actions in this case."

"Very well. We'll see. Continue, Mr. Yates."

The District Attorney sits down grudgingly. We won one small skirmish. Now for the whole war. You never know what will convince a jury. Even with all the right evidence in the world on your side, sometimes juries come back with the wrong verdict and put a killer back on the streets. The wrong verdict here will send me to prison and take away my pension. I've got my whole life riding on this trial. Come on, Yates. Come on, Aldo.

"And now, Aldo, would you mind removing your jacket and shirt?"

"No, not at all."

As Aldo removes his shirt, gasps of horror pop out of the jury box. His arms are twisted with the skin of grotesque, needled scars, a folded, blistery mass.

Yates sets course. "Will you please explain to the Court what has caused the disfigurement of your arms?"

"These are needle tracks. They're real bad ones. I was a heroin addict. They're from shooting heroin into my arms. I got them on my legs too. If it wasn't for my cousin Mike there, I'd be dead now. My cousin Mike set me straight. He saved my life. I tried, but I couldn't get off the needle until he helped me. He's helped a lot of people."

"Aldo, where did you get your heroin?"

"I used to buy it from Donny Dixon down in Harlem. He had a nickel bag operation going in a candy store. A lot of kids I know used to buy from him until he got busted."

"Tell me about your last purchase from Dixon."

"That was on the same day that Dixon got busted. Some cops grabbed me. But I mentioned my cousin Mike and they let me go with a warning never to come back there; to go for help; and that they were going to talk to my cousin. And thank God they did, because that's when he turned me around."

"Aldo, do you know who supplied Dixon?"

"Sure, everybody on the street knows. His connection is Albie Simmons. I've seen Simmons and Dixon pass cash and junk plenty of times in Dixon's candy store. Cousin Mike knew that too. That's when he said he was going to get Albie Simmons for what he did to me, if it was the last thing he did."

"Thank you, Aldo. You can put your shirt and jacket back on now. No further questions. Your witness, Counselor."

Simon has no questions.

Yates has one final witness. Me.

"The Defense calls Michael A. Palermo to the stand."

I'm sworn in and identify myself as if nobody up to this point knows who I am.

"Detective Palermo, how long have you been on the Police Force?"

"Almost eighteen years."

"And how long did you work in the Narcotics Bureau?"

"Fifteen years."

"In that period of time, how many arrests would you say you participated in?"

"Over two thousand."

"Did you suspect that it was through Albie Simmons that your cousin, your godson, was being destroyed by narcotics?"

"I knew that it was Simmons' operation that was supplying Aldo. That's why Albie Simmons was special to me."

"Special?"

"He was special. There was no way he was ever going to get away from me. He was impossible to catch. He was being tipped off by somebody on the inside."

Robert Scott moves uneasily in his chair. I see his fingers tapping his knees under the table. I can feel the tiny ripples of skin raise up in pocked points along the back of his neck.

"You mean there was a security leak?"

"That's right. But nothing we could prove conclusively. But I was working on a strong lead before I was arrested on Mr. Scott's allegations."

Ross Simon stares at Scott. "Why wasn't I told about this?"

Scott weasels back. "I didn't even know about it myself. I'll check it out personally."

"Be sure you do!" orders Simon as he rises.

"Objection, Your Honor. The witness is guessing. This is mere conjecture."

Birnbaum sustains.

Yates is ready to sum it up. "One final question, Detective Palermo. Did you attempt to bribe Assistant District Attorney Robert Scott in regards to any aspect of the Albie Simmons case?"

"No! I never tried to bribe Mr. Scott or anyone else. That charge is an absolute lie. As far as I was concerned, all the money in the world couldn't buy Simmons' freedom if I could stop it. Especially not after what he did to my cousin Aldo."

Simon rises again. "Objection, Your Honor. The defendant is not answering the question. He's giving a speech."

But Birnbaum is satisfied.

"I think we have an answer that is more than sufficient. Overruled."

Yates is finished. "Thank you, Detective Palermo. No further questions. Your witness, Mr. District Attorney."

Ross Simon gets up slowly and comes toward me.

"Detective Palermo, didn't you tell Detective Marshall that you wished you had taken Albie Simmons' bribe?"

Yates jumps to his feet. "Objection. No foundation. The Prosecution must confine its cross-examination to those issues which were testified to in direct examination. Detective Palermo's testimony did not cover anything that Detective Marshall said or did."

"Your Honor," says Simon, "Detective Palermo has testified that he did not try to bribe Mr. Scott, and the Prosecution holds that this area of Mr. Scott's attempted bribe by Detective Palermo contains the conversation that Detective Palermo had with Detective Marshall and therefore a foundation has been laid for this question. The whole area of the bribe attempt is open for the Prosecution to explore."

"Objection sustained. Try a new area, Mr. Simon," says Judge Birnbaum.

"Detective Palermo, where is the tape that you say you made of your meeting with Mr. Scott?"

"Objection. No foundation. The witness has never testified that he made a tape," says Yates.

Scott looks at Yates as if to say, "You dirty bastard, you tricked me. There is no Palermo tape, is there?"

Yates just smiles back at him. Simon really has nothing to ask. Yates was very tight with his area of questioning and the D.A. can't question me on anything that Yates didn't open up.

"No further questions." Simon sits down.

Yates gets up. "The Defense rests, Your Honor."

There are spirited summations on both sides with Simon reaching for an Academy Award which is beyond his grasp.

Finally, after four hours, the jury reaches its verdict.

"Has the jury reached a verdict?" asks Judge Birnbaum.

Time is suspended in a gossamer whirlwind which stands still and spins about in my mind and in the pit of my stomach all at the same time. I feel woozy from head to toes.

"We have, Your Honor. We find the defendant, Michael A. Palermo, NOT GUILTY."

A sudden, strange silence freezes the courtroom for an instant. Time stands still in a twilight zone. Then slowly lips whisper and arms embrace. People hug and kiss each other. I never saw anything like it. I feel like I'm above the whole courtroom, floating there, watching everybody cheer. My mother and Mrs. Coletti cry. Cops shake hands with wise guys. Wise guys with politicians. Politicians with me.

Oscar Birnbaum peers down his glasses at a beaten District Attorney. His eyes say, "I told you so, smartass."

Ross Simon has twisted the knife and spilled his own blood. He never fully recovers and never becomes governor. Instead, he becomes a State Supreme Court Judge.

I go back to the job and business as usual. I put in my twenty and get the hell out of there before somebody else tries to pin a bum rap on me.

Now some of the guys are starting to call me THE MAFIA COP. That's all the new District Attorney has to hear. He'll wind up bringing me back to Court again.

I start my own security business. Who knows, some day I may even get some hard evidence on the new District Attorney, Robert Scott, and bring HIM to Court.

EPILOGUE

Albie Simmons serves nine months in Sing Sing State Penitentiary in Ossining, New York. When he returns to the streets, he finds that Nicky Barnes has been murdered and that Monroe Benson has taken over. Shortly after that, Monroe Benson is gunned to death as he walks to his apartment, and Albie Simmons takes over the Harlem drug trade and runs drugs through Inspector O'Hagan's District like a sewer rat.

Robert Scott retires as District Attorney and goes into private practice representing accused and convicted drug felons. He also acts as the payoff man to inside contacts in law enforcement. He assumes the same role played by his friend and fellow defense attorney, Marcus Brown, who becomes a State Senator.

Augie Coletti serves one year in federal prison in San Quentin. He returns to the streets and resumes a successful career in organized crime.

Carmine Canicatti continues his business dealings and becomes an underboss in the Marcante Family. He is now active in the Family business in Las Vegas, Nevada.

Federal Agent Johnny Napolitano is promoted to a district supervisor position.

Jimmy Sorelli resolves his differences with Buck Truccolini and resumes a successful singing career. When this author meets him at his Jersey City building which he is renovating with marble walls and ceilings and with display cases of Capo Di Monte figurines, he is cooking us fresh pasta fagiola that he's making especially for me on his stove. As we look out across the Hudson River at the New York skyline, I say innocently, "You know, Mike Palermo is a friend of mine."

He says, "Oh, yeah, I just sang at his wedding."

I say, "He didn't just get married."

He says, "Oh, yes he did."

I say, "Mike Palermo, the New York City Narcotics cop?"

And then he goes crazy and screams, "I don't know no cops. I don't have nothin' to do with cops. I don't go near cops."

Then I find out that there is a wise guy, a capo regime, a big man in the New Jersey mob, whose name is also Mike Palermo. Different guy. Same name. You figure it. I eat my pasta fagiola and hope I don't bite down on a stone in the beans.

Buck Truccolini dies five years later of natural causes. He overeats.

Old friends on the Police Force retire. Some of them go into business for themselves and some take private jobs. Others die.

Some years later, Ross Simon walks into The Grotto Restaurant on Mott Street with his girlfriend, Tania. They eat a heavy meal. Before dessert, the girl gently kisses his lips and goes to the ladies' room. While she is gone, the waiter serves Simon apple pie and coffee. He finishes his meal and is suddenly stricken with crushing pains in his chest. He sinks back into his chair, with his face, eyes open, to the ceiling. Tania's worried face looks down at him from above. He hears nothing but his heart thundering in his ears. He reads her silent lips, "I'm sorry." And then she runs away.

His failing heart pounds softer and softer and then stops. For the last three seconds of his life, Ross Simon knows that he is dead. The waiter removes the apple pie laced with sodium morphate.

Carmine Canicatti watches everything from his table in the rear of his restaurant. There is more than one way to fill a contract, he thinks.

"Remember that no matter what you are or what you may become, you will never be anything more than the seeds of two families. One is made of clay, the other of honor."

—R.S.C.

Books from Skyhorse Publishing

To see our complete catalog or to order online, please visit www.skyhorsepublishing.com.

The Little Black Book of Mafia Wisdom: Secrets, Lies, Tricks, and Tactics of the Organization That Was Once Bigger Than U.S. Steel
By Wesley Jacques
Delve into the inner workings of the Mob and the mindset of those who run it through these mesmerizing quotes from some of the smoothest and most dangerous criminals, real and fictional, who ever made headlines.

The Mafia at War: The Shocking True Story of America's Wartime Pact with Organized Crime
By Tim Newark
Drawing on a wealth of eyewitness accounts, contemporary reports, and declassified intelligence documents, some never published before, The Mafia at War reconstructs the relationships between the Mafia and Allied intelligence organizations. Uncovering the extraordinary secrets of this collaboration, Newark provides crucial insight into both the history of World War II and how the Mafia came to dominate global crime in the post-war world.

Young Al Capone: The Untold Story of Scarface in New York, 1899-1925
By William Balsamo and John Balsamo
The first biography of Capone to focus on his youth in Brooklyn and the events that shaped him into one of history's most notorious criminals.

The Tangled Web: The Life and Death of Richard Cain—Chicago Cop and Mafia Hitman
By Michael J. Cain
"One of the most important mob books ever written."—Ray Gibson, *Chicago Tribune*
The Tangled Web tells the dramatic story of detective Richard Cain's criminal career as revealed by his half-brother, Michael. Cain led a double-life—one as a well-known cop who led raids that landed on the front pages, and the other as a "made man" in one of Chicago's most notorious mob families. Eventually executed by shotgun, Dick Cain lived and died in a world of bloodshed and violence, leaving behind a story so outlandish that he has even been suspected of being involved in the assassination of John F. Kennedy.